Information Sharing

Information Sharing

Reference and Presupposition in Language Generation and Interpretation

Kees van Deemter & Rodger Kibble

CSLI PUBLICATIONS
Center for the Study of Language and Information
Stanford, California

Center for the Study of Language and Information
Leland Stanford Junior University
Printed in the United States
06 05 04 03 02 5 4 3 2 1

Library of Congress Cataloging-in-Publication Data

Information sharing : reference and presupposition
in language generation and interpretation /
edited by Kees van Deemter and Rodger Kibble.
p. cm. – (CSLI lecture notes ; no. 143)
Includes bibliographical references and index.

ISBN 1-57586-404-5 (pbk. : alk. paper)
ISBN 1-57586-403-7 (alk. paper)

1. Reference (Linguistics) 2. Presupposition (Logic)
3. Computational linguistics.
I. Deemter, Kees van. II. Kibble, Rodger, 1956–
III. Series.
P325.5.R44 I54 2002
401′.41—dc21 2002006892
CIP

∞ The acid-free paper used in this book meets the minimum requirements of the American National Standard for Information Sciences—Permanence of Paper for Printed Library Materials, ANSI Z39.48-1984.

CSLI was founded early in 1983 by researchers from Stanford University, SRI International, and Xerox PARC to further research and development of integrated theories of language, information, and computation. CSLI headquarters and CSLI Publications are located on the campus of Stanford University.

CSLI Publications reports new developments in the study of language, information, and computation. In addition to lecture notes, our publications include monographs, working papers, revised dissertations, and conference proceedings. Our aim is to make new results, ideas, and approaches available as quickly as possible. Please visit our web site at
http://cslipublications.stanford.edu/
for comments on this and other titles, as well as for changes and corrections by the author and publisher.

In memory of Rosemary Stevenson

Contents

Contributors

Antonella De Angeli LORIA Laboratory, Vandœuvre-lès-Nancy, France. Antonella.De_Angeli@ncr.com

John Bateman Angewandte Linguistik, Universität Bremen, Germany. bateman@uni-bremen.de

Norman Creaney University of Ulster, Coleraine, N. Ireland, UK. n.creaney@ulst.ac.uk

Cassandre Creswell Department of Linguistics, University of Pennsylvania, Philadelphia, USA. creswell@ling.upenn.edu

Kees van Deemter Information Technology Research Institute, University of Brighton, U.K. Kees.van.Deemter@itri.brighton.ac.uk

John Gurney Adelphi Laboratory Center, Adelphi, Maryland, USA. gurney@arl.army.mil

Herman Hendriks Utrecht Institute of Linguistics (OTS), Utrecht University, The Netherlands; and ILLC/Department of Philosophy, University of Amsterdam, The Netherlands. Herman.Hendriks@let.uu.nl

Pamela W. Jordan Learning Research and Development Center University of Pittsburgh, Pennsylvania, USA. pjordan@pitt.edu

Rodger Kibble Department of Mathematical and Computing Sciences, Goldsmiths College, University of London, U.K. r.kibble@gold.ac.uk

Elizabeth Klipple Adelphi Laboratory Center, Adelphi, Maryland, USA. klipple@arl.army.mil

Emiel Krahmer Computational Linguistics, Tilburg University, The Netherlands. e.j.krahmer@kub.nl

Geert-Jan Kruijff Computerlinguistik, Universität des Saarlandes, Saarbrücken, Germany. gj@coli.uni-sb.de

Ivana Kruijff-Korbayová Computerlinguistik, Universität des Saarlandes, Saarbrücken, Germany. korbay@coli.uni-sb.de

Frédéric Landragin LORIA Laboratory, Vandœuvre-lès-Nancy, France. Frederic.Landragin@loria.fr

Patrice Lopez LORIA Laboratory, Vandœuvre-lès-Nancy, France. Patrice.Lopez@loria.fr

Ivandré Paraboni Information Technology Research Institute, University of Brighton, U.K. Ivandre.Paraboni@itri.brighton.ac.uk

Craige Roberts Department of Linguistics, Ohio State University, Columbus, Ohio, USA. croberts@ling.ohio-state.edu

Laurent Romary LORIA Laboratory, Vandœuvre-lès-Nancy, France. Laurent.Romary@loria.fr

Jennifer Spenader Computational Linguistics, Department of Linguistics, Stockholm University, Sweden. jennifer@ling.su.se

†**Rosemary Stevenson** Department of Psychology, University of Durham, U.K.

Mariët Theune Parlevink Language Engineering Group, Department of Computer Science, University of Twente, Enschede, The Netherlands. theune@cs.utwente.nl

Frédéric Wolff LORIA Laboratory, Vandœuvre-lès-Nancy, France. Frederic.Wolff@fr2.vdogrp.de

Henk Zeevat Institute for Logic, Language and Computation (ILLC), University of Amsterdam, Netherlands. henk.zeevat@hum.uva.nl

Preface

Academic communities are sometimes separated by artificial boundaries. The linguistic community is no exception: some linguists insist on a theoretical perspective, others prefer a data-oriented or computational approach. It has often been observed that boundaries between disciplines or scientific approaches can become counterproductive if they become rigid; the present volume is an attempt to show what happens when they are taken with a pinch of salt. The papers contained in this volume might be partitioned into the three categories mentioned above, but such a partitioning would tend to obscure existing commonalities. In our view, the most important common element is what we will call *Information Sharing*.

When we express ourselves, we share information. Information sharing involves distinguishing between parts of an utterance that express *given* information (e.g., because the information has been shared before) and parts that express *new* information. Information sharing is crucial to all the papers collected in this book, regardless of their methodology. And even if we look at specific aspects of Information Sharing, such as salience, presuppositionhood, or deixis, the same picture emerges: A reader interested in how *salience* influences the form and position of a referring expression, for example, could consult papers representing each of the three types: she could read the chapters by Hendriks (theoretical), Stevenson, Jordan, and Landragin (data-oriented), or those by Kruijff et al., or Krahmer & Theune (mainly computational). A similar picture would emerge for someone interested in *deixis*: such a person would be equally likely to turn to Roberts, or to Gurney & Klipple (mainly theoretical) as to Paraboni & van Deemter (mainly computational) or Landragin et al. (data-oriented). *Presuppositions* take up a slight different position in this volume, since they are mainly studied from a theoretical perspective (Zeevat) or a data-oriented one (Spenader), but the reader will have little difficulty finding computational approaches elsewhere (e.g., Johan Bos (2001), "DORIS 2001: Underspecification, Resolution and Inference for Discourse Representation Structures", In Proceedings of ICoS-3, Inference in Compuational Semantics.)

A few additional observations may be worth reporting. Firstly, the book contains a large number of papers that address linguistic issues from the perspective of language *generation*. A focus on language generation is manifest not only in each of the computationally oriented chapters, but also in those by Stevenson, Jordan, Landragin et al., and Creswell. Language *interpretation* has long been the dominant perspective in semantics; yet, a majority of the chapters of this volume represent the opposite perspective, asking how and under what circumstances a particular kind of expression can be produced, or how a particular kind of information is best expressed. In generation, the distinction between given and new information is as crucial as it is in language interpretation. This is evident in the generation of referring expressions, for example: when a speaker wants to say something about an object, she has to use properties whose extensions are known by the hearer (i.e., *given* properties), in order to distinguish the target from a set of contextually available (i.e., given) 'distractors'. The distinction between given and new lies at the heart of all algorithms in this area, but the papers in this volume (most notably those by Krahmer and Theune and by Creaney) elaborate on it in nontrivial ways, by making givenness a graded notion (i.e., incorporating degrees of salience) and by applying the distinction between givenness and novelty to quantified noun phrases.

Secondly – and relating to the theme of givenness and novelty in a different way – the book counts a large number of new departures. Some of the linguistic phenomena addressed here have received little attention in the literature. This is true, for example, for the work on deixis to properties (Gurney and Klipple: 'I'd like to fly *that* high'), and for the work on emphatic reflexives (Creswell: 'The president *herself* led the discussion'). It is also true for Paraboni and van Deemter's study of document deixis (as in 'The algorithms in *the concluding section of this paper*'), and for Creaney's investigation of the computational generation of quantified noun phrases. In other cases it is mainly the methodology that is new. This holds, for example, for Spenader's chapter, which confronts Van der Sandt's theory of 'presuppositions-as-anaphors' with corpus data, and it is equally true for Jordan's corpus study of referring expressions, as well as Zeevat's application of Optimality Theory to the generation of presupposition triggers. In these latter cases, the subject of study is kept constant, but it is precisely the above-mentioned methodological perspective that the authors bring to bear on this particular subject (i.e., theoretical, computational, or data-oriented) that is novel. Although a majority of the chapters focus on the study of nominal expressions, the present collection contains a number of papers (most notably those by Spenader, by Zeevat, by Klipple & Gurney, by Kruijff et al., and by Landragin et al.) that set their eye beyond the noun phrase. The results are interesting, we believe, and we hope that they will prove seminal.

The idea for this book came to us after the 11th European Summer School 'Logic Language and Information' (ESSLLI) in Utrecht in 1999, when three research workshops turned out to be remarkably similar in their scope and purpose. One of the three, which was concerned with the *Generation of Nominal Expressions*, was organized by us. We are grateful to Elisabeth André, Massimo Poesio, and Hannes Rieser (who organized the workshop on *Deixis*), and to Bart Geurts, Manfred Krifka, and Rob van der Sandt (who organized the workshop on *Focus and Presuppositions*). Without their efforts, this book would have lacked its present breadth. Particular thanks are due to Bart Geurts and Paul Piwek for their editorial advice. In addition, we believe that many of the virtues that we would like to see in this volume can be traced back to the multidisciplinary spirit of the yearly ESSLLI, which has grown into so much more than just a summer school. We thank the people who reviewed the papers in this volume during any stage of their bibliographic lives: when submitted to one of the workshops, when submitted for inclusion in the book proposal, and during review of the book itself. In particular (and not counting reviewers who are also contributors to this book), we thank *David Beaver, Robert-Jan Beun, Daniel Bűring, Lynne Cahill, John Carroll, Hua Cheng, Judy Delin, Christy Doran, Miriam Eckert, Bart Geurts, Jonathan Ginzburg, Tony Hartley, Petra Hendriks, Renate Henschel, Ruth Kempson, John Lee, Alice ter Meulen, David Milward, Jon Oberlander, Daniel Paiva, Paul Piwek, Massimo Poesio, Richard Power, Ehud Reiter, Rob van der Sandt, Mark Steedman, Matthew Stone, Michael Strube, Marc Swerts,* and *Jacques Terken* for their reviews.

We hope that, by sharing the information in this volume with CSLI Publications' readership, the different approaches to Information Sharing are brought a small step closer to integration.

Kees van Deemter and Rodger Kibble.

1

Information Packaging: From Cards to Boxes

HERMAN HENDRIKS

This paper is organized as follows. First, in Section 1.1, an outline is given of the theory of information packaging—i.e., the structuring of propositional content in function of the speaker's assumptions about the hearer's information state—as it is presented by Vallduví (1992, 1993, 1994). Vallduví identifies the informational primitives *focus* and *ground*, *link* and *tail*, adapted from the traditional pragmatic focus/ground and topic/comment approaches, and concludes—as is explained in Section 1.2—that the exploitation of information states of hearers by the information-packaging strategies of speakers reveals that these states have at least the internal structure of a system of file cards along the lines of Heim (1982, 1983). Links, which correspond to what are traditionally known as topics and which are typically marked by L+H* pitch accents in English, say *where*—on which file card—the focal information goes, and tails indicate *how* it fits there. This conclusion is challenged in Section 1.3, where it is argued that it begs the question. *If* file card systems are assumed, *then* the information-packaging strategies do seem to contribute to efficient information exchange. The question, however, is whether this assumption itself is justified. Moreover, it will be shown that the idea that links specify a locus of update in information states that are systems of file cards is problematic for various reasons. Therefore, Section 1.4 offers an alternative account in terms of the discourse representation structures of Discourse Representation Theory (see Kamp

Information Sharing: Reference and Presupposition in Language Generation and Interpretation.
Edited by Kees van Deemter and Rodger Kibble.

1981, Kamp and Reyle 1993), which are ontologically less committed than the 'dimensionally richer' file card systems, since discourse representation structures do not come with locations. The latter aspect raises the question what purpose links *do* serve if they do not serve to specify a locus of update: a different perspective on the function of links is required. According to the perspective offered in Section 1.4, linkhood—and hence L+H* pitch accent in English—serves to signal non-monotonic anaphora: the discourse referent Y of a link is anaphoric to an antecedent discourse marker X such that $X \not\subseteq Y$. This hypothesis affects a wide range of phenomena. In addition to its contribution to an analysis of (non-)association with focus, it is shown to subsume 'non-identity' anaphora, contrastive stress, correction, pronoun referent resolution, and restrictiveness of relatives and adjectives. In Section 5, finally, it is pointed out that the account of links given here is consistent with and can actually be considered a partial execution of the intonational-informational research program that is outlined in Pierrehumbert and Hirschberg (1990).[1]

1.1 Information Packaging

The notion of information packaging is introduced in Chafe (1976), where the phenomena at issue are said to 'have to do primarily with how the message is sent and only secondarily with the message itself, just as the packaging of toothpaste can affect sales in partial independence of the quality of the toothpaste inside' (Chafe 1976: 28).

The basic idea is that speakers do not present information in an unstructured way, but that they provide a hearer with detailed instructions on how to manipulate and integrate this information according to their beliefs about the hearer's knowledge and attentional state: 'to ensure reasonably efficient communication, [t]he speaker tries, to the best of his ability, to make the structure of his utterances congruent with his knowledge of the listener's mental world' (Clark and Haviland 1977: 5).

On all levels the crucial factor appears to be the tailoring of an utterance by a sender to meet the particular assumed needs of the intended

[1]The present paper is a merged, updated and extended version of 'Links without Locations' and 'Information Packaging: From Cards to Boxes', which appeared in P. Dekker and M. Stokhof (eds.), *Proceedings of the Tenth Amsterdam Colloquium*, Institute of Language, Logic and Computation, University of Amsterdam, pp. 339–358, and in T. Galloway and J. Spence (eds.), *Proceedings of Semantics And Linguistic Theory VI*. CLC Publications, Ithaca, New York, pp. 75–92, respectively. Section 1.3 of the present paper is largely based on joint work of Paul Dekker (ILLC/Department of Philosophy, University of Amsterdam) and the author, who would like to thank Paul Dekker, Elisabet Engdahl, Fritz Hamm, Sieb Nooteboom, Tanya Reinhart, Enric Vallduví and two anonymous referees for cooperation, discussion and stimulation.

receiver. That is, 'information packaging in natural language reflects the sender's hypotheses about the receiver's assumptions and beliefs and strategies' (Prince 1981: 224).

For instance, sentences such as (1.1) and (1.2) are truth-conditionally equivalent in that they express the same proposition, but each of them 'packages' this proposition in a prosodically different way:[2]

(1.1) *The* **teacher** *loves* ICE CREAM

(1.2) *The* **teacher** LOVES *ice cream*

Typically, speakers will use (1.1) if the hearer at the time of utterance knows nothing about or is not attending to the teacher's relation to ice cream, while they will use (1.2) if the hearer at the time of utterance knows that there exists a relation between the teacher and ice cream, is attending to this relation, but does not know what it is.

Apparently, speakers are sensitive to such differences in the hearer's knowledge and attentional state, and hearers rely on this: 'speakers not using this device systematically give their listeners a harder time' (Nooteboom and Terken 1982: 317).

Truth-conditionally equivalent sentences which encode different information packaging instructions are not mutually interchangeable *salva felicitate* in a given context of utterance: for example, of the above sentences, only the first one is a felicitous answer to the question *What does the teacher love?* It is this context-sensitivity that has traditionally placed information packaging within the realm of pragmatics, where two influential approaches can be distinguished, the 'topic/comment' approach and the 'focus/ground' approach.

According to the focus/ground approach, sentences consist of a 'focus' and a 'ground'.[3] The focus is the informative part of the sentence, the part that (the speaker believes) makes some contribution to the hearer's mental state. The ground is the non-informative part of the

[2] *Italics* are used for unaccented expressions; SMALL CAPS for expressions that bear a H* pitch accent; and **boldface** is used for expressions that bear a L+H* pitch accent. This is the terminology of Pierrehumbert (1980). H* accent and L+H* accent are called A accent and B accent, respectively, in Jackendoff (1972). Occasionally, when the prosody of an example sentence is irrelevant for the discussion, it will be rendered in non-italic non-boldface lower case.

[3] The ground is also known as 'background', as 'presupposition' and as 'open proposition'. In phonology, the term 'focus' is often used for intonational prominence. That is, any constituent which bears pitch accent is said to be a focus. Although in general, (part of) the informational focus is marked by prosodic prominence, not every accented constituent is a focus in the informational sense. In particular, accented constituents may also be topics/links.

sentence, the part that anchors the sentence to what is already established or under discussion in (the speaker's picture of) the hearer's mental state. Although sentences may lack a ground altogether, sentences without focus do not exist.

The topic/comment (theme/rheme) approach splits the set of subexpressions of a sentence into a 'topic', the—typically sentence-initial—part that expresses what the sentence is about, and a 'comment', the part that expresses what is said about the topic. Topics are points of departure for what the sentence conveys, they link it to previous discourse. Sentences may be topicless: so-called 'presentational' or 'news' sentences consist entirely of a comment.

In Reinhart (1982), it is argued that the dimension of 'old'/'new' information is irrelevant for the analysis of sentence topics. Instead, the notion of 'pragmatic aboutness' is defined in terms of the organization of information. The set $\mathrm{PPA}_{(\mathrm{S})}$ of Possible Pragmatic Assertions that can be made with a sentence S expressing proposition φ is defined as follows:

(1.3) $\mathrm{PPA}_{(\mathrm{S})} = \{\varphi\} \cup \{\langle a, \varphi\rangle \mid a \text{ is the interpretation of an NP in S}\}$

A pragmatic assertion $\langle a, \varphi\rangle$ is assumed to be *about* a. The possibility for an NP interpretation a to serve as the topic of a pragmatic assertion $\langle a, \varphi\rangle$ is subject to further syntactic and semantic restrictions, cf. footnote 10 below.

Notice, by way of example (adopted from Dahl 1974), that the sentence *The* **teacher** *loves* ICE CREAM gives rise to parallel topic/comment and ground/focus partitions as indicated in (1.4) if it answers the questions *What about the teacher? What does he feel?*, whereas it induces the partitions specified by (1.5) in the interrogative context *What about the teacher? What does he love?*

(1.4)

<table>
<tr><td>topic</td><td>comment</td></tr>
<tr><td>The teacher</td><td>loves ICE CREAM</td></tr>
<tr><td>ground</td><td>focus</td></tr>
</table>

(1.5)

<table>
<tr><td>topic</td><td colspan="2">comment</td></tr>
<tr><td>The teacher</td><td>loves</td><td>ICE CREAM</td></tr>
<tr><td colspan="2">ground</td><td>focus</td></tr>
</table>

The fact that the two informational articulations correspond to different partitions in (1.5) shows that neither of them is by itself capable of capturing all the informational distinctions present in the sentence. Therefore, the two traditional binomial articulations of focus/ground and topic/comment are conflated into a single trinomial and hierarchical one in Vallduví's account of information packaging (1992, 1993, 1994). The core distinction is the one between new information and anchoring, between focus and ground. In addition, the ground is further divided into the 'link', which corresponds approximately to the topic in the traditional topic/comment approach,[4] and the 'tail'.[5] In a picture:

(1.6) $\gg$

topic	comment		'aboutness'
link	tail	focus	
ground		focus	'old'/'new'

Given this articulation, the answer *The* **teacher** *loves* ICE CREAM to the questions *What about the teacher? What does he love?* will receive the following analysis:

(1.7)

The **teacher**	*loves*	ICE CREAM
link	tail	focus
ground		focus

Roughly speaking, the different parts—focus and ground, link and tail—of a sentence S have the following informational functions in Vallduví's theory. The focus encodes I_{S}, the *information* of S, which can be metaphorically described as ϕ_{S}, the proposition expressed by S, minus K_{h}, the information (the speaker presumes) already present in the hearer's information state. The ground performs an *ushering* role—it specifies the way in which I_{S} fits in the hearer's information state: links indicate *where* I_{S} should go by denoting a location in the hearer's information state, and tails indicate *how* I_{S} fits there by signaling a certain mode of information update.

Of course, talking about ushering information to some location in the hearer's information state presupposes that this information state has some sort of internal structure. In this respect, Vallduví purports to agree with Heim that there has to be some additional internal structure in the hearer's model of the common ground that plays an important role in natural language interpretation, even if this internal structure

[4]To the extent that links correspond to the *topic* in the traditional topic/comment distinction, Vallduví's theory is quite similar to the analysis of sentence topics presented in Reinhart (1982), in whose formalization of a pragmatic assertion of φ about a as $\langle a, \varphi \rangle$ the topic a could be construed as a kind of 'locus of update' for φ (see below). The two approaches differ in that Reinhart allows assertions without a 'locus of update' (since also $\varphi \in \mathrm{PPA}_{(\mathrm{S})}$) and topics that express new information.

[5]The hierarchy does not imply constituency or (even) continuity. In particular, the two parts (link and tail) of the ground may not constitute a linear unit at the surface. Moreover, sentences may have more than one link, and more than one element may constitute the tail.

is of tangential relevance in truth value computation. 'It is this internal structure of information states which is, in fact, crucially exploited by the different information-packaging strategies used by speakers in pursuing communicative efficiency' (Vallduví 1994: 7).

1.2 Files in Focus

In fact, Vallduví takes the metaphor of Heim's file change semantics (1982, 1983) literally, in that he assumes that the information in the hearer's model is organized in files, i.e., collections of file cards. Each file card represents a discourse entity: its attributes and its links with other discourse entities are recorded on the card in the form of conditions. Such a discourse entity may be known to the hearer but not salient at the time of utterance, it may be salient at the time of utterance, it may be completely new to the hearer, it may be inferable from what the hearer knows, etc. Discourse entities mediate between referring expressions (noun phrases) and entities in the real world: indefinite noun phrases prompt hearers to create a new file card, and definite noun phrases incite them to retrieve an already existing file card. Both definites and pronouns denote already existing file cards, but pronouns denote salient file cards, whereas (other) definites refer to non-salient ones. File change comprises the above aspects of file card management, but it also involves content update, i.e., the incorporation of information conveyed by a given sentence into records on novel and familiar file cards, and this is where Vallduví lets information packaging come in. Links are associated with so-called GOTO instructions. In file change semantics, the target location of such a declaration is a file card *fc*. A tail points at an information record—normally a (possibly underspecified) condition—on such a file card, RECORD(*fc*), and indicates that it has to be *modified* (or further specified) by the focus information I_S of the sentence. The associated instruction type is called UPDATE-REPLACE. In the absence of a tail, the focus information I_S of a sentence is simply *added* at the current location. The associated instruction type is called UPDATE-ADD.

Sentences may lack links and tails (recall that the focus is the only non-optional part of a sentence), so the following four sentence types can be distinguished:

(1.8)
a. link-focus
b. focus
c. focus-tail
d. link-focus-tail

The respective sentence types in (1.8) are associated with the (compound) instruction types in (1.9):

(1.9) *a.* GOTO(*fc*)(UPDATE-ADD(I_S))
b. UPDATE-ADD(I_S)
c. UPDATE-REPLACE(I_S,RECORD(*fc*))
d. GOTO(*fc*)(UPDATE-REPLACE(I_S,RECORD(*fc*)))

The sentence and instruction types in (1.8) and (1.9) can be illustrated with the following examples, where links, tails and foci are specified by means of [$_L$...], [$_T$...] and [$_F$...] brackets, respectively, and accented expressions in foci and links are—as above—written in small caps (representing H* pitch accent) and boldface (for L+H* pitch accent), respectively:

(1.10) *a.* link-focus: [$_L$ *The* **boss**][$_F$ *hates* BROCCOLI]
GOTO(*fc*)(UPDATE-ADD(I_S))
b. focus: [$_F$ *He always eats* BEANS]
UPDATE-ADD(I_S)
c focus-tail: [$_F$ *He is* NOT][$_T$ *dead*]
UPDATE-REPLACE(I_S,RECORD(*fc*))
d. link-focus-tail: [$_L$ *The* **boss**][$_F$ HATES][$_T$ *broccoli*]
GOTO(*fc*)(UPDATE-REPLACE(I_S,RECORD(*fc*)))

As regards the first example, suppose that a newly appointed temp is ordering dinner for the boss and asks the executive secretary whether there is anything that he should know about the boss' taste. The executive secretary gives the following answer:

(1.11) [$_L$ *The* **boss**][$_F$ *hates* BROCCOLI]

Example (1.11) is a link-focus construction, and as such it is associated with a GOTO(*fc*)(UPDATE-ADD(I_S)) instruction. The link subject *the* **boss** specifies a locus of update *fc*, viz., the card representing the boss—card #25, say. The focus verb phrase *hates broccoli* specifies the information I_S that has to be added to this card. Suppose that broccoli is represented by card #136. Then, passing over some formal details, the UPDATE-ADD(I_S) instruction associated with the focus *hates broccoli* amounts to adding the condition 'hates(25,136)' to the locus of update, i.e., the boss' card #25. Moreover, the record '$\boxed{\mapsto 25}$', a pointer to the locus of update, is added to card #136, rendering the condition 'hates(25,136)' on card #25 'accessible' from card #136. Vallduví says that this linking mechanism, which designates a unique location for content update, is 'much more efficient' than straightforward multiple recording of information on cards.

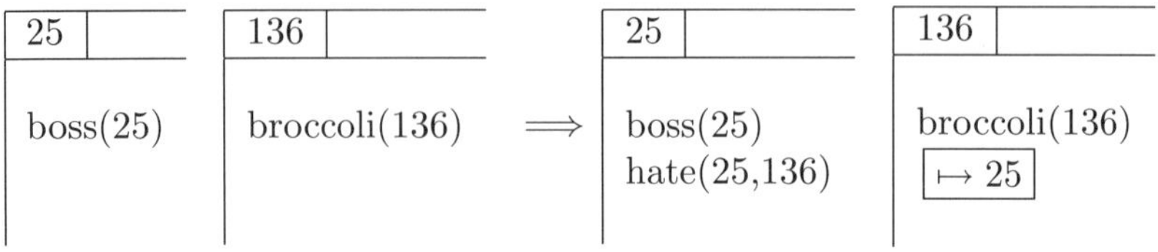

(1.12) [$_\text{F}$*He always eats* BEANS]

Example (1.12), an all-focus construction, is associated with a simple UPDATE-ADD(I_S) instruction. Here, this instruction involves the addition of the focus information I_S that the value of the current card always eats beans. That is: if it is interpreted immediately after example (1.11) and if its adverbially modified transitive verb phrase is left unanalyzed for simplicity, it amounts to adding the condition 'always eats beans(25)' to card #25.

The presence of a tail in a sentence signals a mode of update different from the straightforward UPDATE-ADD(I_S) instruction. A tail indicates that a (possibly underspecified) record on a file card has to be replaced (or specified further). The material in the tail serves the purpose of determining *which* record. Suppose, for example, that (1.13) is a reaction to the statement *Since John is dead, we can now split his inheritance*:

(1.13) *I hate to spoil the fun, but* [$_F$*he is* NOT][$_T$*dead*]

With this focus-tail example, the speaker instructs the hearer to replace the record on the current locus of update—card #17, say, for John—expressing that the value of card #17 is dead by one saying that he is not dead. In short, the tail serves to highlight a condition on file card #17, the one saying its value is dead. This condition is then modified in the way specified by the material in the focus.

In addition to the option of replacing a record on a file card, there is the possibility of further specifying an underspecified record, something which is assumed to be going on in the link-focus-tail example (1.14) given below. Suppose now that the newly appointed temp asks the executive secretary whether it was a good idea to order broccoli for the boss, and that the executive secretary gives the following answer:

(1.14) [$_\text{L}$ *The* **boss**][$_\text{F}$HATES][$_\text{T}$*broccoli*]

The idea is that the temp has an underspecified record on his card for the boss, which says that the boss has some attitude towards broccoli. The lack of information about the nature of this attitude is reflected by the record 'ATT', and it is this record which is replaced by 'hate' after hearing the executive secretary's answer (1.14):

25	136		25	136
boss(25) ATT(25,136)	broccoli(136)	$\Longrightarrow$	boss(25) hate(25,136)	broccoli(136) $\boxed{\mapsto 25}$

Different languages choose different structural means to spell out the same informational interpretations. Vallduví studies the manifestation of information packaging in several languages, with an emphasis on Catalan and English. Cross-language comparison shows that in expressing information packaging, languages exploit word order and prosody in various ways. Roughly speaking, English structurally realizes information packaging by means of alternative intonational contours of identical strings, whereas Catalan has a constant prosodic structure and effectuates information packaging by means of string order permutations. In fact, Vallduví argues that languages such as Catalan supply empirical support for the representation of information packaging sketched above, since these languages package their information in a more salient way than, for example, English. Thus, while informational interpretations may be expressed exclusively by prosodic means in English, information packaging instructions in Catalan are straightforwardly reflected in syntax.

In English, the focus is associated with a H* pitch accent (written in small caps), links are marked by a L+H* pitch accent (written in boldface), and tails are structurally characterized by being deaccented.[6] One and the same string may be assigned different intonational phrasings in order to realize different informational interpretations. In particular, the focal pitch accent may be realized on different positions in the sentence. This is illustrated by the sentences (1.16), (1.18) and (1.20), construed as answers to the questions (1.15), (1.17) and (1.19), respectively:[7]

[6]This may wrongly suggest that the relation between L+H* accent and linkhood and between H* accent and focus is deterministic and obligatory. Rather, probability seems to be the key word here, given that Ross and Ostendorf (1996) have shown that no two professional speakers produce their utterances with the same intonational pattern in a corpus of read-aloud texts, and that, more in general, intonational choices are optional, as argued by, e.g., Nooteboom and Terken (1982), who observe that the probability that a word will be accented varies as a function of the preceding linguistic context. See also Section 1.5 of the present paper.

[7]The intonational 'facts' presented in (1.15) through (1.20) and elsewhere in the present section were questioned by an anonymous referee: 'I find the claim that links such as in example (1.18) get an L+H* accent rather counterintuitive. I have tested this with some linguists in my institute, and NONE of them thought an accent on *the boss* would be appropriate. Instead, a more natural reading would be with *the boss* deaccented in (1.18) and accented in (1.16). As a matter of fact, the latter would

(1.15) What did you find out about the company?

(1.16) $[_{\mathrm{F}}$ *The boss hates* BROCCOLI]

(1.17) What did you find out about the boss?

(1.18) $[_{\mathrm{L}}$ *The* **boss**]$[_{\mathrm{F}}$*hates* BROCCOLI]

(1.19) What does the boss feel about broccoli?

(1.20) $[_{\mathrm{L}}$ *The* **boss**]$[_{\mathrm{F}}$HATES]$[_{\mathrm{T}}$*broccoli*]

In Catalan, the situation is as follows. Metaphorically speaking, one can say that Catalan focal elements remain within a so-called 'core clause', but that ground elements are 'detached' to a clause-peripheral position. In particular, links are detached to the left, and non-link ground elements undergo right-detachment. As a result of detaching both links and tails, the core clause (CC) is left containing only the focus of the sentence:

(1.21) LINKS $[_{\mathrm{CC}}$ FOCUS] TAILS

Consider the Catalan counterparts (1.22), (1.23) and (1.24) of (1.16), (1.18) and (1.20), respectively. The all-focus sentence (1.22) displays the basic verb-object-subject word order. In (1.23) and (1.24), the link subject *l'amo* has been detached to the left. In (1.24), moreover, the tail direct object *el bròquil* has been detached to the right, leaving a clitic (*l'*) in the focal core clause. Note that intonational structure plays a part in Catalan too, albeit 'a rather lame one' (Vallduví 1993: 33): a focal H* pitch acent is invariably associated with the last item of the core clause.

(1.22) $[_{\mathrm{F}}$ *Odia el bròquil* L'AMO]

(1.23) $[_{\mathrm{L}}$ *L'amo*]$[_{\mathrm{F}}$ *odia el* BRÒQUIL]

(1.24) $[_{\mathrm{L}}$ *L'amo*] $[_{\mathrm{F}}$L'ODIA]$[_{\mathrm{T}}$ *el bróquil*]

The above observations provide confirmation that information packaging involves syntax as well as prosody; hence any attempt to reduce information packaging to either syntax (for Turkish, cf. Hoffman 1995) or

be in agreement with the author's NAH hypothesis [to be presented in Section 1.4 below, HH], because only in (1.16) does *the boss* represent a non-monotonic anaphora, whereas links in sentences such as in example (1.18) clearly fail to do so.' Indeed!

prosody (for English, cf. Steedman 1991, 1992, 1993) is inadequate from a cross-linguistic point of view.[8] Accordingly, Hendriks (1996) treats the range of variation in the structural realization of information packaging as displayed by Catalan and English by means of the sign-based categorial grammar formalism of Hendriks (1994), which takes its inspiration from Oehrle's (1988, 1993) work on generalized compositionality for multidimensional linguistic objects and shares characteristics with HPSG (Head-Driven Phrase Structure Grammar—see Pollard and Sag 1987, 1994). Basically, this formalism is a both intonationally/syntactically and semantically/informationally interpreted version of a double 'dependency' variant (see Moortgat and Morrill 1991) of the non-associative Lambek (1961) calculus, enriched with the unary operators of Moortgat (1994). The signs, the grammatical resources of this formalism, are Saussurian form-meaning units which reflect the fact that the dimensions of linguistic form and meaning contribute to well-formedness in an essentially parallel way:

(1.25) intonational term $\triangleleft$ type $\triangleright$ informational term

The treatment of information packaging in this formalism differs from many of its predecessors (including other extensions of standard Lambek calculus such as Oehrle 1991, Van der Linden 1991, and Moortgat 1993), in that it does not employ focusing operators, but, instead, makes use of 'defocusing' operators that license the presence of links and tails. According to most approaches, focused constituents are semantic functors which take the non-focused part of the sentence as their argument. This analysis is based on such assumptions as made in Szabolcsi (1981, 1983) and Svoboda and Materna (1987), where focus is not only considered an information-packaging primitive but also an implicit truth-conditional exhaustiveness operator, and on semantic studies of the phenomenon of 'association with focus' as provided by Jacobs (1983), Rooth (1985), Krifka (1991), and others who have argued that the quantificational structure of so-called focus-sensitive operators is crucially determined by the traditional pragmatic focus-ground partition. However, Vallduví argues convincingly that 'the claim that focused constituents truth-conditionally entail exhaustiveness leads to extreme

[8]Note, moreover, that the structural realization of information packaging in Catalan involves *both* syntax *and* prosody. E.g., the informationally non-equivalent sentences [$_F$ *Odia el bròquil* L'AMO] and [$_F$ *Odia* EL BRÒQUIL] [$_F$ *l'amo*] differ only prosodically. The same holds for English, where the structural realization of information packaging also may involve syntax: Reinhart (1982: 63) notes that a fronted NP such as *Felix* in the sentence *Felix, it's been ages since I've seen him* must be a topic (i.e., link).

positions' (1992: 170), and Vallduví and Zacharski (1993) show that 'association with pragmatic focus' is not an inherent semantic property of 'focus-sensitive' operators, which may express their semantics on partitions other than the focus-ground one—witness obvious cases of association with subsegments of the informational focus, with links, and with other parts of the ground. This dissociation of the pragmatic focus-background distinction from issues of exhaustiveness and focus-sensitivity dispels the need of analyzing focused constituents as operators which semantically take scope over the non-focused parts of the sentence, which can be considered an advantage. As sentences may lack links and tails, such analyses do not immediately reflect the core status of the focus, which is the only non-optional part of a sentence. In some sense, then, all-focus sentences constitute the basic case, and the cases where there is a ground are derived from such basic all-focus structures.

1.3 Cards and Boxes

Vallduví has it that 'a proper understanding of information packaging, i.e., of the actual strategies used by human agents in effecting information update by linguistic means, will help us gain further insight into the structural properties of the cognitive states these dynamic strategies manipulate' (Vallduví 1994: 24).

As we have seen, the basic idea of information packaging is that in discourse, speakers not only present information to their interlocutors, but also provide them with detailed 'instructions' on how to manipulate and integrate this information. With respect to the role of these instructions in the determination of those aspects of the structure of information states which are relevant to natural language interpretation, Vallduví claims that the 'use of these instructions reveals that speakers treat information states as highly structured objects and exploit their structure to make information update more efficient for their hearers' (Vallduví 1994: 3).

More specifically, with respect to 'the internal structure of information states which is, in fact, crucially exploited by the different information-packaging strategies used by speakers in pursuing communicative efficiency' (1994: 7), it is argued that information packaging instructions contribute in two ways to the optimization of information update, since they provide means to

- designate a file card as the locus of information update and hence circumvent the redundancy of multiple update; and
- identify the information of the sentence and its relation to information already present in the hearer's model.

(Recall that the information of the sentence, I_S, is expressed by the focus, and that the ground has an ushering role with respect to I_S: links indicate where I_S goes, and tails indicate how it fits there.) So, summing up, Vallduví concludes that information states constitute systems that have at least the internal structure of a collection of file cards connected by pointers.

Though the presented arguments may appear to be intuitively quite appealing, it can be argued that, strictly speaking, they are not as compelling as they seem. Somehow, Vallduví is begging the question: 'talking about ushering I_S to a location in the hearer's model K_h [...] does not make much sense unless one assumes some sort of rich internal structure for K_h' (Vallduví 1994: 7). The relevant question, however, is whether this assumption of 'some sort of rich internal structure' itself makes sense of anything besides the ushering function of links.

If file card systems are assumed, *then* the information-packaging instruction types apparently do contribute to efficient information exchange. And if this assumption is warranted, it may even serve as an explanation of the fact that we do appear to find these ways of packaging information in a variety of languages. Nonetheless, the more theoretical question is whether this assumption itself is warranted, and whether the organization of linguistic information exchange really presupposes such information states. After all, ushers can be very useful, but there are also halls that have unnumbered seats! Maybe links really make no sense without files, but, for that matter, maybe we simply fail to understand what links do. The notion of 'ushering I_S to a location' may be just as metaphorical as the notion of 'file card collection'. For instance, files are, as Vallduví puts it, 'dimensionally richer' than the card-less discourse representation structures of Discourse Representation Theory (see Kamp 1981, Kamp and Reyle 1993), since each file card introduces its own 'representational space' where all its records are to be found while there is no sensible notion of location in discourse representation structures. Still, a hearer who employs discourse representation structures has an easier job from a bookkeeping perspective than a hearer whose information states are collections of file cards connected by pointers.

This can be illustrated as follows. Imagine an utterance made by Irene, a speaker who organizes her utterances on the basis of the assumption that her audience stores information using collections of file cards connected by pointers, to Hans, a hearer who employs discourse representation structures. Clearly, it would be inappropiate to say that Irene uses links to usher I_S to a location in the hearer's model K_S, since there is no sensible notion of location in Hans' discourse representation structures. Still, this does not at all preclude Hans from updating his discourse representation with the proposition that Irene attempts to get through. And worse, he has even got considerably less to do than a hearer who uses collections of file cards connected by pointers. Compare the following link-focus example:

(1.26) $[_L$**Frank**$_5][_F$*flew from Amsterdam*$_9$ *to Oslo*$_8$ *via* STUTTGART$_2]$

Neglecting various details, if a file clerk is to update her file in order to represent the information expressed by example (1.26) in the way sketched above, she has to carry out the following sequence of instructions:[9]

(1.27) GOTO(5)(UPDATE-ADD(flew(5,9,8,2)))
GOTO(9)(UPDATE-ADD($\boxed{\mapsto 5}$))
GOTO(8)(UPDATE-ADD($\boxed{\mapsto 5}$))
GOTO(2)(UPDATE-ADD($\boxed{\mapsto 5}$))
GOTO(5)

Hans, on the other hand, only has to carry out the following instruction:

(1.28) UPDATE-ADD(flew(5,9,8,2))

This example may serve as an indication that none of the data discussed above precludes the use of, say, Kampian discourse representation structures instead of Heimian files. Clearly, there may be evidence for assuming there to be files at work, and one of the last things this paper would like to claim is that people organize their information in simpler systems than collections of file cards (or discourse representation structures, for that matter). On the contrary. The only point is that the use of files does not appear to be imperative so far.

Notice that Vallduví's conclusion is, in some sense, unfalsifiable. Discourse representation structures can model precisely the same informa-

[9]Assuming that establishing links to the locus of update is done via packaging instructions—of course, these links have to be established *some*how. Note, by the way, that the file clerk's task would not be made easier by structure sharing (something suggested by Enric Vallduví (personal communication)), because also the structure sharing will itself have to be established somehow—in the following way, for example:

GOTO(5)(UPDATE-ADD($\boxed{1}$ flew(5,9,8,2)))
GOTO(9)(UPDATE-ADD($\boxed{1}$))
GOTO(8)(UPDATE-ADD($\boxed{1}$))
GOTO(2)(UPDATE-ADD($\boxed{1}$))
GOTO(5)

tion as file card systems, except for one small difference. The only thing that discourse representation structures lack is a marked discourse referent corresponding to the file notion of 'current locus of update', i.e., the location where the file clerk happens to find herself. If we assume that discourse representation structures have a way of marking such a discourse referent j—by a condition 'CLERK_AT(j)', say—, then the two systems differ only in the way in which they display their information: in one big box, or on several cards connected by pointers. But, moreover, one can show that given Vallduví's specific use of pointers to file cards, there is actually a bijective correspondence between his files and the class of discourse representation structures with atomic conditions and one marked discourse referent for the current locus of update. For note that conditions 'REL($i_1, \ldots, i_n$)' are invariably added on card i_1, inducing pointers '$\boxed{\mapsto i_1}$' on the cards $i_2, \ldots, i_n$. Hence the following correspondence can be established:

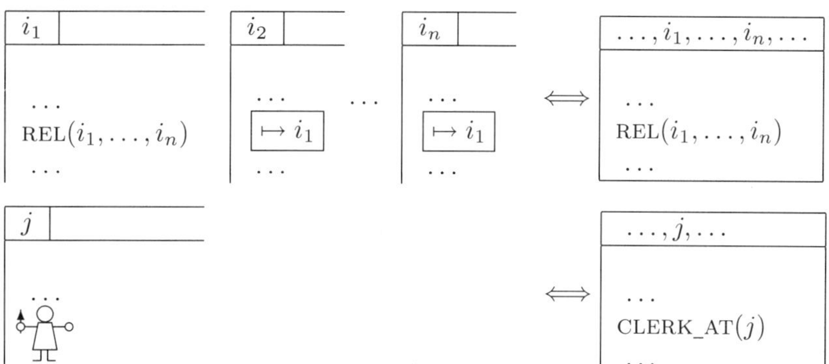

The idea that links specify a locus of update in information states that are collections of file cards connected by pointers is problematic for various reasons. First, it is unclear what locus of update must be associated with quantified, negative and disjunctive links, or—more in general—where and how quantified, negative and disjunctive information has to be put. Second, the existence of sentences with more than one link is enigmatic. Third, the replacement operation triggered by the presence of tails is complicated by the use of file cards. And fourth, the approach leads to the counterintuitive conclusion that pronouns form part of the focus. These issues will be addressed in the remainder of this section.

(a) Vallduví observes that files are 'dimensionally richer' than the discourse representation structures (DRSs) of Discourse Representation Theory. Now, this is true to the extent that each file card introduces its own 'representational space' where all records concerning that file card are to be found. In order to be actually richer, nonetheless, files must be adapted to model more than merely atomic conditions—i.e., individuals having properties and standing in relations at various spatio-temporal locations. Among other things, they should be able to model quantified, negative and disjunctive information. Discourse Representation Theory allows the construction of complex conditions from sub-DRSs, and these conditions—by an appropriate semantic interpretation procedure—model precisely such information. Now, Heim, who explicitly speaks of files and file cards as metaphors (1982: 276 and 302ff.), spells out quantified, negative and disjunctive information in purely semantic terms, i.e., in terms of the domains and satisfaction sets of files. However, it is not clear how such information must be expressed in the non-metaphorical file card set-up of Vallduví (1994).

For one thing, what loci of update are specified by the links of sentences such as (1.29) and (1.30)?[10] On what file card(s)—if any—should the information expressed by these sentences be put?

(1.29) $[_{\text{L}}$**Every man**$][_{\text{F}}$WALKS$]$

(1.30) $[_{\text{L}}$**John or Mary**$][_{\text{F}}$WALKS$]$

For another, how should this information be put? One might think of using sub-files, but then, where must these be put? Are they attached to a main file, or must they be attached to a main file's file card? Which one? Interestingly, Heim raises similar questions in her 1983 paper:

> Take a simple sentence [...]: *It is raining*. In the context of the file metaphor, one doesn't quite know how to deal with this sentence. As an informative sentence, it ought to call for an updating of the file somehow: but what exactly is the file clerk supposed to do? The information that it is raining does not belong on any particular file card, it seems, since each file card is a description of an individual, but *It is raining* is not about any individual. Should the file clerk perhaps write on some arbitrary card: 'is such that it is raining'? Or

[10]Though 'links tend to be definite NPs' (1992: 77), Vallduví notes the 'restricted existence of indefinite links' (1992: 46). 'Sentences with *quantifier links* are' claimed to be 'less natural than others, causing raised eyebrows among some Catalan speakers. Sentences like *A tots els estudiants*$_i$ *els*$_i$ *donen un* CARNET t_i "To all students they give an ID" or *A tothom*$_i$ *no el*$_i$ *tracten* t_i IGUAL "Everybody they don't treat the same" are extremely natural, some other sentences sound odder. Most sentences, however, are felicitous once the right context is construed, although in some cases it may require some sophistication' (Vallduví 1992: 153). Analogously, Reinhart notes that if they 'can be interpreted (pragmatically) as denoting sets, universally quantified NPs, as well as specific and generic indefinite NPs, can serve as topics' (1982: 65–66).

> should he write that on all cards? And what if the file so far doesn't contain any cards yet? [...] Quantified and negated propositions are similarly puzzling if we are so ambitious as to want to say what exactly the file clerk does in response to them. Under the modest aspect of domain and satisfaction set change, however, they pose no problem. (Heim 1983: 183–184)

It should be noted here that such a 'modest' position cannot be retained in the set-up of Vallduví (1994), because there the entities to be updated must be *files*, and *not* their domains and their satisfaction sets.

(*b*) Vallduví (1992: 104) notes that there is no structural restriction on the number of links in Catalan. 'Sentences may have more than one link, as in the Catalan example (1.31).

(1.31) $[_{\text{L}}$*El bròquil*$]$ $[_{\text{L}}$*a l'amo*$]$ $[_{\text{F}}$*l'hi van* REGALAR$]$
the broccoli to the boss *obj-iobj 3p-past* give
Approx.: 'The broccoli the boss (they) gave it to him (for free)'.

In these cases the speaker directs the hearer to go to two addresses and enter the information under both.' (Vallduví 1992: 60, example number adapted). So, assuming that 'they' have card #3 and that the boss and broccoli still possess their respective cards #25 and #136, this means that the sentence is *not* associated with the instruction (1.32),[11] but with an instruction along the lines of (1.33).

(1.32) *GOTO(136)(GOTO(25)(UPDATE-ADD(give(3,136,25)))

(1.33) GOTO(136)(UPDATE-ADD(give(3,136,25))
GOTO(25)(UPDATE-ADD(give(3,136,25))

But this raises questions. What is the current locus of update after (1.33) has been carried out? Is the file clerk suddenly simultaneously working on two different file cards? If she isn't (suppose she is only working on card #25), does this then mean that (1.33) is equivalant to (1.34), the instruction associated with the one-link sentence (1.35)?

(1.34) GOTO(25)(UPDATE-ADD(give(3,136,25))
GOTO(136)(UPDATE-ADD($\boxed{\mapsto 25}$))
GOTO(25)

[11]Note, by the way, that the 'GOTO(136)' constitutes a superfluous detour in instruction (1.32).

(1.35) [$_L$*A l'amo*] [$_F$*hi van regalar el* BRÒQUIL]]

But if (1.33) and (1.34) are equivalent, then why does Catalan allow multiple links at all? And how could (1.33) and (1.34) be non-equivalent—what sense could multiple loci of update make that pointers cannot?

(*c*) Above an informal sketch was given of Vallduví's analysis of tail-containing sentences in terms of UPDATE-REPLACE instructions. It can be expected that various complications will arise when it comes to giving an explicit formalization of the replacement instructions associated with tails. Any attempt at giving an appropriate and fully general definition of these instructions will have to confront a number of questions. Thus, how exactly do you know which record has to be replaced or specified further? Is there guaranteed to be such a record? Is there a unique one, and what happens if there are more? Is it always one record that has to be replaced, or do we sometimes need to replace a group of records? What kind of match must there be between the material in a tail, and the material in the target record? Of course, these are tough nuts that have to be cracked when it comes to coming to theories of belief revision.

Here we will just present a simple example which illustrates that the replacement operation triggered by the presence of tails is specifically complicated by the idea that information is organized in file card systems. Suppose that Louis van Gaal utters (1.36), whereupon Johan Cruijff reacts with saying (1.37):

(1.36) [$_L$**Ajax**][$_F$WON]

(1.37) [$_F$*No*, BARCELONA][$_T$*won*]

Assume the file cards #1 and #2 for Ajax and Barcelona, respectively. Now, clearly, Johan Cruiff here instructs Louis van Gaal to replace his record according to which Ajax won by one according to which Barcelona did. Presumably, this should not (only) be done on the card for Ajax. Instead of the straightforwardly simple (1.38), then, the complex instruction given in (1.39) seems to be needed.

(1.38) *UPDATE-REPLACE(won(2),won(1))

(1.39) UPDATE-REPLACE(,won(1))
GOTO(2)(UPDATE-ADD(won(2)))

(*d*) An example typical of the way in which Vallduví analyzes pronouns can be obtained by combining the above example sentences (1.11) and (1.12) into one text:

(1.40) $[_{\mathrm{L}}$ *The* **boss**$][_{\mathrm{F}}$*hates* BROCCOLI$]$
$[_{\mathrm{F}}$*He always eats* BEANS$]$

The first sentence is a link-focus construction, and therefore associated with an instruction to go to the file card of the boss, thereby turning it into the current locus of update, and to enrich that file card with the information that the boss hates broccoli (and the broccoli file card with a pointer to the file card of the boss). The second sentence is an all-focus construction, associated with the simple instruction to add the focus information that the value of the current locus of update always eats beans to the current locus of update. Hence if it is interpreted immediately after the first sentence, it amounts to adding the information that the boss always eats beans to the card of the boss.

Note that the pronoun *he* obviously does not induce replacement or shift the locus of update. Hence it cannot be a link or a tail, and this inevitably leads to the conclusion that it forms part of the focus.[12] This is a counterintuitive result, however, since it is also clear that the interpretation of the pronoun is provided by the value of the current locus of update—which does not constitute new information, but can be assumed to be already present in the hearer's information state.

1.4 Non-Monotonic Anaphora

Let us wind up the discussion so far. It has been argued that the data discussed above do not enforce the conclusion that information states have at least the structure of a collection of file cards connected by pointers. For that matter, the phenomena can also be accounted for in terms of discourse representation structures, and it is very well possible that circumventing file cards might lead to the avoidance of the complications that were outlined in the previous section.

In view of these considerations, a card-less alternative will be defended in the present section, according to which information states are modeled by means of discourse representation structures, which are ontologically less committed than the 'dimensionally richer' file card system, in that discourse representation structures do not come with locations.

But if, as was argued above, the use of files does not appear to be

[12] As an anonymous referee pointed out, Vallduví's analysis of pronouns might be due to some (implicit) circular argumentation: 'If one would analyse the second sentence of (1.40) in a more intuitive way as consisting of a link (*he*) and a focus part (*always eats* BEANS), then one would have to predict, according to Vallduví, that the pronoun gets an L+H* accent—*quod non*. So it seems that the pronoun *he* is construed as a part of the focus *because* it does not get an accent, and this seems like a circular argument to me.'

imperative, then a question must be faced: what purpose *do* links serve if they do not serve to specify a locus of update by ushering to locations? What does 'ushering to a location' mean if representations do not come with locations? Thus a different perspective on the function of links is required. Below a tentative answer will be suggested that carries less presuppositions than the file metaphor.

This alternative perspective has its heuristic starting point in Kamp and Reyle (1993), who note that processing a plural pronoun does not always involve equating the discourse referent it introduces with one introduced earlier through the processing of some other plural NP. Kamp and Reyle consider the following example:

(1.41) John took Mary to Acapulco.
They had a lousy time.

Here, the plural pronoun *they* does not have a single NP for its antecedent. Rather, the 'antecedent' has to be 'constructed' out of various parts of the preceding text. Such examples, which are very common, seem to suggest that plural pronouns can pick up any antecedent that can be obtained from antecedent information by logical deduction. However, the deductive principles that are permitted in this context turn out to be subject to restrictions.

(1.42) Eight of the ten balls are in the bag.
They are under the sofa.

The pronoun *they* in (1.42) cannot be understood as referring to the two balls that are missing from the bag. Apparently, subtracting one set from another is not a permissible operation for the formation of pronominal antecedents.

The permissible process of antecedent formation displayed by (1.41) is called Summation: a new discourse referent is introduced which represents the 'union' of individuals (John and Mary) and/or sets represented by discourse referents that are already part of the discourse representation structure. Other permissible processes are Abstraction, exemplified by (1.43), which allows the introduction of discourse referents for quantified NPs (compare also footnote 10 above), and Kind Introduction, which introduces discourse referents for a certain 'genus' explicitly mentioned in the text by a (simple or complex) noun. If *they* in (1.44) refers to the (few) men who joined the (conservative) party, we are dealing with Abstraction. The more natural reading, where *they* refers to men in general (and the party is presumably non-conservative), is a case of Kind Introduction.

(1.43) I found every book Bill needs.
They are on his desk.

(1.44) Few men joined the party.
They are very conservative.

In their discussion of the inferential processes available for the construction of antecedents for (plural) pronouns, Kamp and Reyle suggest the following generalization:

> What sets the admissible inference processes of Summation, Abstraction and Kind Introduction apart from an inadmissible inference pattern such as set subtraction is that the former are [...] strictly *positive* (Kamp and Reyle 1993: 344),

or

> 'cumulative' in the following sense: the newly created discourse referent represents an entity of which the discourse referents used in the application of the rule represent (atomic or non-atomic) parts (Kamp and Reyle 1993: 394).

Notice that, when this generalization is taken in conjunction with a principle that anaphora invariably involves the addition of an equational condition 'X = Y' for an anaphoric expression with discourse referent Y and a—possibly inferentially created—antecedent discourse referent X (and such an equational approach is standard practice in Discourse Representation Theory), the necessary result will be that anaphora is always (upward) monotonic: if an expression with discourse referent Y is anaphorically dependent on an expression with discourse referent X, then X ⊆ Y.[13]

The latter result, however, does not seem to be borne out by the facts. For example, Van Deemter (1992, 1994a) presents cases of 'non-identity anaphora' along the lines of (1.45), as well as minimal pairs such as (1.46) and (1.47):

(1.45) *Our neigbours are extremely nice* PEOPLE.
He *is a* TEACHER, **she** *is a* HOUSEWIFE.

(1.46) *John fed the* ANIMALS. *The cats were* HUNGRY.

[13]Let sets A and B be partially ordered by $\leq_A$ and $\leq_B$, repectively. In mathematics, a function $f : A \rightarrow B$ is called *monotonic* iff $a \leq_A b$ entails that $f(a) \leq_B f(b)$ for all a and b in A. Note that the same notion is involved here for (*i*) the function $f : \mathrm{NP} \rightarrow \mathrm{DR}$ which associates every occurrence of a noun phrase a with its discourse marker $f(a)$; (*ii*) $\leq_{\mathrm{NP}}$ such that $a \leq_{\mathrm{NP}} b$ iff a is the antecedent of anaphor b; and (*iii*) $\leq_{\mathrm{DR}}$ such that $X \leq_{\mathrm{DR}} Y$ iff $X \subseteq Y$.

(1.47) *John fed the* ANIMALS. *The* **cats** *were* HUNGRY.

It can be observed that the pronouns **he** an **she** are anaphorically dependent on *our neighbours* in (1.45), but that the discourse referents of the pronouns represent entities which are proper subsets of the entity represented by the discourse referent of the antecedent: obvious cases of non-monotonic anaphora.

Moreover, whereas the reading of (1.46) where *the cats* is anaphoric to *the* ANIMALS strongly and monotonically suggests that all animals fed by John were cats, the reading of (1.47) where *the* **cats** is anaphoric to *the* ANIMALS does not. It even seems to imply that John fed at least one non-cat.[14] Again, we are dealing with non-monotonic anaphora.

Note that the texts (1.46) and (1.47) differ only in the assignment of L+H* accent to the noun phrase *the cats*, which is the distinguishing mark of links in English. Hence our alternative hypothesis concerning links:

(1.48) *Non-Monotonic Anaphora Hypothesis* (*NAH*):
Linkhood (marked by L+H* accent in English) serves to signal non-monotonic anaphora. If an expression is a link, then its discourse referent Y is anaphoric to an antecedent discourse referent X such that X $\not\subseteq$ Y.

This hypothesis affects a range of phenomena. In Hendriks (*draft*) it is argued that a discourse-representational approach of information packaging such as the one sketched here provides a sound background for an adequate theory of the phenomena commonly referred to as 'association with focus' (Jacobs 1983; Rooth 1985, 1992; Krifka 1991), thereby contributing to the integration of pragmatic theories of information packaging with contemporary research in formal semantics. More in particular, the approach is capable of handling the non-marginal cases of association of 'focus-sensitive' operators such as *only* with non-focal parts of the sentence that have been attested in the literature (Vallduví 1992; Partee 1994; Vallduví and Zacharski 1993). That is, not only the phenomenon of 'second occurrence focus' is accounted for, but also the link-sensitive behaviour of 'focus-sensitive' operators is given an analysis of which the approach to links given here is an essential ingredient. Below it will be shown that, in addition to this, the *NAH* subsumes not only the so-called 'non-identity' anaphora just exemplified and analyzed in Van Deemter

[14]'Strongly suggests' and 'seems to imply' instead of 'entails', since though the effects are quite strong, they are of a pragmatic, rather than a logico-semantic, nature. See also (*c*), on pronoun referent resolution, below.

(1992, 1994a), but also the cases of contrastive stress discussed in Rooth (1992) and Vallduví (1992, 1994), and the corrections mentioned by Pierrehumbert and Hirschberg (1990). It contributes to an explanation of the effect of pitch accenting on pronoun referent resolution noted in Cahn (1995), Kameyama (1994), Vallduví (1994), among many others, and it sheds light on the distinction between restrictive and non-restrictive relative clauses and adjectives (see Kamp and Reyle 1993).

(*a*) The relationship between non-identity anaphora and linkhood can be demonstrated even more saliently with relational nouns:

(1.49) *Ten guys were playing basketball in the* RAIN.
The fathers were having FUN.

(1.50) *Ten guys were playing basketball in the* RAIN.
The **fathers** *were having* FUN.

Thus, whereas (1.49) has an 'identity' reading where *the fathers* is anaphoric to *ten guys* which—monotonically—suggests that all ten guys playing basketball in the rain were fathers who were having fun, the reading of (1.50) where *the* **fathers** is anaphoric to *ten guys* does not. This reading seems to—non-monotonically—imply that the fathers who were having fun constitute a proper subset of the ten basketball-playing guys. Since *father* is a relational noun, there is, next to this 'subsectional' reading, also a—non-monotonic—'relational' reading of (1.50) on which the fathers *of* the ten guys playing basketball in the rain were having fun.

Observe, by the way, that Kamp and Reyle's example (1.41) of Summation, a case of monotonic non-identity anaphora in which the pronoun *they* typically appears unaccented, shows that it is not so much the 'non-identity' as the 'non-monotonicity' of the anaphora which is responsible for the L+H* accent (that is: the linkhood) of the anaphor.

(*b*) According to Rooth, contrast is the cornerstone of the interpretation of focus phenomena: 'Intonational focus has a semantic import related to the intuitive notion of contrast within a set of alternative elements' (1992: 113), and Vallduví gives the following example of 'contrastive' links (1993:14):

(1.51) Where can I find the cutlery?
The **forks** *are in the* CUPBOARD, *but*
The **knives** *I left in the* DRAWER.

Note, however, that contrast is not really necessary for L+H* accent:[15]

[15]Nor is contrariety (as proposed in Van Deemter 1994b), witness:

(1.52) Where can I find the cutlery?
The **forks** *are in the* CUPBOARD.

Mere non-monotonicity suffices.

(*c*) As Pierrehumbert and Hirschberg (1990) observe, L+H* accent often arises in corrections. Thus, sentence (1.54) is a natural way of correcting (1.53).

(1.53) *John was stung by* MOSQUITOS.

(1.54) *He was stung by* **bees**.

Interestingly, it can be observed that non-monotonicity plays a role here too. Notice that a sentence such as (1.55) is less naturally uttered in the context of (1.53), even though, semantically (i.e., truth-conditionally) speaking, this sentence is an impeccable expression of the proposition entertained by a speaker who believes that John was actually stung by bees as well as mosquitos.

(1.55) *He was stung by* **insects**.

In fact, a speaker of (1.53) who is 'corrected' by someone's utterance of (1.55) might very well react by uttering (1.56):

(1.56) *Mosquitos* ARE *insects*.

Apparently, it is the fact that mosquitos are insects that thwarts the assignment of L+H* accent to *insects* in sentence (1.55).

(*d*) Many authors have paid attention to the effect of pitch accenting on pronoun referent resolution. The examples below stem from Lakoff (1971).

(1.57) Paul called Jim a Republican. *Then he* INSULTED *him*.

(1.58) Paul called Jim a Republican. *Then* **he** *insulted* **him**.

For grammatical reasons (syntactic parallellism), the preferred antecedents for the unstressed pronouns *he* and *him* in (1.57) are *Paul* and

---

Where can I find the cutlery?
The **forks** *are in the* CUPBOARD, *and the* **knives** TOO.

(Examples such as this one are addressed in Van Deemter (1994a: 12), where equivalence modulo identifying substitutions is proposed as a further source of accent.)

Jim, respectively. The preferences are reverse for the stressed pronouns **he** and **him** in (1.58).[16]

In the theory of Kameyama (1994), this phenomenon is accounted for in the following way:

- A grammar subsystem represents the space of possibilities and a pragmatics subsystem represents the space of preferences;
- Stressed and unstressed pronouns have the same 'denotational range', i.e., the same range of *possible* values;
- *Complementary Preference Hypothesis* (*CPH*): A stressed pronoun takes the complementary preference of the unstressed counterpart.

However, the *NAH* formulated in (1.48) is capable of *predicting* the *CPH* effects: adding L+H* accent to pronouns means the addition of a pragmatic signal that the anaphora involved is non-monotonic. In the case of singular antecedents with entity-representing discourse referents,[17] this means that the anaphor does not *corefer* with its antecedent. Correspondingly, we have that pronominal stress turns the pragmatically determined preference for a certain grammatically possible antecedent into a pragmatically determined preference for non-coreference with that antecedent.[18]

(*e*) The sentences (1.59) and (1.60) (taken from Kamp and Reyle 1993: 255) illustrate the familiar rule of English orthography that non-restrictive clauses are set apart from the surrounding text by commas, but that restrictive clauses are not.

(1.59) The son who attended a boarding school was insufferable.

(1.60) The son, who attended a boarding school, was insufferable.

Note that (1.59), in which the relative clause is used restrictively, suggests that there is more than one son, but only one who is boarding. In (1.60), where the relative clause is used non-restrictively, the suggestion is rather that there is only one son, of whom it is said not only that he

[16]The fact that (1.58) insinuates that calling someone a Republican is an insult is essentially due to the de-accenting of *insulted* in the second sentence of (1.58).

[17]Or, equivalently, singleton-set-representing discourse referents.

[18]Thus let $\{p\}, \{j\}, \{x\}, \{y\}$ constitute the respective discourse referents of the noun phrases *Paul*, *Jim*, **he** and **him**. Then the grammar subsystem specifies $\{\{p\}, \{j\}\}$ as the range of possible values for $\{x\}$ and $\{y\}$, and the pragmatics subsystem (building on syntactic parallellism) specifies $\{p\}$ and $\{j\}$ as the respective preferred antecedents for the pronominal discourse referents $\{x\}$ and $\{y\}$. Since the pronouns are stressed, however, the respective preferences of $\{x\}$ and $\{y\}$ for $\{p\}$ and $\{j\}$ mean that $\{p\} \not\subseteq \{x\}$ and $\{j\} \not\subseteq \{y\}$, that is: $x \neq p$ and $y \neq j$.

was insufferable but also, parenthetically as it were, that he attended a boarding school. If the prosody of these sentences is taken into account, it will be clear that this pragmatic difference is in keeping with the *NAH* as formulated in (1.48). Similar observations can be made with respect to the (non-)restrictiveness of the adjectives and nouns in (1.63) (Kamp and Reyle 1993: 372).

(1.61) *The* **son who attended a boarding school** *was* INSUFFERABLE.

(1.62) *The* **son**, *who attended a* BOARDING SCHOOL, *was* INSUFFERABLE.

(1.63) *John fed the* ANIMALS. *The young cats were* HUNGRY.
John fed the ANIMALS. *The young* **cats** *were* HUNGRY.
John fed the ANIMALS. *The* **young** *cats were* HUNGRY.
John fed the ANIMALS. *The* **young cats** *were* HUNGRY.

1.5 Conclusion

In Pierrehumbert and Hirschberg (1990), 'The Meaning of Intonational Contours in the Interpretation of Discourse', it is proposed that speakers use tune to specify a particular relationschip between the 'propositional content' realized in the intonational phrase over which the tune is employed and the mutual beliefs of participants—speaker *S* and hearer *H*—in the current discourse, where tune, or *intonational contour*, is taken to be a sequence of *low* (L) and *high* (H) tones, made up from pitch accents, phrase accents and boundary tones, and tune meaning is assumed to be built up compositionally. *Pitch accents* mark the lexical items with which they are associated as prominent: accented items are salient, not only phonologically but also from an informational standpoint. Pierrehumbert and Hirschberg follow Beckman and Pierrehumbert (1986) in distinguishing six pitch accents: two simple tones, H* and L*, and four complex ones, L*+H, L+H*, H*+L and H+L*, where the '*' indicates that the tone is aligned with a stressed syllable. Pitch accents are believed to convey information about the status of the individual discourse referents, modifiers, predicates and relationships specified by the lexical items with which the accents are associated.

(*a*) 'In general, we believe that all accent types can be used to convey information to *H* about how the propositional content of the (perhaps partially) instantiated expression corresponding to the utterance is to be used to modify what *H* believes to be mutually believed' (1990: 289).

With respect to the two L+H pitch accents (L*+H and L+H*), it is observed that:

(*b*) '[The L+H pitch accents] are employed by *S* to convey the salience of some *scale* (defined here [...] as a partial ordering) linking the accented item to other items salient in *H*'s mutual beliefs' (1990: 294), and '*S* employs the L+H* accent to convey that the accented item—and not some alternative related item—should be mutually believed' (1990: 296).

Finally, the most common use of L+H* in the data collected by Pierrehumbert and Hirschberg

(*c*) 'is to mark a correction or contrast. In such cases *S* substitutes a new scalar value for one previously proposed by *S* or by *H*—or for some alternative value available in the context' (1990: 296).

By way of conclusion, we may observe that the account of links detailed in the present paper can actually be considered a partial execution—viz., for L+H* pitch accent—of the intonational-informational program outlined in Pierrehumbert and Hirschberg (1990), for note that on the present account the following analogous claims are assumed to hold:

(*a*) Pitch accent is an aspect of information packaging—i.e, the structuring of propositional content in function of the speaker's assumptions about the hearer's knowledge and attentional state;

(*b*) L+H* pitch accent does invoke a scale, viz., the partial ordering '$\subseteq$' on discourse referents, and conveys that the antecedent the accented item finds itself 'linked to' is associated with a discourse referent that is not a subset of the discourse referent of the accented item; and

(*c*) Correction and contrast are among the manifestations of the non-monotonic anaphora signaled by L+H* pitch accent, which were argued to involve (non-)association with focus, 'non-identity' anaphora, contrastive stress, correction, pronoun referent resolution, and restrictiveness of relatives and adjectives.

However, two provisos should be added to this conclusion.

First, it must be noted that the *NAH*, the hypothesis that linkhood—and hence L+H* accent in English—serves to signal non-monotonic anaphora, is not accompanied with a theory of anaphora resolution. Thus, taking up the issue mentioned in footnote 7 above, it is true that a deaccenting of *the boss* in the context (1.17) of (1.18) and an accenting of this expression in the context (1.15) of (1.16) would be in agreement with the *NAH*, 'because only in (1.16) does *the boss* represent a non-monotonic anaphora, whereas links in sentences such as in example

(1.18) clearly fail to do so', but note that also an accenting of *the boss* in the context (1.17) could in principle be accounted for, e.g., by the assumption that the utterer of the anaphoric sentence has access to an appropriate antecedent in a previous utterance of the person who asked (1.17). With respect to non-monotonic anaphora resolution, there are various interesting phenomena that deserve closer attention. Consider, for example, the following contrast:

(1.64) *The children and their parents went to the* FAIR.
The **children** ENJOYED *it.*

(1.65) *The children and their parents went to the* FAIR.
The **small** *children* ENJOYED *it.*

In (1.64) the relevant accessible discourse referent for the non-monotonic anaphor is apparently the one associated with *the children and the parents*, which accounts for the accenting of *children* in the second sentence of that example. In the second sentence of (1.65), on the other hand, this expression does not undergo accenting: this time the relevant accessible discourse referent for the non-monotonic anaphor is apparently not the one associated with *the children and their parents*, but—presumably—the one associated with *the children.* For further discussion of non-monotonic anaphora resolution the reader is referred to Piwek (1997) and (1998).

Second, the *NAH* in its present form associates *only* L+H* accent with non-monotonic anaphora. However, this time taking up the issue that was mentioned in footnote 6 above, it was noted above that no two professional speakers produce their utterances with the same intonational pattern in a corpus of read-aloud texts and that, correspondingly, the distinction between H* accent and L+H* accent is a frequent point of disagreement among transcribers (Pitrelli *et al.* 1994). Since the distinction is far from straightforward and unproblematic, Ross and Ostendorff (1996), among others, typically give it up: if hearers have great difficulty hearing the difference, how can it play a role in information packaging? Maybe the crucial factor is *whether* or not words get accented, so that the question *which* kind of accent has been used is at best of secondary importance. At this point we would like to refer the reader (again) to Hendriks (*draft*), in which a modified version of Rooth (1992)'s 'strong' theory of focus and H* pitch accent interpretation is defended. On such a strong theory, focus interpretation essentially involves some kind of (presuppositional) anaphora. More specifically, it is claimed that association with focus is an epiphenomenon of the fact that, due to the particular lexical semantics of focusing adverbs, this anaphora is non-trivial if and only if it is 'non-monotonic'. This is more or less obvious for items such as *only* and *even*, where the non-monotonic anaphora displays the characteristics of the contextual restriction that is known to play a role in the interpretation of quantificational determiners and adverbs, but with items such as *also*, *too* and *not* it surfaces as a contrast with a parallel element in the 'active context'. Two of the simplifying modifications proposed in Hendriks (*draft*) eliminatively affect both the 'individual case' clause in the interpretation of Rooth's focus operator and his requirement that the contextually restricted focus semantic value always contain the ordinary semantic value. In addition to this, it is argued that the resulting simplified theory of focus interpretation should be raised to the level of *sets* of Roothian alternatives. Motivation for this type shift can be based on general considerations regarding the semantics of questions and the pragmatics of answers, but the resulting theory has, moreover, the advantage of providing a fully uniform, i.e., isomorphic, analysis both of topic—L+H* accent—and of focus—H* accent—interpretation. This analysis is also capable of accounting for cases where focusing adverbs do NOT associate with the focus of the sentence in which they occur. Thus, given raised alternatives, the hypothesis of lexically induced non-monotonic anaphora will turn out to be able to provide a unified explanation, not only for the ubiquity of association with focus but also for the various cases of association with *non*-focus, where focusing adverbs express their semantics on partitions other than the focus-ground one: besides the phenomenon of association with 'second occurrence focus', these include instances of association with subsegments of the informational focus, with non-focal topics and with other parts of the ground.

References

Beckman, M., and J. Pierrehumbert (1986). 'Intonational Structure in Japanese and English'. *Phonological Yearbook* **3**, 15–70.

Bosch, P., and R. van der Sandt (eds.) (1994). *Focus and Natural Language Processing. Proceedings of a Conference in Celebration of the 10th Anniversary of the Journal of Semantics.* Working Papers 6 (Vol. 1: Intonation and Syntax), 7 (Vol. 2: Semantics), and 8 (Vol. 3: Discourse) of the IBM Institute for Logic and Linguistics, Heidelberg.

Cahn, J. (1995). 'The Effect of Pitch Accenting on Pronoun Referent Resolution'. Manuscript. MIT, Cambridge (Mass.).

Chafe, W.L., (1976). 'Givenness, Contrastiveness, Definiteness, Subjects, Topics and Point of View'. In C.N. Li (ed.) (1976), *Subject and Topic*, 25–55. Associated Press, New York.

Clark, H.H., and S.E. Haviland (1977). 'Comprehension and the Given-New Contract'. In R.O. Freedle (ed.) (1977), *Discourse Production and Comprehension*, 1–40. Lawrence Erlbaum Associates, Hillsdale (New Jersey).

Dahl, Ö. (1974). (1974). 'Topic-Comment Structure Revisited'. In Ö. Dahl (ed.) (1974), *Topic and Comment, Contextual Boundedness and Focus. Papers in Text Linguistics 6*. Helmut Buske, Hamburg.

Deemter, K. van (1992). 'Towards a Generalization of Anaphora'. *Journal of Semantics* **9**, 27–51.

Deemter, K. van (1994a). 'What's New? A Semantic Perspective on Sentence Accent'. *Journal of Semantics* **11**, 1–31.

Deemter, K. van (1994b). 'Contrastive Stress, Contrariety and Focus'. In P. Bosch and R. van der Sandt (eds.), 39–49.

Engdahl, E. (ed.) (1994). *Integrating Information Structure into Constraint-based and Categorial Approaches*. ESPRIT Basic Research Project 6852, Dynamic Interpretation of Natural Language. Deliverable R1.3.B. ILLC, University of Amsterdam.

Heim, I. (1982). *The Semantics of Definite and Indefinite Noun Phrases*. Ph.D. Dissertation University of Massachusetts, Amherst. Published in 1989 by Garland. New York.

Heim, I. (1983). 'File Change Semantics and the Familiarity Theory of Definiteness'. In R. Bäuerle, C. Schwarze and A. von Stechow (eds.) (1983), *Meaning, Use and Interpretation of Language*. De Gruyter, Berlin, 164–189.

Hendriks, H. (1994). 'Information Packaging in a Categorial Perspective'. In Engdahl (ed.), 89–116.

Hendriks, H. (1996). 'Intonation, Derivation, Information'. In C. Casadio (ed.), *Proceedings of the Third Roma Workshop on Proofs and Linguistic Categories*. University of Bologna.

Hendriks, H. (*draft*). 'Information Packaging and "Association with Focus" '. Manuscript, Utrecht University.

Hoffman, B. (1995). 'Integrating "Free" Word Order Syntax and Information Structure'. Manuscript, University of Pennsylvania.

Jackendoff, R. (1972). *Semantic Interpretation in Generative Grammar*. MIT Press, Cambridge (Mass.).

Jacobs, J. (1983). *Fokus und Skalen: Zur Syntax und Semantik von Gradpartikeln im Deutschen*. Niemeyer, Tübingen.

Kameyama, M. (1994). 'Stressed and Unstressed Pronouns: Complementary Preferences'. In P. Bosch and R. van der Sandt (eds.), 475–484.

Kamp, H. (1981). 'A Theory of Truth and Semantic Representation'. In J. Groenendijk, T. Janssen and M. Stokhof (eds.) (1981), *Formal Methods in the Study of Language*. Mathematical Centre, Amsterdam. Reprinted in J. Groenendijk, T. Janssen and M. Stokhof (eds.) (1984), *Truth, Interpretation and Information. Selected Papers from the Third Amsterdam Colloquium*. Foris, Dordrecht.

Kamp, H., and U. Reyle (1993). *From Discourse to Logic. Introduction to Modeltheoretic Semantics of Natural Language, Formal Logic and Discourse Representation Theory*. Kluwer, Dordrecht.

Krifka, M. (1991). 'A Compositional Semantics for Multiple Focus Constructions'. *Linguistische Berichte, Suppl.* **4**, 17–53.

Lakoff, G. (1971). 'On Generative Semantics'. D. Steinberg and L. Jacobovitz (eds.) (1971), *Semantics*. Cambridge University Press, Cambridge, 232–296.

Lambek, J. (1961). 'On the Calculus of Syntactic Types'. In R. Jakobson (ed.) (1961), *Structure of Language and its Mathematical Aspects*. Providence.

Linden, E.-J. van der (1991). 'Accent Placement and Focus in Categorial Logic'. In S. Bird (ed.) (1991) *Declarative Perspectives on Phonology*. Edinburgh Working Papers in Cognitive Science. ECCS, Edinburgh.

Moortgat, M. (1993). 'Generalized Quantification and Discontinuous Type Constructors'. In W. Sijtsma and A. van Horck (eds.) (1993), *Proceedings of the Tilburg Symposium on Discontinuous Dependencies*. De Gruyter, Berlin.

Moortgat, M. (1994). 'Residuation in Mixed Lambek Systems'. In M. Moortgat (ed.) (1994), ESPRIT Basic Research Project 6852, Dynamic Interpretation of Natural Language, DYANA-2 Deliverable R1.1.B. ILLC, University of Amsterdam, and to appear in IGPL Bulletin.

Moortgat, M., and G. Morrill (1991). 'Heads and Phrases. Type Calculus for Dependency and Constituent Structure'. OTS Research Paper, University of Utrecht.

Nooteboom, S.G., and J.M.B. Terken (1982). 'What Makes Speakers Omit Pitch Accents?'. *Phonetica* **39**, 317–336.

Oehrle, R. (1988). 'Multidimensional Compositional Functions as a Basis for Grammatical Analysis'. In R. Oehrle, E. Bach and D. Wheeler (eds.) *Categorial Grammars and Natural Language Structures*. Reidel, Dordrecht.

Oehrle, R. (1991). 'Prosodic Constraints on Dynamic Grammatical Analysis'. In S. Bird (ed.) *Declarative Perspectives on Phonology*. Edinburgh Working Papers in Cognitive Science. ECCS, Edinburgh.

Oehrle, R. (1993). 'String-based Categorial Type Systems'. Manuscript. Department of Linguistics, University of Arizona, Tucson.

Partee, B. (1994). 'Focus, Quantification, and Semantics-Pragmatics Issues. Preliminary Version'. In P. Bosch and R. van der Sandt (eds.), 363–378.

Pierrehumbert, J. (1980). *The Phonology and Phonetics of English Intonation*. Ph.D. Disertation. MIT, Cambridge (Mass.). Distributed by the IULC.

Pierrehumbert, J., and J. Hirschberg (1990). 'The Meaning of Intonational Contours in the Interpretation of Discourse'. In P. Cohen, J. Morgan and M. Pollack (eds.) *Intentions in Communication*, MIT Press, Cambridge.

Piwek, P. (1997). 'Accent Interpretation, Anaphora Resolution and Implicature Derivation'. In P. Dekker, M. Stokhof and Y. Venema (eds.), *Proceedings of the 11th Amsterdam Colloquium*. University of Amsterdam, ILLC/Department of Philosophy.

Piwek, P. (1998). *Logic, Information and Conversation*. Dissertation Technical University Eindhoven.

Pitrelli, J., M. Beckman, and J. Hirschberg (1994). 'Evaluation of Prosodic Transcription Labelling Reliability in the ToBI Framework'. *ICSLP94*, Vol. 1, 123–126.

Pollard, C., and I. Sag (1987). *Information-Based Syntax and Semantics. Vol. 1: Fundamentals*. CSLI, Stanford.

Pollard, C., and I. Sag (1994). *Head-Driven Phrase Structure Grammar*. University of Chicago Press, Chicago, and CSLI, Stanford.

Prince, E. (1981). 'Toward a Taxonomy of Given-New Information'. In P. Cole, *Radical Pragmatics*. Academic Press, New York, 233–255.

Reinhart, T. (1982). 'Pragmatics and Linguistics: An Analysis of Sentence Topics'. *Philosophica* **27**, 53–94.

Rooth, M. (1985). *Association with Focus*. Ph.D. Dissertation University of Massachusetts, Amherst.

Rooth, M. (1992). 'A Theory of Focus Interpretation'. *Natural Language Semantics* **1**, 75–116.

Ross, K., and M. Ostendorf (1996). 'Prediction of Abstract Prosodic Labels for Speech Synthesis'. *Computer, Speech and Language*, **10**, 155–185.

Steedman, M. (1991). 'Structure and Intonation'. *Language* **67**, 260–296.

Steedman, M. (1992). 'Surface Structure, Intonation and "Focus" '. In E. Klein and F. Veltman (eds.) *Natural Language and Speech. Symposium Proceedings, Brussels, November 1991*. Springer, Berlin.

Steedman, M. (1993). 'The Grammar of Intonation and Focus'. In P. Dekker and M. Stokhof (eds.) (1993), *Proceedings of the Ninth Amsterdam Colloquium, December 14–17, 1993*, Part III. ILLC, University of Amsterdam.

Svoboda, A., and P. Materna (1987). 'Functional Sentence Perspective and Intensional Logic'. In R. Dirven and V. Fried (eds.) *Functionalism in Linguistics*. John Benjamins, Amsterdam.

Szabolcsi, A. (1981). 'The Semantics of Topic-Focus Articulation'. In J. Groenendijk, T. Janssen and M. Stokhof (eds.) (1981), *Formal Methods in the Study of Language*. Mathematical Centre, Amsterdam.

Szabolcsi, A. (1983). 'Focussing Properties, or the Trap of First Order'. In *Theoretical Linguistics* **10**, 125–145.

Vallduví, E. (1992). *The Informational Component*. Garland, New York.

Vallduví, E. (1993). 'Information Packaging: A Survey'. Report prepared for *Word Order, Prosody, and Information Structure*. Centre for Cognitive Science and Human Communication Research Centre, University of Edinburgh.

Vallduví, E. (1994). 'The Dynamics of Information Packaging'. In Engdahl (ed.), 1–27.

Vallduví, E., and R. Zacharski (1993). 'Accenting Phenomena, Association with Focus, and the Recursiveness of Focus-Ground'. In P. Dekker and M. Stokhof (eds.) (1993) *Proceedings of the Ninth Amsterdam Colloquium, December 14–17, 1993*, Part III. ILLC, University of Amsterdam.

2

Presupposed Propositions in a Corpus of Dialogue

JENNIFER SPENADER

2.1 Introduction

Why and when do speakers presuppose? A possible answer to this question is that speakers presuppose information that they expect to be known, or alternatively, wish to be treated as known by other discourse participants. In corpus analysis of spoken language, this translates into the expectation that presupposed information should be found in the earlier discourse context, should be generally known or should be relatively uncontroversial new information.

Therefore, understanding presupposition is an important element in understanding information exchange in extended discourse. And vice versa, for studying presuppositional information, examining extended discourse through corpus work seems to be a particularly appropriate methodology. Presupposition interpretation is highly context dependent, which means that single sentences or a short context of several utterances are often inadequate for giving a true picture of how presupposed information functions. Corpus study can also give insights into what naturally produced presuppositions look like, how frequently speakers use them, and what their function is in relation to the rest of the discourse. Another advantage of corpus study is that many examples which are difficult to interpret in isolation are often disambiguated when a context is available.

This study looks at a small group of lexical and syntactic presup-

Information Sharing: Reference and Presupposition in Language Generation and Interpretation.
Edited by Kees van Deemter and Rodger Kibble.

position triggers in the London-Lund Corpus of Spoken English: *factive verbs, factive adjectives, change-of-state verbs,* and *it-clefts.* Each trigger was excerpted and classified according to how the presupposed information would be interpreted within the binding theory of presupposition, developed by van der Sandt (1992). First, the discourse context was examined for the presupposed information to determine if presuppositional binding was possible. When not, the most appropriate level of accommodation was determined.

This group of triggers has two characteristics in common that make them particularly interesting to study. First, all of them signal the presupposition of a full proposition, and it will be seen that these present special problems for determining binding relationships. This differentiates them from triggers such as definite NPs and possessive pronouns, where binding is relatively straightforward because only individuals are involved. Second, as far as I know, except for *it-clefts* (see Collins 1991), none of these triggers have been the subject of a large corpus study.

The triggers studied were used rather infrequently, with accommodation at top level being the preferred interpretation for most examples. Problems encountered in applying the anaphoric theory to naturally occurring spoken language presuppositions, and especially the special problems involved in working with propositional presuppositions, are discussed. Areas where the theory could be made more operational for use with empirical data are suggested.

The goal of the study is therefore two-fold, to examine the appearance and frequency of propositional presuppositions signaled by the above triggers in spoken discourse, and to evaluate the descriptive adequacy of the anaphoric theory as a tool for interpreting these presuppositions. Section 2.2 gives a short overview of other work and an introduction to the anaphoric theory. Section 2.3 presents the corpus and method used, section 2.4 presents the results and section 2.5 discusses the findings and some ideas for future studies are given.

2.2 Background

The 90's has seen a revival of interest in presupposition theory, perhaps in part because of advances in formal methods to handle discourse.

The amount of literature on presuppositions is enormous, though surprisingly little discusses naturally occurring presuppositions in context and even less looks at presuppositions in spoken discourse. The only corpus work I am aware of has focused on it-clefts (Prince 1978; Delin 1995; Collins, 1991) and definite NP's (Fraurud 1990, Poesio and Vieira, 1998), though few of these studies have discussed these items from a presuppositional perspective and only some look at spoken language examples (e.g. Collins 1991, Prince 1978). Also, almost all of this work was done before the development of several new presupposition theories, among which one of the most well-known is the anaphoric theory developed by van der Sandt (1992).

This theory argues that presuppositions are anaphoric expressions and as such can be interpreted in the same way as other anaphora within a dynamic semantic theory such as Discourse Representation Theory (DRT) (Kamp and Reyle, 1993). When a presupposition trigger is encountered there are two ways in which the presupposed information can be interpreted: it can be bound or accommodated. If the previous discourse context contains a suitable antecedent the presupposed information can be bound; that is, a discourse referent earlier in the discourse that is similar enough to the presupposed information so that it can function as an antecedent. When the presupposed information is not given in the previous context, it is assumed that the speaker's use signals his desire that his audience treat the information as already given. This leads to a process called accommodation (Lewis, 1979), whereby the presupposition is added to (or integrated in) the discourse record.

The accommodation process is more than just the creation of a discourse referent that can serve as an antecedent. In DRT, whether or not a discourse referent is accessible depends on where in the DRS structure it is, with e.g. referents and conditions in embedded DRSs having access to discourse referents in the main context, but not vice-versa. When a presupposition is triggered in a structure that gives an embedded DRS, accommodation also involves determining in what DRS the presupposed information should be added, which in turn means determining how accessible the presupposed information will be in the rest of the discourse. For non-bindable presuppositions occurring in simple sentences (i.e. no embeddings) the information can be added to the main DRS, and this can be termed main accommodation to differentiate it from cases where there is more than one potential level of accommodation. In these cases, resolving to the main DRS is termed global accommodation. Local accommodation means the addition of the presupposed information into the DRS in which the trigger originated and intermediate accommodation is any point of attachment between these two extremes. Looking at an example may make things clearer.

(1) IF JOHN GAVE ANN A ROSE, THEN HE REGRETS BETRAYING MARY.

>> John betrayed Mary

1. **global:** John betrayed Mary. If he gave Ann a rose then

he regrets betraying Mary.
2. **intermediate:** If John gave Ann a rose and John betrayed Mary then he regrets betraying Mary.
3. **local:** If John gave Ann a rose, then John betrayed Mary and regrets that he betrayed Mary.

In the example above, the presupposition occurs in the consequent of a conditional, which means that all three levels of accommodation are possible because there are three structural positions that are accessible. Global accommodation would add the presupposed information to the main DRS, which means that a relationship between the betrayal and the giving of the rose is not specified in the sentence. Intermediate accommodation would mean adding the presupposed information to the antecedent of the conditional. Local accommodation would place the presupposed information in the consequent of the conditional, which here seems somewhat strange in that we must assume that the betrayal of Mary and the regretting are not suggested as being ordered in time in relation to each other, i.e. we cannot place the betrayal before the regretting because that would accommodate it either intermediately or globally.

We can see from this example that where the presupposition is resolved is dependent on our interpretation of how the different events above are related. Here, no context is given to keep the example simple, but context will naturally also play a large role in determining what level is most plausible.

Before going into more detail about the anaphoric theory a few words should be said about its main competitor, the satisfaction theory. This theory's roots go back to Karttunen (1974), Stalnaker (1974) and Heim (1983) and an interested reader can find a more detailed description in Beaver (1997) and Geurts (1999).

The satisfaction theory needs a form of semantics that allows information update, such as Groenendijk and Stokhof's DPL (1991). In the satisfaction theory, presuppositions are requirements placed on contexts. They require that the information they presuppose is already satisfied in the local context in which the carrier sentence is used. In other words, the sentence is not felicitous if the presupposed information is not already true before the use of the carrier sentence. When information is presupposed that is not already satisfied by the context, it can be accommodated. The context is updated with the presupposed information and then the remainder of the carrier sentence is processed.

It may seem as though examining a context to see if presupposed information is satisfied and examining a representation to see if a suitable and accessible discourse referent is present are the same tasks, regardless of which theory the results are described in (cf. Zeevat 1992). However, despite some similarities, there are several reasons for using the anaphoric theory for this study rather than the satisfaction theory.

First, most agree that the anaphoric theory has the best empirical coverage (Geurts 1999, Asher and Lascarides 1998a). The theory is written very procedurally, making it easy to use when doing corpus analysis. It is implemented in DRT as is a large amount of work on anaphora, making it easier to relate the results of this other work to the current study, a clear plus when evaluating the idea that presuppositions are anaphoric. Finally, the anaphoric theory has a more developed and functional set of guidelines for determining binding and level of accommodation than the satisfaction theory has for determining satisfaction and accommodation. The rest of this section goes into more detail about what these guidelines are.

But the most important reason to prefer using the anaphoric theory rather than the satisfaction theory is that the satisfaction theory only requires presuppositions to be satisfied within the context, but how, or what the satisfaction is based on is not relevant for contextual update to be possible. As van der Sandt (1992) has pointed out, it does not take into consideration that hearers may have more than one reason to consider a presupposition satisfied, i.e. more than one potential antecedent. The anaphoric theory predicts that there may be more than one potential antecedent and which is suitable will have to be determined. In this fundamental way the anaphoric theory aims to relate the presupposition to the rest of the discourse more explicitly than the satisfaction theory and it is this type of representation that will be most useful for applications.

2.2.1 Binding

What could the relationship between a presupposed proposition and its antecedent look like? Van der Sandt(1992) states that the antecedent should subsume the presuppositional information, and that in some cases we should expect that more than one potential antecedent will be available, but the theory itself does not give guidelines on how to determine the most suitable antecedent.

But presuppositions, because they contain more information, are going to have quite a different relationship to their antecedents than e.g. pronouns, which usually are in an identity relationship with their antecedents. In van Deemter (1992) a general definition of anaphora is developed by incorporating many non-traditional anaphoric NP relationships that are central in establishing discourse coherence, and these are the kind of relationships that we will probably see in presuppositional binding. These are non-identity relationships and they are quite varied and as such difficult to characterize. Possible relationships include subsumption, which he defines as 'a subset of a set, part of a quantity, substructure in a given structure.' (p. 35), as well as concepts invoked by so-called relational nouns, such as *the book-the author*. Many of these have been termed bridging anaphora, but definitions differ widely. Van Deemter concentrates his discussion to full NP-anaphora but he also mentions anaphoric predicate relations between verbs. Many non-identity relationships do not easily fall into one of the categories mentioned above and this makes recognizing them a problem. Krahmer and van Deemter (1998) develop a procedure for identifying non-identity relationships, which they term *partial matching*. They associate each discourse referent with a value set, which is the set of individuals of the common noun type to which the referent belongs. If the intersection of the value set of two discourse referents is non-empty then a partial match exists and it is possible that the one referent may serve as an antecedent for the other.

One drawback with these methods is that they have difficulty identifying bridging relationships that are not based on lexical relationships, where at the same time they have a very high potential to overgenerate possible anaphoric relationships. In a discourse concepts talked about are usually related to each other in some way, so the number of potential antecedents could get very high.

Asher and Lascarides (1998b) handle bridging by attempting to identify rhetorical relations that hold between the antecedents and the anaphoric expression. Knowing the rhetorical relationship allows them to compute other semantic information that in turn helps identify the bridging relationship. They apply their method to definite NPs and show how it would work with an it-cleft and the temporal adverb (and presupposition trigger) *again*. However, using this method to help determine antecedents requires that there is already a method for unambiguously determining rhetorical relations.

However, the triggers studied in this investigation result in presupposed propositions. When examples in the literature do show propositional presuppositions binding this is illustrated with presupposed propositions that are identical with their antecedent. We can probably expect non-identity to be more the rule than the exception. With propositions, not only arguments but even predicates can be in some type of synonymous, subsumption or relational noun relationship, or even a combination of all of the above.

A possible procedure to deal with these potential relationships would be to allow two propositions that differ in, for example one argument, to be considered to be in an anaphoric relationship. If the relationship between the arguments that differ, e.g. two NPs, is such that it would be considered a bridging relationship according to the work outlined above, then it should be considered bridging at the level of the proposition. For example, the proposition, 'The car is broken' could then be considered similar enough to 'The motor is broken' that the one could function as an antecedent for the other. However, before examining the presupposed propositions in the corpus it is difficult to say how well this procedure will work.

2.2.2 Accommodation

Accommodation is a process by which hearers will accept presupposed information that does not have an antecedent, adding it to their discourse record. For the triggers studied here, this means adding either a full proposition, or the individual discourse referents and relevant conditions found in the presupposed information, to the discourse record. The original formulation of the idea of accommodation is usually credited to Lewis (1979). There are two views on the communicative nature of accommodation. It has been characterized as a hearer repair strategy which can be exploited by the speaker and it has been argued to be a more general communication strategy which is necessary due to the fact that two or more discourse participants can never be quite certain as to what information they share (Beaver 1999).

As explained above, accommodation can occur at three possible levels, at the level of the main DRS, or at the DRS where the presupposed information was introduced, i.e. local accommodation, or somewhere in between, i.e. intermediate. Van der Sandt (1992) outlined criteria for deciding what type of accommodation is possible and preferred, and these have then been reinterpreted/reorganized and given names by Beaver (1997). It is this latter categorization that is presented below.

1. TRAPPING: If presupposed information contains a discourse referent that is bound, i.e. occurs in the scope of a quantifier, it can only be resolved at a site where the binder is accessible. This constraint sometimes blocks global accommodation.

2. GLOBAL INFORMATIVITY: This insures that a discourse record makes sense and is not redundant: information that is already in the main discourse should not be globally accommodated. This information has an antecedent and should have been interpreted as a case of binding.

3. LOCAL INFORMATIVITY: This constraint prohibits accommodation of information at a local level when it already occurs in an acces-

sible DRS superordinate to the local level. This information is accessible so its addition would be redundant.

4.CONSISTENCY: Finally, accommodation of a proposition cannot occur at a level where the information will contradict information that has already been integrated into the discourse record. For example, if global accommodation would explicitly contradict information already in the context, then global accommodation is no longer an option.

In addition to these constraints, Heim (1983) has argued that there is a preference for global accommodation while van der Sandt (1992) has argued that there is a preference for higher levels of accommodation over lower levels. The advantage of a high level of accommodation is that the information is more accessible from the rest of the discourse.

Corpus work should therefore be able to say something about how well the above guidelines aid in determining level of accommodation as well as perhaps give some empirical evidence to support or deny the proposed preference for higher levels.

2.3 Method

50 dialogues between 2-7 speakers taken from the London-Lund Corpus of Spoken English[1] (LLC) were analyzed. LLC is a computerized transcribed corpus of spoken British English and the selected dialogues contained approximately 233,000 words. Tone units have often been considered a kind of 'sentence' for spoken language and the selection contained 36,432 tone units. Twelve of the dialogues were so-called 'conversations between disparates' while the remainder were 'conversations between equals'. See Svartvik (1990) for more information about the corpus.

Six well known trigger groups that presuppose propositions were selected as the object of study. The triggers chosen easily lend themselves to automatic recognition within untagged text, because they are limited to one or two lexical signals and/or because the syntactic structure associated with the lexical clue is predictable, making the identification of the presupposition more automatic.[2] Each trigger and the examples from each group that were studied are presented in table 1.

The trigger is not the lexical item alone, but the lexical item together with a specific syntactic structure. For example, factive adjectives, factive verbs and change of state verbs are triggers only when these lexical

[1]The London-Lund Corpus of Spoken English can be obtained at http://www.hit.uib.no/icame/icame.hmtl

[2]For example, *too* is a well known trigger but the syntactic structure that accompanies it can vary greatly, and what it presupposes varies according to its focus structure, which in turn means identification of the presupposition is a more complicated process.

TRIGGER		EXAMPLES
factive verbs	subject comp	count, make sense, suffice, amuse, bother, matter
	object comp	know, realize, resent, find out, discover, see, notice
factive adjectives	subject comp	significant, odd, tragic, exciting, relevant
	object comp	glad, proud, lucky
COS-verbs		begin, start, stop, finish, cease, continue, carry on
it-clefts		it is/was C_i which/whom/in which/for whom/when where/that/ $\emptyset$ $S - C_i$

TABLE 1 Presupposition Triggers Studied

items occur with a sentential complement. When these lexical items are used without the required syntactic structure, they are not presupposition triggers. Examples of each trigger with the presupposition identified are given in table 2.

Note that the presupposition of a change-of-state verb differs according to the meaning of the verb. Also, the definition for *it-clefts* given in 2 was modified for the study, so that only examples where the clefted constituent was an NP, PP or ADV were analyzed. For *it-clefts*, the clefted element is not part of the presupposed proposition. When this is an obligatory argument to the presuppositional portion, an indefinite NP such as *someone* or *something* replaces it in the presupposition.

Because the corpus is untagged, two subgroups of the above had to be excluded because analysis would require studying a substantial amount of data by hand.[3] The excluded groups were *know* without an explicit *that* to introduce the sentential complement and *it-clefts* used without a relative pronoun.

A key-word-in-context excerption of each presupposition trigger was made. Classification of the presuppositions was a two step-process: first, the presupposition, as it could be understood in the clause in which it appears, was identified and second, the most suitable interpretation of the presupposition was determined, which in this study meant categorizing the presupposition as bound or accommodated. No constraints were made on how much of the previous discourse could be examined to look for potential antecedents. If the presupposition was not bound, the pre-

[3]The author intends to analyze these groups at a later date.

TRIGGER		EXAMPLES
factive verbs	subject comp	a. That John stole the money matters. b. John's stealing the money matters. >> John stole the money
	object comp	a. Everyone knows that John stole the money. >> John stole the money
factive adjectives	subject comp	a That John is a thief is relevant. >> John is a thief.
	object comp	b. I'm not glad that John's a thief. >> John is a thief.
COS-verbs	example: start	a. Subject started VERB ing when he was a child. b. Subject started VERB -infinitive when he was a child. Let t be reference time of utterance >> Subject didn't VERB at time before t
it-clefts		It is/was C_i which/whom/who/in which/for whom when where/that $S - C_i$ (C = NP, PP or ADV only) >>(Someone/somewhere/somehow/something S

TABLE 2 Identification of Presuppositions in their Local Context for Each Trigger

TRIGGER	NO OF PRESUPPOSITIONS TRIGGERED
factive verbs - subject comp	0
factive verbs - object comp	57
factive adjectives	0
COS-verbs	78
it-clefts	31

TABLE 3 Number of Presuppositions Found Signaled by Triggers Studied

ferred level of accommodation was determined, making reference to the criteria presented earlier in 2.2.2, and on the basis of the most plausible interpretation according to the discourse meaning. Embedded contexts were considered to arise because of negatives, conditionals, disjunctives, explicitly given *probably* or *maybe* and other easily identifiable modals and for cases of modal subordination.[4]

2.4 Results

2.4.1 Frequency of presupposition triggers

Each excerpted trigger instance was examined and cases where the syntax was not that of presuppositional usage were discarded. From the remaining data, incomplete examples where the speaker was interrupted or changed structures mid-way were also removed. As can be seen in table 3, the presuppositional triggers studied were rather infrequent, and for some categories, e.g. factive verbs with subject complements and factive adjectives, non-existent. The numbers given also err on the conservative side. When it was unclear if a presupposition trigger was followed by a sentential complement or merely a new clause it was analyzed as a new clause.

2.4.2 Interpretation of presuppositions

After determining the presupposition according to the patterns given in table 2, all examples were classified into one of four categories: binding, main DRS accommodation, global accommodation, or as local accommodation. Table 4 presents these results.[5] Main DRS accommodation (MAINACC) describes accommodation in the main DRS in cases where there were no other potential accommodation sites. Global accommodation (GLOBAL) here is any presupposition accommodated into the top

[4]For simplicity, the subordinating nature of verbs marking propositional attitude was not taken into consideration, though this should perhaps be looked at more closely in future studies.

[5]The discrepancy between the numbers in table 3 and table 4 is due to the removal of examples where the speaker's utterance was too incomplete or vague for analysis.

Trigger	Total	binding	mainacc	global	local
fact verbs - obj	54	6	38	1	9
COS-verbs	68	10	43	13	2
it-clefts	31	19	10	2	0

TABLE 4 Interpretation Given

DRS when there was at least one other potential accommodation site. Local and intermediate accommodation were collapsed here into one category termed LOCAL. This was done in part because of the low frequency of examples with a potential intermediate accommodation site, as well as the difficulty involved in determining the interpretation differences between these two levels in the examples found. A more detailed description of how binding was determined is given in 2.4.3, and examples of different levels of accommodation and how they were determined is described starting in 2.4.4.

2.4.3 Binding

For binding to be possible, there must be an antecedent for the presupposed information in the previous discourse. The method used was to first determine the presupposed information and then examine the discourse content up to its introduction. If the presupposed information was felt to be already known, the utterances where the information was contained were identified as accurately as possible and some general observations about the differences in form between this/these potential antecedent/s and the presupposed information were made.

No examples were found where the presupposed information was an identical match with earlier introduced information. The following example is the closest to this ideal that was found in the data.

(2) >> SHE IS UNUSUAL(1 3 1190[6])

Speaker c: `- [m] - - but <she . at> the same time she seems unusual, doesn't she.`
Speaker A: `Yes. Yes. And everybody NOTICES that she's unusual`

Here, Speaker c (male) suggests 'she is unusual' and Speaker A (female) replies with a very similar proposition, that the person referred to as 'she' is unusual, and this proposition is presented as presupposed information by virtue of the fact that it is used in the sentential complement of the

[6]The number given after each example refers to the dialogue and line number of the first line of the example in the London-Lund Corpus.

factive verb *notice*.

The *seems* in Speaker c's statement could be interpreted as a modal operator which then makes the potential antecedent inaccessible. However, it seems clear that these two propositions are related despite the non-identity relationship between them. If the function of Speaker A's utterance is also taken into consideration, then the relationship becomes even morc obvious. From a speech-act perspective, Speaker c and Speaker A's utterances form an adjacency pair. Speaker c expresses an assessment and Speaker A expresses her agreement by presenting via presupposition a similar proposition. Speaker c's original, and somewhat weaker assertion, that 'she' only *seems* unusual, can be interpreted as a kind of hedging, i.e. an unwillingness to express a negative opinion. So speaker A's presupposition serves the discourse function of letting Speaker c know that she agrees with his assessment, and the identification as non-identity binding is fairly clear.

The simplest cases involved small differences, as above, or where clear synonyms were used. Most examples, however, were not this straightforward. In the example below, the synthesis of several utterances, made by several different speakers, plus world knowledge, would need to be taken into account to identify a binding relationship. Note that Speaker A and B (=Debbie) are married and Speaker d (female) is going to get married.

(3) >> PEOPLE GIVE YOU THINGS BEFORE YOU GET MARRIED (210 927)

Speaker d:(1) Doesn't seem much different *except for* trying to answer these awful conundrums about what shall we give you and trying to fit it in (laughs).
Speaker B: (2) THAT'S, THAT'S nice.
Speaker d: (3) Yes but,
Speaker A: (4) THAT'S the bit Debbie enjoyed enormously.
Speaker B: (5) Oh THAT'S much the <cos> THAT won't [haep] THAT won't yes THAT won't happen again so I should enjoy IT very much
Speaker d: (6) Yes THAT'S true.
Speaker B: (7) Cos THAT stops very rapidly after you get married actually.
ALL: (laugh)
Speaker B: (8) People STOP giving you things after you get married actually.
ALL: (laugh)

Here the presupposition that people no longer give couples gifts/things after marriage can be partially understood from the earlier context, including especially Speaker d's remark in line (1). In (1) Speaker d mentions the difficulties she has had in telling people what she would like as wedding gifts. This is the introduction of the topic, and the abstract object anaphoric reference with THAT in Speaker B's statement in (2) seems to refer to the situation of being able to say what you would like as a gift. Notice how this idea is 'floated' and developed through the dialogue using several abstract object anaphoric references, THAT in (2), (4), (5) (6) and (7) and IT in (3), before finally being made more explicit in Speaker B's statement in (8). Speaker A and B repeat and add attributes and comments to the idea and all participants acknowledge their understanding of each statement. The utterances (5) and (7) are very instrumental in making the idea given, though neither alone functions well as an antecedent. Perhaps by (8) it is no longer clear what exactly is being discussed and therefore the statement in (8) with its presupposition is an important clarification of an idea that in this multi-speaker setting may have been unclear to all participants. This is the only point in the discourse where the idea is made explicit, (even in (1) it is implicit!) and without the additional information supplied by utterances (2)-(7) the presupposed information in (8) would be too implicit in (1) to be treated as a potential antecedent. In this case, it seems necessary to consider the information provided by several utterances made by several speakers as being the source of an antecedent for the presupposed information.

The next example illustrates that very long distances may exist between a potential antecedent and a presupposition, here an 895 line gap.

(4) >> HE IS ENTHUSIASTIC (HE = PROF. PITT) (2 1@ 120)

Speaker A: `Also Pitt has talked about it a good deal.`
`Professor Pitt here, and he has supported.`
`(SEVERAL LINES)`
`Yes, he has supported you is it with the Cambridge`
`Press. He has supported you quite strongly and we had`
`(895 LINES: UNTIL LINE 1015)`
Speaker A: `You could indeed but I should continue`
`also to give Professor Pitt's since I know that`
Speaker B: `KNOW that he is enthusiastic.`
Speaker A: `Yes, quite. He supported you very strongly.`

Whether or not this should be considered a case of binding depends on how similar *he is enthusiastic* is to the sum of the earlier propositions in the same discourse about Professor Pitt's strong support of Speaker B. Functionally, it seems as if Speaker B uses his statement to show his agreement or acknowledgment of Speaker A's earlier assessment.

2.4.4 Accommodation

Presuppositions that are not bound must be accommodated. Accommodation can take place in the main DRS (listed as MAINACC in table 4) or, if there are several possible accommodation sites, globally, intermediately or locally. When there is a choice between more than one level of accommodation, the highest level should be considered first. The constraints given in section 2.2.2 were utilized in determining the correct level of accommodation.

2.4.5 Accommodation in the Main DRS

When the presupposed information occurred within the Main DRS, i.e. not in a subordinate DRS, there is only one potential accommodation site, the main DRS itself. This was by far the most frequent interpretation for all presuppositions. See the two examples below.

(5) >> EVERYBODY ELSE IN THE COLLEGE WAS USING (VISUAL AIDS) ALL THE TIME. (MAINACC) (211B 1312)

Speaker d: `And a few more of them came back and I gradually REALIZED that everybody else in this college was using them all the time. You know, visual aids, prompts, this sort of lark.`

(6) >> HE WAS WRITING HIS THESIS EARLIER (MAINACC) (210 991)

Speaker B: `Just casually toss <them> a banana, to a three month old child - tossed across the room, CARRY ON writing his thesis (laughs). It was an absolute pigsty.`

For both examples, binding was not an option. In the discourse from which example 5 is taken there is no information in the discourse about other college employees using visual aids, or the suggestion that the other participants share this idea. In example 6 there is no information that the subject of Speaker B's utterance had been working on a thesis prior to the time of the utterance, and in fact it is clear from the presentation that the intended interpreter does not know the individual because the story begins with "I have a cousin a bit like you..."

2.4.6 Global Accommodation

For some cases there was more than one site for accommodation available, as in the example below, where the 'if-then' structure makes all three levels of accommodation available.

(7) >> ADDRESSEE HAD NOT BEGUN TO REARRANGE HIS ASSESSMENT OF LAWRENCE'S NOVELS PRIOR TO THE REFERENCE TIME OF THE UTTERANCE (GLOBAL) (3 1c1260)

Speaker B: `Well, if you apply that criterion, then surely you must START to rearrange your estimates of Lawrence's novels, surely.`

Based on the criteria for determining level of accommodation there does not seem to be anything blocking global accommodation. Note that the statement could be interpreted both as a generic statement and as a more specific question to the addressee about how applying 'the criteria' affected his assessment (note the adverb 'surely'), and based on the greater context (not given here), I believe the latter is a more accurate description of what is going on.

2.4.7 Local Accommodation

Local and intermediate accommodation proved to be infrequent and difficult to distinguish. They were therefore collapsed into one category.

(8) *I AM GOING TO BE A VAST AMOUNT OF HELP TO YOU (LOCAL) (2 2A 16)

Speaker A: `But I don't really KNOW that I'm going to be a vast amount of help to you`

The main clause in examples with a negated first person subject and 'know' function to deny their sentential complements and always are interpreted as LOCAL (see Kiparsky and Kiparsky 1970). There were 5 cases of this specific structure.

(9) >> THINGS ARE BLOCKED UP 'IN X-RAY'(2 9 1132) (LOCAL)

Speaker B: `Signs are the only things you can observe, like if you took an X-ray and SAW that things were blocked up or something.`

Example 9 above is an excerpt from a discussion concerning the difference between 'signs' and 'symptoms' in which the general usage of the terms is discussed. A hypothetical X-ray and what you could see in it is used as an example. Possible interpretations with accommodation are:

Global: Things are blocked up. If you look at an X-ray you see this.
Local: If you take an X-ray then things are blocked up and you see this.

There is no X-ray before the clause beginning with 'if'. If you believe that the X-ray is what allows you to see that things are blocked up, then global accommodation does not seem to be an option. It seems to violate the constraint on trapping, discussing information we can have only by virtue of the reference to an X-ray that does not yet exist at that point in the discourse. On the other hand, if you interpret the example as suggesting that we earlier, by other means than the X-ray, have been party to information that things were blocked up, then global accommodation would be preferred. I think the order of presentation of the events, e.g. X-ray then the information that things are blocked up, seems to support the former interpretation, i.e. local accommodation.

Notice that the presupposition occurs within a sentence beginning with 'if', signaling the beginning of a hypothetical context. Consider a similar example.

(10) >> SOMEBODY IS A CELEBRATED STRIKER (LOCAL)(214 799 B)

Speaker A: `It might be - that if you KNEW that somebody was a celebrated striker - you might try hard not to employ him.`

Here the hypothetical situation is marked very clearly with surface clues such as 'it might be' and 'if' as well as what seems to be impersonal 'you', plus the use of simple past tense. Local accommodation seems to be required because the discourse referent for 'somebody' (identified in the same clause as "a celebrated striker") is only created in the complement, also the site of the presupposition. Consider another example:

(11) >> A PATTERN IS NOT WORKING AT TIME T-1 (LOCAL) (1 2@ 649)

Speaker A: `When we've got a bit more [inf] information, and if we've seen a pattern <that> that BEGINS to work [@m] With [@m] with an Austrian university`

Speaker A and another are discussing setting up some kind of program between their university and universities abroad. Whether the program will occur or not is still unclear at the time of the discussion. Up until the sentence 'and if we've seen a pattern' they are discussing which Italian universities would make possible partners and that the pattern would have to first work with these universities. After this, something else will be implemented 'with an Austrian University'. Here it is necessary to read a great deal of the previous context to understand that the pattern referred to is a discussion of how the exchange will work in practice between their university and the Italian universities.

The trapping rule applies here - the presupposed proposition 'a pattern is not working earlier' contains reference to the discourse referent for 'a pattern'. Only local accommodation is possible because global accommodation would make the presupposition undefined because the discourse referent for *a pattern* wouldn't be accessible from a DRS outside the hypothetical discussion.

Many of the cases where local accommodation was preferred were in hypothetical discussions similar to so-called modal subordinating contexts discussed by Roberts (1989). These were hypothetical contexts that may or may not have be explicitly marked as such throughout, and determining when one ends posed a challenge for determining the correct interpretation for the presupposition because information introduced within the hypothetical context should not be accessible from outside the context. An example from the corpus is given in 12 below.

(12) >> He's (= your scientist) going for question one (1 1 942) (local)

Speaker B `And let's have your literature question, let's have it in the same position every time so that your scientist will KNOW that he's going for question one, your literature person will go for question two`

B is discussing his ideas for how an examination could be improved to make it more relevant for students from the natural sciences ('your scientist') (contrasted here with students from the liberal arts, 'your literature person') and the discussion begins several lines previous to his statement. Future tense, as well as phrases such as 'let's have' are both signals of the modal subordinating context.

Global accommodation would lead to an interpretation where the natural science student ('your scientist') knows he/she is going for question one even before the new format for examinations has been mentioned, making it a rather illogical choice. The entire discussion focuses on making a clear distinction in questions between those that are for literature students and those that are for natural science students. The assertional meaning of the sentence is that the scientist will be 'aware' of which question he is going for, and not that he will be going for an already existing question. We understand from the earlier context (not presented here) that natural science students prefer to answer questions dealing with non-fiction texts, and standardizing the order of questions will make it easier for these students to quickly find this question.

Local accommodation could also be argued to be preferred because the existence of a 'question one' is first referenced in the presupposed proposition, which would make it a case of trapping. But it may also be that the discussion of how the exam will be set up is sufficient enough for the discourse participant to infer the existence of two questions.

2.5 Discussion

The small number of presupposition triggers found was unexpected considering the amount of dialogue searched. One reason may be that the triggers studied required clearly identifiable sentential complements. In many cases the speaker's intended syntactic structure was often difficult to determine. If a potential complement was not marked with *that* nor was it part of the same tone unit, it was indistinguishable from a sequence of two sentences and the conservative identification criteria used here may have lead to an undercount of trigger occurrences. Examining prosody might increase accuracy here. Another reason may be that informal spoken discourse has a low number of complex sentences.

The categories local and intermediate accommodation were collapsed into one category, LOCAL. This was done because the actual number of examples was small and it was in many cases difficult to determine which level was really reflective of speaker meaning. The simplification can also be justified on the grounds that the differences between these two categories seem only to be meaningful when discussing an individual example, and not in comparison with accommodation or binding. The low number of examples of LOCAL accommodation was not unexpected. These examples require that the presupposition is triggered under some kind of embedding, for example within a modal subordinating context, or within a conditional sentence. They correspond to what would earlier be described as presuppositions that failed to project outside the complex sentence in which they appeared. Presenting information or ideas using these types of contexts may be less frequent than concrete references to the past or to the here and now in informal conversation.

Accommodation in the main DRS (MAINACC) and global accommodation (GLOBAL) were found to be the most frequent interpretations. This was also in many ways a predictable result. Accommodation at top level is what has been termed 'presuppositional' or 'presupposing' reading of the sentence, and should then be relatively uncontroversial discourse new information.

Both Heim and van der Sandt have suggested that higher levels of accommodation will be preferred over lower (see 2.2.2). This should have resulted in GLOBAL being more frequent than LOCAL. However, both types were present in about the same number. This result could have something to do with the nature of presupposed propositions. If one element of a presupposed proposition is first introduced in the embedded context then this suffices to make the entire presupposed proposition 'unprojectable' and many of the examples of LOCAL accommodation were in fact cases of trapping. However, GLOBAL accommodation may still be more common than LOCAL accommodation for other triggers, though this needs to be studied empirically.

Different trigger types also displayed different tendencies to bind or accommodate. For example, presuppositions triggered by the *it-clefts* studied never led to LOCAL accommodation. This doesn't mean that they can never occur with this type of meaning; we can easily construct an example by, e.g. embedding them in a conditional sentence. But the usage didn't appear in the corpus and it may be that the *it-cleft* is a construction that is functionally used in discourse to present highly factual information. This suggests that there may be distributional differences in the kind of information different triggers are associated with, something that more empirical work could shed light on.

2.5.1 Determining Binding for Propositions

A recurring problem in the study which affected all results was that it was difficult to determine reliably what a potential antecedent for a propositional presupposition could be.

The examples found were quite different from most examples of bound presupposed propositions given in the literature,[7] where the presupposition is usually identical with an earlier proposition. But if such a strict definition had been used, no cases of binding would have been found in the corpus for the triggers studied here. In some cases potential antecedents were spread out over several utterances but none alone could uniquely serve as an antecedent.

In both example 3 and example 4 there was more than one utterance that could function as a potential antecedent, though several of them do not completely express the entirety of the proposition, making it difficult for any one of them to uniquely function as an antecedent. Binding then requires synthesizing information from several sources, or accommodating part of the information.

It may be that the relationship we are looking for between presup-

[7] All of which seem to be constructed examples, i.e. not taken from a corpus but created by the author for illustration.

positions and their potential antecedents is not really as analogous to that found between more traditional anaphoric expressions and their antecedents as first thought. The relationship antecedent-personal pronoun is very strong, in that the pronoun is almost completely dependent on its antecedent for an interpretation. But for non-identity relationships such as bridging anaphora, the dependence is less, so the link is likely to be weaker. The greater the semantic independence, the weaker the relationship because the relationship is less necessary to the interpretation. Many presuppositions, especially the propositional presuppositions studied here, have a rich semantic content, the argument used to explain why they may be accommodated. This same quality is an argument for them being more independent from their antecedents than other anaphoric expressions.

It could be that the type of anaphoric relationship is closer to that between what has been called discourse-deixis anaphora (Webber 1991) or abstract object anaphora (Eckert and Strube 1999) and their antecedents. Like presupposed propositions, these often take propositional antecedent, or sometimes a synthesis of several propositions. They differ from presupposed propositions in that they *must* find an antecedent in order to get an interpretation, whereas presupposed propositions have the option of being accommodated.

Relevant to this comparison is Webber's (1991) suggestion that the discourse context can supply entities 'whose propositional content is the source of new intended referents' (Webber 1991, p. 133), e.g. the context may be clearly understood as being the source of a referent but the referent itself may not have been perceived as such before the use of the presupposition. An example of this could be example 3.

Consider that binding literally means the presupposed proposition must be given information in the discourse. For other triggers it seems appropriate to believe that they will often be used with a binding interpretation. For example, objects and actors are introduced in a discourse and they are referred to repeatedly as the discourse develops and more information about them is given. It is quite common for these entities to be referred to using definite noun phrases or another presuppositional expression, as they are referred to several times. But what is the point of repeating already given propositions?

Examining the usage found in the corpus, three explanations suggest themselves. First, speakers seem to presuppose information that has been contributed by several speakers across several utterances, as in example 3. This functions as a kind of summing up of what everyone has agreed on, expressed as one clear proposition. We can imagine that this is more common in spoken discourse than written text due to the greater need to actively negotiate meaning. Second, speakers also seem to presuppose propositions that may have only been indirectly suggested in the earlier discourse, sometimes dependent on all participants making the same connection or inference, such as in example 4. Presupposing the proposition makes the idea clearer, but asserting it would be somewhat unnecessary, because it is not really new information. Finally, speakers seem to presuppose an already introduced proposition when this serves a different pragmatic function, as in example 2. Here the function seems to be to show agreement with the initial speaker. For this third category of usage it seems likely that the presupposition of the proposition will be made by a different speaker than the one who initially introduced it.

This explanation seems to correctly describe the corpus data, and also explains why binding of propositional presuppositions is infrequent, and difficult to determine. The information may be implicit, underspecified, split among speakers and utterances, and not synthesized until the moment the presupposition is introduced, similar to coerced referents. However, perhaps because it can from a certain perspective be considered given information, it is more appropriate to presuppose it than assert it.

2.5.2 Accommodation vs. Binding after Processing

Another problem in applying the theory to empirical data was that for some examples it was unclear if accommodation or binding was the correct interpretation. That some presuppositions can equally be given an interpretation of binding as accommodation is one of the many ways van der Sandt (1992) has suggested ambiguity can arise. However, in such cases it should be clear that two interpretations result. Here it seemed more as if the lack of an unclear procedure for determining propositional binding was the root of the problem.

Of course, accommodation and binding have to do with individual processing strategies. All discourse participants will not perceive everything in the same way. In terms of processing demands on the listener, it could be argued that binding is probably cognitively easier than accommodating when binding is easy to identify. Because accommodation is usually initiated after an inability to bind, it may always need more processing time. Additionally, accommodated information is not just *added*, it must be integrated. On the other hand, when binding is difficult to identify, for cases like many found in the corpus, often several utterances have to be synthesized, and several inferences have to be made. This may mean that it may be equally processing intensive.

Accommodated material cannot differ so greatly from information that can be bound in the degree to which it is related to the discourse either, because speakers will seldom presuppose information that is unrelated. Even if they did as pointed out in Asher and Lascarides (1998a), hearers will always try to maximize the coherency of the message by searching for a relationship. It is this characteristic of discourse that creates a dilemma when interpreting presupposed information in context: it is always possible to find similar or related propositions in the preceding discourse but it is not clear that these are similar enough to license binding. Again, a better procedure for determining binding would help here.

From a computational semantics perspective, what we are after is a discourse representation that is usable, and we can ask how different accommodation and binding are in the representation they will result in after processing. Both processes affect the discourse record in almost identical ways: the presupposed proposition is added to the main DRS, or it is already there and identifying binding results in a potentially more coherent representation. Considering if there are other relevant differences should be the subject of future empirical study.

2.5.3 Role of Shared Knowledge and World Knowledge

Two additional problems became apparent when working with the corpus: it was not clear how shared knowledge and world knowledge should be integrated in the analysis and it was not clear how shared knowledge and information that is new to the hearer could be distinguished.

When working with the corpus, the need to make reference to non-discourse based knowledge in interpretation became very clear, though most discussions of presupposition focus on discourse based information, and modelling more is beyond the ambitions of, e.g. DRT. Strictly speaking, only information that is represented in the discourse is available for 'binding', and not knowledge shared between discourse participants or even general knowledge about the world. For example, if a speaker says something about 'my wife' the information that the speaker has a wife may be common knowledge between the participants but not part of the discourse record and as such will be classified as accommodation. However, we can expect that the listener will, in a sense 'bind' this presupposed information with some sort of non-discourse based antecedent. 'Binding' of this type can surely occur both with this kind of shared private information and with information that is general world knowledge, e.g. when the speaker refers to the president of the United States. This is also another difference between presuppositions and other anaphoric expressions. It seems likely that presuppositions can be bound to non-discourse based antecedents (if these should be called antecedents), but anaphora, which are much more semantically reduced, either cannot or tend not to be, because they won't be identifiable.

Prince (1981) discusses this general problem and makes a distinction between information that is truly new to the hearer or reader and what she termed 'new-unused' information; that is, known to the hearer or reader but not 'active' at the time of use. What is considered new and new-unused, will vary from individual to individual depending on background knowledge. In new-given theory, focus is placed on information as having a certain status, whereas the binding theory discusses information in terms of how it will be processed. New information clearly coincides with information interpreted by accommodation. The difficulty lies in determining what is done with new-unused information – Is it accommodated, or is it sufficiently familiar to be bound to some non-discourse based antecedent? If we say it is bound, it differs considerably from other bound information in that it is non-salient in the current conversation.

For the material studied, the difficulty found in distinguishing new from new-unused was partly due to the corpus used. First, the participants generally knew each other, and therefore had some degree of shared knowledge, and secondly, the transcript was not always a complete record of the conversation, e.g. it begins in the middle, participants come and go, etc, which means the results do not correctly portray the burden of interpretation of a conversational participant. What is, however, interesting is that even if the information is not shared it could still be interpreted. Speakers tended to give hearers enough information to make sense of what they were saying, whether it was needed or not, something they may not always be able to determine.

2.5.4 Conclusions

Was the anaphoric theory functional enough to use as a description of natural language presuppositions? The answer is yes and no. The procedure for analysis seems to be intuitively functional, in that they can be used by a researcher to try to describe and explain the interpretation of presuppositions in natural language data. However, the theory is still too general to serve as an explicit guideline for dealing with the varied and complex examples that are common in informal dialogue. Determining the potential antecedents of presupposed information, especially for propositional presuppositions, is one important example. How world knowledge and common ground should be dealt with is another. Also, even with more specific guidelines many interpretations will always be influenced by the hearer/transcript reader's own, subjective understanding of how they believe the different events in the transcript are interrelated.

Was corpus research an appropriate method to study presuppositions? Absolutely. Very few examples ever allowed an interpretation to be established with certainty from a context of one or two utterances, and for many of the examples given above, not only is a larger context necessary to even present the example, but also the greater context of the discussion had to be described in order for the interpretation to be clear. The next step in a corpus study would be to look at other trigger types, such as *too*, aspectual adverbs like *still* and *already*, and even definite NPs, where there is also very little corpus work on spoken language.

Acknowledgements I wish to express my very warm thanks to Rob van der Sandt and Henk Zeevat for invaluable discussion and comments on this work. Also thanks to Bart Geurts, Kees van Deemter and the anonymous reviewers for many useful comments. All errors are my own.

References

Asher and Lascarides 1998a: N. Asher and A. Lascarides: The Semantics and Pragmatics of Presupposition, Journal of Semantics, 15 (3), pp. 239-300

Asher and Lascarides 1998b: N. Asher and A. Lascarides: Bridging. Journal of Semantics, 15 (1), pp. 83-113

Beaver 1997. D.I. Beaver: Presupposition, In *Handbook of Logic and Language*, J. van Benthem & A. ter Meulen (Eds), 939-1008

Beaver 1999. D.I. Beaver: Presuppositions Accommodation: A Plea for Common Sense. In L. Moss, J. Ginzburg & M. de Rijke (Eds). *Logic, Language and Computation*, vol. 2, CSLI Press.

Collins 1991. P. Collins: *Cleft and Pseudo-cleft constructions in English.* Routledge, London. London.

van Deemter 1992. K. van Deemter: Towards a Generalization of Anaphora. Journal of Semantics 9, pp. 27-51

Delin 1995. J. Delin: Presupposition and shared knowledge in it-clefts. Language and Cognitive Processes, 10, 97-120

Eckert and Strube 1999. M. Eckert and M. Strube: Dialogue Acts, Synchronising Units and Anaphora Resolution, Proc. of Amsterlogue 1999, Amsterdam University, 7-9 May.

Fraurud 1990. K. Fraurud: Definiteness and the processing of NP's in natural discourse, Journal of Semantics, 7, (4) pp. 395-433

Geurts 1999. B. Geurts: *Presuppositions and Pronouns*, Current Research in the Semantics/Pragmatics Interface: Vol 3., Elsevier Science Ltd., Oxford, London.

Groenendijk and Stokhof 1991. J. Groenendijk and M. Stokhof. Dynamic Predicate Logic. Linguistics and Philosophy 14. pp. 39-100

Heim 1992. I. Heim: The Semantics of Definite and Indefinite Noun Phrases. Doctoral dissertation, University of Massachusetts, Amherst.

Heim 1983. I. Heim: On the Projection Problem for Presuppositions. In *Proceedings of the Second West Coast Conference on Formal Linguistics*, D. Flickinger et al. (Eds], Stanford University Press, CA, pp. 114-125

Kamp and Reyle 1993. H. Kamp and W. Reyle: *From Discourse to Logic: Introduction to Modeltheoretic Semantics of Natural Language, Formal Logic and Discourse Representation Theory.* Dordecht: Kluwer Academic Publishers.

Karttunen 1974. L. Karttunen: Presuppositions and Linguistic Context. Theoretical Linguistics 1, pp. 181-194

Kiparsky and Kiparsky 1970. C. Kiparsky and P. Kiparsky: Fact, In *Progress in Linguistics* , M. Bierwisch and K. Heidolph, eds. The Hague, Mouton, 143-173

Krahmer and van Deemter 1998. E. Krahmer and K. van Deemter: On the Interpretation of Anaphoric Noun Phrases: Towards a Full Understanding of Partial Matches, Journal of Semantics, 15(4), 355-392

Lewis 1979. D. Lewis: Scorekeeping in a Language Game, Journal of Philosophical Language, 8, Reidel Publishing Co. 339-359

Poesio and Vieira 1998. M. Poesio and R. Vieira: A Corpus-based Investigation of Definite Description Use, Computational Linguistics.

Prince, 1978. E. Prince: A comparison of WH-clefts and it-clefts in discourse. Language 54, 883-906

Prince 1981. E. Prince: Toward a Taxonomy of Given-New Information. In Radical Pragmatics. Cole, P., Ed. Academic Press, London.

Roberts 1989. C. Roberts: Modal Subordination and Pronominal Anaphora in Discourse. Linguistics and Philosophy, 12, pp. 683-721

van der Sandt 1992. R. van der Sandt: Presupposition projection as anaphora resolution. Journal of Semantics, 9, pp. 333-377

Stalnaker 1974. R. Stalnaker: Pragmatic Presuppositions. In *Semantics and Philospy*, M.Munitz and P. Unger, Eds, New York University Press, pp. 197-214

Svartvik 1990. J. Svartvik (Ed.): *The London-Lund Corpus of Spoken English, Description and Research*, Lund Studies in English, '82, Lund University Press.

Webber 1991. B. Webber: Structure and Ostension in the Interpretation of Discourse Deixis. Language and Cognitive Processes, 6 (2), pp. 107-135.

Zeevat 1992. H. Zeevat: Presupposition and Accommodation in Update Semantics. Journal of Semantics, 9. pp.379-412

3

Explaining Presupposition Triggers

HENK ZEEVAT

3.1 Introduction

Traditional theories of presupposition treat the phenomenon of presupposition as a unified whole. They can be described as uniformly characterising the consequences for the interpretation of sentences of a class of lexical items, syntactic constructions and intonational phenomena: the presupposition triggers. There are some minor exceptions: Karttunen (1974) and Karttunen & Peters (1979) discuss the double presupposition of factive attitude verbs. According to their proposal, a trigger like "x is glad that " would presuppose both that the complement is true and that x believes the complement. Stalnaker (1973) notes that the falsity of the presupposition of certain triggers does not result in the loss of truth value of the assertion as such. This happens with triggers like *even* and *too*. According to Stalnaker's view, a sentence containing such particles can be true, even if the presupposition is false, but it will be infelicitous. In the same paper Stalnaker also observes that not all triggers accommodate with the same ease. Van der Sandt (1992) notes in his discussion of anaphoric pronouns that while they should be counted as triggers, they still do not accommodate. Zeevat (1992) makes a distinction between a class of triggers that trigger lexical presuppositions and a class of triggers that are anaphoric, claiming that the first class accommodates as predicted by his reconstruction[1] of Heim (1983)

[1]Under this speculative reconstruction of Heim, accommodating the presupposition means adding it to all contexts surrounding the trigger, until a context is reached where it causes an inconsistency. The accommodation concept of Van der Sandt on

Information Sharing: Reference and Presupposition in Language Generation and Interpretation.
Edited by Kees van Deemter and Rodger Kibble.

whereas the second class accommodates as Van der Sandt would have it. Gazdar (1979) notes that his generalisation that simplex sentences with a trigger occurrence entail their presuppositions has exceptions. These exceptions are attitude verbs like "be glad that" that in a context as in (1) do not entail the truth of their complement.

(1) John thought that Mary had left him. He was glad she had.

These differences have however not been treated systematically.

Second, while there is a wide range of default-like devices in the different presupposition theories, from the satisfiable incrementation of Gazdar (1979), the mysterious pragmatic strengthening invoked by Karttunen (1974) and Beaver (1995) to the "preferences" of Heim (1983), Van der Sandt (1992) and Geurts (1995), no successful explanation for these preferences and defaults has been offered so far. Third, the treatments are uniformly based on a notion of context for resolution or satisfaction where the content of the context is what the speaker knows (Gazdar (1979)), an information state derived by the previous exchanges (Karttunen (1974), Heim (1983), Zeevat (1992), Beaver (1995)), the common ground (Stalnaker (1978)) or the old discourse representation structure (Van der Sandt (1992), Geurts (1995), Kamp & Rossdeutscher (1994)). This is a wide range, but it does not include inaccessible presuppositions or antecedents of presupposition triggers, such as suggestions by a third party in the common ground or DRS or a possibility introduced by one of the conversational partners. Yet, these suffice for licensing the use of triggers such as *wh*-questions, clefts, intonationally marked topic and particles such as *too* or *indeed*.

This paper tries to make progress in refining our understanding of presuppositions in these three directions. First, we reduce the preferences and defaults to optimality theory (OT), a theory that has been successfully applied in phonology and syntax, and is currently finding more and more applications in semantics and pragmatics. Our treatment is an extension of Blutner (2000)'s reformulation of Van der Sandt's theory in OT by the two constraints: **Do Not Accommodate** and **Strength**. We add two further (generation) constraints: **Parse Old** and **Parse Other**. The resulting theory is successful in capturing the defaults, in explaining the obligatory occurrence of certain triggers and in accounting for the absence of accommodation for a wide range of triggers, including pronouns, *too*, *indeed* and intonationally marked topics. We also develop a general account of the differences between triggers in terms of their semantic requirement.

---

the other hand requires only a single addition to the highest context to which it can be consistently added.

3.2 The Particle "Too"

The particle *too* is a good starting point for our discussion. (2) is the example in Kripke (MS) to show that (at least some) presupposition triggers must be taken as anaphors to specific information in the context. If we do not make this assumption, given that millions of people dine in New York every evening, the presupposition is trivial, which conflicts with our intuition about the example, which says that it can only be used in certain contexts.

(2) John is having dinner in New York too.

But this example has other interesting properties as well. *Too* is a presupposition trigger that does not accommodate (against most theories of presupposition that predict the general availability of accommodation as an option). If it would accommodate, then —given the millions that have dinner in New York every evening— the occurrence of the particle "too" would again be allowed in all contexts since this accommodation would add only information already true in the context. This again conflicts with the intuition that "too" only occurs in certain contexts.

Second, the antecedent need not be a direct ingredient of the context. It is sufficient that the other person who has dinner in New York is only reported or suggested. E.g. (3):

(3) Harry may well stay in New York for dinner.

provides a good antecedent. Also (4):

(4) Bill believes that Mary will eat in New York.

(4) also illustrates a third property: partial resolution. The antecedent only mentions eating and does not imply that a dinner is involved (a lunch or a quick snack would also do). The process of finding the antecedent adds the additional information that Mary will have dinner, at least according to Bill. This process is one of finding an antecedent that only partly meets the specification and of adapting it to become a full antecedent.

A fourth property of the particle *too* is that it cannot be omitted when it has a suitable occurrence in the context. When it is omitted the total discourse becomes strange, though perhaps not always to the same degree. It can sometimes be replaced by other markers (e.g. *also*) but the bare version of the sentence is usually not appropriate if the version with *too* is. This is hard to show by just a few examples, one really needs to go through a substantial body of natural text and try to omit the *toos*[2].

All these four properties are unexplained by the best presupposition theories on the market (Heim (1983) and Van der Sandt (1992)). Inaccessible antecedents are out, accommodation is allowed without restriction, partial resolution is ruled out in the two formalisations and the theories have nothing to say about the obligatory nature of *too*.

The work of Kamp & Rossdeutscher (1994) on *wieder* (German: again) is interesting in this connection. On the basis of a detailed study of *wieder*, they conclude that accommodation is extremely rare and that partial (and not full) resolution is the case that is most frequently found. In an early presentation of this work, Kamp also tended to the view that there was something seriously wrong with the received view of presupposition. As we shall see, this is not the right conclusion. A theory that omits the possibility of accommodation and has only partial resolution instead will not do as a general theory of presupposition, but, at the same time, the pattern observed for *wieder* is typical for the class of presupposing discourse particles. Like *too*, *wieder* marks that the reported event or state is not the only one of its kind reported or assumed in the context, although *wieder* has the additional content that the other entity is temporally anterior to the reported one. This additional content seems to be responsible for the one difference in their presuppositional behaviour: *wieder* does not take inaccessible antecedents, such as suggestions or possibilities. I come back to this point later on when discussing *immers*.

3.3 Old Material

In order to deal with inaccessible antecedents, it seems necessary to allow propositional and other antecedents that are not in the common ground as such but that are only believed or suggested as possibilities in the common ground. It may be the speaker who believes the presupposition or entertains its possibility, but it may also be the hearer or another person to whom beliefs have been attributed in the common ground. It is also not necessary that the attitude is belief or knowledge. Dreams, presentations of plans, desires and possibilities all seem to provide proper antecedents for at least some triggers.

A corrects her conversation partner *B*:

(5) B: The king of France is bald.
A:The king of France is not bald, France is a republic.

[2]My student Tim Kliphuis and later myself have carried out an overview of this kind for a series of Dutch particles in the text of Multatuli's Max Havelaar, a famous 19th century Dutch novel.

In her correction, A presupposes that there is a king of France, even though she has not the slightest inclination herself to assent to the statement that there is such a person. The natural solution is to think that the statement A is correcting, representing B's beliefs only and not the common ground, supplies the antecedent.

The following examples illustrate a wider range of contexts that can provide such antecedents.

(6) A: John thinks Mary has gone to Bill's party.
B: Carol has gone there too.

A: John dreamt that his car was stolen.
B: My car was stolen too.

A: John said that he is going to the concert.
B: Bill is going too.

A: John thinks that Mary ate the cake.
B: It was Bill who ate the cake.

A: John suggested that he might come tonight.
B: I will come too.

A: Maybe John will sing tonight.
B: I will sing too.

The possibility of such antecedents[3] (*inaccessible* is borrowed from Discourse Representation Theory) appears to have been neglected in the more formal presupposition literature simply because many of the key triggers in that literature do not seem to allow such antecedents. Definite descriptions, names, factives, and lexical presuppositions prima facie do not take such antecedents at all. Anaphoric pronouns clearly also belong to this group. But questions, many particles (but not *wieder*), clefts and intonationally marked topic typically do take other antecedents as well. The range of attitudes that generate inaccessible antecedents is roughly[4]

[3]I have been unable to spot proper references for the first observations of these weaker antecedents for presupposition triggers, but the observation is not due to me. I believe they came up first in discussing the presuppositions of intonationally marked topic and in discussions around the presupposition of questions, but I have not been able to find references or to find people who knew about them.

[4]There is a considerable overlap with the distribution of negative polarity items, but there is not an exact match: e.g. *suggest* in Modern Greek takes negative polarity items. This should not worry us unduly, since there is a lot of variation in the distribution of different negative polarity items, also between languages.

what Giannakidou (1998) has labelled the veridical contexts: those that do not license negative polarity items. That class can be characterised in a quasi-logical way as the closure of the simple sentences under operators that entail the truth of their arguments (e.g. *and*, *necessary*) but also under such operators as *maybe*, *dream*, *belief* etc. At one point, I thought an independent characterisation could be developed starting from the rather particular semantics for belief sentences I developed in Zeevat (1996). There the discourse markers of belief sentences are discourse markers of the DRS that represents the belief sentence and not of the DRS representing its complement. If this approach could be generalised to the other operators for which it seems plausible, the veridical operators would be just those that put their discourse markers in the context that surrounds them. Negations and quantifiers, on the other hand, block this outward movement of markers. This may be a correct point of view, but as a characterisation it is not worth much: it quite obviously just restates the fact that the complements of these operators generate inaccessible antecedents. It perhaps reflects the intuition that the objects and facts of the veridical contexts are ones that the common ground is committed to in some way or other as possibly relevant, without necessarily being committed to their proper existence.

3.4 Requirements and Anaphora

If we have a sentence S containing a trigger T with a presupposition P, the presupposition P must be resolved or accommodated. If neither is possible (usually because the context entails the negation of the presupposition) the sentence cannot be properly interpreted, does not define a proper update or —in terms of discourse representation theory— the development algorithm gets stuck. Our old information state (or DRS) is preserved, it just did not get updated.

Contrast this with what happens to a proposition p if $p \models q$ and we try to update an information state σ such that $\sigma \models \neg q$ with p. The interpretation is successful, a proper update is possible and the DRT development algorithm does not block. But we obtain an inconsistent information state.

This comparison should suffice to establish that —following Stalnaker and Gazdar (and more recently Geurts)— one cannot say that simple sentences S containing a trigger presupposing P also entail P. If that were true, it would follow that adding S to an information state σ entailing $\neg p$ would result both in undefinedness and the empty information state. What we should rather say —and this insight goes back to Heim— is that the fact that the simple sentence S has a presupposition

P explains the intuition that S entails P. After all, for all information states σ that can be updated with S, it holds that $\sigma[S] \models P$. If S just entailed P and S contains no other triggers it would hold for all σ for which $\sigma[S]$ is defined that $\sigma[S] \models P$, which is close to the standard way of defining entailment in update semantics. But it is not entailment, as we saw. The presupposition causes undefinedness in those cases where entailment would cause inconsistency.

Generalising this insight, one arrives at the most basic form of the satisfaction theory of presupposition: the trigger has a semantics which requires the truth of the presupposition for the update with the trigger to be defined at all. But this theory brings problems that are hard to solve. The first is the *locality* problem. It is hard to see why the satisfaction of the requirement should consist in the presupposition appearing in the global context —which it mostly does— when the requirement only arises in the local context of the trigger. Much energy has been devoted to the explanation of this aspect of the satisfaction theory, with very little result. The second is the *rationality* problem. This is the fact that it is often hard to see why the presupposition is required by the semantics of the trigger. Following fairly standard views, names presuppose the existence of something or somebody bearing that name. Since names are often taken to be directly referential, it is hard to see why the local context should require that there is something or somebody bearing that name: the existence of a referent as such seems sufficient for the semantic contribution of the trigger in the local context. And, third, there is the *identification* problem. The identification of the presupposed material in a higher context does not guarantee that the presupposition is locally satisfied.

We are confronted with the locality problem almost all the time. In (7), the presupposition is required in the scope of the negation. Yet, there is agreement that most of the time it ends up in the context of the sentence itself.

(7) John does not regret that Mary left.

(7) just does not mean (8) in contexts that are not committed to the falsity of *Mary left.*

(8) It is not the case that Mary left and that John regrets that.

The rationality problem is perhaps less controversially illustrated by Stalnaker's observation that "John left too", just continues to mean what "John left" means, even if nobody else left. As we saw just now, *too* has no nontrivial semantical properties other than presupposing some other event of the same type (under compositional semantics we would have to represent its semantic content as the identity function over type t or et).

And the identification problem is perhaps best illustrated by considering propositional attitudes.

(9) John believed that Mary regretted that Bill left.

(9) presupposes that Bill left —normally. But the fact that Bill left is no guarantee that Mary believes that and so does not guarantee that the presupposition of *regret* is satisfied where it matters, i.e. locally, in the scope of the belief operator.

These problems merely underpin the thesis that it does not suffice to say that the presupposition is given by the requirement of the semantic content of the trigger. I want to make a still stronger claim: I want to deny that the requirement is the presupposition. What I want to say is that sometimes it is, that sometimes the requirement is only a part of the presupposition and that sometimes there is no requirement at all. For this we need to make some assumptions about the semantic role of different categories of triggers.

I take it that in natural language we sometimes find the situation that a predicate only applies to an arrangement of entities that already meets certain conditions. One can make an analogy here with the preconditions of certain actions. For example, it is not possible to post a letter before it is written and it is not possible to write a letter if one does not have a pen or a pencil and paper. In much the same way, one can say only of an adult male that he is a bachelor. This fact plays an important role in our interpretation of sentences containing the word *bachelor*. If we say (10) about a four-year old:

(10) Tommy is a bachelor.

it will be interpreted metaphorically. Tommy wants to walk to kindergarten with a different girl every day, maybe. The same happens if we say (11) about an 18-year old girl:

(11) Susanna is a bachelor.

Here we may refer to her general lifestyle, or the state of her apartment. And Seuren (1988) observes that lexical presuppositions play a role in disambiguation. *A bald tyre* (unlike dutch: *een kale band*, french: *un pneu chauve*) describes a tyre that has lost its profile, whereas a treeless mountain in Dutch (but not in English or French) can be called *een kale berg* (french: **une montagne chauve*, english: **a bald mountain*). Apparently the word *kaal* has a different set of presuppositions evoking different concepts than *bald* has. And the different readings are selected by presupposition satisfaction. (And it is very likely that the metaphorical interpretations due to presupposition violation are responsible for the emergence of different specialised concepts expressed by the word.)

Lexical items that have such requirements become presupposition triggers presupposing precisely the requirement. The process of resolution and accommodation is how they manage to meet the requirements. This is characteristic for what are normally called lexical presupposition triggers.

The other triggers are different. Referential devices such as names, pronouns, definite descriptions, demonstratives and others supply referents for predications. The way in which they do that is by searching the context by a variety of criteria. These criteria are their presuppositions and it is by no means clear that the role these referring expressions play in defining the thought expressed by the sentence in which they occur depends much on the content of their presuppositions. Kaplan (1989) is largely devoted to showing that many of these expressions are directly referential and that their descriptive meaning serves only to fix the reference and does not enter the proposition they express. Zeevat (2000) generalises this to all of the referential devices mentioned, with the possible exception of some uses of definite descriptions. Indeed, it might be argued that these expressions do not have any part of their presupposition as a requirement: the existence presuppositions standardly assumed for them can be attributed (as lexical presuppositions) to the predicates whose argument places they fill. This, however, is problematic.

(12) a. Russell and Strawson argued about the king of France.
b. Russell and Strawson argued about the father of Jane.

While in the first case of (12) the existence presupposition does not emerge as a presupposition of the sentence as a whole, in the second case, in the absence of information that Jane does not exist or that she is fatherless, we standardly assume the existence of the object. Since the predicate *argue about* does not presuppose the existence of its object, we cannot explain the presupposition of (12b) in this way. It thus seems that we must assume that existence of the referent is required for referential expressions and explain it as a precondition for a referential expression fulfilling its semantic role. Typically, the varied conditions by which these expressions search the context are not required for their semantic contribution. Indeed, in the case of pronouns, deicticals and demonstratives, these conditions do not seem much like contents at all: they refer to the position of the referent in the context (recent mention, position in the visual field, role in the conversation) and do not give any inherent characterisation of the object.

It is again clear that the presupposition resolution and accommodation process is the means by which the referential expressions fulfill their requirement. But it would be wrong to assume right away that that is why they are presupposition triggers. It is rather the other way around: these expressions' primary function is to collect old and given material from the context in order to say new things about it. They are primarily anaphors and it is because they are anaphors that they have presuppositions and the existence requirement. This category can be described as the referential anaphoric presupposition triggers.

The final category comprises particles and intonationally marked topics. It is usually the case that the particle or the intonation does not make a contribution to the truth conditions of the sentence in which it occurs. With a different intonation or without the particle the sentence means much the same. It follows that the trigger places no requirement on the context. The particles are anaphoric devices and basically position the sentence in the context. I propose to call this category of triggers the non-referential anaphoric triggers.

The following table draws some concrete conclusions from the abstract considerations above.

trigger	**presupposition**	**requirement**
$bachelor(x)$	$adult(x) \wedge male(x)$	idem
he	$salient(x)$	x
the king	$king(x)$	x
John	$named(x, john)$	x
$regret(x, p)$	p	$believe(x, p)$
$know(x, p)$	p	$p \wedge believe(x, p)$
$too(e)$	$e', e' \neq e$	none
$again(s)$	$s', s' < s$	s'

What we said is still problematic. If we think in terms of the DRT development algorithm, any failure of both resolution and accommodation for a presupposition will throw the algorithm into a dead-end street. The difference with the pure satisfaction theory is that we can in some cases unblock the algorithm and end up with an interpretation after all, i.e. when the requirements are still met. In the case the presupposition overlaps with the requirement this does not do: deblocking the algorithm after presupposition failure does not do any good: the interpretation results in garbage. A version of the algorithm which —perhaps after sending an error message— gives up on the resolution or accommodation and continues with its other work will fail because of failing the requirements only. This explains Stalnaker's observation about *even* and *also*.

It is my view that requirements are fully given by the presupposition and the semantic content of a trigger. The requirement of the trigger is what the presupposition has to contribute to the semantics of the trigger for it to carry out its semantic role. I have tried to argue the point that there is no other way in which the trigger's semantics can obtain that contribution: entailment is just something else. It may be confusing because we are not used to thinking about the semantic role of e.g. *know* or *John* without the contribution that their presuppositions make. But that is precisely the point: when the requirement is not fulfilled by resolving or accommodating the presupposition, there is no semantic role. The semantics of triggers can be analysed only by taking them seriously as triggers. And in that sense, but in that sense alone, indicating the trigger's requirement is a task of the lexicographer.

The difference between presupposition and requirement explains the different behaviour of triggers with respect to inaccessible antecedents. An inaccessible antecedent is fine if its existence and identification suffices for meeting the requirement of the trigger in its local context. This happens standardly with triggers that lack requirements. An interesting case arises when the requirement is strictly weaker than the presupposition. Some inaccessible antecedents are then allowed, but not all of them. Compare (13).

(13) John believes that p and he regrets that p.

Here a resolution to an inaccessible antecedent occurs and the requirement is met. But we do not predict that accommodation of *John believes that p* is possible when there is no inaccessible antecedent. Thus if (14) occurs in isolation, we must still infer that p is true, and not just that p is believed by John.

(14) John regrets that p.

On the other hand, (15)

(15) John believes that p and he knows that p.

allows the same resolution, but this resolution is not sufficient for entailing the requirement. In this case, the only option left is global accommodation or global resolution (combined with local accommodation).

In (16), we see the same phenomenon with names.

(16) In the 18th century, some astronomers assumed the existence of a planet Vulcan within the orbit of Mercury and Bill now thinks he has discovered evidence that Vulcan is really there.

The inaccessible antecedent for Vulcan is sufficient for meeting the requirement in the second context if we take it that the assumption of the planet (and possibly of its name) is part of Bill's beliefs. The existence of the planet is part of the requirement and is therefore locally entailed by the occurrence of the name. It is, however, not the kind of entailment that comes from conceptual relations, like the relation between *bachelor* and *unmarried*. It is a presupposition of the expression fulfilling its semantic role, in this case providing a referent for a predication. If the local existence of Vulcan is not given, the context has to contain the information that Vulcan exists, possibly after accommodation. Only if the context already has the information that Vulcan does not exist, a local accommodation in Bill's beliefs is possible.

Another example is (17).

(17) Bill thought that John had finally solved the problem. The solution however turned out to be mistaken.

Here we have a partial resolution to an inaccessible antecedent, to whatever Bill thought that John thought was the solution. The requirement is met by the existence of such an object, even though the referent does not meet the condition expressed by the noun in the description.

My earlier example about the king of France finds a similar explanation. B denies the existence of the king of France and, within that denial, the belief of A is sufficient to meet the requirement of the trigger. The other examples in the last section are of particles that have no requirement since they lack a proper semantical content. There are subtle differences between the particles in their acceptance of inaccessible antecedents. *Indeed* is the particle that seems most willing to take inaccessible antecedents whereas *too* is much less gregarious.

(18) John dreamt that he failed and indeed he did.
(?) John dreamt that Bill went to Spain, and, in fact, he went too.
(?) John dreamt that Bill went to Spain but, in fact, he went instead.

These subtle differences may be treated under the heading of the requirement of the particles involved, thus leading to the view that *too* and *indeed* have some non-trivial semantical content. But there are other possibilities. *Too* but not *indeed* has another particle with which it stands in complementary distribution: *instead*. If we try to spell out the communalities between *instead* and *too* we find that they both presuppose another element of the same kind in the context. The sentence with *instead* implicates that the other element of the same kind does not exist, whereas the sentence with *too* implicates that it exists next to the current element. We can obtain these effects by making the (non-

)existence of the antecedent part of the presupposition of the particles. The implications —if they are not already given by the context— are then a result of a partial resolution. The implications are clearly not a part of the content, because of the example (19), mimicking Heim's example.

(19) A: My parents think that I won the gold medal for my essay.
B: My parents think that I won it instead/too.

The differences between the acceptability and obligatoriness of *too* versus *indeed* can perhaps be explained by the failure of certain environments to give a good answer for the choice between *too* and *instead.* E.g. a dream that John had an icecream, when we want to report that Bill had an icecream, does not clearly make a distinction between *next to* and *instead of.* Notice that the absence of a particle is not a good alternative either.

(20) Mary dreamt that John had an icecream. Bill had one ?∅/*?too/*?instead.

3.5 Optimality Theory

Blutner (2000) was the first to notice that the defaults and preferences that are so characteristic of presupposition theories can be adequately captured by the soft constraints and the constraint ordering of optimality theory. He proposes two constraints: **Do Not Accommodate** and **Strength**, ordered as indicated. The accommodation constraint prevents accommodation when it is not necessary, the strength constraint prefers the reading of the sentence that gives most information. An absolute constraint of **Consistency** can be added to obtain local accommodations, when global ones are not consistent, though this could also be expressed as a demand on the candidate set of updates as in Blutner & Jäger (1999). The system provides a reconstruction and an improvement of the theory of Van der Sandt (1992). The advantages of the OT version are that it makes accommodation in downward entailing contexts less preferred and that partial resolution is smoothly incorporated.

If optimality theory can be applied to presupposition interpretation, it is natural to ask whether it can be applied to the generation of presupposition triggers as well. In fact, one might first want to be sure that the so-called interpretation principles are not really generation principles in disguise. But it seems impossible to think of a principle like **Do Not Accommodate** as a generation constraint. Looking at different contexts, we get different interpretations of (21). Yet we do not find a difference in form if we consider the generation in each of the interpretational possibilities. I.e. all four readings (two resolutions and two accommodations) of (21) just give us (21).

(21) Bill believes that John regrets that Mary left.

The best we can do is to say that an intended local accommodation is bad when the context does not yet explicitly rule out global accommodation. A constraint against the use of a trigger in a local context where its presupposition holds according to the speaker, but where global accommodation is possible but not intended by the speaker would be a possibility. But this would capture only a small part of the effects of **Do Not Accommodate**.

The decision to relegate the communication of some content to presupposition accommodation rather than to a separate prior assertion involves considerations of efficiency and even politeness. Though the reconstruction of these considerations plays a role in the interpretation of accommodating examples, their recognition does not seem to be the crucial factor: that is the absence of an antecedent. **Strength**, likewise, is so much a question of choosing between possible interpretations that a corresponding generation principle is hard to imagine. If a weaker reading is intended it can only be obtained by *but*s and *however*s. The need for these *but*s and *however*s seems a consequence of **Strength** as an interpretation principle.

There is a class of presupposition triggers which are obligatory in the sense that if the local context has the appropriate antecedent, the trigger must occur. Intonational marking, discourse particles, pronouns, *another*, *a different*, and some uses of definite descriptions all seem to fall into this class.

The basic observation is that (22) normally cannot be replaced by the sentence without *too* in a context where *too* appears.

(22) John is in Spain too.

This is familiar from the generation of referential expressions. There seems to be a hierarchy of referential devices which can be selected only if the application criteria of the classes appearing above in the hierarchy do not apply. This is not the place for a detailed discussion of all of the application criteria, but there are at least two relevant principles that can be taken from the provisional hierarchy, as given by the table below.

NP type	**selection condition**
reflexive	c-command
1st or 2nd person pronouns	conversation participant
demonstratives	presence in current attention space
anaphoric	high salience through mention
short definites	old, dependence on high salient

other marking NPs	other element of same type
long definites	new and unique
indefinites	new

Grice (1975) observed that in (23)

(23) I saw John in town with a woman.

the woman cannot be known to be John's wife or his mother, even though, strictly speaking, either of them would suffice for the truth of the example. We can also add, on the basis of the hierarchy, that she is also not the speaker or the hearer, or John herself (if the name John could be used for women as well). It can also be assumed that she was not mentioned in the discourse before and specifically not in the last sentence. Grice's two short definites should win from the indefinite, because in that case there is dependence on the highly salient John.

The first principle we can extract from the referential hierarchy is that when some object or event is already in the common ground of the conversation this has to be marked by the choice of the device by which we refer to it. This is the case when we look for a referential device for an object that we need to refer to. This can be an old object or it can be an object that belongs to an old object (it is the restaurant's waiter, one of the playing children, three of the students in the bar etc.). All devices in the hierarchy fulfill the principle except for long definites and indefinites. I want to call the constraint **ParseOld**. It is a parse constraint because it forces the expression of a feature appearing in the input.

The second principle is that the presence of an old but different object of the same type must always be marked. This is the business of *another*, *a different*, *too*, *also* and presumably other elements as well. The constraint is **ParseOther**. We must assume that these two constraints are ranked equally in order to explain the combination of devices as in *another* or *the other*, *this other* etc. (There is no *other me* or *other you*, but they do not seem to be needed).

Both constraints seem to have a primarily psychological explanation. If we assume that the perceptual system is biased to the identification of what is similar, then nothing seems more functional than a controlled use of this bias: inhibit it when necessary and reinforce it when identifications need to occur. **ParseOld** also increases efficiency, since the old marking NPs and VPs are generally much shorter.

The generation constraints affect the distribution of triggers: they force the use of an item from the relevant class of triggers when the conditions for its application occur.

One additional remark about **ParseOther**. Compare (24)

(24) Bill ate from the cake
John did too

and (25)

(25) Bill ate from the cake
No, John did .

It might seem that the second example is a clear violation of **Parse-Other**, in fact, *too* is not even allowed there. But this fits what the second speaker wants to achieve: his proposal is to remove Bill as a cake-eater and replacing him by John. This can in some contexts be marked by *instead*, as in (26). (Not necessarily always: the correction is itself a marker of the *instead* type.)

(26) Bill says that John ate the cake but Harry says that Charles ate it instead.

3.6 Blutner's Theorem

Blutner (2000) provides the following explanation of the fact that intonationally marked topic-focus articulation gives rise to a non-accommodatable presupposition. Given an interpretational constraint **Do Not Accommodate**, the use of topic-focus intonation where the presupposition is not resolvable loses out to the other candidate generations that do not presuppose: they do not violate the accommodation constraint. And it is necessary[5] to include those intonational variants in the candidate set that do not give rise to the presupposition.

The explanation uses a novel way of thinking about the application of optimality theory to the syntax and interpretation of natural languages. We have both interpretation constraints and generation constraints that simultaneously apply to pairs of generations and interpretations. A pair $< g, i >$ can be suboptimal even if the interpretation is an optimal interpretation of the input, because there is a g_1 that can be interpreted with less violations of the interpretation constraints. (Similarly, a generation g can be optimal for the interpretation i by the generation principles but fail because there is a better interpretation i_1 than the intended i available for g.)

I use *Blutner's Theorem* for the general principle: if a trigger context has simple non-triggering expression alternatives with the same meaning, it does not accommodate. The simplicity of the alternative expressions guarantees that they are considered in the optimality contest so that

[5] Necessary because it is impossible to think of any answer to the hard question which alternatives to include that would omit the intonational variants.

Blutner's reasoning applies to them. If the context lacks a suitable antecedent and non-presupposing means of expression are available, the principle forces us to choose those means of expression rather than the presupposing ones, which would force an accommodation.

The only alternative explanation of non-accommodation of certain triggers that I know of is Van der Sandt's. He argued that pronouns do not accommodate because they lack sufficient semantic content. Now it is not clear that this does the job for pronouns. In English, the morphology of "her" gives exactly the same semantic content as "a female person", which can be added to the context without any problems, like the even less contentful "somebody" or "something". But the explanation is untenable for particles like "indeed" in a sentence "indeed p". The presupposition in that case is "p" itself. If Van der Sandt's explanation were extended to "indeed", it would follow that the presupposition of factive verbs cannot be accommodated anymore, since "John regrets that p" has exactly the same presupposition as "indeed p".

Blutner's theorem is a strong principle and trying to refute it is a rewarding game. The game is so rewarding that one is sometimes tempted to go to the weaker[6] alternative constraint: **Obligatory Triggers Do Not Accommodate**. So far neither me nor Blutner nor anybody else has come up with a good optimality theoretic reason why this constraint should hold and it is also quite unclear why Blutner's reasoning should be correct in the case of intonation and fail for presupposition triggers. So I want to stick here to the full strength of Blutner's Theorem and use it to draw some non-trivial conclusions about the semantics of the apparent counterexamples.

Occurrences of presupposing particles are unproblematic. One clearly must take the view that the same sentence without them is an alternative to them of the required simplicity. This is largely borne out by the facts, though interestingly not entirely. For example, in (27) in the absence of suitable antecedents, we get, instead of a free accommodation, the inference that it is the speaker who wants coffee. This may be partial resolution based on the naturally highly salient speaker or an idiomatic fact about *too*.

(27) Context: out of the blue
Do you want coffee too? (speaker)
(??)Do you want coffee instead?

More problematic is the case of *knowledge* and *belief*. It seems that *belief* provides *knowledge* with a simple non-presupposing expression al-

[6]The alternative constraint only applies to particles and other obligatory presupposition triggers and thus avoids the counterexamples.

ternative, but *knowledge* still accommodates as well as any trigger. I have to follow here the opinion of most theorists of knowledge that it is simply false that knowledge equals truth plus belief. It is also necessary that the known fact played an appropriate causal role in the genesis of the belief.

A similar case is the putative counterexample (Geurts p.c.) (28).

(28) John managed to break the lock.

Of course *managing* accommodates well and (28) has the simple expression alternative *John broke the lock* but it now just follows from Blutner's theorem that they do not mean the same. This counterexample bites, because it forces us on the slippery slope of having to claim that *manage to* X expresses the subject's ability to do X, which X by itself does not express, even though it entails it. Reasoning of this kind is familiar from the literature on metaphors. (29a) implies (29b) and inversely but they do not express the same since the image in (29a) is missing in (29b.) It is rather clear that truth-conditional equivalence is not a guarantee of the psychological identity of meaning and it is psychological identity that is required for the workings of Blutner's theorem.

(29) a. Henk blew his top.
 b. Henk got rather angry

The most interesting counterexample is provided by the opposition between *a(n)* and *the*. There are uses of *the* that easily accommodate, like: *the inventor of electrical power* and there are cases that follow Blutner's theorem in being nearly unaccommodatable, like *the man* in (30).

(30) The man told me that he was going to get angry.

The choice for a definite description is more complex than just the choice between a presupposing and a non-presupposing article. In fact, it is by no means clear that all uses of definite descriptions are presupposing, compare e.g. the interpretation of (31) under which it is false, in a context where Bill is married to Jane. (Bill clearly could have preferred to stay a bachelor or to marry another person.)

(31) It is necessary that Bill's wife is Jane.

Resolving to the global context to pick up Jane would lead to a true interpretation, quite contrary to intuition. (I am assuming that *necessary* is used in the sense where it rules out that things could have gone differently. Under that operator, the name Jane rigidly refers to Jane.)

Short definite descriptions can meet the requirement of **ParseOld** both when they obtain a bridging interpretation and when they are anaphoric. In other uses —mostly using long definites so that accommodation is allowed— they reflect the speaker's opinion that she has managed to provide sufficient descriptive material to make the reference unique. In these cases the indefinite article is ruled out or extremely marked. It seems then that the opposition between definite and indefinite article is a double one: uniqueness versus non-uniqueness when a new entity is involved, as well as old versus new.

We may perhaps say that all definite descriptions presuppose. But they only accommodate when they are unique descriptions. The combination of a definite article with a non-unique description is a trigger that has the indefinite article as a simple expression alternative. The combination of the definite article with a unique description does not have the indefinite article as a simple expression alternative. Therefore, only the anaphoric and the bridging uses of definites fall under Blutner's theorem.

Viewed from the perspective of the referential hierarchy, this connects the definite article to three parse constraints: **ParseOld**, **ParseDependent** and **ParseUnique**, with **ParseUnique** ranked lower than the other two and **ParseOld** ranked above **ParseDependent**. In (32), *the man* is selected because pronouns and demonstratives do not apply and the next possibility in the referential hierarchy is the default old-marker *the*.

(32) A girl pushing an old man in a wheelchair came down the path. The man/*he was smoking a cigar.

He is not possible here because the antecedent is not an argument of the main clause and thereby not highly salient. In (33) *the waiter* is selected because it is functionally related to a highly salient item. Choosing *Tim*, or *a waiter* would violate **ParseDependent**. The waiter is a new referent in the story.

(33) We entered the restaurant. The waiter brought us the menu.

Finally, in (34) we find a case where the third constraint applies.

(34) The director of Tim's school is organising a meeting.

A full discussion of these cases within a serious optimality theoretic reconstruction of the referential hierarchy must be deferred to another paper, but it is possible to illustrate what is going on with some OT diagrams.

I am assuming that there are a set of tied constraints at work in NP-selection. The relevant ones for the choice between definites and indefinites are the following: **ParseSalient**, **ParseAttention**, **ParseOld** and **ParseUnique**. I am further assuming that pronouns are parsing salience and oldness, demonstratives attention and oldness, and the definite article uniqueness and oldness. The problem can be given as generating an NP for a discourse referent x that is a book by the author Anna. We assume a further constraint **FaithInt** that marks candidates if their interpretation would lead to the assumption of a feature in the input that is not there. We also need an economy constraint preferring shorter expressions and **Do Not Accommodate** for punishing unresolvable old-marking expressions if we want a fuller treatment.

In the first context x has just been mentioned and it is now salient.

input: x	**Salient=**	**Attention=**	**Old=**	**Unique >**	**FaithInt**
it					
this					*
this book	*			*	
this book by Anna	*				*
the book	*				
the book by Anna	*				
a book by Anna	*				

The winner is *it* in this context, but *this* would win if x were in the centre of visual attention as well, because of the extra mark that *it* would then receive and the mark that *this* would lose.

The second context we consider is that the book has been mentioned before, but is not currently salient.

input: x	**Salient=**	**Attention=**	**Old=**	**Unique >**	**FaithInt**
it					*
this					**
this book					*
this book by Anna					*
the book					
the book by Anna					
a book by Anna			*		

The winner is now *the book* (by economy) but would be replaced by *this book* if it were the case that the book is also in the centre of the visual field.

In the third context, the book is neither old nor in the visual field. It is moreover true in the context that Anna has written a single book only.

input: x	Salient=	Attention=	Old=	Unique >	FaithInt
it					*
this					**
this book					*
this book by Anna					*
the book					
the book by Anna					
a book by Anna				*	

Do Not Accommodate now decides for *the book by Anna*, because *the book* is not resolvable either in the context of the conversation (it is not old) or in the general context (there are many books).

And the fourth context is one where Anna is a prolific author. Again the book is new.

input: x	Salient=	Attention=	Old=	Unique >	FaithInt
it					*
this					**
this book					*
this book by Anna					*
the book					*
the book by Anna					*
a book by Anna					

The definite descriptions fail because they give the feature Old or Unique, which are not features of the input. Alternatively, they can be ruled out by **Do Not Accommodate**. So the winner is *a book by Anna.*

I am giving these diagrams with a great deal of hesitation, because I think the precise treatment of NP selection needs much more work and I am aware of quite a number of problems with the present treatment. These diagrams are only meant to illustrate the approach I am tentatively adopting in this paper to underpin my treatment of presupposition triggers. What they do bring out, I hope, is that the idea of a double function of definite descriptions does not forcibly lead to the view that the definite article is ambiguous. The article marks two different features which guide us to a correct resolution or accommodation. Apart from that function, the definite article has no proper semantic content.

3.7 Inderdaad toch wel immers

The theory I have been sketching in the sections above offers a good basis for the study of discourse particles. The title of this section is formed by four Dutch particles[7].

They typically accompany assertions that came up earlier in the conversation. In this situation —schematically— we can distinguish four different cases: $+S+H$, $+S-H$, $-S+H$ and $-S-H$, depending on the attitude of the speaker and the hearer towards the statement[8]. The speaker and hearer can agree that the statement is true, the speaker can support it while the hearer is against it, the speaker can oppose the hearer's opinion that the statement is true and, finally, they can agree that it is false. All four cases are exceptions to *Stalnaker 1978*'s theory of assertion which requires of assertions that they be both informative and consistent with the common ground at the point of the assertion. $+S, +H$ and $-S, -H$ are straightforward violations, but the other two go against the spirit of the approach as well. $-S, +H$ and $+S, -H$ make the proposal that the assertion be common ground inconsistent with the common ground as it was developed so far. So in all four cases, the statement is not a proper assertion.

The following is a natural correlation. $+S+H$ *immers*, $+S-H$ *wel*, $-S+H$ *inderdaad*, $-S-H$ *toch*. My first hypothesis was that the particles in fact mark the abnormal assertions for their particular kind of abnormality. But this is easily shown to be false: the four particles can be used all at the same time as in (35).

(35) Jan is toch inderdaad immers wel gekomen.
As you know, John DID indeed come after all.

If we look at more examples, we see that the distribution is not determined by the four conversational situations: the particles have a far wider distribution.

Much better is the following analysis: *wel* p triggers $\neg p$ and the high salience of $\neg p$ (*salient*($\neg p$)). *Toch* p (in one important reading) triggers $\neg\ p$, without the high salience. *Inderdaad* p triggers p and so does *immers* p.

Immers is special because it also indicates that the most salient statement is true because of p. An *immers* statement is normally an argument for the statement that comes immediately before it. This gives *immers* a requirement that puts it in the same context as the motivated statement: normally the global context, i.e. the common ground. A proposition that is not common ground cannot justify why another

[7] *inderdaad* is equivalent to *indeed*, the others lack a clear English counterpart. *Wel* can be rendered by emphatic *do*, *toch* is sometimes *after all* and *immers* can mostly be rendered by *as you know*.

[8] Neutrality is atypical. One would expect parties to react to each others' statements.

proposition should be in the common ground. This makes *immers* unique among the four particles in not taking inaccessible antecedents and in having an unproblematic relation with the Stalnaker conditions: an *immers* sentence can only be used when the common ground does not yet contain the causal or evidential connection it expresses. The fact that *immers* is obligatory for expressing a causal or evidential connection from a common-ground item to a common ground item, even when other causal markers are around, leads to the following curious fact: a presupposition trigger occurrence that cannot resolve.

(36) Omdat Piet naar huis ging, kon hij niet meehelpen.
Because Piet went home, he could not help.

Omdat is a presupposition trigger like its English counterpart *because*. Yet, when it is resolvable to the common ground, the sentence would require an occurrence of *immers*. So it follows that the presupposition of *omdat* cannot resolve without the presence of *immers* and must therefore accommodate[9].

Immers lacks inaccessible antecedents for the same reason as *again*: its semantic content relates the current clause to an earlier one.

Wel, *toch* and *inderdaad* presuppose the negation, the falsity and the truth of the clause they mark. *Wel* does that over a short distance only: there must be a relation of parallelism between the negation and the occurrence of *wel*. But unlike *immers*, they also take inaccessible antecedents. The speaker's beliefs, the hearer's beliefs, and suggestions by any other party all provide good antecedents, as is shown in (37).

(37) Jan droomde dat hij het tentamen niet gehaald had, maar hij is wel geslaagd.
John dreamt that he did not pass the exam, but he made it allright.
Jan dacht dat hij het tentamen niet zou halen, maar hij is toch geslaagd.
John thought that he would not pass the exam, but he made it

[9]In an earlier paper, Zeevat 1997, I claimed that the indefinite article was a trigger which obligatorily accommodates, and supported this by the analogy to Latin and Russian that do not have the grammatical obligation of putting an article. The behaviour of indefinites can in the current context be characterised by letting them be presupposing without marking the referent as old. This, by the principle **Parse-Old**, entails that they cannot be resolved: if they were, they would be replaced by an old-marker such as the definite article. Bare Latin or Russian NPs behave like normal presupposition triggers because these languages lack the definite article as an old-marker. Other cases of non-resolving triggers can be obtained by giving the lexical material of the presupposition of a trigger the intonation that indicates they are new material.

allright.
Jan droomde dat hij het tentamen niet zou halen, en hij is inderdaad gezakt.
John dreamt that he would not pass the exam, and indeed he failed.

This means that our initial hypothesis is just a special case. Apart from *immers*, there is no marker that specialises in a combination of a speaker and a hearer attitude. The other particles can be used in the indicated combination of attitudes, but that is not a requirement for their use at all.

Combining things, we can indeed come up with a context that combines the use of the four items at the same time, as in (38).

(38) We weten dat Jan thuis is. Ik begrijp niet waarom Piet beweert dat Jan er niet is want hij is immers inderdaad toch wel thuis.
We know that Jan is home. I do not understand why Piet claims that Jan is not there, because as you know, he IS indeed at home allright.

There are many issues that must remain undiscussed in this section. Which class of particles can be treated as presupposition triggers taking inaccessible antecedents? Does the treatment cover all uses of *toch*, *inderdaad*, *wel* and *immers*? These questions are difficult and have to be deferred to another paper[10].

3.8 Classifying Triggers

I claim that triggers are fully determined when three properties are known: what they presuppose, what they require from their presupposition and whether they have a simple expression alternative.

The answer to the first two questions determines to what extent the trigger can take inaccessible antecedents. The answer to the third question determines whether or not they can accommodate. In addition, there are generation constraints responsible for obligatory occurrence and the absence of obligatory old-markers (or new marking) may force non-resolving readings of certain triggers.

trigger	**presupp.**	**requir.**	**inacc.**	**oblig.**	**resol.**	**accom.**
the_1 N	$x, N(x)$	x	some	yes	yes	no
the_2 N	$x, N(x)$	$\exists! x N x$	no	no	yes	yes
a(n) N	$x, N(x)$	x	no	no	no	yes
regret p	p	Bp	some	no	yes	yes
bachelor(x)	man(x)	man(x)	no	no	yes	yes

[10]A more extended treatment of these particles can be found in Zeevat (2000)

manage to X	difficult(X)	none	no	no	yes	yes
because p	p	p	no	no	yes	yes
omdat p	p	p	no	no	no	yes
omdat immers p	p	p	no	yes	yes	no
know p	p	p,Bp	no	no	yes	yes
destressed X	X	none	yes	yes	yes	no
too(S(x))	$S(y)$	none	yes	yes	yes	no
instead(S(x))	$S(y)$	none	yes	yes	yes	no
wieder(X(e))	$X(e')$	$e' < e$	no	yes	yes	no
inderdaad p	p	none	yes	yes	yes	no
wel p	$\neg p$	none	yes	yes	yes	no
toch p	$\neg p$	none	yes	yes	yes	no
immers p	$p, salient(q)$	$reason(p, q)$	no	yes	yes	no

This table lists the trigger, its presupposition, its requirement, taking of inaccessible antecedents, obligatory occurrence of the trigger, whether it resolves or not and finally whether it accommodates or not. In the table *destressed* stands for intonationally marked topic, the columns *resolving* and *accommodating* indicate whether the trigger's presupposition can be handled by resolution or accommodation respectively. The theories of Heim and Van der Sandt posit the identity of the presupposition and the requirement and put the last two columns uniformly to *yes*. They have nothing to say about the variation in the fourth and fifth column.

3.9 Conclusion

I have presented the outlines of a presupposition theory that is more linguistically inspired than the standard theories and that is a good tool for understanding of those triggers that are only marginally considered in traditional theories, like discourse particles and intonationally marked topic. Further research is needed to determine the potential of this approach for other discourse particles. A full formalisation is feasible for the current approach, but has not yet been carried out. Blutner's theorem and the curious behaviour of *immers* seem beautiful illustrations of Saussure's view that the semantics of a natural language is partly determined by its inventory of items.

Acknowledgment

I wish to thank Antje Rossdeutscher and Robert van Rooy for talking me out of the confused state of mind which started this paper, Reinhard Blutner and Rob van der Sandt for their encouragement and critical comments, Bart Geurts, David Beaver, Irene Heim and an anonymous reviewer for valuable and valid objections and Anna Pilatova for critically reading my last version. And Jennifer Spenader for some last minute corrections. All errors are my own.

References

Beaver 1995. D. Beaver. *Presupposition and Assertion in Dynamic Semantics.* PhD Thesis. University of Edinburgh.

Blutner 2000. R. Blutner: Some Aspects of Optimality Theory in Interpretation. *Journal of Semantics*,**17**,p. 189-216.

Blutner & Jäger 1999. R. Blutner & G. Jaeger. Competition and interpretation: The German adverbs of repetition. MS 1999.

Gazdar 1979. G. Gazdar. *Pragmatics. Implicature, Presupposition and Logical Form.* Academic Press, New York.

Geurts 1995. B. Geurts. *Presupposing.* PhD Stuttgart University.

Giannakidou 1998. A. Giannakidou. *Polarity Sensitivity as (Non)Veridical Dependency*, John Benjamins.

Grice 1975. H.P. Grice. Logic and Conversation. In *P. Cole & J.L. Morgan (eds.): Syntax and Semantics 3: Speech Acts* New York, pp. 41-58.

Heim 1983. I. Heim: On the projection problem for presuppositions. WCCFL, 2, pp. 114-26.

Kamp & Rossdeutscher 1994. H. Kamp. & A. Rossdeutscher: Remarks on Lexical Structure and DRS Construction. Theoretical Linguistics, 20, pp. 97-164.

Kaplan 1989. D. Kaplan: Demonstratives. In *J. Almog, J. Perry, H. Wettstein (Eds.) Themes from Kaplan.* Oxford, pp. 481-563.

Karttunen 1974. L. Karttunen: Presupposition and linguistic context. Theoretical Linguistics, 1, pp.181-94.

Karttunen & Peters 1979. L. Karttunen & S. Peters: Conventional Implicature. In *C. K. Oh & D. Dineen. (Eds.) Syntax and Semantics 11: Presupposition.* Academic Press, New York, pp. 1-56.

Kripke, S. Presupposition. MS.

Van der Sandt 1992. R. van der Sandt: Presupposition projection as anaphora resolution. Journal of Semantics 9, pp. 333-377.

Seuren 1988. P. Seuren: Lexical meaning and Presupposition. In *W. Hüllen & R. Schulze (eds.). Understanding the lexicon.* Niemeyer, Tübingen, 170-187.

Stalnaker 1973 R.C. Stalnaker: Presuppositions. *Journal of Philosophical Logic*, 2, pp. 447-457.

Stalnaker 1978. R.C. Stalnaker: Assertion. In: P. Cole (Ed.): *Syntax and Semantics 9: Pragmatics.* New York, p315 - 332.

Zeevat 1992. H. Zeevat: Presupposition and Accommodation in Update Semantics. *Journal of Semantics* **9** (1992), p. 379-412.

Zeevat 1996. H. Zeevat: A Neoclassical Analysis of Belief Sentences. In: *Proceedings of the 10th Amsterdam Colloquium.* ILLC, University of Amsterdam, 1996, part III, p. 723-742.

Zeevat 1997. H. Zeevat: The Mechanics of the Counterpart Relation. In: Kuenne, W., A. Newen & M. Anduschus (eds.) Direct Reference, Indexicality and Propositional Attitudes. CSLI Publications, 1997, p. 155-185.

Zeevat 1999. H. Zeevat 1999: Demonstratives in Discourse. *Journal of Semantics* **16** p. 279-315.

Zeevat 2000. H. Zeevat: Discourse Particles as Speech Act Markers. LDV-Forum, Zeitschrift für Computerlinguistik und Sprachtechnologie, Journal for Computational Linguistics and Language Technology, **17**, 1/2, 2000, p. 74-91.

4

Demonstratives as Definites

CRAIGE ROBERTS

4.1 Introduction[1]

It has always seemed to me that definite NPs in English — pronouns, definite descriptions, and demonstratives — are simple things, and that there's something amiss in those accounts which would treat them as ambiguous or, as in the E-type approach to pronouns, as only apparently simple disguises for more complex logical forms.

In a recent paper (Roberts, to appear), I argue that English definite descriptions and pronouns are uniformly interpreted as carrying presuppositions of existence and uniqueness. The existence presupposition is anaphoric; definites presuppose the existence of an antecedent in discourse, a familiar entity that is, moreover, unique among familiar discourse referents in satisfying the NP's descriptive content (as given by its head noun and modifiers, if any). But this antecedent is neither a preceding NP, nor an individual in (a model for) the world. Instead, and crucially, it is a discourse referent.

A **discourse referent** is an abstract entity in the common ground

[1]This paper was presented at the conference on Mapping the Semantics-Pragmatics Boundary: Context-Dependence, at Cornell University, in March, 1999. Thanks to Sally McConnell-Ginet, Irene Heim, David Dowty, Shravan Vasishth, David Kaplan, and especially Zoltán Szabó, as well as the members of the OSU pragmatics working group, whose comments and suggestions were extremely helpful in developing the ideas presented here. Thanks also to three anonymous reviewers for the current volume, whose detailed comments were extremely helpful in making improvements, and to the editors for their assistance and patience. But of course, any errors are mine alone.

Information Sharing: Reference and Presupposition in Language Generation and Interpretation.
Edited by Kees van Deemter and Rodger Kibble.

of the interlocutors in a discourse, where the common ground (following Stalnaker (1979), Heim (1982)) is the information which the interlocutors (presume to) have in common in the discourse. Just as the propositions in the common ground may or may not be true, the discourse entities, those entities which may be alluded to in the discourse, may or may not actually exist. It is in this sense that they are not referents in the standard semantic sense of this term. Karttunen (1976) introduced the notion, arguing that it was needed, *inter alia*, to provide "referents" for NPs in cases where the existence of the entities in question is only hypothetically entertained, as in (1). Heim (1982) proposed that discourse referents could serve as the "referents" to which the pronouns "refer" in quantificational or conditional contexts like (2):

(1) Bill says he saw a lion on the street. He claims that <u>the lion</u> had escaped from the zoo.

(2) a) Every farmer who owns a donkey beats <u>it</u>.
b) If a farmer owns a donkey, he beats <u>it</u>.

In (1) since the speaker isn't committed to the existence of Bill's lion and can even sensibly follow up with a denial of its existence, we cannot talk about the referent of *the lion* in the standard sense. In (2a) and (2b), even if we assume that there are farmers who own donkeys, still there are (presumably) many, and not a single referent for *it*, even for a given farmer. Example (3) is closely related to cases like (2b):

(3) In the past, if a married woman wanted to take out a loan, she had to ask <u>her husband</u> for permission.

We pick out an arbitrary married woman and say something about her obligations to her husband; so again, there can be no question of a referent for *her husband*. Moreover, in (3) there is no NP antecedent for *her husband*. The existence of the arbitrary woman's husband is entailed (under the current laws of the United States) by the fact that she is married, and it is this entailment which licenses the use of the definite description. [2] We can capture the obvious similarities between (3) and (2b) in a unified analysis, by taking the entailment of existence of a husband in (3) to trigger existence of a corresponding discourse referent in the interlocutors' common ground. We take discourse referents, then, as the abstract antecedents of NPs. Following Heim (1982), we realize this informational notion of discourse referent as a constraint on contexts of interpretation, technically a uniformity across the assignment functions available for interpretation at a given point in discourse. For example,

[2] Whether this license is direct or indirect is a matter of controversy, which I will touch on later in this paper.

suppose that in (1) *Bill* is associated with the index *7*. Thereafter (if not before), the set of assignment functions which may be used to interpret utterances in the discourse in question will include only those which assign the intended individual named Bill to the seventh variable. This is a way of encoding the fact that the interlocutors have information about the existence of an individual with the relevant properties. [3]

Since the uniqueness presupposition associated with definite descriptions and pronominals in Roberts (to appear) is informational, requiring uniqueness of a corresponding discourse referent relative to information in the common ground, unlike Russell's uniqueness entailments for definite descriptions, on this account it is not surprising that the semantic uniqueness effects predicted by Russell for definite descriptions are only found in certain types of contexts. Pronouns differ from definite descriptions in carrying presuppositions of maximal salience of their familiar discourse referent in the context of interpretation. But otherwise the meaning of definites is simple and uniform. What is complex in their interpretation isn't the logical forms of these NPs themselves, or even their anaphoric presuppositions; it is the multi-faceted pragmatic process of anaphora resolution. Understanding this process casts light on the notion of a *context of interpretation*, and on how we collectively negotiate what that context is at any point in a given discourse.

Here I will propose an extension of this analysis to cover the interpretations of demonstrative NPs with *this* and *that*. I will argue for treating these NPs as a species of definite NP, and hence as uniformly anaphoric in the sense just defined. Like definite descriptions and pronouns, demonstrative NPs occur bound by quantificational antecedents and in examples of what I call discourse deixis, as well as in standard deictic use. However, just as pronouns differ from definite descriptions in carrying presuppositions of salience, demonstrative NPs differ from pronouns and definite descriptions in presupposing an accompanying demonstration. This is a presuppositional recasting of David Kaplan's thesis that a demonstration is part of the demonstrative's semantic content. But the theory does not follow Kaplan in assuming that demonstrative NPs themselves are directly referential. Rather, it is the presupposed demonstrations themselves which are direct in the way that they pick out some entity. Hence, direct reference in demonstrative NPs is actually indirect, via their accompanying demonstrations.

In Section 4.2 I will lay out some facts about the use and distribution of demonstrative NPs in English. In Section 4.3 I summarize Kaplan's

[3]This notion bears a close resemblance to the technical notion of a parameter in the Situation Semantics of Barwise and Perry (1983), though those authors (p.c., 1987) may have had something slightly different in mind.

theory of demonstratives in canonical uses and sketch some problems for extending that theory to a general account of English demonstratives. In Section 4.4 I lay out the general theory of definite NPs which underlies the treatment of demonstratives I then propose in Section 4.5. Section 4.6 offers some brief conclusions.

4.2 English demonstrative NPs: some facts

The focus of this essay is the semantics and pragmatics of English demonstrative noun phrases (NPs), especially those dedicated demonstratives with *this* and *that*, or their plural forms *these* and *those*. The dedicated demonstratives may be used alone, pronominally; or as determiners, accompanied by a Common Noun (CN) Phrase. We see canonical uses of these NP types exemplified in (4)–(7): [4]

(4) [holding up an Adena Indian artifact from 200BC:] This is beautiful craftsmanship.

(5) [pointing at some stuffed peppers in a restaurant display case:] Those look particularly delicious.

(6) [salesman on a car lot, nodding in the direction of a nearby cluster of trucks:] These vehicles have four-wheel drive.

(7) [policeman, pointing in the direction of a man running through a crowd:] Stop that man!

In each of these uses, the speaker plainly indicates the intended referent (in the standard semantic sense), either by actually pointing or by a similar gesture which helps to pick out the referent in the space surrounding the speaker. When a demonstrated entity is human, or sufficiently human-like that use of an accompanying grammatically neuter pronominal form would seem odd, pronominal *this* and *that* are replaced by *s/he*, pronominal *these* and *those* by *they*. I will assume here that such uses of third person personal pronouns are demonstratives, as well.

Demonstratives can also be used to make reference to constituents of the text (uttered or written) of a discourse itself, as illustrated by (8):

(8) This sentence is short.

One might utter such examples accompanied by a demonstration, not unlike the one involved in (4). But there are other uses of demonstra-

[4]Maclaran (1982:15-23) also offers an analysis of examples of demonstrative degree modifiers as in her (i) and (ii):

(i) I need about this much.

(ii) Does it bother you to be that tall?

Like her, I will assume that the semantics of these is basically the same as that of the determiners, although I won't have any more to say about them here.

tive NPs which could not be plausibly said to involve an accompanying gestural demonstration of the intended referent. Many of these have an NP antecedent, as in (9):

(9) I saw one quilt which was quite abstract, with lots of asymmetric diagonals. Another one was more traditional, worked in an old Amish pattern. This quilt was less busy than the other, but just as bold.

In some of these cases, the antecedent is a quantified NP but the demonstrative is not within its scope. Examples of this sort are parallel to the so-called E-type uses of personal pronouns:

(10) The Russians had allowed few pieces from their collection to go on show in the West, but these were the highpoint of the exhibition. (Maclaran 1982)]

And some demonstratives have a bound variable interpretation. The is illustrated by both (11) and (12), the latter an example of telescoping (Roberts 1989):

(11) Every dog in my neighborhood, even the meanest, has an owner who thinks that that dog is a sweetie.

(12) On every team there is one player who is not as strong as the rest. That weakest member is the one to play hardest against. (Maclaran 1982)

Demonstratives may also take narrow scope with respect to modals or other operators, as in the modal subordination interpretation of the second sentence in (13) or the donkey-type anaphora in (14):

(13) Michelin is hoping to find ten more tyre inspectors. These new employees would be required to work the night shift for the first three weeks. (after Maclaran 1982)

> modal subordination interpretation: 'if more tyre inspectors were hired, they would be required to work the night shift. . .'

(14) When a professional athlete sprains an ankle, that injury usually gets special treatment.

In (13), following the analysis of modal subordination in Roberts (1989,1996), the buletic proposition that Michelin finds ten more tyre inspectors serves to restrict the domain of the modal *would*, yielding the implicitly conditional interpretation suggested. In (14), *that injury* is understood to be under the scope of the adverb of quantification *usu-*

ally. The understood antecedent is only an existential entailment of the antecedent clause, the injury that results from spraining an ankle.

Thus, in several respects considered so far, demonstrative NPs display a range of behavior which is typical of definite descriptions and pronouns, as well— they may be interpreted as anaphoric to an NP or as a bound variable, as E-type, or under the scope of a modal or other operator. But demonstrative NPs are known to contrast with definite descriptions in important respects. One is in the relationship between the NP and an accompanying demonstration; such accompaniment is quite common with demonstrative NPs, as their name would suggest, as in (4)–(7) above. But this is not the case with definite descriptions, a contrast illustrated by the following pair due to Sally McConnell-Ginet (p.c.):

(15) You [nodding to Mary] sit in that chairk [pointing to chair *a*], and you [nodding to Jonathon] sit in that chairl [pointing to chair *b*].

(16) You [nodding to Mary] sit in the chairk [pointing to chair *a*], and you [nodding to Jonathon] sit in the chairl [pointing to chair *b*].

(15) is acceptable and unremarkable, but (16) is clearly infelicitous. While being accompanied by distinct demonstrations may sufficiently enrich the descriptive content of two type-identical demonstratives so that they may be taken to denote different entities, it is not sufficient to distinguish the intended referents of two type-identical non-demonstrative definite descriptions.

Another respect in which demonstratives, at least when accompanied by a deictic gesture, differ from definite descriptions is in their potential scope behavior, as illustrated by the following minimal triplet:

(17) Context (CG): Charles is from Charleston, West Virginia. Paul is from St. Paul, Minnesota. δ is a pointing by the speaker in the direction of Paul, who is seated on a chair in front of the speaker:

Look over here [δ, the gesture held throughout the next sentence]. If Charles and Paul had changed chairs, then

a) the man being pointed at would be from Charleston
b) he[δ] would be from Charleston.
c) this man being pointed at [δ] would be from Charleston.

Many speakers judge (17a) to be felicitous and true. [5] We can take the definite description to mean something like 'the man I would be pointing at in that (counterfactual) situation', who would be Charles. But this reading isn't possible for (b) or (c), which mean that Paul would be from Charleston. Discussing an example very similar to (17b), Kaplan (1977) notes that intuitively this is patently false in the context suggested — whether or not Charles and Paul change chairs should have nothing to do with Paul's being from Charleston.

I take it that all of the above facts need to be accounted for by an empirically adequate theory of the semantics of English demonstratives. Of course, we needn't assume that demonstratives are unambiguous. However, there are both empirical and theoretical reasons to attempt an analysis of each demonstrative form as univocal, with a shared core of meaning between the various forms. Empirically, the diachronic evidence strongly argues that the contemporary demonstratives evolved from a deictic usage, and, moreover, that the contemporary definite article *the* and the personal pronouns evolved from the ancestor of the non-proximal demonstrative *that* (per Lyons (1977), the unmarked member of the +/- proximal pair). Theoretically, we would prefer an account that, drawing upon the common etymological origins of demonstratives and definite descriptions, can account for both their similarities and their differences in a maximally simple and insightful way. Surely it is not an accident that the demonstratives in (4)–(8) and (17c), and those in the remaining examples have the same forms. For example, the specification for +/- proximality is critical in examples like (9), which are unacceptable with proximal *this* replaced by the definite article:

(9′) I saw one quilt which was quite abstract, with lots of asymmetric diagonals. Another one was more traditional, worked in an old

[5] There is another way of minimally contrasting the role of a definite description in this context with that of a demonstrative description. Assume the same context as in (17):

(i) If Charles and Paul had changed chairs, then

a) the man who I'd be pointing at [δ] would be from Charleston.
b) this man who I'd be pointing at [δ] would be from Charleston.

Even speakers who are uncomfortable with the felicity or truth of (17a) tend to accept (ia) as felicitous and true. But the consensus is that (ib) is quite odd unless we take the relative clause to be non-restrictive, and then the utterance is false in the context suggested. Space does not permit extended discussion of the reasons why the relative clause must be interpreted as non-restrictive. Suffice it to say that it seems that the restrictive descriptive content of a demonstrative must subserve the identification of the intended demonstratum, and that counterfactual assumptions do not generally subserve that identification.

Amish pattern. #The quilt was less busy than the other, but just as bold.

This same distinction is important in helping to pick out the demonstratum in the canonical demonstrative uses; cf. (4)–(8), where replacing the proximal by non-proximal forms, or *vice versa*, would result in very different meanings. And conceptually, proximity and the direction involved in demonstration are two facets of the same process, that of picking out the intended referent in the situation of utterance. [6] Hence, we might expect that the proximity feature of the meanings of all demonstratives points at a common origin in deixis, whether the demonstrative is being used with a canonical demonstration or not.

4.3 Kaplan's theory of demonstratives

Responding to examples like (17b) above, Kaplan (1977) developed a theory of English demonstrative NPs in their canonical usage, i.e. accompanied by a demonstration. He assumes that a demonstration like δ has a "standard form" which is basically like that of the descriptive content of a definite description like that in (17a). The general form he suggests is given in (18), instantiated for (17b) in (19):

(18) "the individual that has appearance A from here now"

(19) "the individual who I appear to be pointing at from my perspective now"

If we take (19) to be part of the descriptive content of a demonstrative use of *he*, adding also the information suggested by the pronoun's gender, then we get a complete descriptive content for (17b), in (20), which is very close to that of the demonstrative description in (17c):

(20) "the male individual who I appear to be pointing at from my perspective now"

Moreover, this appears to be very close to the pragmatically enriched (liberalized) descriptive content of (17a). The question then is how to differentiate these examples. Kaplan's theory is summarized in (21); (21b) should be understood to hold in a theory of propositions as structured entities, so that the meaning of an NP used in an utterance remains itself a component of the proposition expressed:

[6] So far as I know, most (?all) languages make use of the distinction between proximal and non-proximal in reference, and in some, the distinction is refined even further. For example, in Japanese this is a three-way distinction, as we see in *kono*, 'this', *sono* 'that', and *ano* 'that over there'.

(21) **Kaplan's theory of English demonstrative NPs:**

(a) Demonstratives are incomplete expressions which must be completed by a demonstration. . . Thus each demonstrative, *d*, will be accompanied by a demonstration, δ, thus: d[δ] (Kaplan 1977, Section XV)

(b) Demonstratives are directly referential. "I intend to use '*directly referential*' for an expression whose referent, once determined, is taken as fixed for all possible circumstances, i.e., is taken as *being* the propositional component." For such expressions, "The rules do not provide a complex which together with a circumstance of evaluation yields an object. They just provide an object." "the semantical rules. . .provid[e] a way of determining the *actual* referent and no way of determining any other propositional component." (Kaplan 1977, Section VI)

Demonstrative NPs are contrasted with definite descriptions, since the latter *do* "provide a complex which together with a circumstance of evaluation yields an object", via the descriptive content embodied in their Common Noun Phrase (CN), i.e. the head noun and any complements or modifiers thereof. Another way of capturing the distinction might be to say that definite descriptions have a Fregean sense, so that their reference on a given occasion depends upon the circumstance of evaluation. But demonstrative NPs do not: Their reference depends not on the circumstance of evaluation, but solely upon the situation of utterance. To underline this difference, Kaplan suggests that interpretation takes place in two stages:

(22) Kaplan's two stage interpretation:

- Character: a function from contexts (of utterance) to contents

- Content: a function from worlds/circumstances of evaluation to denotations; e.g., individual concepts, propositions, etc.

Using this two-stage approach to interpretation, we can differentiate two kinds of rigid designators. Proper names have the same content in any given context, hence have "rigid characters". On the other hand, demonstratives and other indexical expressions don't generally have the same content in different contexts; but in a given context, the content is always rigid.

Given this general theory, Kaplan can account for the examples in (17) as follows: The demonstrative NPs in (17b) and (17c) are directly referential, and hence will be rigid designators in any given context, their referent being directly given as the demonstratum of δ. The descriptive content of δ (plus that of the NP, if any) will be interpreted solely with reference to the situation of utterance, i.e. in the first phase of interpretation, and hence pick out Paul in both cases, so that the consequent would correctly be interpreted as denoting the false proposition that Paul would be from Charleston. But a definite description like that in (17a) isn't directly referential. This is reflected in the fact that the accompanying demonstration δ does not play a role in the interpretation of the definite description, and so its referent isn't "fixed" on Paul, the actual demonstratum, but can vary with the circumstance of evaluation, in accord with the descriptive content as interpreted in that circumstance (in the second phase of interpretation). This explains the apparent anomaly (or falsity) of (17b/c) and the sense that (17a) can be true, while still getting at the similarity in content of the three NPs. They effectively have the same descriptive content but different modes of reference.

There are several problems with embedding Kaplan's account within a more general account of demonstratives, which I'll briefly sketch here. The first, theoretical problem is that given (21a), Kaplan's theory is only applicable to demonstrative NPs in their canonical usage, accompanied by a demonstration of some sort. Even permitting a fairly wide range of speaker's behaviors to count as demonstrations, this rules out several of the common uses of demonstratives, i.e., the anaphoric-to-NP, narrow scope, and bound variable uses in Section 1 above. Presumably, non-demonstrative uses of NPs with the form of demonstratives are not directly referential, as this would be incompatible with bound variable or narrow scope interpretations. This ambiguity leaves unexplained common factors in the intuitive meanings across the full range of uses, such as the proximal/non-proximal distinction seen in *this/that*. And it leaves unexplained the obvious etymological relations between the forms used in demonstrative and non-demonstrative uses, on the one hand, and between demonstrative NPs and definite descriptions, on the other. Perhaps one could come up with a story that would explain the switch from direct reference in the presumably primitive deictic ancestors of the contemporary demonstratives to 'indirect' reference in their non-demonstrative uses and in their cousins the definite descriptions. I can imagine various forms such a story might take, but since all of them are more complex and less satisfying than the story I will propose below, I won't speculate further here.

Another, empirical problem for the generalization of Kaplan's theory is pointed out in unpublished work by Irene Heim (1985). Consider her example (23):

(23) Context: The speaker sees two images of chairs in the room where she sits, one to her left, the other image to her right. The image to the right is either a reflection in a mirror or else behind a piece of clear glass. δ_1 is a pointing by the speaker to the image to her left, δ_2 is a pointing to the image to her right:

That[δ_1] is that[δ_2].

Now consider two different possible contexts of utterance for (23), c and c'. c is the mirror world, so that δ_1 and δ_2 are in fact gestures which pick out the same chair. On Kaplan's theory, (23) expresses the necessarily true proposition in c. c' is the glass world, where the speaker is pointing at different chairs, so that, again on Kaplan's theory, (23) expresses the necessarily false proposition. But our intuitions tell us that in neither case does utterance of (23) seem trivial. Kaplan (1977, 1978) explains this apparent non-triviality for related examples as follows: The audience for (23) trusts that the speaker is saying something true. However, they don't know which context they're in, c or c'. From the character of (23), they know that it expresses either a necessarily true or a necessarily false proposition. Hence, they conclude that they're in a context like c, not c', hence acquiring new information, even though the proposition expressed was not contingent.

However, Heim points out that although this might seem a plausible explanation for the informativeness of (23), this type of explanation doesn't seem to be extendable to examples like her (24) and (25):

(24) That[δ_1] might well be that[δ_2].

(25) If that[δ_1] were that[δ_2], there would be only one chair in the house.

Kaplan argues that the content of a sentence in any given context is a function of the contents of its parts in that same context ("There are no monsters."). Therefore, since (23) is a part of both (24) and (25), the propositions they express should be calculable on the basis of the proposition expressed by (23). But this is not the case. E.g., consider (24). Suppose its LF is $\Diamond$(23), and that it is uttered in context c. Since $|(23)|^c$, the proposition expressed by (23) in context c, is the necessarily true proposition, $|(24)|^c$ should be the same. And the same agreement would hold for c', where both (23) and (24) would express the necessarily false proposition. But intuitively, (23) and (24) have different meanings. Similarly, given the counterfactual mood of the antecedent of (25), we might felicitously utter it in a situation known by the interlocutors to be like c'. Then the antecedent would be necessarily false, on Kaplan's theory. If we take the meaning of a counterfactual to be basically that of Lewis (1973), then the sphere of worlds in which the antecedent would be true (which are closest in other respects to the actual world c') would be the empty set, and (25) would be trivially true, since the consequent would be trivially true in all those worlds in that sphere. But (25) seems to be contingent, instead, its truth dependent on other facts about the household in question.

Another empirical problem for Kaplan's approach arises in connection with a phenomenon I will call **discourse deixis**, illustrated in (26):

(26) Melanctha has a dog and a cat. The latter is her favorite, but the former is more loyal.

Discourse deixis is closely related to the textual deixis illustrated by (8) above, where *this sentence* was used to refer to the sentence in which the demonstrative itself occurred. In discourse deixis, the relative proximity in question is that of a constituent or constituents in the immediately preceding discourse — in the case of *former* or *latter*, a pair of maximally salient NPs. But reference is not to those NPs themselves, but to the entities which the NPs denote. [7] In (26), the referent of *the latter* is the referent of the second member of the ordered (by order of utterance) pair <*a dog,a cat*>, while the referent of *the former* is that of the first element of that pair. Relevant here is the fact that we can observe direct reference effects with discourse deixis, as in (27):

(27) Melanctha has a dog and a cat, both of whom are getting very old.
The cat is her favorite, but the dog is more loyal.
If I hadn't uttered the last sentence, the latter would spit up hairballs and the former would bark.

The last utterance here is quite odd, and surely false: *the latter* and *the former* can only be taken to refer to the dog and the cat, respectively, on account of their being the referents of the most salient pair of NPs, those in the second sentence, <*the cat, the dog*>. But the counterfactual antecedent asks us to imagine that we hadn't uttered that second sentence; and in addition, the properties predicated of the discourse deictic NPs are clearly more appropriate to the entities which the deictic NPs would have referred to if the second sentence hadn't been uttered. Just as in (17), where Paul's provenience surely wouldn't vary as a function of his changing places with someone in the situation of utterance, in (27) the dog couldn't reasonably be expected to start spitting up hair-

[7] Of course, indefinite NPs arguably do not denote, nor do definites. I use the term loosely here, and in what immediately follows, for simplicity of expression. One might say, more precisely, that in using *the former* and *the latter* the speaker intends to pick out the same pair of referents which she intended in uttering the antecedent NPs. See Grice (1957), Kripke (1977) on the notion of a Speaker's referent; more on this below.

balls because the speaker hadn't uttered the second sentence What this example shows is that discourse deixis is potentially just as direct as canonical demonstrative use. However we account for direct reference effects in the latter had better extend to the former, as well.

But the reference in discourse deixis is not direct. Even if we grant that discourse deixis is based on the textual deixis displayed in (8) and that this use of a demonstrative involves a demonstration, in discourse deixis the demonstratum is distinct from the deictic NP's referent. One might still try to maintain the direct reference account by taking the deictic element in NPs like *the former* to be only part of the logical form of the noun*former*, which one might represent roughly as in (28):

(28) λx.speaker's_referent_for(x,dthat[the non-proximal member of the maximally salient pair of uttered NPs in prior discourse])

Kripke (1977) introduces the notion of a *speaker's referent* to explain the type of example noted by Donnellan (1966), who noted apparent exceptions to Russell's (1905) arguments that definite descriptions do not denote, i.e. that unlike proper names, they have no referents but are basically quantificational. The speaker's referent in a given use of a definite description is an entity (in the world) which the speaker has in mind in using the definite; we might say that this is an entity which the speaker takes to truthfully instantiate the existential quantification associated with the definite. Thus, the speaker's referent is an actual entity pragmatically related to the use of the definite description, but the latter itself still does not refer. Kaplan's *dthat* (Kaplan 1978) directly refers to the unique entity which satisfies the description in brackets following it. Taking the property denoted by (28) to be the argument of the definite article, the resulting definite description will pick out the speaker's intended referent (in the context of utterance) in uttering the first NP of the pair. Thus, the definite description *the former* is interpreted *as if* directly referential, although it itself is not. What's directly referred to is the NP *the cat* itself, although *the former* is understood to be anaphoric to that NP in the usual sense. Note that on the assumption that Russell was basically correct that definite descriptions do not refer, [8] it cannot be that the structured proposition expressed by the consequent of the conditional in (27) is singular by virtue of containing the semantic referent of *the cat.* We might try to indirectly retrieve an actual cat, the speaker's intended referent which justifies the claim that Melanctha

[8]This assumption is not contradicted by contemporary theories like those of Kamp (1981) or Heim (1982), and subsequent work in dynamic interpretation wherein definites are treated as variables. For variables are certainly no more referential in themselves than the Russellian definite description.

has a cat. But the relationship of that animal to the NP *the cat* would be pragmatic, not be that of direct reference. Suppose we said that the proposition expressed by (27) includes, instead of the intended cat, the actual NP used to refer to that cat. The problem then is that it isn't the English NP itself which has as speaker's referent the cat. Rather, it is the use of the NP in the particular discourse in question which has that intended speaker's referent. Can we construct a singular proposition which contains a use of an NP? I imagine one could try to entify a use in such a way as to define such a singular proposition, though it strikes me as stretching the original conception of singularity to do so. But even if we could, examples like the following demonstrate that this would not be adequate:

(29) Everyone in my neighborhood who owns both a dog and a cat tells me that the latter intimidates the former, not the other way around.

(29) presents a problem for the use of the logical form in (28) for *former*, because there is no way to pick out a speaker's referent for *a cat*, which is under the scope of the universal quantifier. I.e., such a generalization does not pertain to any particular cat which the speaker might have in mind. So, (27) and (29) argue that we need to extend the account of the direct reference effect in (17) to cover non-canonical uses of demonstratives, and that we cannot use the notion of a speaker's referent to do so. We seem to need something more abstract for such cases, something like Karttunen's (1976) notion of a discourse referent (more below).

In what follows, I will argue that English demonstrative NPs are a type of definite NP, a class which also includes definite descriptions and personal pronouns. The view I propose will lead me to defend a variation of Kaplan's (21a) against apparent counterexamples, while arguing that (21b) is incorrect. In particular, I will argue that demonstratives do presuppose an accompanying demonstration, though we must take the notion of demonstration to be rather broader than is sometimes assumed. But there is good evidence that demonstratives are no more directly referential than definite descriptions, and I will offer an alternative explanation for the facts which led Kaplan to claim that they are.

4.4 Background: Definite NPs in a Context Change Semantics

Before I can defend the thesis that demonstrative NPs are a species of definite NP, I need to explain what I take to characterize the class of

English definite NPs, a class which includes the personal pronouns as well as definite descriptions. Though my views about definites are themselves quite simple, a subtle but significant variation on the Russellian view, the facts which must be explained in order to support these views, and the theories which must be rebutted to defend them, are many and complex. Hence, I can only hint here at the full story. For a detailed exposition and arguments, please see Roberts (1999).

Over the past twenty years, there has been a good deal of work on the semantics of definite descriptions and pronouns. Very briefly touching on a few highlights: Evans (1977, 1980) proposed extending the Russellian analysis of the definite description (Russell 1905) to certain uses of personal pronouns, the so-called E-type pronouns. Heim (1982) argued that the Russellian treatment was empirically incorrect even for definite descriptions, as well as for pronouns, and proposed replacing Russell's uniqueness clause with a presupposition of familiarity, satisfied when interlocutors have in their common ground a discourse referent (in the sense discussed above) corresponding to the definite. Since discourse referents are numerals (the indices on variables), technically this amounted to a requirement that the referential index on the definite NP be the same as the discourse referent. Kadmon (1990) and others argued that although definites, both descriptions and pronominals, do have familiarity presuppositions, they also presuppose Russellian uniqueness in the world (or model), a claim with which Heim (1990) herself agreed. A number of others (see especially Löbner 1987, Neale 1990, 1990b) have weighed in on this matter, but there is evidence which appears to favor both analyses, so that it has been difficult to draw any firm conclusions.

Consider the following evidence for the two positions (from Roberts, to appear, unless otherwise noted). In (30), we see the use of the definite description in a title. According to the history of the institution concerned, this was intentionally made part of the title by its nineteenth century trustees to counter the impression that another institution with the word *Ohio* in it was an institution of the state, hence relying on an implication of uniqueness long before Russell noticed it. In (31), a student who turns the page in question can reasonably expect to find exactly one clown, not more than one, again reflecting the uniqueness effect. And (32) strikes native speakers as infelicitous while (33) is felicitous, presumably reflecting the fact that cars have more than one tire, whereas unicycles have exactly one wheel.

(30) The Ohio State University is in Columbus.

(31) Teacher, giving directions: On the next page, you will find a puzzle. Find the clown in the puzzle.

(32) Every car had a puncture in the tire.

(33) Every unicycle had a spoke missing from the wheel.

However, Heim (1982) pointed out a number of problematic types of examples for Russellian uniqueness. In (34), if the sage plant were unique in being purchased by a given individual, that would be contradicted by its being purchased along with either others. The example ought to sound contradictory, but it does not. Marilyn Walker (p.c.) has observed that the Russellian account would predict that (35) and (36) should be synonymous, whereas in fact they are not. This can be seen by the felicity of following (35) with (37), but the infelicity of following (36) with (37):

(34) Everyone who bought a sage plant or a rosemary planted the sage plant with extra bone-meal or the rosemary in a well-limed soil, (and if it was a sage plant, bought eight others along with it).

(35) Among the members of his class at Eton, John was the cricket player.

(36) Among the members of his class at Eton, John was the only cricket player.

(37) Several others played cricket for fun, but he was by far the best and most dedicated.

So, neither the Russellian account on which definite descriptions display semantic uniqueness nor the familiarity-based account is entirely satisfactory from an empirical point of view. The question is how to capture the clearly valid intuitions of both parties while escaping the problems just illustrated, as well as others.

The analysis in Roberts (to appear) presupposes a dynamic theory of interpretation, in which the conventional meaning of a natural language expression is the potential it has to update information that the interlocutors share, or behave as if they share. This is modeled as a function from contexts to contexts, the expression's Context Change Potential.

On this view, the context of an utterance is a body of information, that information which the interlocutors have in common, i.e. their common ground. Note that this is a significantly different conception of the notion of context than we find in some other work, including, as I understand it, Kaplan's. There, it seems that context is understood to be something like the actual, physical circumstances in which the utterance takes place. Those physical circumstances, with a speaker, other interlocutor(s), location and time of utterance, etc., are reflected in the present Context Change Semantics notion of context in the information which the interlocutors share, but the informational conception of context goes well beyond these circumstances. It includes, as well, information about the way the world is, a set of propositions which may or may not be true. And, crucial for our present discussion, it includes information about the entities which the propositional information pertains to, the discourse referents. [9]

There are two facets of the Context Change Potential for any given expression: its **presupposed content** and its **proffered content**. The presupposed content specifies what a context must be like in order for the Context Change Potential to be defined for that context. The proffered content — what is asserted in an assertion, but also the non-presupposed meaning of an interrogative or imperative — reflects the information which utterance of that expression adds to a context in which it is felicitously uttered.

The general view of presupposition assumed is that of Stalnaker (1974, 1979) as realized and extended in Heim (1982, 1992). An utterance is felicitous in a given context if and only if all of the utterance's presuppositions are satisfied in that context. Presuppositions may be propositional; in that case, they are satisfied if and only if they are entailed by the interlocutors' common ground, the set of propositions which they (behave as if they) hold in common to be true. But the common ground is only one facet of the context in which a discourse occurs, and presuppositions may put constraints on other facets of the context besides the common ground. Heim (1982) defines the context of utterance as an ordered pair consisting of a **Domain** — the set of familiar discourse referents — and a **Satisfaction Set** which captures the information in the interlocutors' common ground about the corresponding discourse referents. Discourse referents may be introduced into the domain by utterance of an indefinite NP, as well as on the basis of common familiarity with the corresponding entity in the world, e.g. on the basis of acquaintance by perception.

(38) Heim's (1982) notion of Context
Given:

- a model $M = < W, A, Int >$, W a set of worlds, A a set of individuals, Int a function from basic expressions to functions from worlds to extensions
- the set of natural numbers N, and

[9]Roberts (1996b) argues that the interlocutors' common ground also includes a great deal of information about the structure of the discourse itself: what it's about and how it's related to other goals and plans of the interlocutors. I will stick in the present paper to the simpler notion which ignores this type of information, but believe it is ultimately quite important for understanding the notion of relevance, and hence for determining what is being demonstrated on a given occasion.

- G, a set of assignment functions from N into A,

C is a **Context** (relative to M) iff $\mathrm{C} = <\mathrm{Sat}, \mathrm{Dom}>$, where:

> Dom $\subseteq N$ is the **Domain** of C, the set of familiar Discourse Referents, and
> Sat $\subseteq$ WxG, the **Satisfaction Set** for C, $= \{<\mathrm{w}, \mathrm{g}>$: for all i $\in$ Dom, g(i) is an individual which verifies in w all the information the interlocutors share about i$\}$.

If in $C = < Sat_C, Dom_C >$ the interlocutors know that i is a cat, then every $<\mathrm{w}, \mathrm{g}>$ in $\mathrm{Sat_C}$ will be such that $\mathrm{g(i)} \in \mathrm{Int}(cat)(\mathrm{w})$, in the model in question. [10]

Note that in adopting Heim's general framework for interpretation, one need not, and I do not, follow her in assuming that definite and indefinite NPs are interpreted as variables which may be unselectively bound by operators in whose scope they fall. This assumption was central to Heim (1982); however, many authors have subsequently argued against this aspect of her theory, notably Heim herself in subsequent work (Heim 1990). Definite, as well as indefinite NPs can be treated, e.g., as (the dynamic counterparts of) generalized quantifiers with existential force (see Chierchia 1995).

Within this general framework, the theory of definite NPs which I develop in Roberts (to appear) is an informational counterpart of the classic Russellian logical form for definite descriptions. As in Russell's treatment, the interpretation of a definite NP contains both an existence clause and a uniqueness clause. However, these are both part of the presuppositional content of the definite, rather than its proffered content (contra Russell and more in line with Strawson's observations). [11] The existence and uniqueness presuppositions of a definite description are not claims about an individual in a model, but about a discourse referent in the domain of discourse. Thus, the existence presupposition amounts

---

[10] See Heim (1982) Chapter three for rules which yield a recursive, extensional definition of satisfaction for formulae of increasing complexity; Chapter 2 for discussion of how this model may be made intensional. Heim (1982) talks about Files instead of Contexts, but Heim (1992) equates those notions.

[11] Briefly, the presuppositional character of the uniqueness associated with definites is supported by the following example, discussed by Kadmon (1987):

(i) A strange man lives here. If he/the strange man who lives here sees a cat, he screams.

As she points out, if we assumed the Russellian interpretation of the definite description *the strange man who lives here*, or the related E-type interpretation of the pronoun *he*, this would yield truth conditions for the conditional which are too weak: 'If there is a unique strange man who lives here, he screams.' Instead, if there is uniqueness associated with these NPs at all, it must be presuppositional.

to (a variation on) Heim's (1982) Familiarity Presupposition for definite NPs, and the uniqueness presupposition is about the status of the familiar discourse referent in the Domain of the Context of discourse. Use of a definite description does not entail that there is some entity in the model/world which uniquely bears the descriptive content of the NP, but only that there is a familiar discourse referent in the context which is the only element of the Domain that's entailed by the common ground to bear the NP's descriptive content.

(39) and (40) give the informational existence and uniqueness presuppositions of definite NPs, both informally and in terms of the framework given in (38). In (40), clause (i) is the informational counterpart to Russellian existence, while (ii) is the counterpart to uniqueness:

(39) **Informational Existence and Uniqueness of Definite NPs** (informal):
Given a context *C*, use of a definite description NP_i presupposes that there is a discourse referent *i* in the Domain of *C* which is the unique familiar discourse referent contextually entailed to satisfy the (possibly liberalized) descriptive content of NP_i.

(40) **Familiarity and Uniqueness Presuppositions of Definite NPs** (formal):
For context $\mathrm{C} = < \mathrm{Sat_C}, \mathrm{Dom_C} >$, if a definite NP with (possibly liberalized) descriptive content *Desc* is felicitous in C then

(i) $\exists \mathrm{i} \in \mathrm{Dom_C}[\forall < \mathrm{w}, \mathrm{g} > \in \mathrm{Sat_C}[\mathrm{Desc(w)(g(i))}]$ &
(ii) $\forall \mathrm{k} \in \mathrm{Dom_C}[\forall < \mathrm{w}, \mathrm{g} > \in \mathrm{Sat_C}[\mathrm{Desc(w)(g(k))}] \rightarrow \mathrm{k} = \mathrm{i}]]$,

where *Desc(w)(g(i))* is true iff the individual assigned to *i* by *g* has the property denoted by *Desc* in world *w*.

(40) gives a set of necessary conditions for utterance of a definite NP to be felicitous. We know that these conditions will not be sufficient in cases where the descriptive content of the NP carries other presuppositions; we have seen one such case above, where *former* and *latter* presuppose a pair of maximally salient NPs in prior discourse. We'll see in the following section that when a definite is also demonstrative, an additional presupposition is imposed.

The proffered content of definite descriptions can be taken to be nearly identical to that of a pronoun, e.g., in static terms, with a logical form something like $\lambda P[P\{x\}]$; or it may have redundant existential force, as in $\lambda P[\exists y(P(y) \;\&\; y = x)]$. The presupposition will guarantee that the free variable in this proffered content gets appropriately bound, given standard mechanisms of (selective) binding in such dynamic theories (e.g., see Chierchia 1995). The relationship between indefinites and definites is this: While an indefinite has existential force, proffering the existence of a discourse referent with a certain descriptive content (which is presupposed to be novel relative to the Context, as in Heim (1982)), a definite presupposes the existence of such an entity, and moreover that the descriptive content is not known to hold of any other familiar discourse referent. This does not preclude that in fact there is some other entity in the world (or model of interpretation) which has that property, but only that the existence of such an entity is not entailed by the interlocutors' common ground. Hence, the uniqueness associated with definites is **informational uniqueness**.

Although weaker than the Russellian semantics for definite descriptions, the present theory can still account for robust semantic uniqueness effects in examples like (30) and (31):

(30) The Ohio State University is in Columbus.

(31) Teacher, giving directions: On the next page, you will find a puzzle. Find the clown in the puzzle.

The definite description in (30) is a title, like *the King of France*. Titles are created with a view to their potential use in a variety of contexts. Their creators know that they may at some point be used in conversations in which the interlocutors are well-enough informed that they are in a position to be familiar with all the entities in the world which satisfy the title's descriptive content. In such a case, the common familiarity of the interlocutors will license discourse referents for all these entities, so that the definite description title will only be felicitous, by (40), if there is in fact only one entity in the world which it describes. Taking this into account, those who create a title make sure that it satisfies semantic, Russellian uniqueness, in order to guarantee its felicity. (31) involves directions intended for use in a future situation in which the hearer will presumably be in a position to have perceptual access to full information about the page in question, and in particular to know how many clowns there are in the puzzle which they've found on that page. At that point, the hearer and speaker will have in their common, perceptually gleaned information knowledge of the existence of those clowns, and hence in the context there will be a discourse referent for each of them. If there were more than one clown (or puzzle) on that page, the definite description would be infelicitous, its uniqueness presupposition unsatisfied in the intended situation of use. So, once again, the speaker takes this into account and guarantees felicity by only using the definite when the clown is (so far as she knows) unique on the page.

The last example illustrates another facet of (40): We automatically take *the puzzle* and *the clown* to bear what Evans (1977, 1980) called a *liberalized* descriptive content. That is, we assume that the speaker intends to refer to the 'puzzle that's on the next page of the book you're holding' and 'the clown that's in the puzzle on the next page in the book. . .', and not to the sole thing in the whole world that's a puzzle or a clown. Such liberalization is an instance of domain restriction, a phenomenon whereby the quantificational domain of an operator (here, the existential) is pragmatically restricted with reference to what is relevant in the context. [12] But (40) does not predict that semantic uniqueness effects like those predicted by Russell, where we understand the speaker to convey the information that the intended referent is unique in the world under its description, will always be associated with the use of a definite description. This result is desirable, because although Russell's observations were correct about examples like (30), he didn't look at enough types of examples to see that semantic uniqueness effects in definite descriptions only arise in certain types of contexts. In (30) and (31), the contexts involve special epistemic assumptions. In other types of examples, there is a conversational implicature associated with the choice of a definite description when a pronoun would have sufficed (see Roberts (to appear) for more discussion). When these conditions do not obtain, as in (34), repeated here, no uniqueness effects arise:

(34) Everyone who bought a sage plant or a rosemary planted the sage plant with extra bone-meal or the rosemary in a well-limed soil, (and if it was a sage plant, bought eight others along with it).

The definite description *the sage plant* in the predicate satisfies informational familiarity and uniqueness; at the time of utterance, there is a corresponding discourse referent in the domain, introduced by the indefinite *a sage plant*, and it is the only discourse referent which satisfies the NP's liberalized descriptive content 'the sage plant that x bought', for some x instantiating the subject in any given world in the (satisfaction set of the) common ground. But this doesn't preclude there being other such sage plants in that world which were purchased by x, and in fact the conjoined VP pertains eight other sage plants x purchased, without any hint of infelicity or contradiction. Neither Russellian, semantic uniqueness for definite descriptions nor Löbner's (1987) and Heim's (1990) functional accounts of the semantics of definite descriptions can explain the felicity and non-contradictoriness of such examples, while the present account can.

[12]Note that this is not the same notion as that of the Domain of the Context. Rather, it has to do with restricting the set of entities (or the proper sort) over which the operator ranges. See Roberts (1995, 1999), von Fintel (1994) for discussion of the pragmatics of domain restriction.

Although many of the authors who have recently worked on definites propose uniform conditions over definite descriptions and pronouns, semantic uniqueness effects almost never occur with pronouns. This is associated with a difference in the distribution of pronouns and definite descriptions. Consider the contrasts in the following:

(41) A woman entered from stage left.
Another woman entered from stage right.
#The woman/$\surd$The FIRST woman/$\surd$The SECOND woman was carrying a basket of flowers.

(42) A woman entered from stage left.
Another woman entered from stage right.
SHE was carrying a basket of flowers, while /#the woman/$\surd$the FIRST woman/#the SECOND woman led a goat.

In (41) and (42), the first two sentences set a scene in which there are apparently two women, distinguished only by which side of the stage they have entered from. We see in (41) that we cannot felicitously use the definite description *the woman*, apparently because it refers non-uniquely in the scene in question. The more specific NPs are felicitous; *first* and *second* may either be taken to allude to the order of a woman's entrance on the stage or the order of our mention of her and her entrance, with the same results. (42) shows that the pronoun *she*, while even less contentful than *the woman*, may be felicitously used, but it can apparently only refer to the second woman, as shown by the possible references to the other woman in the adjunct clause. Note that we cannot argue that the first woman is simply not salient by the time we interpret the pronoun; in the same relative linear position in discourse, *she* in (43) can take the first NP as its antecedent:

(43) A woman entered from stage left.
There was a basket of flowers in the middle of the stage.
She picked it up.

The difference in (42) seems to be that a pronoun takes as its antecedent the *most* salient entity in the context at the time of its utterance which is of a sort compatible with the pronoun's features. But a definite description doesn't take relative salience of potential antecedents into account.

It would take me too far afield in the present paper to attempt to spell out in any detail what it is for a discourse referent to be salient in a given context of utterance. See Roberts (1998, to appear) for discussion and relevant references on the subject. Here, I must simply assume that in a given context C we can pick out a group of discourse referents as being salient at that point in the discourse. Let us call this set *Sal(C)*, the salient set in the context *C*, and assume that it is a subset of the set of familiar discourse referents in *C*, Dom(C). Further, I will assume that there is an order of relative salience on Sal(C), $>_{Salient}$, enabling us to capture which discourse referents are most salient in *C*.

The sensitivity of pronominal interpretation to salience is captured in the presuppositions of pronouns spelled out in (44) and (45):

(44) **Presuppositions of Pronouns** (informal):
Given a context *C*, use of a pronoun Pro_i presupposes that there is a discourse referent *i* familiar and salient in *C* which is the most salient discourse referent satisfying the descriptive content suggested by the person, number and gender of Pro_i.

Informational uniqueness of the presupposed discourse referent antecedent for the pronoun is entailed in (44) by the superlative *most*. So if we take the person, number and gender of a pronoun, suitably liberalized, to constitute its descriptive content, then (44) amounts to (39) plus the presupposition of maximal salience of the antecedent discourse referent. The latter is encoded as a restriction on the comparison class for the determination of informational uniqueness (clause (ii)) to the set of discourse referents that are at least as salient as that corresponding to the antecedent:

(45) **Familiarity and Uniqueness Presuppositions of Pronouns** (formal):
For context $\text{C} = <\text{Sat}_\text{C}, \text{Dom}_\text{C}>$, with the salient discourse referents $\text{Sal}_\text{C} \subseteq \text{Dom}_\text{C}$, if a pronoun with descriptive content Desc (given by its person, number and gender) is felicitous in C then
(i) $\exists \text{i} \in \text{Sal}_\text{C}[\forall <\text{w}, \text{g}> \in \text{Sat}_\text{C}[\text{Desc(w)(g(i))}]$ &
(ii) $\forall \text{k} \geq_{\text{Salient}} \text{i}\,[\forall <\text{w}, \text{g}> \in \text{Sat}_\text{C}[\text{Desc(w)(g(k))}] \rightarrow \text{k} = \text{i}]]$,
where *Desc(w)(g(i))* is true iff the individual assigned to *i* by *g* has the property denoted by *Desc* in *w*, and $\geq_{\text{Salient}}$ is a partial order over $\text{Sal}_\text{C} \, \text{x} \, \text{Sal}_\text{C}$ s.t. $\text{x} \geq_{\text{Salient}} \text{y}$ iff x is at least as salient as y.

These presuppositions effectively restrict the search space for pronominal antecedents to the set of maximally salient entities at the time of utterance. Hence, the uniqueness presupposition, unlike that for definite descriptions, generally does not obtain over the entire domain of discourse referents, and semantic uniqueness effects do not arise.

Before moving on to argue that demonstrative NPs are definite, and hence subject to (40), we need to address briefly the issue of what it means for an NP to be familiar, i.e., what licenses the search for a discourse referent antecedent for that NP. Consider the following taxonomy of ways we might understand familiarity, and hence of ways in which the introduction of a familiar discourse referent into the common ground may be licensed:

(46) **Taxonomy of familiarity**:

- **(a)** strong familiarity: the NP has as antecedent a discourse referent introduced via the utterance of a (usually) preceding NP[13]
- **(b)** weak familiarity:
  - **(i)** the entity referred to is globally familiar in the general culture or at least among the participants in the discourse (e.g. through perceptual acquaintance), although not mentioned in the immediate discourse (see (47) below)
  - **(ii)** introduction of the NP's discourse referent is licensed by contextual entailments alone (see (48) below)
  - **(iii)** weak familiarity is guaranteed by giving a functional interpretation to the definite description (which function may have to be accommodated); see (49)–(51) and (52), (53) below)

When someone says that an NP is used anaphorically, they often seem to mean that the NP is strongly familiar, as defined in (17a). Heim (1982) makes it clear that the notion of familiarity she has in mind subsumes both strong familiarity and the first type of weak familiarity; this is the type of familiarity guaranteed by deictic gestures in discourse, which could be characterized as directly acquainting the interlocutors with the existence of the relevant entity, as well as making it maximally salient at that time. In Roberts (to appear), I argue that the familiarity presuppositions of definite NPs can be satisfied by the other types of weak familiarity, as well. This is intended to counter authors like Fraurud (1990), Birner and Ward (1994), and Poesio and Vieira (1998), who offer what they take to be counter-examples to the claim that definite descriptions have familiarity presuppositions. In most of those examples weak familiarity is satisfied, although strong familiarity fails. A few illustrations will have to suffice here:

(47) One stranger to another: <u>The sun</u> is especially hot today.

(48) I dropped ten marbles and found only nine of them. <u>It</u>/<u>the missing marble</u> is probably under the sofa.

[13] I want to leave open the possibility of treating cataphora, generally involving a pronoun in a subordinate clause in the same sentence as the antecedent NP, as yielding strong familiarity. But I won't have anything to say about those cases here.

(49) John read a book about Schubert and wrote to the author. (Heim 1982)

(50) I walked into the room. The windows looked out to the bay. (Clark 1977)

(51) Context: One detective to another, after stumbling over a strangled body at a crime scene:
The murderer must be far away by now.

If (47) is an out-of-the-blue utterance between perfect strangers, presumably *the sun* will fail to be strongly familiar. However, in such cases there is no sense of accommodation or awkwardness. Rather, even strangers, if they take each other to be sane, normal adult humans, can assume that they share the same environment, on a planet which revolves around a single sun; hence they can assume that the information they share entails the existence of exactly one sun. Under weak familiarity, this existence entailment licenses a discourse referent corresponding to the (actual) sun, which satisfies the familiarity presupposition of the definite description. Uttered out of the blue, (48) is generally unacceptable with the underlined pronoun, as noted by Partee (cited in Heim 1982). But unnoted there is the fact that it is quite unremarkable with the full definite description. The first sentence only entails the existence of a missing marble without mentioning it, making the discourse referent for the marble (merely) weakly familiar but not salient. This satisfies the presuppositions of the definite description, but not of the pronoun. In (49) the existence of a book, in combination with our general knowledge about how books come into being, entails the existence of an author, who is thereby weakly familiar; we can take *author* to be interpreted as a function, with the discourse referent corresponding to *a book about Schubert* serving as implicit argument. Our understanding of (50) involves default knowledge about rooms, that they generally have windows in them. In (51), the detectives know a crime scene when they see one, and each knows that the other knows that a strangled body entails the existence of a murderer. Hence, many examples which were treated by Heim and subsequent authors as requiring accommodation do not on the present account, since they are licensed by a corresponding discourse referent which is (merely) weakly familiar. However, weak familiarity which is licensed solely by contextual entailment does not by itself suffice to make the corresponding discourse referent salient, so that in such cases a definite description is generally preferred over a pronoun. *He*, *they*, *he* would be unacceptable (on the intended interpretations) if replacing the definite descriptions in (51).

However, accommodation is sometimes required to satisfy the presupposition of familiarity. In general, wherever there are presuppositions there is the possibility of accommodating them even though strictly speaking they fail in the context of utterance, so long as it is perfectly clear what is presupposed. [14] Taking weak familiarity to be the relevant notion for the definitions in (40) and (45) radically cuts down the number of cases which call for accommodation. However, we still see the need in examples like (52) and (53):

(52) (To a European friend who knows nothing about West Virginia:)
Last weekend we climbed <u>the biggest mountain in West Virginia</u>.

(53) (One stranger to another:)
Well, I have to go. <u>The little woman</u> is waiting for me.

In these examples, presumably the audience had no idea prior to the utterance that there existed thing as a mountain in West Virginia (52) or that the speaker was married (53). So weak familiarity fails. But since the mountain in question is described in superlative terms, then it will be semantically unique under that description. And we know that if a man is married in this culture, he can have only one wife. That is, these examples illustrate semantic uniqueness, or Löbner's (1987) semantically functional interpretations. So if we accommodate the existence of a mountain or a wife, then the informational uniqueness of the corresponding discourse referent is assured. Note that these examples argue against a theory of definite descriptions built solely on familiarity, since such a theory would not be able to account for the infelicity of an indefinite article in such examples:

(54) #Last weekend we climbed a biggest mountain in West Virginia.

One probable reason why weak familiarity has not heretofore been seriously taken into account is the difficulty of specifying just when a discourse referent which is merely weakly familiar is introduced into the common ground. If, e.g., a discourse referent i is licensed by an existence entailment alone, when is this licensure "calculated" and i introduced into the domain of the common ground, Dom(C)? I grant that this is a difficult problem from a computational point of view, a sub-case of the problem discussed at length by Sperber and Wilson (1986): When does a potential entailment get drawn in discourse — as soon as the discourse context is sufficient rich to entail it, or only if and when it becomes evident that it is relevant? In all such cases, as they illustrate in great detail, the amount of inference required to keep up with the pos-

[14] That is to say, when we place contextual constraints on accommodation, the result is a much tighter theory, making clearer predictions about when accommodation is acceptable and when it is not. For general discussion, see Roberts (1995,1996).

sible entailments would be computationally intractable. Walker (1993) suggests that often redundancy is acceptable in discourse precisely because it helps to remind the hearer of already familiar information (e.g., propositions in the common ground) just when that information permits one to draw inferences relevant for the current discussion. This, in turn, suggests that we don't just continually whirr through all the information in our common ground looking for inferences which can be drawn; it is likely that in general these are actually drawn only when their relevance is brought to our attention. In the case of weak familiarity, this would mean that in the record that a hearer attempts to keep of the common ground there might be no pre-existing discourse referent, one being inserted after the fact just when it becomes clear that it is both licensed by entailment and required to satisfy the familiarity presupposition of a definite. But as in presupposition satisfaction generally, we wouldn't want to say that this involved accommodation — a violation repaired after the fact; e.g., see Karttunen's (1973) discussion of presupposition satisfaction satisfied by entailed information, a very straightforward and common phenomenon.

Thus, the problem of when to introduce entailed information, including merely weak discourse referents, is a processing matter, a reflection of the limitations of the human beings who process language. Such cases do not involve accommodation in the sense of a repair, as introduced in Lewis (1979). We generally don't even notice the necessity of this licensure noticed-after-the-fact in cases like (48)–(51).

In summary, a range of examples, of which (34) illustrates only one type, argue that either Russellian proffered semantic uniqueness or its presuppositional counterpart place too strong a requirement on the semantics of definite descriptions, while pronouns generally fail semantic uniqueness. Yet familiarity alone does not suffice to explain the semantic uniqueness effects observed in (30), (31) and a range of other examples. If we adopt weak familiarity and assume that the uniqueness displayed in definites is informational uniqueness rather than semantic, the full range of examples can be explained, including the examples which cause problems for the theories of semantic uniqueness or familiarity alone. Far fewer types of examples now require accommodation, and given the presuppositional character of informational uniqueness, we would expect some such examples in any case.

4.5 Demonstratives without direct reference or ambiguity

In this section, I will present a theory which treats English demonstrative NPs as a type of definite NP, a subclass which cuts across the other two sub-classes, the definite descriptions and the pronouns. The theory I offer gives a unified account of all the types of demonstratives considered above: pronominal and descriptive, accompanied by canonical demonstrations or textual deixis, and, with only minor variation, discourse deixis, as well.

There is only one type of use of demonstrative NPs which the present theory cannot account for, so far as I can see. This is what Maclaran calls the 'specific indefinite' use of proximal demonstratives, illustrated by (55):

(55) [excited teenager on the phone to a friend:] I met this great looking guy on the bus this afternoon!

Such uses seem to fail familiarity altogether, so that they aren't plausibly definite; further, there is an apparent failure of proximity of the guy in question in the actual discourse context. [15] I speculate that the proximal might be used to indicate some sort of empathetic proximity, but otherwise have nothing of interest to say about these. [16] After offering in Section 4.5.1 a characterization of the presuppositions which differentiate the demonstratives from the other types of definite discussed, in Section 4.5.2 I'll briefly discuss what it means for a demonstrative NP to be accompanied by a demonstration. Then in Section 4.5.3 I'll return to the question of how to account for the direct reference effects observed by Kaplan.

4.5.1 The presuppositions of demonstrative NPs

I begin with the assumption that demonstrative NPs with *this*, *that*, *these*, and *those* are all definite, whether descriptions or pronouns. Thus, they all carry the presuppositions of familiarity and informational uniqueness noted in (40) for definite NPs in general. Following Kaplan, I assume that demonstratives, including demonstratively used personal pronouns, carry an additional assumption which neither definite descriptions, nor

[15] I also understand (Arantxa Martin-Lozano, p.c.) that though Spanish has demonstratives whose uses otherwise seem to closely parallel those of the English demonstratives as spelled out here, they are not used in the way illustrated by (55). This suggests that this use has developed as a special feature in some language(s), rather than as a direct reflection of the demonstrative's ordinary meaning.

[16] But see Dekker (1997) for some interesting speculation about specificity and definiteness, which may bear on such uses as well as on specific indefinites and the like.

pronouns in general, do: They presuppose an accompanying demonstration, whose demonstratum is correlated with the discourse referent that satisfies their familiarity. Further, I will assume that this presupposition of a demonstration is general for all the uses of demonstratives noted in Section 1, and not just for those canonical uses which involve a deictic gesture. And I will argue that given the presupposition of a demonstration, we can explain the direct reference effects associated with demonstratives without assuming that they have a special, direct mode of reference. Insofar as we say that any NP has a Context Change Potential, which is the counterpart in a dynamic, context change semantics of a Fregean sense, we can say that demonstratives, like other definites, have senses.

(56) **Presuppositions of Demonstrative NPs** (informal):
Given a context C, use of a (non-)proximal demonstrative NP_i presupposes (a) that there is an accompanying demonstration δ whose unique demonstratum, correlated with a weakly familiar discourse referent by virtue of being demonstrated, lies in the direction indicated by the speaker at a (non-)proximal distance to the speaker, and (b) that the weakly familiar discourse referent for the demonstratum is the unique familiar discourse referent contextually entailed to satisfy the (possibly liberalized) descriptive content of NP_i.

Comparing (56) to (39) from above, we see that the Presuppositions of Demonstrative NPs include those of definites more generally:

(39) **Informational Existence and Uniqueness of Definite NPs** (informal):
Given a context C, use of a definite description NP_i presupposes that there is a discourse referent i in the Domain of C which is the unique familiar discourse referent contextually entailed to satisfy the (possibly liberalized) descriptive content of NP_i.

Moreover, if we assume, as seems natural, that the accompanying demonstration serves to make the intended demonstratum, and hence its discourse referent, maximally salient, then the presuppositions for pronouns in (45) are satisfied, as well. Hence, all demonstratives satisfy the presuppositions for both demonstratives generally and for pronouns, while satisfying others in addition.

Maclaran (1982:159) argues that the proximity feature of a demonstrative is presupposed, not entailed, since this facet of a demonstrative's meaning can't be "sensibly denied", as argued by the infelicity of B's reply in her example (57):

(57) A: I've had three slices of this cake.
B: No, you haven't. It's not near you.

In the formal version of (58), I adopt the dynamic counterpart of a dual indexing system (Kamp 1971), so that interlocutors can keep track both of the global common ground (CG) and the local context of evaluation at any given point in the discourse (the local context *C*). When the two differ, as under the scope of an operator or in the course of interpretation of a conditional, I will assume that interpretation of a demonstrative is anchored directly to the common ground. This and the directness of demonstrations themselves are the keys to explaining the so-called direct reference effects noted by Kaplan.

(58) **Presuppositions of Demonstrative NPs** (formal):
Given a context of evaluation C, with common ground CG s.t. $\mathrm{Dom_{CG}} \subseteq \mathrm{Dom_C}$, and discourse referent S s.t.
$\forall \mathrm{i} \in \mathrm{Dom_{CG}}\, \forall < \mathrm{w}, \mathrm{g} > \in \mathrm{Sat_{CG}}[\mathrm{speaker(w)(g(i))} \leftrightarrow \mathrm{i} = \mathrm{S}]$,
if a [+(-)proximal] demonstrative $\mathrm{NP_i}$ with (possibly liberalized) descriptive content Desc is felicitous in C, then

(i) $\exists\delta[\delta \in \mathrm{Dom_{CG}}$
$\& \forall < \mathrm{w}, \mathrm{g} > \in \mathrm{Sat_{CG}}[\mathrm{demonstration(w)(g(\delta))}\ \&$
$\mathrm{accompanies(w)(g(\delta),\ utterance(NP_i))}]\ \&$

(ii) $\exists \mathrm{j} \in \mathrm{Dom_{CG}}[\forall < \mathrm{w}, \mathrm{g} > \in \mathrm{Sat_{CG}}[+(-)\mathrm{proximal(w)(g(j), g(S))}$
$\&\ \mathrm{demonstratum\ (w)(g(j), g(S), \delta)}]\ \&$
$\forall \mathrm{k} \in \mathrm{Dom_{CG}}[\forall < \mathrm{w}, \mathrm{g} > \in \mathrm{Sat_{CG}}[+(-)\mathrm{proximal(w)(g(k), g(S))}$
$\&\ \mathrm{demonstratum(w)(g(k), g(S), \delta)}] \rightarrow \mathrm{k} = \mathrm{j}]\ \&$
$\mathrm{Desc(w)(g(j))}]\ \&$

(iii) $\mathrm{j} = \mathrm{i}]]$

where *Desc(w)(g(i))* is true iff the individual assigned to *i* by *g* has the property denoted by *Desc* in world *w*; and *+(-)proximal(w)(g(j),g(S)) & demonstratum(w)(g(j),g(S),δ)* is true iff the individual assigned to *j* by *g* is in the set of entities (non-) proximal to the speaker *g(S)* and is the demonstratum intended by *g(S)* for the demonstration *g(δ)*.

Again, comparing (58) with the formal statement of the presuppositions of definites in (40) above, we see that the former incorporates the presuppositions in the latter:

(40) **Familiarity and Uniqueness Presuppositions of Definite NPs** (formal):
For context $\mathrm{C} = < \mathrm{Sat_C}, \mathrm{Dom_C} >$, if a definite NP with (possibly liberalized) descriptive content *Desc* is felicitous in C then

(i) $\exists \mathrm{i} \in \mathrm{Dom_C}[\forall < \mathrm{w}, \mathrm{g} > \in \mathrm{Sat_C}[\mathrm{Desc(w)(g(i))}]\ \&$

(ii) $\forall k \in Dom_C[\forall < w, g > \in Sat_C[Desc(w)(g(k))] \rightarrow k = i]]$, where *Desc(w)(g(i))* is true iff the individual assigned to *I* by *g* has the property denoted by *Desc* in world *w*.

Clause (58i) tells us that there's a demonstration that is familiar in the CG, that is, whose existence is common information for the interlocutors; the familiar discourse referent is δ, and hence the demonstration (in any give world) is $g(\delta)$. Clause (ii) says that there's a discourse referent familiar in the CG which is the unique demonstratum of this demonstration and which satisfies the NP's descriptive content, and clause (iii) that the discourse referent for this demonstratum, *j*, is the same as that for the demonstrative NP, *i*. Note that no matter the context in which the demonstrative occurs (e.g., under the scope of a modal, hence irrealis), the demonstratum is always determined with respect to the CG, i.e. the information about actual circumstances of utterance. Hence, following Kaplan, demonstrata cannot be shifted in modal contexts; there are no monsters.

The heart of this proposal is the claim that a demonstrative NP conventionally presupposes that the familiar discourse referent for the demonstratum of its associated demonstration is the same as the discourse referent which satisfies the NP's familiarity presupposition. In (58), this identity is guaranteed by clause (iii). I might instead have simply used *i* in place of *j* throughout, but I wanted to emphasize that the demonstration alone makes its demonstratum weakly familiar, and that what the NP's presupposed content does is equate that discourse referent with its own.

But what is a demonstration? How can this notion be made sufficiently broad to capture the sense in which not only canonical uses of demonstratives, but discourse deixis as well involves a demonstration?

4.5.2 Demonstrations

Demonstrations are communicative devices, used to bring an audience's attention to something. But they are not themselves linguistic. That is, though an expression in a given language may presuppose an accompanying demonstration, the demonstration itself is not a part of that language. Rather, it is part of the actual world as experienced by the interlocutors, its demonstratum singled out in that world. [17] Hence, demonstrations are insensitive to linguistic stipulation about

[17] One reviewer wondered what type of ontology is presupposed by (58), where satisfaction sequences can map discourse referents onto demonstrata in the world. But I see nothing any more difficult in assuming that demonstrations are real entities in the world than in assuming such status for events, facts, behaviors, and other abstract entities generally conceded to be spoken of as if they exist.

their demonstrata. If we point at something, it doesn't matter if we say we're pointing at something else; there are no linguistic "shifters" which can take scope over a demonstration. The demonstratum is the actual demonstratum in the space in which we point. In this sense, demonstrations themselves are direct.

The demonstrations presupposed by demonstratives are fundamentally locative, demonstrating their intended referent via indication of its location. While a deictic gesture is surely the prototypical demonstration, as in deixis more generally such spatially-realized gestures find analogies in non-spatial domains. When an entity obviously lies in the physical space surrounding the speaker, indication of its location is a conventional part of the meaning of a demonstrative used to refer to it. But conceptually the speaker lies at the zero-point of a system of coordinates, only one of which is spatial. Other dimensions include temporal proximity, proximity in the temporally aligned space of use or mention in the discourse, and even what Lyons calls *empathetic* proximity, pertaining to the speaker's identification with the entity referred to (Lyons 1977, Maclaran 1983). As is quite common in natural language, expressions which involve reference to the spatial dimension may be extended by analogy to other dimensions in this system of coordinates, always from the egocentric perspective of the speaker. There is a great deal of discussion of this type of extension in the linguistic literature, e.g. use of spatial prepositions for temporal and modal loci, similar extensions of verb senses (e.g., for *approach*), etc. See Anderson (1971), Fillmore (1975), Lyons (1977), Comrie (1981), and Jackendoff (1983), among others, for extensive discussion.

What I have called canonical uses of demonstratives, as in (4)–(7) above, are accompanied by demonstrations in actual space. Since this space is three dimensional, the demonstratum might lie in any of an infinite set of directions from the speaker. In the absence of any other indication of the direction in which the hearer is to search, a deictic gesture (pointing, glance, nod, etc.) by the speaker will provide the required orientation. Along the line suggested by the gesture, the hearer will search for the intended referent within a region which is (non-)proximal to the speaker, in accordance with the proximity presupposition of the demonstrative. But even in actual space, it is important to distinguish a demonstration from a deictic gesture. The former only requires giving adequate evidence to enable a hearer to infer the speaker's intended demonstratum. [18] A deictic gesture is neither necessary nor sufficient

[18]This broader sense of *demonstration* is suggested by standard dictionary definitions like the following in the *American Heritage Dictionary*:

to guarantee that this requirement is satisfied. Successful demonstration isn't so much a question of following specific conventions as of adopting effective strategies for pragmatically picking out the intended referent in the relevant space (see Clark, Schreuder and Buttrick 1983). To see that a deictic gesture by itself is insufficient, consider again the following examples:

(5) [pointing at some stuffed peppers in a restaurant display case:] Those look particularly delicious.

(7) [policeman, pointing in the direction of a man running through a crowd:] Stop that man!

(5) might be uttered in a situation where the speaker is pointing in the direction not only of the intended referents, the peppers, but of some flies on the glass of the display case. What makes this a successful demonstration is a combination of the deictic gesture itself, plus the understood goals of the speaker (to pick out something to eat) and the meaning of the predicate (which is unlikely to be held to be true of the flies). In (7), the policeman is pointing into a crowd of people, which presumably contains a number of men. The success of the demonstrative *that man* in picking out the intended referent depends upon both the descriptive CN *man* and the higher salience of the referent by virtue of his frantic attempt to escape, as well as on the deictic gesture in the right general direction.

And if an entity is sufficiently salient, a deictic gesture is not necessary. Consider a situation in which two friends are sitting in a coffee shop when a man comes in and begins to noisily harass the personnel at the counter. Not wanting to draw attention to herself by staring or pointing, one friend might whisper (59) to the other:

(59) That guy is really obnoxious.

Here, the distal feature of the demonstrative, plus its descriptive content, plus (say) the fact that the hearer has obviously been distracted since the man began his behavior, pick out a most likely intended referent. In this type of context, the pronoun *he* might substitute for *that guy*, although the richer descriptive content of the demonstrative description makes it a safer bet to pick out the intended referent if one isn't sure

---

demonstrate:

1. To prove or make manifest by reasoning or adducing evidence
2. To describe or illustrate by experiment or practical application
3. To manifest or reveal

as well as by colloquial uses of the term e.g., *Shawn will demonstrate how the new operating system works, I have demonstrated that my client cannot be guilty, Mary has demonstrated that she is trustworthy*, etc.

he's already maximally salient. But *the guy* wouldn't suffice because, due to its lack of demonstration (unlike the demonstrative) and its relative insensitivity to salience (unlike the pronoun), it wouldn't pick out a unique entity in the situation described.

The devices we can use to demonstrate an intended (discourse) referent along the temporal or textual coordinates are more restricted than those we can use in actual space, because these spaces themselves are only two-dimensional (for the textual, because of its temporal realization). Then by this same token, there are only two directions in which the demonstratum might lie relative to the speaker's position (the time of utterance): prior to or after, so the restricted means are generally sufficient. In these uses, demonstratives are often used as contrasting pairs, indicating relative proximity to the speaker. Assumption of the temporal space is illustrated by (60), while (8), repeated from above, illustrates textual deixis:

(60) George ran a fever one evening last week. <u>That time</u> he ignored it. But it happened again last night, and <u>this time</u> he called the doctor.

(8) This sentence is short.

The discourse deixis illustrated by *former* and *latter* is based on textual deixis. In a textual or discourse deixis, given the nature of presupposition and the interlocutors' (usual) lack of access to text following the time of utterance, demonstratives tend to lend themselves better to anaphora than to cataphora. For cataphora, we are limited to the use of the proximal demonstratives, and the intended referent must immediately follow, as in the textual deixis in (61) and the discourse deixis in (62):

(61) This is an ugly word: *hippopotamus*.

(62) Do you know these new rose hybrids, Meidiland and Peace?

All of the examples where demonstratives are used anaphorically to a preceding NP or as bound variables, as in (9)–(14) above, can be viewed as instances of discourse deixis. The proximity associated with the pronoun may be helpful in picking out an antecedent NP, based on its relative proximity in the text to the time of utterance of the demonstrative; but unlike textual deixis, the intended discourse referent of the demonstrative is the antecedent's discourse referent, and not the antecedent itself.

Discourse deixis and the anaphoric use of demonstratives differ from canonical demonstrative use in this respect: The demonstratum is a linguistic constituent, e.g. an NP or Sentence (for anaphora with *this*). And there is a slippage of the relationship between the demonstrative and its demonstratum, so that instead of presupposing the equation of the discourse referent for the demonstrative with that for the demonstratum itself, as in (58iii), it is equated with the discourse referent introduced by the demonstratum, its "referent". That is, we use the proximity presupposition in the demonstrative to pick out (demonstrate) a maximally salient NP or other constituent. Then it is the (already familiar) discourse referent which corresponds to this demonstrated NP that satisfies the familiarity presupposition of the demonstrative NP itself. So for discourse deixis, we need to replace (58) by (58^d). The only differences are indicated here in boldface; note especially the revised clause (iii):

(58^d) **Presuppositions of Discourse Deictic Demonstrative NPs** (formal):
Given a context of evaluation C, with common ground CG s.t. $\mathrm{Dom_{CG}} \subseteq \mathrm{Dom_C}$, and discourse referent S s.t. $\forall \mathrm{i} \in \mathrm{Dom_{CG}} \forall < \mathrm{w}, \mathrm{g} > \in \mathrm{Sat_{CG}}[\mathrm{speaker(w)(g(i))} \leftrightarrow \mathrm{i} = \mathrm{S}]$, if a [+(-)proximal] demonstrative $\mathrm{NP_i}$ with (possibly liberalized) descriptive content Desc is felicitous in C, then

(i) $\exists \delta[\delta \in \mathrm{Dom_{CG}} \;\&\; \forall < \mathrm{w}, \mathrm{g} > \in$
$\mathrm{Sat_{CG}}[\mathbf{demonstration\_in\_discourse}(\mathrm{w})(\mathrm{g}(\delta))$
$\&\; \mathrm{accompanies(w)(g(\delta), utterance(NP_i))}] \;\&$

(ii) $\exists \mathrm{j} \in \mathrm{Dom_{CG}}[\forall < \mathrm{w}, \mathrm{g} > \in \mathrm{Sat_{CG}}[+(-)\mathrm{proximal(w)(g(j), g(S))}$
$\&\; \mathrm{demonstratum(w)(g(j), g(S), \delta)}] \;\&$
$\forall \mathrm{k} \in \mathrm{Dom_{CG}}[\forall < \mathrm{w}, \mathrm{g} > \in$
$\mathrm{Sat_{CG}}[+(-)\mathrm{proximal(w)(g(k), g(S))}$
$\&\; \mathrm{demonstratum(w)(g(k), g(S), \delta)}] \rightarrow \mathrm{k} = \mathrm{j}] \;\&$
$\mathrm{Desc(w)(g(j))}] \;\&$

(iii) $\boldsymbol{\forall < \mathrm{w}, \mathrm{g} > \in \mathrm{Sat_{CG}}[\mathrm{discourse - referent(w)(g(j))} =}$
$\mathbf{i]]}$,

where:

demonstration-in-discourse is true of an individual at a world just in case that individual is a constituent (e.g., NP) in the linguistic structure of the discourse in question;

Desc(w)(g(i)) is true iff the individual assigned to *i* by *g* has the property denoted by *Desc* in world *w*;
+(-)proximal(w)(g(j),g(S)) & demonstratum(w)(g(j),g(S),δ) is true iff the individual assigned to *j* by *g* is in the set of entities (non-) proximal to the speaker *g(S)* and is the demonstratum intended by *g(S)* for the demonstration *g(δ)*, and

discourse-referent is a function which maps a world and a linguistic constituent to the discourse referent whose introduction into Dom(CG) the constituent licenses in the discourse in that world, so that *discourse-referent(w)(g(j))* = *i* is true iff the entity assigned to *j* by *g* is a constituent which has triggered the introduction of the discourse referent *i* into CG in *w*.

The difference between canonical and discourse deictic uses of demonstratives is minimal. We do not need to claim, as one must with the direct reference theory, that demonstrative NPs used for discourse deixis have a distinct mode of reference from those used with canonical demonstrations. One can readily see how (58^{d}) evolved as a variation on (58).

There is also a slippage of the role of proximity in discourse deixis. We commonly see the use of the unmarked non-proximals *that* or *those* to indicate not greater relative distance from the speaker, but simple contrast with some other, slightly less salient entity of the same sort. This varies from speaker to speaker, and in general the way that proximity specifications work in discourse deixis is harder to pin down. For example, in (9) we might use *that* instead of *this*, in (10) we might use *those* instead of *these*, and in (12) we might use *This* instead of *That*, without much change, if any, in meaning:

(9) I saw one quilt which was quite abstract, with lots of asymmetric diagonals. Another one was more traditional, worked in an old Amish pattern. This quilt was less busy than the other, but just as bold.

(10) The Russians had allowed few pieces from their collection to go on show in the West, but these were the highpoint of the exhibition. (Maclaran 1982)

(12) On every team there is one player who is not as strong as the rest. That weakest member is the one to play hardest against. (Maclaran 1982)

In these examples, a pronoun or a definite description might be substituted for the demonstrative. But the demonstratives seem to be used for one of two reasons: They tend to carry an implication of contrast, implicating that other members of a relevant contrast set do not have the properties predicated of the demonstrative (this seems to be the case in (9), (10) and (12), for example). And, as noted by Isard (1975) and Maclaran (1982) in slightly different terms, they tend to be used when the discourse referent which satisfies their familiarity is only weakly familiar, based on contextual entailments, especially if it contrasts in this respect with other, strongly familiar discourse referents which are alternative candidates to satisfy that familiarity presupposition. This distinction in degree of familiarity can be used to assist in anaphora resolution, as seems to be the case in (63), while the lack of contrast or novelty in (64) makes the demonstratives seem infelicitous:

(63) First square nineteen, then cube it/that. (Isard 1975)

it: 'nineteen'
that: 'nineteen squared'

(64) A car drew up at the door. Two dark-suited men got out of it/the car/?this/?that, then it/?this/?that disappeared down the drive again. (after Maclaran 1982)

I speculate that the contrast involved is based on the proximity distinctions which are central to demonstratives in their canonical use, while the association with relative novelty comes from the canonical use as well, where the discourse referent which satisfies the demonstrative's familiarity presupposition is only just made weakly familiar via the accompanying deictic gesture at the time of utterance. By a Gricean quantity implicature, use of a demonstrative instead of a pronoun or definite description implicates that one of these two conditions — contrast or weaker familiarity — obtains.

Thus, we see that extension of the use of demonstratives into the more abstract space of discourse leads to a slight shift in their sense, so that proximity ceases to play precisely the same role that it plays in the canonical use. However, even there, implications based on the proximity specifications and on the presupposition of a demonstration play the central role in determining when a demonstrative is felicitous, or even preferred over another type of definite. Hence, I would argue, the central features of the presupposition in (58) are retained in discourse deixis — the presupposition of proximity (if only indirectly, and in the modified form of an implication of contrast) and of demonstration (if only in the form of implication that the intended discourse referent is merely weakly familiar). In other respects, the demonstratives are simply descriptive or pronominal definites, and hence their distribution overlaps significantly in discourse with that of those other NP types.

4.5.3 Accounting for direct reference effects

Given the theory outlined in the preceding sections, we want to show how it can account for the direct reference effects observed by Kaplan in examples like (17b) and (17c), repeated here with indices on the NPs for convenience: [19]

(17) Context (CG): Charles is from Charleston, West Virginia. Paul is from St. Paul, Minnesota. δ is a pointing by the speaker in the direction of Paul, who is seated on a chair in front of the speaker:

Look over here [δ, the gesture held throughout the next sentence]. If Charles and Paul had changed chairs, then

a) the man being pointed at would be from Charleston
b) he[δ] would be from Charleston.
c) this man being pointed at [δ] would be from Charleston.

I will assume a theory of counterfactual interpretation which is a variation on the general approach of Lewis (1973). Roughly, in a static version of the approach, for a given counterfactual *If* ϕ, *then would* ψ, in order for the counterfactual to be true in a given world w, ψ must be true in a set of worlds determined as follows: We first consider all those worlds in which ϕ is true. Now among these worlds, we consider only those in which are true as many as possible of the propositions which are true in w. These are then the ϕ-counterfactual worlds accessible to w, call them $W^{\phi/\mathrm{w}}$. If ψ is true in all the worlds in $W^{\phi/\mathrm{w}}$, then the whole conditional is true in w; otherwise, it is false in w.

For (17b) or (17c), in determining $W^{\phi/\mathrm{w}}$ for a given world of evaluation w, we will only consider worlds in which Charles and Paul have changed chairs. But as many of the other propositions true in w which are compatible with that exchange should be true in each world in $W^{\phi/\mathrm{w}}$. In particular, since Paul is from St. Paul in the actual world, and there is no conflict between the truth of that proposition and the counterfactual exchange, then we should rule out those counterfactual worlds in which (the counterpart of) Paul is from some other place. When we utter the demonstrative *he*$_i$ or *this man being pointed at*$_i$, the demonstrative presuppositions in (58) must be satisfied. In the context specified, we

[19]My discussion of the direct reference effects in intensional contexts is partly inspired by unpublished work of Heim (1985), in which she argues that it is presuppositions associated with the demonstratives which account for the direct reference effects in counterfactual contexts, and not direct reference *per se*. However, in the end the view presented here differs from hers in several important respects. She does not subscribe to the general theory of definites outlined above, nor to the theory of demonstratives as definites with presupposed demonstrations, nor does she explicitly assume, as I do crucially, the non-linguistic nature of demonstration or the use of dual indexing. Hence, my presentation should not be taken to reflect her views on demonstratives.

have a familiar demonstration δ_2 and it is known that its demonstratum in the actual situation is Paul. Technically, the interlocutors have a discourse referent *2* such that for any one of the relevant assignment function/world pairs <w,g> in the satisfaction set of the CG, *g(2)* is entailed by CG to be the demonstratum of δ_2 in w and to be Paul. This satisfies the first two clauses of (58) for the use of a demonstrative like *he* or *this man being pointed at.* But (58iii) requires that the discourse referent corresponding to the demonstratum in CG, *2*, be the same as the discourse referent which satisfies the demonstrative NP's familiarity presupposition. I.e., in (17b) and (17c), felicity requires that $i = 2$. Hence, the demonstrative NP must refer to Paul, the actual demonstratum associated with the discourse referent for the demonstration in the common ground. Since all the worlds in $W^{\phi/w}$ entail that Paul is from St. Paul, the consequent is false in all those worlds, and hence the whole conditional will be false in w.

But in the interpretation of (17a), there is no requirement on the discourse referent for the definite description that it be the same as the demonstratum; it need only be familiar and unique under its (possibly liberalized) descriptive content, satisfying (40). So, for the definite description, we could set $i = 2$, in which case the NP has the sense of 'the man who I'm now pointing at', yielding the same falsity as (b) and (c). In this case, what is going on is that the familiarity presupposition of the definite description is being satisfied globally, with reference to the fact that the speaker is actually pointing at Paul. But we can also set $i = 1$, so that the relative clause has the sense 'the man who I would be pointing at in that counterfactual situation', making the counterfactual true. In the second case, the familiarity presupposition of the definite description is satisfied locally, under the scope of the counterfactual *would*; and the counterfactual assumption that Charles and Paul have changed places will guarantee that in all the worlds in which we consider the truth of the consequent, there will be someone sitting in the chair being pointed at by the speaker, namely (the counterpart of) Charles, who is in fact from Charleston. [20]

As Zoltán Szabó (p.c.) pointed out to me, even when the common ground doesn't contain information about where Paul was from, we still feel that (17b) or (17c) would be false in a given world, so long as he wasn't from Charleston (in that world). This is true. In such a case, in some worlds in the common ground of the interlocutors Paul might

[20] I emphasize that the use of indices in this explanation is merely a bookkeeping device, to help keep the different possible discourse referents straight; the semantic result is a consequence of the way that presupposition projection works in this type of theory (see Heim 1983), and not some sort of representational magic.

be from Charleston, in others from St. Paul, etc. The counterfactual would be true in those worlds in which Paul was from Charleston, false in the others. But the truth of the entire conditional in any given world would be purely a function of the truth of the consequent in that world; hence, the conditional itself would be judged infelicitous because the counterfactual antecedent would be irrelevant to the conditional's truth.

Recall that in (27) we observed direct reference effects with discourse deixis, instead of spatial deixis:

(27) Melanctha has a dog_1 and a cat_2, both of whom are getting very old.
The cat_2 is her favorite, but the dog_1 is more loyal.
If I hadn't uttered the last sentence, the $\text{latter}_\text{i}[\delta_j]$ would spit up hairballs and the $\text{former}_\text{k}[\delta_m]$ would bark.

The antecedent of the conditional sets up a counterfactual situation in which the structure of the preceding discourse is different than it actually is, i.e. in which the only preceding utterance is the first sentence. Yet, as the discussion of demonstrations above predicts, in picking out the intended demonstrata for the demonstrative head nouns in *the latter* and *the former* we directly consult the actual space of the discourse, ignoring that counterfactual discourse structure in which the third, conditional sentence directly follows the first. In keeping with the general character of discourse deixis, however, as given in (58^d), instead of equating the discourse referent for the demonstrative *the former* with that for the demonstrated NP *the cat* itself, we equate it with the discourse referent which satisfies the familiarity presupposition of that (definite) NP, which, in any mapping of the information in the common ground onto a model, will always map onto a cat. Then, the counterfactual is false, assuming that Melanctha's cat wouldn't start barking just because the speaker had omitted uttering the second sentence. [21] On this account of (27), we do not need to worry about singular propositions or their constituents, something which appeared to pose a problem for the direct reference approach.

Finally, let us reconsider Heim's problem for Kaplan's theory, where (23) and (24) are incorrectly predicted to be synonymous, both either necessarily true or necessarily false. Recall that the context is such that δ_1 is a pointing by the speaker to an image of a chair to her left, δ_2 is a pointing to an image of a chair to her right, the latter perhaps only a

[21] Alternatively, one might assume that *the former* itself is interpreted counterfactually, so that it takes its referent to be the dog. But it would still presuppose that its discourse referent was that of the actual demonstratum, the latter being *the cat*, thus leading to a contradiction.

reflection in a mirror:

(23) That[δ_1] is that[δ_2].

(24) That[δ_1] might well be that[δ_2].

(25) If that[δ_1] were that[δ_2], there would be only one chair in the house.

The present theory avoids this prediction by eschewing direct reference. In (23), the two demonstratives are merely two definite NPs. Each is conventionally linked to the discourse referent corresponding to the demonstratum of the accompanying demonstration. But whether or not the demonstrata are identical is a contingent fact, dependent on facts about the demonstrations and other factors in the world, so (23) will be true in some circumstances, false in others. But even when (23) is, in fact, false, its truth is compatible with all that's known in the situation of utterance Heim describes and, hence, (24) is true. Therefore, as desired, (23) and (24) are not truth conditionally synonymous on the present account. Further, even though (23) is false, the truth of (25) is still contingent on other facts about the furnishings of the house in question; e.g. if there are other chairs in the next room, (23) might be false and (25) false as well.

None of this assumes that a demonstrative NP itself is directly referential, and in fact it would be difficult to make sense of that notion in the present framework, in which meaning has to do with the information an utterance contributes to a given context of utterance. However, demonstratives do presuppose a demonstration, and in the canonical cases involving a deictic gesture, the demonstratum of that demonstration, an individual in the actual world, will serve to anchor the interpretation of the demonstrative in such a way that it will effectively act like a rigid designator in modal contexts. Because of the actuality of the anchor and the interpretive priority of presupposition satisfaction over updating with proffered information, the demonstrative behaves as if it takes scope over the modal (or any other operator in the proffered content).

Thus, the current theory can account for direct reference effects without the assumption of direct reference as a distinct mode of referring. The direct reference effect is indirect. That is to say, it is demonstrations that are directly "referential", not nominal reference. Although demonstratives, like other definites, do not refer at all, a competent speaker will always use them to pick out, via the associated demonstration, a speaker's referent in some actual space associated with the utterance situation. In discourse, that actual space may be that of the linguistic structure of the discourse itself, in discourse deixis.

Notice that the present account ties together Kaplan's two theses, from (21), which otherwise are logically independent.

(21) Kaplan's theory of English demonstrative NPs:

(a) Demonstratives are incomplete expressions which must be completed by a demonstration.
(b) Demonstratives are directly referential.

Here, the fact that demonstratives behave as if directly referential is due to the fact that they presuppose an accompanying demonstration, which demonstration is directly referential (as it were). Only (a) need be stipulated. And so we can eat our Fregean cake and have (the best of) Kaplan, too.

4.6 Conclusion: Theories of context

According to Kaplan, the difference between a demonstrative and a definite description is that the two types of NP have distinct modes of reference: Demonstratives, which require an accompanying demonstration in order to be semantically complete, have direct reference, picking out the intended referent without the mediation of a Fregean sense. Definite descriptions display non-direct reference, picking out a sense via the NP's descriptive content, with the referent then determined via the world (or circumstance) of evaluation. However, because not all uses of demonstratives are plausibly directly referential, Kaplan appears to be driven to claim that demonstratives are systematically ambiguous, with no account of how the homonyms might have developed out of a common historical ancestor.

On the present account, demonstratives and definite descriptions are both types of definite NPs, and hence both have presuppositions of familiarity and informational uniqueness. The difference between them is this: The demonstrative, but not the definite description, carries a presupposition that the discourse referent which makes it familiar is anchored by information in the common ground to an individual in the world which is directly indicated by the speaker at the time of utterance of the demonstrative NP. This presupposition will have much the same effect as direct reference, so that the demonstrative will behave as a rigid designator in counterfactual contexts. Hence, this theory permits a uniform treatment of demonstrative NPs, both pronominal and descriptive, while accounting for the directly referential effects in certain uses.

It seems to me that at the heart of the difference between the two views of demonstratives considered here, Kaplan's and my own, is a different conception of the notion of context of utterance. To see this, consider the relationship between Kaplan's notion of the Character of an expression, and the view of the meaning of an expression in a dynamic view of interpretation, the latter exemplified here by Heim's (1982,1992) notion of the Context Change Potential of an expression: [22]

Character: a function from contexts of utterance to contents, where contents are the usual functions (individual concepts, propositions, etc.) from circumstances of evaluation (like worlds or situations) to denotations.

Context Change Potential: a function from contexts to contexts; the Context Change Potential is defined for a given argument context iff the context satisfies all the presuppositions of the corresponding expression. The output context is an updating of the input to reflect the proffered content of the expression.

We can see that from the context change perspective, the meaning of an expression has two facets: presuppositional content, used to determine felicity and hence definedness for a given context; and proffered content, the way in which a felicitous input context is updated to yield a new context. If we take a dynamic context to be something like the common ground at a given point in a discourse, the Context Change Potential for an expression can be taken to encode the information in Kaplan's Character. [23] For example, if part of the Character of a given expression, like *I* or *we*, is a specification that it be anchored to the speaker in the context of utterance, then we might say that the Context Change Potential for the expression is only defined for a certain context if in that context the discourse referent which satisfies the expression's familiarity presupposition is the discourse referent for the speaker. If the speaker is pointing at an object in the actual world, then the fact of that demonstration and the identity of the demonstratum are known in the common ground/context, and only such a context can satisfy the presuppositions of an accompanying demonstrative NP. Etc. But the richer notion of Context Change Potential cannot be retrieved from that of Character. The latter seems to be confined to retrieving values for distinguished elements of the context of utterance — speaker, audience, location and time of utterance, etc. The Context Change Potential

[22] One might instead place this account in one of the other contemporary theories of dynamic context, e.g. those of Barwise and Perry (1983), Kamp and Reyle (1993), Groenendijk and Stokhof (1990), or Chierchia (1995). What is crucial here is that context is dynamically updated, rich enough to enable the interlocutors to keep track of different types of information, and relevant for presupposition satisfaction.

[23] Similarly, the Context Change Potential can capture Perry's (1977) "procedure for determining reference from a context", his proposed understanding of the Fregean sense of an utterance containing a demonstrative. As Perry notes, this is closely related to Kaplan's notion of *character*.

and associated notion of context are conceptually much richer than this, designed to permit an account of the full range of conventional presuppositions in language, as well for context update. Since we want a theory of presupposition anyway, and, I would argue, the satisfaction theories of presupposition embodied in Context Change Semantics and its kin are demonstrably superior to any alternatives, the richer notion of Context Change Potential seems to be independently well-motivated. Hence, one might argue, we can dispense with Character *per se*.

But the Context Change Potential and the theory on which it is based *does* presume a conceptually different notion of context than Kaplan's. The latter seems to assume that the context of utterance is the actual physical situation of the discourse, perhaps characterized as a set of distinguished elements like the actual speaker, audience, etc. But in Context Change Semantics, context is a more abstract notion, not directly a physical space or actual entities in the world, although it of course encodes information about the concrete physical situation in which the utterance occurs and about the entities therein. The notion of context independently motivated by facets of the theory of presupposition is that of an organized collection of various types of information. That information is partly propositional, including the interlocutors' presuppositions. But the context also contains information about the discourse itself, including information about what's been referred to therein (the familiar discourse referents), about the questions under discussion in the discourse and the discourse goals and plans which these suggest (Roberts 1996b), and of course, about the interlocutors and their roles at various junctures in the discourse — who's speaker, who's addressee, etc.

How can we decide between these two notions? We need to ask which notion of context yields a theory of demonstratives which is optimal both in empirical adequacy — getting the facts right — and in its generality — accounting for related phenomena in an insightful, succinct fashion. And of course, all things being equal, we would like to adopt a theory of context which is independently motivated by several facets of interpretation. I think that on all these grounds, the notion of context as an organized body of information, abstractly accessible to all interlocutors, is superior to that of context as a concrete situation or collection of concrete entities.

References

Anderson 1971. John M. Anderson: *The Grammar of Case: Towards a Localistic Theory.* Cambridge University Press, London.

Barwise and Perry 1983. Jon Barwise and John Perry: *Situations and At-*

titudes. MIT Press.

Birner and Ward 1994. Betty Birner and Gregory Ward: Uniqueness, familiarity, and the definite article in English. *Proceedings of the Annual Meeting of the Berkeley Linguistic Society*, 93–102.

Chierchia 1995. Gennaro Chierchia: *Dynamics of Meaning: Anaphora, presupposition, and the meaning of grammar*. University of Chicago Press.

Clark 1977. Herbert H. Clark: Bridging. In P.N. Johnson-Laird and P.C. Wason (Eds.) *Thinking: Readings in Cognitive Science*, Cambridge University Press, 411–420.

Clark, Schreuder and Buttrick 1983. Herbert H. Clark, Robert Schreuder, and Samuel Buttrick: Common ground and the understanding of demonstrative reference. *Journal of Verbal Learning and Verbal Behavior*, 22:245–258.

Comrie 1981. Bernard Comrie: *Language universals and linguistic typology: syntax and morphology*. Blackwell, Oxford.

Dekker 1997. Paul Dekker: On denoting descriptions. ILLC Research Report and Technical Notes Series #LP-97-02, Institute for Logic, Language and Computation, University of Amsterdam.

Donnellan 1966. Keith Donnellan: Reference and definite descriptions. *Philosophical Review* 75:281–304.

Evans 1977. Gareth Evans: Pronouns, quantifiers and relative clauses (I). *Canadian Journal of Philosophy*, 7:467–536.

Evans 1980. Gareth Evans: Pronouns. *Linguistic Inquiry* 11(2):337–362.

Fillmore 1975. Charles J. Fillmore: Santa Cruz Lectures on Deixis, 1971. Indiana University Linguistics Club.

Fraurud 1990. Kari Fraurud: Definiteness and the processing of NP's in natural discourse. *Journal of Semantics* 7:395–433.

Grice 1957. H. P. Grice: Meaning. *Philosophical Review* 66:377–88. Reprinted in D.D. Steinberg and L.A. Jakobovits (Eds.) *Semantics: An interdisciplinary reader in philosophy, lingguistics and psychology*. Cambridge University Press., 53–59. And in H.P. Grice, *Studies in the Way of Words*, 217–223.

Groenendijk and Stokhof 1990. Jeroen Groenendijk and Martin Stokhof: Dynamic Montague Grammar. In L. Kálman and L. Pólos (Eds.) *Papers from the Second Symposium on Logic and Language*. Adakémiai Kiadó, Budapest, 3–48.

Heim 1982. Irene Heim: *The Semantics of Definite and Indefinite Noun Phrases*. Ph.D. dissertation, University of Massachusetts at Amherst.

Heim 1983. Irene Heim: On the projection problem for presuppositions. In M. Barlow, D. Flickinger, and M. Wescoat (Ed.), *Second Annual West*

Coast Conference on Formal Linguistics, 114–125. Stanford University.

Heim 1985. Irene Heim: Direct reference explained away. Unpublished ms., University of Texas at Austin.

Heim 1990. Irene Heim: E-type pronouns and donkey anaphora. *Linguistics and Philosophy*, 13:137–177.

Heim 1992. Irene Heim: Presupposition projection and the semantics of attitude verbs. *Journal of Semantics* 9:183–221.

Isaard 1975. Stephen Isaard: Changing the context. In Edward L. Keenan (Ed.) *Formal Semantics of Natural Language*. Cambridge: Cambridge University Press, 287–296.

Jackendoff 1983. Ray Jackendoff: *Semantics and cognition*. MIT Press, Cambridge, MA.

Kadmon 1987. Nirit Kadmon: *On Unique and Non-Unique Reference and Asymmetric Quantification*. Ph.D. dissertation. UMass, Amherst.

Kadmon 1990. Nirit Kadmon: Uniqueness. *Linguistics and Philosophy* 13:273–324.

Kamp 1971. Hans Kamp: Formal properties of 'Now'. *Theoria* 37:227–273.

Kamp 1981. Hans Kamp: A theory of truth and semantic representation. In Jeroen Groenendijk, Theo M. V. Janssen, and Martin Stokhof (Eds.), *Formal Methods in the Study of Language*. Amsterdam: Mathematische Centrum.

Kaplan 1977. David Kaplan: Demonstratives, draft #2. Ms., UCLA Philosophy Department. Revised and published as: Demonstratives: An essay on the semantics, logic, metaphysics, and epistemology of demonstratives and other indexicals. In Joseph Almog, John Perry, and Howard Wettstein (Eds.) *Themes from Kaplan*, Oxford University Press, 1989, pp.481–563.

Kaplan 1978. David Kaplan: Dthat. In Peter Cole (Eds.) *Syntax and Semantics Volume 9*, Academic Press, New York, pp.221–43.

Kamp and Reyle 1993. Hans Kamp and Uwe Reyle: *From Discourse to Logic: An introduction to modeltheoretic semantics of natural language, formal logic and Discourse Representation Theory*. Dordrecht: Kluwer.

Karttunen 1973. Lauri Karttunen: Presuppositions of compound sentences. *Linguistic Inquiry* 4:169–193.

Karttunen 1976. Lauri Karttunen: Discourse referents. In James D. McCawley (Ed.) *Syntax and Semantics, Volume 7: Notes from the Linguistic Underground*. Academic Press, New York, 363–385.

Kratzer 1981. Angelica Kratzer: The notional category of modality. In H. J. Eikmeyer and H. Rieser (Eds.) *Words, Worlds and Contexts*. de Gruyter, Berlin, 38–74.

Kratzer 1989. Angelica Kratzer: An investigation into the lumps of thought.

Linguistics and Philosophy 12:607–653.

Kripke 1977. Saul Kripke: Speaker's reference and semantic reference. In P.A. French, T.E. Uehling and H.K. Wettstein (Eds.) *Contemporary Perspectives in the Philosophy of Language.* University of Minnesota Press, Minneapolis.

Lewis 1973. David Lewis: *Counterfactuals.* Harvard University Press.

Lewis 1979. David Lewis: Score-keeping in a language game. In Rainer Bauerle, Urs Egli and Arnim von Stechow (Eds.) *Semantics from a Different Point of View.* Springer, Berlin.

Löbner 1987: Sebastian Löbner: Definites. *Journal of Semantics* 4:279–326.

Lyons 1977. John Lyons: *Semantics.* Cambridge University Press.

Maclaran 1982. Rose Maclaran: *The Semantics and Pragmatics of the English Demonstratives.* Ph.D. dissertation, Cornell University.

Neale 1990. Stephen Neale: *Descriptions.* MIT Press (Bradford Books), Cambridge, MA.

Neale 1990b. Stephen Neale: Descriptive Pronouns and Donkey Anaphora. *Journal of Philosophy* 87.3:113–150.

Nunberg 1977. Geoffrey D. Nunberg: *The Pragmatics of Reference.* Ph.D. dissertation, City University of New York.

Nunberg 1993. Geoffrey D. Nunberg: Indexicality and deixis, *Linguistics and Philosophy* 16:1–43.

Perry 1977. John Perry: Frege on Demonstratives. *Philosophical Review* 86:474–97.

Poesio and Vieira 1998. Massimo Poesio and Renata Vieira: A Corpus-Based Investigation of Definite Description Use. *Computational Linguistics* 24.2.

Roberts 1987. Craige Roberts: *Modal Subordination, Anaphora, and Distributivity.* Ph.D. dissertation, University of Massachusetts at Amherst. Reprinted with extensive revisions, 1990, Garland Press (Outstanding Dissertations in Linguistics Series), New York.

Roberts 1995. Craige Roberts: Domain restriction in dynamic semantics. In Emmon Bach, Eloise Jelinek, Angelika Kratzer and Barbara H. Partee (Eds.) *Quantification in Natural Languages*, Kluwer, Dordrecht, 661–700.

Roberts 1996. Craige Roberts: Anaphora in intensional contexts. In Shalom Lappin (Ed.) *The Handbook of Contemporary Semantic Theory.* Blackwell, Oxford, 215–246.

Roberts 1996b. Craige Roberts: Information Structure: Towards an integrated theory of formal pragmatics. In Jae-Hak Yoon and Andreas Kathol (Eds.) *OSU Working Papers in Linguistics, Volume 49: Papers in Semantics.* The Ohio State University Department of Linguistics.

Roberts 1998. Craige Roberts: The place of Centering in a general theory of anaphora resolution. In Walker et al. (Eds.), *Centering Theory in Discourse*, Oxford University Press.359–400.

Roberts (to appear). Craige Roberts: Uniqueness presuppositions in definite noun phrases. To appear in *Linguistics and Philosophy.*

Russell 1905. Bertrand Russell: On denoting. *Mind*, 66:479–93.

Sperber and Wilson 1986: Dan Sperber and Deirdre Wilson: *Relevance: Communication and Cognition.* Harvard University Press.

Stalnaker 1974. Robert Stalnaker: Pragmatic presuppositions. In M. Munitz and D. Unger (Eds.) *Semantics and Philosophy.* New York University Press, 197–219.

Stalnaker 1974. Robert Stalnaker: Assertion. In Peter Cole (Ed.) *Syntax and Semantics 9*, Academic Press, New York.

Strawson 1950. P.F. Strawson: On referring. *Mind* 59:320–344.

Von Fintel 1994. Kai von Fintel: *Restrictions on Quantifier Domains.* Ph.D. dissertation, University of Massachusetts at Amherst.

Walker 1993. Marilyn A. Walker: *Informational Redundancy and Resource Bounds in Discourse.* Ph.D. dissertation, University of Pennsylvania.

5

The use of emphatic reflexives with NPs in English

CASSANDRE CRESWELL

5.1 Introduction[1]

Many languages have a special morphological form which can be used with an NP as a marker of emphasis. In English a reflexive pronoun can serve this purpose.[2] The question this presents for natural language generation (NLG) is: Why do speakers choose to use an emphatic with an NP form instead of a "plain" NP?

The claim of this paper is that this emphasis is a pragmatic phenomenon and, as such, the answer to this question is crucially dependent on the beliefs of the speaker and addressee about (1) which entities in the discourse model are important, either because of their properties or because of their role in the discourse, and (2) how what is predicated of these important entities relates to what is predicated of other less important entities. In order to generate these forms, these beliefs must be part of the knowledge base used in the generation of a text.

[1]The analysis here has profited greatly from the comments of many others, including Jim Alexander, Miriam Eckert, Karin Golde, Ellen Prince, Maribel Romero, Matthew Stone, two anonymous reviewers, and the editors of this volume. My investigation of emphatic reflexives began as part of Georgia Green's thesis seminar at the University of Illinois, 1996-1997; as such, additional thanks go to the members of that group, not least to Georgia herself.

[2]See Golde (1999b) for an analysis of the diachronic development of the *self* morpheme in English from solely an intensifying function to both a reflexive and an intensive (emphatic) function.

Information Sharing: Reference and Presupposition in Language Generation and Interpretation.
Edited by Kees van Deemter and Rodger Kibble.

Although the generation of intensive reflexives is only a small part of the larger task of generating nominal expressions, many of the factors that are relevant to the former are also relevant to the more general problem of NLG. Determining and keeping track of how predicates, entities, and events are related to each other is relevant in the generation of scalar particles like *even* and *only* (König, 1991), accent placement signaling contrastive focus (Theune, 2000; Schwarzschild, 1999; among others) or scalar implicature (Hirschberg, 1985), and syntactic forms with special discourse functions, such as topicalization and left-dislocation (Prince, 1998).

The paper is structured as follows. Section 5.2 characterizes the most general conditions motivating speakers' use of the emphatic reflexive form based on a small corpus of naturally occurring data.[3] Section 5.3 discusses infelicitous usages of emphatic reflexives. Previous analyses of emphatic reflexives have claimed that these forms may not be used when referring to discourse new referents or when the referring NP is indefinite or deictic (Leskosky, 1972; Verheijen, 1986; McKay, 1991; Baker, 1995; Kemmer, 1995). In fact, these conditions are not independent, inviolable constraints on the use of emphatic reflexives, rather they follow from what makes the use of an intensive felicitous. Finally, Section 5.4 presents an algorithm for the generation of intensive reflexives based on a discourse entity's membership and role in a set of conceptually-related entities.

5.2 Reasons for the use of intensive reflexives

5.2.1 The phenomenon

Emphatic reflexives may appear in several syntactic positions. This analysis will discuss only appositive reflexives,[4] those that immediately follow their NP antecedent, as in (1),[5] but not those that may appear away from their NP antecedent as in (2).

(1) a. **The president herself** led the discussion at the most recent meeting.

b. Fred lives in the suburbs, not in **the city itself**.

[3]The corpus used for this work consists of approximately eighty tokens. Of these, thirty-three are from home repair manuals, and twelve are from an agricultural extension service web site. The remainder are from news articles and novels. The sources of examples from this corpus are indicated in the footnotes.

[4]Although there have been syntactic analyses of intensive reflexives (Verheijen, 1989), the term *appositive* should not be construed as a description of the syntactic behavior of this form.

[5]The boldface type used in example sentences does not indicate intonational prominence.

(2) a. **He** will **himself** attend the concert.
b. **My dog** knows how to open the gate **himself** if it's left unlocked.
c. **Myself, I** love chocolate cake.

Appositive reflexives may appear following an NP in almost any argument position (subject, object, object of a preposition); the other types of emphatic reflexives can only have an NP in subject position as an antecedent.

5.2.2 Prominence and Contrast: why speakers use emphatics

Speakers use emphatics felicitously only when their addressee can infer from the context that (1) the referent is the most prominent of a set of related entities and (2) the predication they are making about this prominent entity contrasts with some other salient predication in the discourse model. The meaning of these terms *prominence* and *contrast* will be defined as precisely as possible in the following section in order to be incorporated into the algorithm laid out in the final section of the paper.

Because other researchers have arrived at essentially the same two factors, specifically Baker (1991) and Golde (1999a), the contribution of this paper is not the claim that these two factors are the crucial conditions for the use of intensive reflexives. The difference between the present study and previous analyses is that here the role of speaker and addressee beliefs as felicity conditions on the usage of these forms is made explicit. In order to generate these forms and others like it, a way of determining and formalizing these beliefs computationally must be devised. This paper is a preliminary attempt at this determination and formalization.

A map for this section of the paper is as follows. First, it describes what it means to be prominent, and then what it means to contrast with other predications. It ends with a brief discussion of what this prominence and contrastiveness have been confused or conflated—possibly quite reasonably—with in the past.

Prominent member of a set of related entities

Speakers use appositive reflexives to emphasize the particular importance within the discourse of the referent of the reflexive's antecedent NP. This *particular importance* has been referred to variously as discourse prominence, literal prominence, and metalinguistic prominence (Baker, 1995; Kemmer, 1995: Golde, 1999a). For the use of an intensive to be felicitous, the addressee must be able to infer the speaker's beliefs about the referent's prominent status within the discourse model.

In the participants' shared understanding of the discourse context, certain entities are more prominent than others. The speaker assumes that the addressee shares (or can reasonably be expected to understand) the belief that the entity referred to with an intensive is prominent and understands the criteria on which this prominence depends.

Prominence might depend on a variety of possible criteria. The entity referred to might be the **main character** in a text, the narrator, or the character whose point of view is being represented, as in (3), where Archer is both the main character and the person whose point of view is represented. The criteria may be based on sociological prominence, i.e. the entity referred to is **important in the real world**: the boss, the president, the pope, a celebrity, as in (4). The entity can be the main topic of the discourse, that is the **global center of attention** (Grosz and Sidner, 1986),[6] as in (5). The entity could also be some sort of **conceptual focus** (Langaker, 1993; Kemmer, 1995; Golde, 1999a); for example, the word *cigar* in a discussion of slang and terminology related to cigars, as in (6a), or the septic tank in a septic system, as in (6b).

(3) *Context: Archer is the main character of the story and the story is told from his point of view*
'...Archer knew that Mrs. Welland was thinking: "It's a mistake for Ellen to be seen, the very day after her arrival, parading up Fifth Avenue at the crowded hour with Julius Beaufort—"and **the young man himself** [=Archer] mentally added: "And she [=Ellen] ought to know that a man who's just engaged doesn't spend his time calling on married women."'(Wharton)[7]

(4) a. *Context: Article about the way CEO Dan Evans runs the Bob Evans Sausage Company*
'As chairman, Dan Evans cultivates a folksy feeling in the campus-like, red-brick headquarters building, where male executives are required to wear old-fashioned string ties and where **Dan himself** wears cowboy boots.' (*Wall Street Journal* 10/22/96)

b. *Context: Article about George Lucas, director of the* Star Wars *films*
'Forget for a moment the Trilogy's trinity: Obi-Wan, Luke and Yoda. To meet **the deity himself** [=George Lucas], first you

[6]As opposed to the local center of attention; see section 5.2.4 for discussion of this difference.

[7]Wharton: Wharton, Edith. 1993. *The age of innocence.* New York: Collier.

have to make the pilgrimage to Skywalker Ranch, George Lucas's hideaway headquarters 30 minutes north of San Francisco.' (*Newsweek*, 1/20/97)

(5) *Context: Informational page about the effects of the verticillium fungus*
'Verticillium enters the plant through the roots and moves into the vascular system. Vascular tissue carries nutrients and water up and down the plant. **The fungus itself** [= verticillium] may block the vascular system, it may produce a toxin or cause the plant to produce a toxin.' ("Leaf Wilting (Verticillium Wilt)", UW extension service)[8]

(6) a. 'Words descriptive of cigars — including **the word *cigar* itself**, the ultimate etymology of which is uncertain — are typically Spanish, Spain having been the conduit of the cigar's introduction to Europe.' (*The Atlantic Monthly*, 11/1996)

b. 'Once a sanitary permit has been obtained, your septic system can be installed. Since most system failures that occur in less than a year are the result of poor construction methods and materials, careful attention is needed to have a dependable system. **The septic tank itself** must be of a design and construction approved by the State of Wisconsin, whether it is cast in place or purchased ready-made.'("Septic systems: Installation and Inspection", UW extension service)

As can be seen in these examples, the criteria may overlap; the global topic of discussion may in fact also be a sociologically-prominent person, as in (4), where Dan Evans and George Lucas (and their respective enterprises) are in fact the topics of the articles. In (5) the fungus verticillium is the topic of discussion, but in a discussion of a disease, its physical manifestation, its victim, and the symptoms it causes, the disease (in this case the fungus) will be a 'prominent conceptualization'.

Although it is quite easy to illustrate what one means by *prominence* by means of example, formalizing this notion is quite difficult. With the wide range of referents seen in the corpus (and illustrated in the above examples), the most specific characterization possible of what it means to be prominent is the one given at the beginning of this section: 'to be mutually regarded as prominent by the participants in a discourse'. This definition is both self-referential and relativized to both the context of the discourse and the world knowledge of the speaker and addressee, that is the belief sets of the discourse participants about the discourse

[8] UW EXTENSION SERVICE: http://www.uwex.edu/disted/infosrce/index.html

and the world.

Hence, formalizing the concept of prominence necessarily relies on a somewhat ad hoc designation of a feature [prominent]. For generation purposes, entities in a database would be distinguished as [+/- prominent] perhaps based in part on an empirically-derived set of rules. Such rules might be more or less domain specific. One might wish to institute the following rule, for example:

Rule: The global topic/center of attention of a text should be designated as [+prominent].

This rule would be applied in combination with a rule for determining the global topic of a text.

In contrast, one might make a more domain-specific subrule for use in generating texts on home repair:

Rule: The entity to be repaired (e.g. the wall, the roof, the ceiling, the toilet) should be designated as [+prominent].

Other possible 'rules of thumb' for designating a prominent entity will be discussed in Section 4.

One additional aspect of prominence is that an entity can only be important relative to other entities; and so, asserting that the referent of the NP is prominent means it must be a distinguished member of a set of (somehow) related entities. As such the [prominent] attribute would require not only a +/- value but also a subattribute [relative to] whose value would be a set of entities.

5.2.3 Contrast

Prominence is not the only factor in the usage of emphatic reflexives. As mentioned above, a contrastiveness condition also holds. Not every reference to the prominent entity in a set may be marked with an intensive reflexive. An emphatic form is only appropriate when a predication is made of the prominent referent, and a salient and related predication holds of some other entity or entities in the relevant set of contrasting entities.

Here two questions arise: what counts as a relevant set of contrasting entities and what counts as a salient, related predication. The related set of entities will be derived in the course of deciding which entity is prominent because, as mentioned above, prominence is a relative quality. This is discussed further in the final section of the paper. The second issue is not unique to the use of emphatic reflexives. It arises in all analyses of what has been variously termed *contrast, kontrast, contrastive focus*, or *semantic focus* (Theune, 2000; Vallduvi and Vilkuna, 1998; Schwarzschild, 1999). The terms *contrast* and *focus* are used to characterize an array of concepts. Here the term *contrast* is used to refer to the situation described above: one where the predication made of the prominent entity is salient in the discourse because this same predication has been or will be (explicitly or implicitly) made of another entity in the discourse. This is a semantic or conceptual characterization of focus, not a phonological one.[9] We will now examine the different types of contrasting predications that emphatic reflexives are used with by looking at some naturally-occuring examples.

The most basic type of related predication is simply when the same predicate P holds of the prominent entity and some member(s) of its containing set, as in (7).[10] In addition, P may not hold of the prominent entity but does hold of some other member of the containing set (or vice versa), as in (8). Another more complicated possibility is when P holds of the prominent entity and Q, a predicate that is somehow similar to P, holds (or does not hold) of a member of the contrasting set, as in (9). The two predicates Q and P may even be related only as conceptual opposites, as in (10).

(7) a. $P =$ Sold in Tube holds of $x =$ 'the glue' and $y =$ 'a hardener'
'Epoxy adhesives are sold in two tubes, **the glue itself** and a hardener.'(DK)[11]

b. $P =$ Not Safest Place For the Sake Of holds of $x=$ 'the product' and $y =$ 'our children and pets'
'But these may not be the safest places either for the sake of our children and pets, or for **the product itself**.'("Pesticides: Storage", UW extension service)

(8) $P =$ Is Something to Look Forward To holds of $x =$ 'it'; $\neg P$ holds of $y =$ 'lunch'
'It's my lunchtime reading, so progress is slow, but it's something to look forward to everyday (**lunch itself** isn't).' (email, G.G. 121696)

[9]The relation between pitch accent, or phonological focus, placement and emphatic reflexives is complex and falls outside of the strictly written corpus used here. It is briefly touched on at the end of this section. However, because pitch accent placement and semantic focus are closely related, many of the insights on semantic focus derived from the investigation of the generation of pitch accents in English will be relevant to the description of contrast here.

[10]It appears that the two entities should fill the same argument position in their respective predications. See footnote 22 for one exception to this.

[11]DK: McGowan, John and Roger DuBern. 1991. *The DK Pocket Encyclopedia. Home Repair.* London: Dorling Kindersley. Scanned by Joseph Rosenzweig, February 1994.

(9) a. P = Granite holds of x = 'the steps;; Q = Brick holds of y = 'the building'
'We climbed the four granite steps before the Research Laboratory. **The building itself** was of unadorned brick and rose six stories. We passed between two heavily-armed guards at the entrance.'(Vonnegut)[12]

b. P = Split holds of x = 'the wood'; Q = Open Up holds of y = 'the joints'
'Instead of **the wood itself** splitting, the glued joints may open up.' (DK)

(10) a. P = Consider Literature Compromising holds of x = 'they'; Q = Has No Fear of Literature holds of y = 'She'
'She supposed they considered literature compromising. **She herself** had no fears of it.' (Wharton)

b. P = The Women Are Gracious Towards holds of x = 'the person who had caused them harm'; Q = Is Slighted by The Women holds of y = 'Elinor'
'Elinor could not but smile to see the graciousness of the women towards the very person who, unbeknownst to them, had caused them such harm; while **she herself** [= Elinor], who had comparatively little power to wound them, sat pointedly slighted by both.'(Baker's (37)a, Golde (1999a)'s (2)e)

A final type of relation between predications found with emphatic reflexives is when the related predication is only implicit in the discourse. It is part of the discourse model only on the basis of the speakers' and hearers' beliefs and inferences about the discourse context and the world.

For example, in (11), the addressee must infer from the fact that the battens will be nailed to the timber uprights in the walls, that these uprights will be providing support for the battens; this is the predication related to the predicate Not Giving Adequate Support For x that holds of the plasterboard.

(11) P = Give Adequate Support for Battens holds of x = 'the timber uprights'; $\neg P$ holds of y = 'the plasterboard'
'Replacing sheet panelling: ...If, however, you are fitting this type of panelling on to a partition wall, the simplest method is to remove any wallpaper and stick the sheets directly on to the wall. If you prefer to use battens, you should find the timber uprights in the wall and nail the battens to these. **The plasterboard itself** cannot give adequate support for the battens.'(DK)

[12] VONNEGUT: Vonnegut, Kurt. 1998. *Cat's cradle*. Delta.

Another example where the related predication is only implicit is (12). Here, the addressee must have a belief that the book that the narrator is reading could also give a picture of the life of Mona Aamons.

(12) P = Give a Picture Of holds of both x = 'the index' and y = 'the book'
Context: The narrator is reading the index of a book about Mona Aamons.
'CHAPTER 55: NEVER INDEX YOUR OWN BOOK
As for the life of Aamons, Mona, **the index itself** gave a jangling, surrealistic picture of the many conflicting forces that had been brought to bear on her and of her dismayed reactions to them.' (Vonnegut)

In (11–12) the other entities of which something is implicitly predicated have been explicitly evoked in the discourse. Even this, however, is not required. In (13), the first sentence of a newspaper article, not only is the related predication implicit, the entities themselves have not been evoked.

(13) P = Consigned to Scrap Heap holds of both x = 'the program' and y = 'nonrecycled entities'
'Urbana was one of the first cities in Illinois to adopt a recycling program. Now **the program itself** may be consigned to the scrap heap.' ("Recycling: Will Urbana scrap the U-cycle program?" *The Octopus*, 1996.)

For (13) to be felicitous, the addressee must share the belief that entities that are not recycled are thrown away, i.e. consigned to the scrap heap and—in a discussion of recycling—must accommodate the existence of entities that are recycled and entities that are not recycled as part of the discourse model.

The saliency of the related predication about other members of the set may be quite weak. When the distinguished member is somehow important in almost any context, almost any predication about the prominent entity can somehow evoke an implicit related predication, as in (14a–14b).

(14) a. P = Sent Burns Into Their Lives holds of x = 'Fate' and y = ??
'Lite said that [Burns had no business being there] because he [= Lite] was not given the power to peer into the future, and so could not know that **Fate herself** had sent Robert Grant Burns into their lives.'(Golde (1999a)'s (1b))

b. P = Defecated Schiele Into Classroom holds of x = 'the devil' and y = ??

'Cried one professor after a few months of Student Schiele's tantrums and rebellion: "**The devil himself** must have defecated you into my classroom!"'(Golde(1999a)'s (1c); Brown Corpus)

Golde (1999a) accounts for the absence of a contrasting predication in examples like (14) by separating a requirement for prominence into two types: 'literal', prominence based on some discourse-independent criteria; and 'metalinguistic', prominence based on the referent's role in the discourse. In the case of the former, Golde claims there must only be some sort of noteworthiness with respect to (some unspecified set of) more 'humble' figures, rather than some more salient contrastive predication.[13]

Treating this class of usages as a separate type of intensive reflexive may not be not necessary. These apparently 'contrast-less' usages could instead be explained as the speaker expecting the hearer to accommodate the saliency of some related predicate. The requirement of contrast, i.e. that a related predication about some other less prominent entity must be salient, is then met merely on the basis of beliefs that the speaker can reasonably expect the addressee to accommodate.

Support for such a claim can be found in the pitch accent used with intensive reflexives. Intensive reflexives, and in particular the 'prominent in any context' type, as in (14), appear to require the placement of contrastive stress on the intensive. For example, no matter how noteworthy it is for the pope to come to dinner, simply using *the pope himself* without any contrastive accent on the intensive seems infelicitous. In other words, even when 15a is uttered out of the blue, it is odd to mark the subject as thematic and the predicate as new (or the entire utterance as new). To be felicitous, the pitch accent needs to be positioned on the intensive, as in 15b, leaving the predicate as an open proposition with the pitch accent marking the subject NP as the variable to be instantiated (Pierrehumbert and Hirschberg, 1990).

(15) a. #By the way, **the pope himself** is invited for DINner tonight. I think I'll make chicken casserole.

b. By the way, **the pope HIMSELF** is invited for dinner tonight, so you'd better wear a tie and maybe consider shaving for once.

Contrastive stress is licensed in exactly the case where the open

[13]Baker (1995) also implicitly recognizes the fact that in some usages there is no apparent contrast by including emphasis in his Contrastiveness Condition:

Contrastiveness Condition: Intensive NPs are appropriate only in contexts in which *emphasis* or contrast is desired. (italics mine)

proposition (or predication) is given, i.e. discourse or hearer-old. In other words, the hearer is expected to already be considering (or to accommodate) the fact that the given predicate holds of some x. As such, the placement of contrastive stress on the intensified NP is evidence that the predicate, as part of a given open proposition, should be taken as contextually salient; the relevant set of entities are anything else that could be an instantiation of x. The uses of emphatic reflexives that Golde characterizes as lacking contrast in the discourse context may simply depend on intonation to signal an implicit contrast should be accommodated rather than having it provided as part of the previous discourse model.

In fact, the use of emphatic reflexives in general may require the use of contrastive pitch accent. Whether such a usage is informationally-redundant or whether emphatic reflexives in actuality contribute only a 'meaning' of prominence (and the contrastiveness assumed here is contributed by the phonological focus) remains an open question. Because the tokens in the present corpus are all from written texts, an empirically-based characterization of the correlation between contrastive accent placement and emphatic reflexives remains a topic for future research.

5.2.4 What prominence is not

This section revisits the issue of defining prominence. In order to further clarify what discourse prominence is, it is differentiated from what it is not: topichood, referential accessibility, or a shift of an entity from background to foreground.

Topichood

Golde (1999a) defines discourse prominence as 'referentially accessible, e.g. a topic'. *Topic*, however, is a notoriously vague and ill-defined concept. As such, evaluating Golde's claim that discourse prominence correlates with intensive usage is only possible if topichood can be formally defined.[14]

Perhaps the most useful formalization of topichood, in the sense of pragmatic aboutness is to be found in centering theory (Joshi and Weinstein, 1981; Grosz, Joshi and Weinstein, 1995; Walker, Joshi, and Prince;

[14]It should be noted that Golde herself makes no claims about the correlation between local topichood and the use of the intensive form. Following Kemmer (1995), Golde's usage of the term *topic* appears to be in the sense either of global discourse topic or some sort of cognitive anchoring point for a group of conceptually-related entities (Langacker, 1993). This type of topichood appears to be closer to what it means to be prominent for the purposes of intensive marking, as discussed above. However, in light of the predilection to conflate the notions of topichood and discourse prominence, it seems useful, to include this discussion of how local topichood and prominence differ.

1998), which provides an objective way of characterizing coherent discourse in terms of transitions between local centers of attention at each point in a discourse. Prince (1999) uses the concepts of a backward-looking center, C_b, or preferred center, C_p, as a formal correlate of topichood, in the sense of what a given utterance is about (Reinhart, 1981). In English, the usual ranking algorithm for members of an utterance's list of forward-looking centers (a determining factor in what is allowed to be the C_b or C_p of an utterance) is based on grammatical relations, with grammatical subject ranked highest on the list (Brennan, Friedman and Pollard, 1987). Every non-discourse-initial utterance has a C_b, and every utterance has a C_p. According to the Pronoun Rule, if anything in the utterance is pronominalized, the C_b must be.

As mentioned in section 5.2.1, intensive reflexives can modify full NPs or pronouns in any grammatical role. As such, in the absence of any cooccurrence restriction on intensifiers and grammatical subjecthood or pronominalization, one would a priori not expect a connection between local topichood and the use of intensives. This claim must be tested systematically on a set of naturally occurring data. Regardless of whether a correlation is found, however, local topichood cannot be used in characterizing the set of conditions which license the use of an intensive reflexive with an NP.[15]

Referential accessibility

Prominence cannot be reduced to referential accessibility. At a given point in a discourse, there may be numerous entities that are referentially accessible to the participants, but an intensive cannot be used with just any referentially accessible entity. For example, in the second sentence of (16) both *Aunt Sara* and *the Smiths* are pronominalizable. But in the third sentence, only the pronoun referring to Aunt Sara may be used with an intensive reflexive, not the pronoun referring to *the Smiths*.

(16) a. Aunt Sara doesn't approve of the way her neighbors, the Smiths, are raising their children. After their son Timmy crashed his car, they bought him a new one immediately. **She (herself)** would never have done such a thing.

b. Aunt Sara doesn't approve of the way her neighbors, the Smiths, are raising their children. After their son Timmy crashed his car, she would never have bought him a new car right away, but **they (# themselves)** bought him a new one immediately.

[15]A study of the correlation between syntactic position and use of emphatic reflexives could, however, provide a statistical distribution of intensive reflexives that could then be incorporated into a probabilistic generation algorithm.

Under the assumption that the ability to be referred to with a pronoun is a mark of referential accessibility, one would assume that using an intensive should be equally acceptable in (16)a-b. As this is not the case, we can rule out referential accessibility as a factor in the use of intensive reflexives. As will be discussed below, referential accessibility (or cognitive status) is a contributing factor in the felicity of the use of an intensive, but, clearly, not one of the motivating factors in why a speaker chooses to use an intensive.

Foregrounding Referent Used with Emphatic

Kemmer (1995) claims that the contrastive aspect of the use of emphatic reflexives is the result of the intensive being used to signal a shift in attention from some other less important entity back to the entity referred to with the intensive. Support for her claim comes from uses of intensive reflexives that follow a pattern, like that in (17), where a predication P is made of an entity a and then of the prominent entity b (e.g. *Not just* $P(a)$ *but* $P(b$ *itself)*; $P(a)$ *and also* $P(b$ *itself)*; $P(a)$ *rather than* $P(b$ *itself)*; $P(a)$ *but not* $P(b$ *itself))*.

(17) a. 'A summer mulch can be placed in the aisles between rows. Be sure to leave **the row itself** free of mulch.'("Strawberries: Renovation," UW extension service)

b. 'Consider putting outdoor security lights on poles away from your house rather than on **the house itself**.'("Spiders," UW extension service)

In many cases, however, the predication about the distinguished entity takes place *before* the predication about a member of the related set, as in (18a) repeated from above and (18b). In both of these examples, the emphasized NP appears in a sentence-initial subordinate clause. Entities which have a related predication made of them, *the glued joints* and *new supporting battens* respectively, appear in the following main clause.

(18) a. 'Any furniture which has solid panels is designed to cope with the fact that the wood will shrink across the grain. However, if the panel is held too rigidly, shrinkage will occur and the panel will eventually split. You can fill a narrow split by opening it up slightly with the point of a tenon saw, then tapping in a piece of glued veneer and planing it smooth with the surface. In some pieces of furniture, the base frame or drawer runners prevent movement. Instead of **the wood itself** splitting, the glued joints may open up. If the gap is wide enough, choose a strip of matching timber that is slightly wider than the open

joint and plane a shallow taper along it. Scrape out the old glue from the joint with a knife blade, put glue on the strip and tap it into the gap until it jams in tightly.' (DK)

b. 'Panelling provides a simple way of levelling an irregular wall surface and requires little attention...Apart from **the panelling itself**, you will probably need to attach new supporting battens to the wall. These can be unplaned as they will be concealed under the panelling. If the battens are for an exterior wall, it is worth getting the timber treated with preservative so that it will not rot.'(DK)

In neither of these examples is there a shift from some other center-of-attention to the referent of the intensified NP. Example (18a) is from a text about repairing split panels in wooden furniture. The previous context, as shown, discusses these panels. The text that immediately follows the use of the intensive explains how to fill a joint that has opened up. The best characterization of this change is not that *the wood* is now the center of attention, but rather that there is a shift in attention from the panels to the glued joints.

Example (18b) comes from a text segment on replacing panelling. The two preceding paragraphs discuss the use of panelling in general and specific types of panelling. The paragraph introduced with the clause in which the emphatic reflexive appears discusses battens. There is no shift after the use of *the panelling itself* to a focus on panelling.

It seems wrong to characterize either of these uses as a shift in attention from some other entities to the entity referred to with an intensive. If anything, the position of the intensified NPs in these examples—that is in subordinate or adverbial clauses that precede their main clause—is one usually associated with given, presupposed, or backgrounded information (Geis, 1986; Horn, 1986), not with content to be foregrounded. Speakers, then, are not using intensives to signal a shift in the 'center of attention' of a discourse to the intensified NP's referent.

5.3 Infelicitous usages of intensives

This section outlines the conditions under which a speaker's use of an intensive reflexive will be infelicitous. Section 5.3.1 explains why an intensive reflexive will be unacceptable in the absence of understandable beliefs about a referent's prominence or about a contrasting predication. Section 5.3.2 argues that the use of an intensive will also be pragmatically odd when the cognitive status of a referent is such that it does not reasonably allow an addressee to have such beliefs.

5.3.1 Absence of shared beliefs about prominence and contrast

If an addressee does not share the beliefs of the speaker about the referent's place within a set of related entities (prominence), or about the availability of a salient, related predication made of another entity in that set (contrast), that is he either does not understand them, disagrees with them, or cannot accommodate them (Lewis, 1979), then the use of an intensive form will seem odd. A felicitous use of an appositive reflexive depends on the addressee understanding both of these factors. Neither of the factors discussed in section 5.2 are by themselves a sufficient condition for use, but both are necessary for a felicitous usage. When a shared understanding of either prominence or contrastiveness is absent, the usage of an intensive is unacceptable, as the following examples demonstrate.

Example (19) shows that even when an entity has prominence, if the context does not supply an understandable contrast, the usage of an intensive will be unacceptable.

(19) 'When cold water enters a toilet and meets the warm air of the bathroom, the tank or bowl may sweat. To reduce sweating, empty the tank, dry it thoroughly, and line it with 1/2-inch polystyrene or foam rubber. Use a kit or cut your own liners to fit the tank walls and floor. Glue the liners in place with silicone cement, and let the adhesive dry thoroughly (at least 24 hours) before refilling **the tank** (**#itself**).'(Digest)[16]

In a discussion of how to stop a toilet tank from sweating, the tank is a highly salient entity and the most prominent member of the set of parts of a toilet. There is, however, apparently nothing in this discourse that implies that there is something else in the discourse model of which the predicate *needs to be refilled* (or *not refilled*) holds. Without a related predication, the usage of the intensive sounds odd and leaves the addressee wonder what other event of refilling is relevant here.

The following two examples illustrate the infelicitous use of an intensive reflexive in the absence of beliefs about prominence. In (20), a list of many different types of annual flowers is presented. The text is a piece about growing flowers in general. Accommodating a belief that zinnias are prominent in this context is virtually impossible because there is no reason for the reader to believe that this type of flower, zinnia, is prominent here. Therefore, using an intensive with *zinnia* is unacceptable—

[16]DIGEST: *Reader's Digest New Complete Do-It-Yourself Manual.* 1991. Pleasantville, NY: The Reader's Digest Association. Scanned by Joseph Rosenzweig, March 1994.

even though a related predication Is a Recommended Annual holds of other entities in the discourse.

(20) Both annuals and perennials are commonly planted in cut flower gardens. Some recommended annuals include aster, cornflower, cosmos, dianthus, gomphrena, marigold, scabiosa, and **zinnia (# itself)** ("Cut Flowers: Growing," UW Extension Service)

Example (21) is from a catalog advertisement illustrated with pictures of a model wearing woolen sweaters, posed on a rocky beach, with the ocean in the background.

(21) a. 'Enduring elements/ Hardy texture, neutral tone, muted pattern, a sense of the rocky beach and of **the sea itself**' (J. Crew sales catalog; December, 1996)

b. ?? Enduring elements/ Hardy texture, neutral tone, muted pattern, a sense of the sea and of **the rocky beach itself**

In examples (21)a-b, there is certainly the same (somewhat vague) predication made of both the sea and the beach, that the sweaters shown have a sense of them. In this context though, marking the sea as the most prominent entity is fine. In contrast, referring to the beach with an intensive is odd. The belief that would make this use felicitous—that the beach is somehow more conceptually prominent than the ocean—is not a normal belief (Nunberg, 1978).[17] In contrast, the same belief about the sea is easier to accommodate because 'everyone knows' the sea is an inherently important entity. The rocky beach is not, and it is this extralinguistic fact that makes using intensive marking in (21)a fine, but infelicitous in (21)b.

It should be noted that even when there are shared beliefs about an entity's prominence and the salience of some related predication about nonprominent entities, the use of the form is not obligatory, as shown in (23).

(23) 'There is a wide choice of appliances that offer alternatives to central heating. These include an extensive range of portable electric heaters. They are efficient, easy to move and not expensive to

[17]Leskosky (1972) makes a similar point with the following example:

(22) a. I snubbed Spiro Agnew himself yesterday. (Leskosky's 8)

b. (?) I snubbed my paper boy himself yesterday. (Leskosky's 9)

Leskosky's description of the two sentences is that the former means, 'I snubbed one individual whose importance I wish to emphasize.' He states that a similar reading is not possible in the latter, 'unless one has extreme feelings of inadequacy or unless someone like the editor of the *Tribune* delivers one's papers.' In other words, (22b) is only acceptable if one can accommodate some understandable beliefs about why one's paper boy is important.

buy, although **electricity (itself)** is a costly fuel to use for heating.'(DK)

Its presence or absence has no effect on the truth-conditional meaning of an utterance. Instead, the use of this form allows the speaker to make implicatures about what she believes about an entity, its relation to other entities, and what is predicated of them. Usage of an intensive can play a valuable role in communicating more than just truth-conditional meaning because it communicates additional information about what the speaker assumes about the discourse model.

5.3.2 Constraints on cognitive status and linguistic form

The cognitive status of a referent leads the speaker to choose a certain NP-form (Gundel, Hedberg, and Zacharski, 1993). The scale of cognitive status ranges from *in focus* (e.g. whether attention is focused on the referent) to *familiar* (the addressee has a representation of the referent in memory) to *type identifiable* (the addressee is able to access a representation of the type of object described by the NP), including several intermediate points. Gundel, et al. claim that a speaker uses a particular linguistic form to signal what she assumes the cognitive status of a referent to be. In the corpus of naturally occurring data on which this study is based, appositive reflexives are used with referring expressions of any cognitive status (from type identifiable to in focus) and linguistic form (indefinite NP, definite NP, pronoun, etc.).

This distribution is in contrast with the claim made in previous studies that indefinites and deictics are unacceptable forms for use with an intensive (Baker, 1995) as the contrasts in acceptability in (24) and (25) demonstrate. In addition, it has been claimed that intensives are unacceptable when referring to new entities (Leskosky, 1972; Verheijen, 1986; McKay, 1991; Baker, 1995; Kemmer, 1995).

(24) a. # Our delivery boy saw **an old man himself** sitting in the lobby today.

b. Our delivery boy saw **the old man himself** sitting in the lobby today.

(25) a. # I bought my sandwich from **that food truck itself.**(pointing)

b. I bought my sandwich from **the food truck itself.**

These apparent constraints, in fact, follow from the reasons for use explained above. In order for addressees to understand why speakers are using the intensive form, they must have beliefs about the entity's relation to other entities (in the real world or in the discourse model). In other words they must have some belief that the entity is more important than those other entities and a reason to base this importance on. Speakers cannot reasonably expect addressees to share beliefs about unfamiliar entities (Prince, 1992). To the extent that indefinites and deictics are used to refer to hearer-new entities, they will be unacceptable when used with intensives.[18] When speakers expect that their addressee can make the correct inferences about a new entity, then such an entity can be referred to with an intensive. No inviolable constraints in these cases are necessary.

Intensives and indefinites

An indefinite NP usually serves to pick an arbitrary member out a set of entities and establish it as a discourse referent. The use of an indefinite cannot imply that this arbitrary member is more important than any other entity in the set, and in the absence of an appropriate comparison set such a usage will be unacceptable.

Some indefinites do not simply pick out an arbitrary, hearer-new entity from a set (Prince, 1981; Dahl, 1987); as a result, examples of intensified indefinites, though rare, do occur. The indefinite counterexamples in this corpus fall into two categories, hearer-new tokens of a hearer-old type, as in (27a) where the set of hinges is discourse-old, or generic usages, as in (27b) or (27c).

(27) a. *Context: Section of repair manual on fitting hinges on a door*
'Cutting hinge rebates: [Step 1:] Use **a hinge itself** to trace the dimensions and hole positions [of the hinge rebate] and a try square to draw the lines.'(DK)

b. *Context: Army captain lecturing soldier on the importance of behaving as a member of a group.*
'**A man himself** is worth nothing in this world.'(movie, *A Thin Red Line*, 1998)

c. *Context: Section of repair manual on types of metals*
'All kinds of decorative and utilitarian objects are made in metal, and **metals themselves** differ widely in their nature

[18] Because my corpus consists only of written texts, there are no instances of deictics to support the claim that an intensive could be used felicitously with a deictic. The argument for such a claim is similar to that for the usage of indefinites with intensives. As long as the speaker can reasonably expect the addressee to understand why the referent is prominent, then an intensified form should be acceptable, as shown by the constructed example in (26):

(26) Context: The speaker and addressee are at a party where it is reasonably obvious who the guest of honor is.
'No one seems to be having fun at this party. [Pointing at the guest of honor] **He himself** seems to be completely depressed by the look on his face.'

and value—from the expensive silver of engraved salvers to the cheap cast iron of firedogs.' (DK)

These types of indefinites allow the speaker to safely assume that the hearer shares her beliefs about the entity, as in (27b),[19] the set the entity is a member of, as in (27a), or the set of entities, like (27c). In these cases, the shared belief is that the entity is a distinguished member of a (super)set of relevant entities.

Intensives and discourse-new entities

Entities may be simultaneously hearer-old and discourse-new. In addition, entities with the information status of inferrables are apparently discourse-new but often pattern in usage with discourse-old entities (Prince, 1992; Birner, 1994). Not surprisingly, both hearer-old/discourse new status and inferrable status allow references marked with intensives, as in (28)–(29).

(28) 'There is a wide choice of appliances that offer alternatives to central heating. These include an extensive range of portable electric heaters. They are efficient, easy to move and not expensive to buy, although **electricity itself** is a costly fuel to use for heating.'(DK)

(29) 'Hanging from the middle of the beam was a huge iron hook. There was a sign impaled on the hook. "This hook," the sign proclaimed, "is reserved for **Bokonon himself**."'(Vonnegut)

Electricity in (28), repeated from above, is an inferrable entity because electric heaters were evoked in the previous sentence. In (29), the sign presumably counts as a discourse in and of itself, so Bokonon must have discourse-new information status. The sign painter, however, has an understanding of who will be reading the sign; he or she must assume that the sign reader will know who Bokonon is and why he is important.[20]

5.4 Generating emphatic reflexives

In the previous sections, the type of beliefs that both constrain and motivate a speaker's use of an emphatic reflexive have been presented. Discourse participants must share beliefs about a referent's status in relation to other referents in the discourse and what is being predicated

[19] In this token, it may be that the property that makes the individual here prominent is the very property of being singled out from the set of all men.

[20] The context of this example is that Bokonon is the religious leader of a persecuted religious sect whose members are hung on hooks throughout the countryside where this sign and hook are found. Thus, the appropriate contrasting predicate here is Hook Is Reserved For. The related entities are Bokonon's followers.

of all of these entities.[21] In order to correctly generate these forms, then, the propositional content of such beliefs must be part of the knowledge base used in the generation process.

5.4.1 Background on NP Generation

The implementation of an algorithm that decides when an NP should be marked as intensive would best take place during the sentence planning stage, an intermediate generation stage, that takes place after high-level content generation but before surface generation (Reiter, 1994). This sentence planning level is where operations like lexical choice, construction of referring expressions, descriptive explicitness, and semantic focus assignment have been addressed. (See Prevost (1995) for references.) Determination of NP form is essentially independent of whether the form should be marked as an intensive and could take place before or after an intensive-marking algorithm.

5.4.2 Encoding prominence

In order to implement the algorithm given below for assigning intensive marking, the entities in the database must be associated with conceptual groupings where one member is distinguished as prominent. A similar type of grouping, an *ASet*, or set of alternative entities in a discourse model that belong to the same class, is used in Prevost (1995) for generating pitch accent placement for rhematic and contrastive use of intonation. Here, however, the objects grouped together will not necessarily be of the same type (e.g. the set of different kinds of saws) but will instead belong to some sort of unified conceptual grouping (e.g. the saw, its parts, items that are sawed).

Each grouping designated in the knowledge base will be a subset, proper or otherwise, of the set of all entities in the knowledge base. Possibly groupings could be restricted to the subset of discourse entities that have been evoked in prior discourse, as in Prevost (1995). However, as discussed above, inferrables and brand-new entities may be used with intensives. Therefore, the conceptual groupings might be best based on the set of all entities in the knowledge base, rather than the set of discourse entities evoked in the discourse.

Deciding what the comparison set of entities will be composed of and which member should be distinguished as important will often depend on idiosyncratic world knowledge. However, to some extent, grouping entities and designating prominence will be domain-independent. As such,

[21] The term *share* is of course too strong. Speakers can only operate under the *assumption* that their beliefs are held (or at the very least understandable) by the addressee.

these decisions could be automated to some extent. The following section outlines several possible groupings, noting which could potentially be generated with domain-independent algorithms.

Possible types of conceptual groups

A default grouping could include all entities in the knowledge base that are used in the discourse model, with the global discourse topic as the distinguished member of the concept set. Along similar lines, depending on the discourse type to be generated, the narrator or the main character could be the default distinguished member.

Some conceptual groupings will be only a subset of all entities in the knowledge base. One potentially useful type of subset is a partially-ordered set (poset). Posets are sets whose members can be ordered on the basis of a transitive relation that is either asymmetric and irreflexive or antisymmetric and reflexive (e.g. *is a part of, is a subtype of, is a member of*). In such cases, the highest ranked member of the poset could be designated as the distinguished member. For example, in the set of parts of a book, the entire book would be the distinguished member.

Because partially-ordered sets play an important role in the characterization of the conditions that allow the usage of particular linguistic forms and functions, for example topicalization, left-dislocation, and scalar implicature (Hirschberg,1985; Prince,1998), these types of sets need to be part of a natural language generation system's knowledge base in any case. In some cases, subsets of posets will have to be conceptual groupings themselves. For example, in the set of parts of a septic system, if the poset relation is reflexive, the septic system would be designated as the distinguished member. However, for the purposes of intensive marking, it would be important to have a subset where the septic tank could be assigned distinguished status.

Unlike posets, some conceptual groupings seem to have no well-formalized definition. For instance, a reasonable grouping of entities in a database of diseases might be 'entities related to a disease': the disease, the symptoms it causes, its physical manifestation, its victim, and its chemical byproducts. Here, the disease would be the prominent member of the set. The most prominent member of a generalized form of this type of set would be a 'cognitive anchoring point' (Langacker, 1993; Kemmer, 1995; Golde, 1999a). These kinds of set are highly domain-dependent. They would need to be added on an ad hoc basis to a database.

In some cases, groupings could be automatically generated from the knowledge base: an entity defined in terms of another entity should be grouped with that other entity and the definer marked as distinguished, e.g. the house vs. poles away from the house, the row vs. the aisles between the rows, storage on each side of the motor well vs. the motor well.[22] Such algorithms will depend on the structuring of the propositions in question. For example, in the set made up of two entities, a child and a mother, if the mother is identified as *the child's mother*, then one could then refer to *the child itself*; if the relation is defined in the opposite direction, the other member should be intensified, *the mother's child* and *the mother herself*.

Finally, another type of conceptual grouping will, like the posets, be an ordered grouping. Like the scalar particle *even*, intensive reflexives can be used when the referent of the NP they modify is the endpoint on a scale of likelihood of belonging to the predicate the NP is used with. For example, in (31), the relevant scale is either a scale of likelihood of passing up free dope or of possessing the moral fiber that one needs to resist great temptations. Presumably, the pope would be an endpoint on either of these scales.

(31) a. Even the pope wouldn't pass up free dope.

b. **The pope himself** wouldn't pass up free dope. (Leskosky's (4))

To generate this type of use, all entities in a certain predicate would be ranked on the basis of the likelihood of belonging in the predicate. The least likely would be the distinguished member. This type of scalar ranking could then be used for the generation of scalar particles like *even*.[23]

---

[22] These types of grouping appear to allow for a special case of the use of the intensive. It seems that there is no need for some additional related predication in which the contrasting entity is in the same argument position as the prominent entity, when instead the definer and the definee are both arguments of a single two-place predicate, as in (a) and (b):

(30) a. 'Die sizes. Like taps, dies are sized the same as bolts (see facing page), and the size is marked on **the die itself**.' (Digest)

b. 'Written leases are in effect for the period specified in **the lease itself**.'("Written Farm Leases", UW extension service)

These could be represented as Marked-On(size of the die, the die itself) and Specified-In(the period the lease is in effect for, the lease), respectively.

These types of usages appear to be more closely related to the locality-marking functions of reflexive forms, discussed in the syntactic literature on binding.

[23]The difference between the use of *even* and the use of an intensive reflexive is not entirely clear. In some cases, *even* can be replaced by or appear in addition to an intensive reflexive. Possibly, intensives are favored in cases where the distinguished status of the entity is based on more than just its position on a scale of the relevant predicate. See Baker (1995) for discussion.

Variation in groupings as a text progresses

At any given point in the discourse, only a subset of all entities in the discourse model may be salient. As a result, conceptual sets may lose or gain members as the discourse proceeds, or a set that is relevant at one point may no longer be relevant later.

For example, in the first paragraph in (32), it is the work and the blade that are the relevant group; out of these the blade is the prominent member. In the second paragraph, the motor, the blade and the arm of the saw are now the relevant set; here it is the arm that is prominent, not the blade.

(32) 'Although it does much the same work as a table saw, the radial arm saw has distinct advantages. Most important, the blade enters the work from above; thus it is easy to watch the cut being made. In crosscutting, instead of pushing the work past the blade, you move **the blade itself**.

A radial arm saw is a circular saw suspended from a track on a metal arm over a wooden table. The motor and blade can be moved along the arm or locked in any position on it. **The arm itself** can be positioned at any angle for mitered cuts. The blade can be tilted to make bevel cuts or turned to a horizontal position to saw into the edges of stock.'(Digest)

Incorporating changes in grouping as a discourse proceeds will require tracking the saliency of entities and the groups to which they belong. This will be more relevant in generating longer texts with multiple discourse segments.

5.4.3 Encoding contrast

Generating intensive reflexives only when the context provides a related predication requires defining what counts as a salient, related predication. So, for each predicate, there must be (1) a method of tracking which predicates are salient and (2) a designated set of pairs (or sets) of related predicates in the knowledge base.

One possible way of tracking the saliency of predicates is Prevost (1995)'s information structure store (ISstore), an ordered list of abstract semantic representations—open propositions or predicates—of previous utterances. This ISstore could be used in a variety of ways with respect to the generation of emphatics. Only the most recent predicate in the ISstore might count as salient in the discourse, that is only the immediately preceding predication would count as salient for the purpose of determining whether to use an intensive. Saliency could, however, be extended to every predicate in the ISstore. An independent algorithm to calculate saliency would be needed to determine the appropriate portion of the ISstore to remain salient at a given point in a discourse.

Some degree of look-ahead or input from a higher-level text planning module would be needed in the system in order to generate intensive-marked NPs used in predications that precede their related predication. Another issue which an ISstore system could not deal effectively with is the generation of intensive reflexives when the related predication is never explicitly evoked in the discourse, as in (11–13) above.

An additional issue in encoding contrast is defining *related*. Ways of determining which predicates are related were briefly discussed in Section 5.2.3. Because what counts as related for the purposes of generating intensive reflexives is quite similar to the relatedness involved in determining contrastive accent placement, for the former we can use a method designed for the latter. As discussed in Theune (2000), one possible method for determining relatedness is a (possibly multiple-inheritance) sort hierarchy of predicates. The relevant sense of 'related' then will correspond to the following:

Related Two predicates that share a common parent in the sort hierarchy are related.

The algorithm and the example based on it below simply utilize a predicate RELATED that holds of pairs of predicates, abstracting away from the need for a sort hierarchy. Axioms stating that RELATED(Q, Q) and RELATED$(Q, \neg Q)$ always hold could also be included in defining RELATED.

5.4.4 A Generation Algorithm

Once the groupings and relations between entities and predicates are predesignated in the knowledge base, an algorithm to decide when to use an intensive form can be implemented. The most efficient implementation of such an algorithm in an NLG system will depend on how groupings and relations are represented in the knowledge base and how the input to sentence planning is structured. A preliminary formulation of this algorithm is presented here.

Algorithm `Predication P is to be made of an entity x.`

```
If [(∃y∃Q∃S(RELATED(P,Q)∧ SALIENT(Q(y))
        ∧(y,x ∈ S)∧ PROMINENT(x,S))
    ∨(∃y∃Q∃R∃S(RELATED(P,Q)∧ SALIENT(Q(y)))
        ∧(x ∈ R) ∧ (y,R ∈ S)∧ PROMINENT(R,S)))]
Then generate intensive reflexive marked form of x;
Else generate plain NP form for x.
```

First, the algorithm performs a search for a predication Q related to

P the predication in question. Predicate Q must also be part of a salient proposition, $Q(y)$ where y is a member of the set of conceptually-related entities S to which x belongs. If the above conditions hold and x is the most prominent member of S, then $P(x)$ will be generated with an intensive reflexive marking on the NP that refers to entity x.

The second disjunct allows for examples like (27a) and (27b), where the entity is a member of a set that is prominent. In this case, if x is not itself the most prominent member of S but is instead any member of R, and R is the most prominent member of the set S, then the intensive reflexive will be generated. To illustrate, the set S might be composed of several subsets of discourse entities, e.g. Hinges, Try Square, Door, Lines. Although no particular hinge h is prominent, if Hinges are the most important things under discussion, a singular NP used to refer to an arbitrary hinge h could be generated with an intensive reflexive.

This algorithm requires the following sets to be designated in the database, RELATED (holding of pairs of predicates), SALIENT (holding of propositions),[24] and PROMINENT (holding of a pair of a conceptual set and one of its members).[25] In addition, for each of these relations, we must know which entities, propositions, or predicates it holds of. For each entity, we must know which conceptual groupings (or *CSets*) it belongs to and whether it is the member designated as prominent.

5.4.5 Example implementation of algorithm

This section will present a sample running of the algorithm in the previous section. Our database consists of three predicates, P, R, and Q, and six entities, a, b, c, d, e, and f:

P = Is on Tour Now
R = Is Playing at The Sands
Q = Is Playing at Caesar's Palace
a = Dean Martin
b = Frank Sinatra
c = Sammy Davis, Jr.
d = Olivia Newton John
e = Julio Iglesias
f = Frank Sinatra's Backup Band

[24]These are not open propositions or predicates as in Prevosts's ISStore. As demonstrated in the example implementation below, the identity of the entity of which the related predicate is predicated matters; if the entity is not in a conceptually-related grouping with the prominent entity, then the use of an intensive reflexive is not appropriate.

[25]The semantics of PROMINENT will have to be adjusted accordingly so it can take either an entity and a set, or a set and a set as its arguments.

J = The Rat Pack[26]
K = Musicians
L = Frank Sinatra-related musicians
RELATED = $\{(Q,R),(P,\neg P),(R,\neg R),(Q,\neg Q)\}$
PROMINENT = {(b,J),(b,L)}
CSETS = {J={a,b,c}; K={a,b,c,d,e,f}; L={a,b,c,f}}
R = {b}; Q = {a,c,d,e,f} P = {a}

We will now apply the algorithm to *Frank Sinatra is playing at The Sands* in the context of three different $Q(x)$. The generation of the intensive form will depend on for which entity Q holds. We will treat the saliency of $Q(x)$ as given.

(33) a. Generate $R(b)$.
b. RELATED$(Q,R)\wedge$ SALIENT$(Q(a))$ $\wedge(b,a \in J)\wedge$ PROMINENT$(b,J))$
c. Dean Martin is playing at Caesar's Palace. Frank Sinatra himself is playing at The Sands.

(34) a. Generate $R(b)$.
b. RELATED$(Q,R)\wedge$ SALIENT$(Q(f))$ $\wedge(b,f \in L)\wedge$ PROMINENT$(b,L))$
c. Frank Sinatra's backup band is playing at Caesar's Palace. Frank Sinatra himself is playing at The Sands.

(35) a. Generate $R(b)$.
b. RELATED$(Q,R)\wedge$ SALIENT$(Q(d))$ $\wedge\neg\exists S((b,d \in S)\wedge$ PROMINENT $(b,S))$
c. Olivia Newton John is playing at Caesar's Palace. Frank Sinatra is playing at The Sands.

In (33)–(34), the intensive reflexive form is generated. In the final pair, however, *Frank Sinatra* is generated without the emphatic reflexive. The absence of the intensive in (35) results from the lack of a conceptual grouping including both Olivia Newton John and Frank Sinatra, with Frank as the most prominent member. In fact, the same text, but with the intensive reflexive, is certainly less acceptable, as in (36).

(36) # Olivia Newton John is playing at Caesar's Palace. Frank Sinatra himself is playing at The Sands.

[26]The Rat Pack was a group of entertainers whose heyday was in the early 1960s. Frank Sinatra was their unofficial leader.

Context and real-world knowledge are important factors here. In a context, such as the Dean Martin Fan Center webpage, Frank Sinatra might no longer be the most prominent member of the Rat Pack; one would prefer a text where *Dean Martin* was marked with *himself*, and Frank was referred to with a plain NP. Even in a more 'neutral' context, if one's hearer were Dean Martin's biggest fan, he may object to the speaker's utterance of (33). In addition, if Dean Martin's membership in the Rat Pack were unknown to one's addressee, (33) may sound as odd as (36). And in fact, depending on one's beliefs about Frank Sinatra's place in the musical world, perhaps even (36) sounds acceptable; in such a case, any singer could be grouped with Frank Sinatra in the set K, Musicians, and Frank Sinatra would always be designated as the prominent entity. Example (36) would then be acceptable because b, d would both belong to the Cset K, where b is the most prominent member.

The ultimate goal might be to build a system that could take factors like these into account. Such a system would create CSets and PROMINENT pairs based on knowledge of the world, the discourse, and its audience.

5.5 Conclusions

This paper has outlined the conditions that motivate speakers' use of emphatic reflexives and demonstrated how these conditions might be taken into account in generating these forms. Speakers use intensive reflexives in order to signal the prominence of one entity in a group of conceptually related entities. In addition, this emphasis can only be marked when a predication is made of this prominent entity and a related predication about another less important entity is also salient. The use of an emphatic reflexive is infelicitous if the conditions of prominence and contrast do not hold or if the speaker cannot reasonably expect the addressee to share her beliefs that they hold, such as when the entity marked as prominent is unfamiliar to the addressee. In order to generate intensive reflexives, beliefs about how entities are related conceptually, which entities are important, and which predicates are related must be part of the knowledge base used in the generation of a text. The algorithm provided above can only be implemented if these groupings and relations are already determined; determining these groupings and relations is a separate and even more difficult problem.

Generating emphatic reflexives is only a very small aspect of generating nominal expressions. Nonetheless, the issues that arise in characterizing when a nominal expression should be marked with an emphatic are more widely relevant. Deciding which entities and which predicates are related to each other within a discourse model, determining what it means to be important in a discourse or in the real world, and keeping track of what is salient at a given point in a discourse are all tasks that are also necessary for the generation of scalar particles (such as *even*), scalar implicatures, pitch accents, and syntactic constructions with special discourse functions.

References

Baker, C.L. 1995. Contrast, discourse prominence, and intensification, with special reference to locally free reflexives in British English. *Language.* 71:1.

Birner, B. 1994. Information status and word order: an analysis of English inversion. *Language.* 70.2: 233-59.

Brennan, S.E., M.W. Friedman, and C.J. Pollard. 1987. A centering approach to pronouns. In *Proceedings of the 25th Annual Meeting of the ACL*, 155-162.

Dahl, D. 1987. Determiners, entities, and contexts. In Y. Wilkes, ed. *Proceedings of TINLAP, Theoretical Issues in Natural Language Processing*, 133-136.

Geis, M. 1986. Pragmatic Determinants of Adverb Preposing. *Papers from the 22nd Regional Meeting of the Chicago Linguistics Society.*

Golde, K. 1999a. Evidence for two types of English intensive NPs. *Papers from the 35th Regional Meeting of the Chicago Linguistics Society.*

Golde, K. 1999b. Tracing the Functional Expansion of the Self-pronoun. *The Ohio State University Working Papers in Linguistics* 52.

Gundel, J. K., N. Hedberg, and R. Zacharski. 1993. Cognitive status and the form of referring expressions. *Language.* 69: 274-307.

Grosz, B. J. , A. K. Joshi, and S. Weinstein. 1995. Centering: a framework for modeling the local coherence of discourse. *Computational Linguistics* 21.2: 203-25.

Hirschberg, J. 1985. *A theory of scalar implicature.* Ph.D. thesis. University of Pennsylvania.

Horn, L. 1986. Presupposition, Theme and Variations. *Papers from the 22nd Regional Meeting of the Chicago Linguistics Society.*

Joshi, A. K. and S. Weinstein. 1981. Control of inference: role of some aspects of discourse structure—Centering. In *Proceedings of the International Joint Conference on Artificial Intelligence.* Vancouver, B.C., 385-387.

Kemmer, S. 1995. Emphatic and reflexive *-self.* In D. Stein and S. Wright, eds. *Subjectivity and Subjectivisation.* Cambridge: Cambridge University Press.

König, E. 1991. *The meaning of focus particles: a comparative perspective.* London: Routledge.

Langacker, R. 1993. Reference point constructions. *Cognitive Linguistics.* 4: 1-38.

Leskosky, R. 1972. Intensive reflexives. *Studies in the Linguistic Sciences.* 2.1.

Lewis, D. 1979. Scorekeeping in a language game. *Journal of Philosophical Language.* 8: 339-359.

McKay, T. J. 1991. He himself: Undiscovering an anaphor. *Linguistic Inquiry.* 22: 368-73.

McNally, L. 1998. On the linguistic encoding of information packaging instructions. In P. Culicover and L. McNally, eds. *Syntax and Semantics. The limits of syntax.* 29. New York: Academic Press.

Nunberg, G. 1978. *The pragmatics of reference.* Ph.D. thesis. City University of New York.

Pierrehumbert, J. and J. Hirschberg. 1990. The meaning of intonational contours in discourse. In P. R. Cohen, J. Morgan, and M. E. Pollack, eds. *Intentions in communication.* Cambridge, MA: MIT Press.

Prevost, S. 1995. *A Semantics of Contrast and Information Structure for Specifying Intonation in Spoken Language Generation.* Ph.D. thesis. University of Pennsylvania.

Prince, E. F. 1981. On the inferencing of indefinite-*this* NPs. In A. K. Joshi, B. L. Webber, and I. A. Sag, eds. *Elements of discourse understanding,*

231-250. Cambridge: Cambridge University Press.

Prince, E. F. 1992. The ZPG letter: subjects, definiteness, and information-status. In S. Thompson and W. Mann, eds. *Discourse description: diverse analyses of a fund raising text.* Philadelphia/Amsterdam: John Benjamins B. V. 1992.

Prince, E. F. 1998. On the limits of syntax, with reference to Topicalization and Left-Dislocation. In P. Culicover and L. McNally, eds. *Syntax and Semantics. The limits of syntax.* 29. New York: Academic Press.

Prince, E. F. 1999. How not to mark topics: 'Topicalization' in English and Yiddish. Ms. University of Pennsylvania

Reinhart, T. 1981. Pragmatics and linguistics: an analysis of sentence topics. *Philosophica.* 27: 53-94.

Reiter, E. 1994. Has a consensus NL generation architecture appeared, and is it psycholinguistically plausible? In *Proceedings of the Seventh International Workshop on Natural Language Generation*, 163-170.

Rooth, M. 1992. A theory of focus interpretation. *Natural Language Semantics*: 1.

Selkirk, E. 1995. Sentence prosody: Intonation, stress and phrasing. In J. Goldsmith, ed. *The handbook of phonological theory.* Oxford: Blackwell.

Schwarzschild, R. 1999. GIVENness, AvoidF and other constraints on the placement of accent. *Natural Language Semantics.* 7.2: 141-177.

Theune, M. 2000. *From Data to Speech: Language Generation in Context.* Ph.D. thesis. IPO, Center for User-System Interaction. Eindhoven.

Vallduvi, E. and M. Vilkuna. 1998. On rheme and kontrast. In P. Culicover and L. McNally, eds. *Syntax and Semantics 29. The limits of syntax.* New York: Academic Press.

Verheijen, R. 1986. A phrase structure syntax for emphatic self-forms. *Linguistics.* 24: 681-695.

Walker, M.A., A.K. Joshi, and E.F. Prince, eds. 1998. *Centering theory in discourse.* Oxford: Oxford University Press.

6

The Role of Salience in the Production of Referring Expressions: A Psycholinguistic Perspective

ROSEMARY STEVENSON

6.1 Introduction

Successful generation of discourse depends on both the speaker and the hearer (or writer and reader)[1]. The speaker must produce utterances that cohere with what has been said earlier, while the listener must discover how to integrate the speaker's current utterance with what has been said before. Each participant in a discourse maintains a constantly developing mental representation of the current discourse, both the parts they have spoken themselves and the parts in which they have been the listener. The communicative success of an utterance depends on the quality of the links between each utterance and these discourse representations. This discourse representation can be thought of as a mental model, a mental representation of the situation being described (e.g. Johnson-Laird, 1983). The speaker expects the listener to construct a mental model of the situation described by each utterance that is as close to the speaker's mental model as possible. According to Johnson-Laird & Garnham (1980), a minimum requirement for two people to

[1]In the interests of brevity, I will refer to speakers and listeners throughout this paper. However, I intend my comments to apply equally well to writers and readers.

Information Sharing: Reference and Presupposition in Language Generation and Interpretation.
Edited by Kees van Deemter and Rodger Kibble.

co-ordinate mental models in this way is for the speaker to have a model of the listener's model at each point in the discourse. Such a model enables the speaker to decide what is new to the listener, what can be inferred, what is already familiar, and which entity is the currently most salient in the speaker's and the listener's models. The speaker also has to have a plan of the narrative in order to decide who or what to mention at each point in the discourse, a choice that must be co-ordinated with knowledge of the listener's model to decide how to refer to that entity.

In this chapter, I discuss ways in which the relative salience of entities in the speaker's mental model affects the choice of who to refer to next and the choice of referring expression. Early work on salience and the production of referring expressions has tended to concentrate on perceptual salience and the importance of the information to the speaker. For example, Osgood and Bock (1977) identified three kinds of salience: naturalness - the natural order of constituents mirrors the natural order of events (e.g. Agent - action -Patient), vividness - the inherent salience of the semantic features of the entity (e.g. the murderer vs. the man); and motivation-of-speaker - salience attributed by the speaker (e.g. interest, concern, perspective). Among other things, they found that Agents were more likely to be mentioned first than Patients and that entities with high vividness ratings were more likely to be mentioned first than items with low vividness ratings. They cite a study by Ertel (1977) in support of salience through motivation-of-speaker. Ertel carried out a content analysis of sports writers' reports of identical soccer games. Reports were paired so that one writer supported one team and the second writer supported the other team. Only sentences including references to players of both teams were analysed. Ertel found that the player from the favoured team (whichever it was) was more likely to appear in sentence subject position than the player from the opposing team.

Perceptual salience clearly plays a role in the choice of referent, but it is likely to be most evident in descriptions of scenes (as in Osgood and Bock's first experiment and in Ertel's study) or when presented with sentences out of context (as in Osgood and Bock's second experiment). However, the situation is likely to be different in dialogue, where the choice of who to mention first in an utterance and how to refer to them are likely to be at least partly determined by what was said in the preceding utterance. It is this second kind of situation that is simulated in the experiments to be described here. The basic method that is used is a sentence continuation task: Participants are presented with a sentence (or clause) and asked to write a second sentence that continues the theme of the first. The entity mentioned first in the second sentence is then determined. The reason for using this task rather than analysing real dialogues, is that by providing the first sentence, the number of entities and their presumed salience can be systematically manipulated to enable hypotheses about salience to be tested. To go back to the notion of mental models, we assume that the experimental participant constructs a mental model of the situation described by the first sentence. Then, when writing a second sentence that continues the theme of the first, the relative salience of the entities in the mental model will determine the choice of sentence subject and the choice of referring expression. The basic assumption, in agreement with Osgood and Beck, is that the subject of the second sentence is likely to be the most salient entity in the participant's mental model of the situation described by the first sentence[2]. Given this assumption, we need to determine what factors affect salience in a model of the discourse in order to be able to model successfully the generation of referring expressions. This issue is addressed in section 1.2 of this chapter. A plausible further assumption might be that the choice of which referring expression to use is more likely to be affected by coherence and givenness than by salience. This second issue is addressed in section 1.3 of the chapter.

6.2 Choice of Referent

The idea of using sentence continuation tasks to investigate the production of referring expressions, as a function of the relative salience of the discourse entities in a mental model of the preceding discourse, highlights the relation between comprehension and production. The speaker needs to understand the previous contribution to the discourse in order to structure his or her own contribution appropriately. We therefore begin our discussion of how a subject referent is chosen by identifying two kinds of salience that have been discussed in the literature: salience arising from structural aspects of the preceding utterance, as in centering theory, and salience arising from semantic aspects of the preceding utterance, as in research on thematic roles.

6.2.1 Centering Theory

Centering theory relates focus of attention, choice of referring expression, and perceived coherence of utterances within a discourse segment (Grosz, Joshi & Weinstein, 1995). Grosz et al. identify two kinds of local discourse centers: a set of forward looking centers (**Cf**) and a backward

[2]Choice of sentence subject is also likely to affect the choice of sentence voice - active or passive. I do not discuss sentence voice here. However, other work has shown that passives are more likely to be used than actives when the speaker's attention is drawn to the Patient rather than the Agent (e.g. Carroll, 1958; Flores D'Arcais, 1973; Tannenbaum & Williams, 1968; Turner & Rommetveit, 1968).

looking center (**Cb**). It can be argued that the first of these, the **Cf**, concerns salience and hence the choice of referent in the next utterance; whereas the second, the **Cb**, concerns coherence and hence the choice of referring expression in the next utterance. I will discuss the **Cf** and salience here, and postpone discussion of the **Cb** until Section 1.3.

According to centering theory, every utterance in a discourse either introduces entities in the **Cf** or refers to previously introduced entities. Entities in the **Cf** are ranked according to their accessibility in the discourse model; the highest ranked entity is said to be the most salient and is called the "preferred center" (**Cp**). The **Cf** ranking is determined by a number of factors, such as grammatical role, surface position, and information status (Walker, Joshi & Prince, 1998). Grosz et al (1995) proposed that entities that are realised as subjects or are pronominalised are ranked higher in the **Cf** than others. Brennan, Friedman and Pollard (1987) proposed ordering the **Cf** by obliqueness of grammatical role, with subject having the highest rank, object next, followed by other roles.

There is growing psychological evidence to support the idea that entities in the **Cf** are ranked on structural grounds, with the first mentioned entity being more highly salient than the second (Gernsbacher, 1989; Gernsbacher & Hargreaves, 1988). The idea that the first mentioned entity is the **Cp** coincides with the production research discussed earlier which suggests that speaker places the most salient entity in subject or initial position. However, research on thematic role focusing complicates this picture by suggesting that salience may also depend on the thematic role of the entity. Thus, when a listener becomes the speaker, this salient thematic role may be mentioned first in the utterance, rather than the first mentioned entity.

6.2.2 Thematic Roles

Psychological research on thematic roles is rooted in a body of work showing that the interpretation of a pronoun in a *because*-clause depends on the "implicit causality" of the main verb (Garvey and Caramazza, 1974; Caramazza, Grober, Garvey and Yates, 1977). Garvey and Caramazza (1974) coined the term implicit causality to describe a property of transitive verbs whereby the instigator of the action is implicitly encoded. For some verbs this causality favours the subject of the verb as the initiator of the event, for other verbs it favours the object. For example, in the sentence *John cheated Bill*, we usually assume that something John did initiated the cheating, while in the sentence *Mike punished Peter*, we usually assume that something Peter did initiated the punishment. By examining participants' completions of sentence fragments such as

(1) a. John cheated Bill because he ....

b. Mike punished Peter because he ....

Garvey and Caramazza established that, when asked to do so, English speakers reliably interpret the pronoun as referring to NP1 with some verbs and to NP2 with others. For example, *cheat* is an NP1 verb and so people reliably interpret the pronoun in (1a) above as referring to John. By contrast, *punish* is an NP2 verb and so they interpret the pronoun in (1b) as referring to Mike.

Subsequent work has developed along three lines. First, the same method has been used to study the production, rather than the comprehension, of referring expressions. This has been done by removing the pronoun from the end of the fragment to be completed and then identifying the individual referred to in the subject position of the completion (Stevenson et al, 1994). Second, the observed preferences for NP1 or NP2 have been considered in terms of thematic roles (Au, 1986; Stevenson et al, 1994). For example, when people write completions to sentence fragments containing state verbs and ending with *because he* (e.g. *John irritated Bill because he ....*), they assign the pronoun to the Stimulus (John) regardless of its position in the sentence. Thus NP1 is preferred with verbs such as *irritate*, where NP1 is the Stimulus, whereas NP2 is preferred with verbs such as *envy*, where NP2 is the Stimulus (Au, 1986; Stevenson et al, 1994). Third, when connectives other than *because* have been used with verbs describing events (i.e., transfers or actions), the focusing evoked by the implicit causality of the verb is reinforced or reduced depending on the connective (Au, 1986; Ehrlich, 1980; Stevenson, Crawley & Kleinman, 1994).

All three of these developments are shown in Stevenson et al's (1994) study. I will describe one of the experiments reported there to show how focusing evoked by the verb and moderated by a connective affects the choice of who to refer to in the continuation. Stevenson et al (1994, Experiment 3) presented subjects with sentence fragments containing pairs of thematic roles and asked them to write a continuation that continued the theme of the first sentence. They then examined the surface subject of the continuation to discover which of the two referents had been referred to. Three different thematic role pairs were investigated, pairs containing Goal and Source thematic roles, pairs containing Agent and Patient thematic roles, and pairs containing Experiencer and Stimulus thematic roles. The position of the thematic roles in the first clause was also varied. Definitions of these thematic roles were gleaned from

Verb Type	Thematic Role Order	Example sentences
Transfers	GS	John passed the book to Bill so/because ...
	SG	Bill seized the book from Bill so/because ...
Actions	PA	Bill was hit by John so/because ..
	AP	John hit Bill so/because ...
States	ES	John admired Bill so/because ..
	SE	Bill irritated John so/because ..

TABLE 1 Examples of sentences used in Stevenson et al (1994) (taken from Experiment 1). [Note: **GS**=Goal-Source; **SG**=Source-Goal; **PA**=Patient-Agent; **AP**=Agent-Patient; **ES**=Experiencer- Stimulus; **SE**=Stimulus-Experiencer.]

Andrews (1985), Fillmore (1968), Jackendoff (1985) and Radford (1988) and can be found in Stevenson et al (1994). Examples of the materials from Stevenson et al's Experiment 3 are shown in Table 1.

Thematic role order indicates which thematic role was mentioned first in the sentence. For example, The Goal was mentioned first in Goal-Source (GS) sentences whereas the Source was mentioned first in the Source-Goal (SG) sentences. Participants were presented with 48 sentences, 16 for each verb type. In each set of 16, eight sentences were in one thematic role order and the remaining eight were in the other role order. Within each thematic role order, half the sentences ended in *so*, the other half ended in *because*.

Once the data had been collated, two judges, naive as to the experimental hypothesis, examined the continuations to identify the first mentioned referents. Only continuations in which the first mentioned referent was one of the two individuals in the fragment were used in the analyses. If one of these individuals was referred to with a pronoun and the content of the rest of the continuation was not sufficiently explicit to identify the referent, the pronoun was classed as ambiguous and not included in the analyses. All together, 22% of the responses were omitted from the analyses either because they did not refer to one of the two individuals in the fragment (12%) or because they contained ambiguous pronouns (10%).

In a continuation task, the choices of one or the other individual are not independent. That is, the person who begins a continuation with the first mentioned individual cannot, by definition, begin it with the second

		Connective					
		so			because		
		Ant.		1^{st}MS	Ant.		1^{st}MS
		1st	2nd	$1^{st} - 2^{nd}$	1st	2nd	$1^{st} - 2^{nd}$
Verb Type	Role order						
Transfer	GS	62	26	+36	60	22	+38
	SG	15	70	-55	50	35	+15
Action	PA	65	19	+46	57	30	+27
	AP	15	71	-56	32	57	-25
State	ES	72	12	+60	12	82	-70
	SE	10	85	-75	80	12	+68

TABLE 2 Percentage of references to each antecedent and first mention scores in Stevenson et al's (1994) Experiment 3.[Note: **Ant** = Antecedent Order; **1st MS** = 1st Mention Score]

mentioned individual. Because of this lack of independence, the number of continuations that mentioned the second mentioned individual was subtracted from the number of continuation that mentioned the first mentioned individual. This resulted in a positive number when there were more continuations referring to the first mentioned individual and a negative number when there were more continuations referring the second mentioned individual. For ease of reference, we will refer to these derived scores as *first mention scores*, since the higher the score, the greater the tendency to refer to the first mentioned individual. A shift in the first mention score from one role order to the other indicates a thematic role effect that is independent of sentence position, since the position of the two roles reverses in the two orders while first mention remains constant. Table 2 shows both the percentage of references to each individual in the subject position of the continuations and the percent first mention scores.

To analyse the data, analyses of variance on the first mention scores were carried out separately for each verb type. Consider first the transfer verbs. Inspection of the first mention scores in Table 2 shows that the Goal was the preferred referent with *so* (the first mention score was positive in the GS order and negative in the SG order), whereas the first mentioned individual was the preferred referent with *because* (the first mention scores were positive in both orders). The statistical analyses confirmed both of these observations. Inspection of the first mention sores for the action verbs in Table 2 show that the Patient was the preferred referent overall (over both connectives, the first mention score was positive in the PA order and negative in the AP order), and that this preference is greater with *so* than with *because* (the first mention scores are larger with *so* than with *because*). These observations were also confirmed by the statistical analyses. Finally, inspection of the first mention scores for state verbs shows that the Experiencer was preferred with *so* (the first mention score was positive in the ES order and negative in the SE order), whereas the Stimulus was preferred with *because* (the first mention score was positive in the SE order and negative in the ES order). Once again, the statistical analyses confirmed these observations.

These results demonstrate three phenomena. First, they show the role of the connective in maintaining or shifting the pre-existing focus evoked by the verb. Second, they show a focusing effect evoked by the verb (as long as it describes an event). Third, they reveal a difference between verbs describing events and verbs describing states. The choice of subject referent in the continuation was influenced by all these factors.

To begin with the effect of the connectives, the function of a connective is to signal the coherence relation that holds between the two clauses. Consider first, the connective *because. Because* signals the Explanation relation in which a reason is given for the event or state described in the main clause. It is natural, therefore, that the reason predicates something of the causal Agent of an action (e.g., *Anne cheated John because she wanted the extra money*) or of a transfer (e.g. *Anne passed the book to John because he wanted to read it*) or the Stimulus of a state (e.g. *Anne envied Lucy because she had so many accomplishments*). By contrast, *so* signals either a Result relation or a Purpose relation (Knott, 1996). Continuations to action and state fragments containing *so* are mainly Results (e.g. *Anne cheated John so he went to the police*; *Anne envied Lucy so she tried to imitate her*), whereas continuations to transfer fragments containing *so* are mainly Purposes (e.g. *Ann passed the book to John so that he could read it*) (Stevenson, Knott, Oberlander & McDonald 2000)[3]. It seems most natural for the Result of an action or state to involve the person acted upon or the person who experiences

[3]When continuations to fragments containing *and* were examined, the choice of coherence relation also differed between transfers on the one hand and actions or states on the other. The continuations were mainly Narratives when the fragment described a transfer and mainly Results when the fragment described either an action or a state. Stevenson et al interpreted these findings with transfer fragments containing *so* and *and* as indicating that participants tried to avoid expressing Results of transfers because results violated the meaning of the transfer verb - that it enables a subsequent event rather than causes it.

the state, and for the Purpose of a transfer to involve the Goal. Hence, the person involved in the coherence relation is also the focused thematic role. On the basis of these and other observations, Stevenson et al (2000) concluded that people aim to keep the focused entity, the coherence relation and the referent of the pronoun in alignment. Of course, they also found examples where such alignment did not occur, indicating that these constraints on interpretation act as pressures that favour one pronominal referent over the other, not as hard constraints.

Turning to the focusing properties of the verbs describing events, it is important to note that connectives, by signalling a coherence relation, either maintain or shift a pre-existing focus evoked by the verb in sentences describing events. Consider again the first mention scores for transfer sentences in Table 2. The shift from a preference for the Goal with *so* to a preference for the first mentioned individual with *because* can be interpreted as a shift towards the Agent brought about by *because*[4]. Notice that the preference for the Agent with *because* is stronger when the Goal is mentioned first than when it is mentioned second (the first mention score is larger in the GS order than in the SG order). This pattern of first mention scores supports the idea that *so* reinforces an already existing preference for the Goal, whereas *because* shifts the pre-existing focus towards the Agent, resulting in competition between the pre-existing focus on the Goal and the new focus on the Agent. A similar case can be made for the action sentences. Returning again to Table 2, recall that there is an overall preference for the Patient with both *so* and *because* (with both connectives, the first mention score is positive in PA sentences and negative in AP sentences). However, when we move from *so* to *because*, there is a shift towards the Agent (the absolute size of the first mention scores is reduced with *because* compared to *so*). This pattern of first mention scores also supports the idea that *so* reinforces an already existing preference for the Patient, whereas *because* shifts the pre-existing focus towards the Agent.

Finally, the difference between events and states can be seen by examining again the data for state sentences in Table 2. Unlike event sentences (transfers and actions), state sentences show no evidence of a pre-existing preference evoked by the verb. Instead, there is a pure effect of connective: When the connective is *so*, the Experiencer is preferred; when the connective is *because*, the Stimulus is preferred. Stevenson et al.

[4]There are problems with this analysis of transfer verbs because it assumes that the subject of a transfer sentence has two thematic roles: Agent and either Goal or Source, depending on the order of the latter two roles. However, Jackendoff (1972) has argued that an NP in a single sentence can bear more than one thematic role (see also Cowper, 1992).

(1994) explained this difference between events and states by proposing that when people encounter an event verb, they construct a tripartite mental representation of the action. This representation consists of a pre-condition (which may be the cause), the action itself, and the end-point of the action (Moens & Steedman, 1988). Stevenson et al. claim that the focus evoked by the verb in clauses describing events is on the thematic role associated with the endpoint of the event, a focus that is attenuated when the connective directs attention to the cause. On the other hand, a state has no such tripartite representation since it has no pre-condition and no result (Moens & Steedman, 1988). According to Stevenson et al., therefore, no focus is evoked by state verbs. A focus only appears when a subsequent connective *converts* the state into an event having an initial condition and a consequence. If the connective directs attention to the initial condition, as with *because*, then the Stimulus is preferred. If the connective directs attention to the consequence, as with *so*, then the Experiencer is preferred. These proposals have since been supported by reading time studies (Stevenson & Urbanowicz, 1995; submitted). Thus, the choice of who to refer to is determined not simply by the **Cp** as defined in centering theory. It also depends on thematic role focusing, which clearly acts as an alternative influence on salience. Whether or not an utterance induces focusing based on initial mention (as proposed by centering theory) or focusing based on thematic roles (as in studies of thematic role focusing) most likely depends on whether or not the utterance contains an implicit causality verb (McKoon, Greene & Ratcliff, 1993).

McKoon et al (1993) claim that implicit causality is a feature of interpersonal verbs, which they define as those that "describe a relationship between two people that has a psychological component: At least one of the people must have some mental representation of the other" (p.12), and they define implicit causality as identifying "the argument that initiates an action or evokes a response" (p.12). McKoon et al (1993) found thematic role focusing in state sentences containing implicit causality verbs but not in sentences containing non-implicit causality verbs (e.g. *scratched*, *went to visit*, *waited to see*)[5]. All together,

[5]Thematic role focusing is not the only additional influence on salience, and hence the choice of who to mention first in an utterance. Others have found that the topic character or the referent most closely related to the topic is more focused than a non-topic character or a referent not closely related to the topic (Anderson, Garrod & Sanford, 1983; Garrod & Sanford, 1988; Karmiloff-Smith, 1980, Marslen-Wilson, Tyler & Koster, 1993). Syntactically marked information (e.g. deer in deer hunting) is also more focused than unmarked information (deer in hunting deer) (McKoon, Ward, Ratcliff, & Sproat, 1993); and a named character is more highly focused than one described by a referring expression (Sanford, Moar & Garrod, 1988).

therefore, a speaker's choice of sentence subject depends on the relative salience of the entities in the speaker's mental model of the prior utterance. This salience may be determined by a range of factors, including being mentioned first in the sentence, being the thematic role associated with the endpoint of an event, and being the entity upon which the coherence relation expressed in the new utterance is predicated.

6.2.3 Animacy as a factor influencing salience

Animacy has long been regarded as a salient feature of noun phrases (e.g. Clark & Begun, 1971). Thus, animacy may also be a determinant of which entity a speaker chooses to mention first. A series of sentence continuation studies carried out in collaboration with Massimo Poesio and Jamie Pearson investigated this issue. We began by noting that Sidner's (1979) theory of focusing proposes that the discourse focus in transfer sentences is the object transferred (e.g. *the book* in *John gave the book to Bill*). By contrast, as we saw above, Stevenson et al (1994) argued that the default focus of a transfer sentence is the Goal, because the Goal is the thematic role associated with the endpoint of the described event. According to Sidner, each utterance in a discourse consists of a discourse focus and an actor focus. The discourse focus is introduced by special syntactic constructions or by serving as Theme (in the thematic role sense) of a sentence. Agents of sentences serve as preferred antecedents for pronouns that also fill the Agent role. Agents are therefore tracked by a separate mechanism, the actor focus. For Sidner, the discourse focus was closely related to the notion of 'discourse topic' and it received the most attention. Thus, the Theme is normally the discourse focus, which means, contrary to Stevenson et al's (1994) data, the Theme should be the most salient entity in transfer sentences.

To distinguish between animacy and Agency in the Actor Focus, Pearson, Stevenson & Poesio (in preparation) conducted a detailed study of focusing in transfer sentences in which the pattern of animate and inanimate entities in the sentence was systematically varied. In Stevenson et al's (1994) study, the transfer sentences contained two animate participants and an inanimate Theme (e.g. *John gave the book to Bill*). Since Stevenson et al (1994) found a preference for the animate Goal in these sentences, Pearson et al considered the possibility that the Goal was preferred because it was the Actor Focus. Such a possibility could be the case if the Actor Focus contains an animate entity but not specifically an Agent, as suggested by the evidence cited above. At the same time Pearson et al also considered the possibility that the Theme (i.e. the Discourse Focus) might be the preferred referent in a continuation if the pattern of animate and inanimate entities was changed.

To examine the role of animacy, Pearson et al first conducted a study in which the sentence fragments contained a single animate entity, as shown in (2) to (4) below:

(2) (a) GS: Barbara bought the clock from the store. AII
(b) SG: Barbara returned the clock to the store.

(3) (a) GS: The shop obtained Ann from the agency. IAI
(b) SG: The shop returned Ann to the agency.

(4) (a) GS: The hospital received a letter from John. IIA
(b) SG: The hospital sent a letter to John.

The (a) member of each pair is a GS sentence, meaning that the Goal is the first mentioned entity and the Source is the third; the (b) member of each pair is an SG sentence, meaning that the Source is the first mentioned entity and the Goal is the third. As indicated by the ordering of the letters A (animate) and I (inanimate) to the right of the (a) sentences, the first mentioned entity (Goal or Source) is animate in sentence pair (2), the second mentioned entity (the THEME) is animate in (3) and the third mentioned entity (Goal or Source) is animate in (4). Participants were presented with booklets containing sentences like the ones above and asked to write a second sentence for each one that continued the theme of the first.

The choice of entity in the subject position of each continuation was then identified by one of the Experimenters in the same as was done in Stevenson et al's (1994) Experiment 3. The resulting categorisations were then checked by a second experimenter. Disagreements between the two experimenters were either settled by discussion or discarded as ambiguous. Table 3 shows the number of times each referent was the subject of the continuations.

We carried out two different statistical analyses on the results. First we determined which of the three entities was mentioned significantly more often than would be expected by chance [6]. We concluded that whichever entity was mentioned significantly more often than chance was the preferred entity. Second, we checked whether or not there was also a preference for the Goal, as would be expected on the basis of Stevenson et al's data. To do this, we first obtained a *Goal preference score* for each sentence by subtracting the number of times the third mentioned entity was chosen from the number of times the first mentioned entity was chosen. This derived measure is also shown in Table 3. If there is

[6] Four response categories were used: the continuations could refer to the 1st mentioned entity, the 2nd mentioned entity, the 3rd mentioned entity or some other entity. Thus, with 4 response categories and 8 sentences per condition, chance level was 2 for each role order.

Animacy of entities	Role Order	Ant. 1st	2nd	3rd	GPS $1^{st} - 3^{rd}$	Statistically Significant Results
AII	GS	**5.41**	1.78	0.56	+4.85	1st entity (Goal)
	SG	**4.84**	1.63	0.94	+3.90	
IAI	GS	1.94	**5.01**	0.44	+1.50	2nd entity (Goal)
	SG	1.09	**5.31**	0.78	+0.31	
IIA	GS	1.66	1.25	**5.46**	- 3.80	3rd entity (Goal)
	SG	0.62	0.97	**6.31**	- 5.69	

TABLE 3 Number of Times each Referent was the Subject of the Completions In Experiment 1 of the Animacy Study. Difference scores (1st minus 3rd) are also shown. [Note: the order of the letters A (animate) and I (inanimate) in column 1 indicate the positions of the animate and inanimate entities in the sentence. **Ant** = Antecedent Position; **GPS** = Goal Preference Score]

a Goal preference, we should find a significant difference between the two Goal preference scores, with the score for GS sentences being higher than the score for SG sentences. One-tailed t-tests were used to test for such a difference. The outcomes of these analyses are shown in the right hand column of Table 3. The preferred entity, as identified by the comparison with chance level, is shown first in this column; then the Goal is listed in parentheses if it was referred to significantly more often than the Source. As can be seen in Table 3, the effect of animacy was clear cut: Participants predominantly referred to the animate entity in each case, giving support to the idea that the Actor Focus favours animate entities, but not specifically an Agent. The data for the animate entity is highlighted in the table. In addition, there was also a small but significant preference for the Goal over the Source in all three animacy patterns.

Having established that the animate entity is preferred in sentences containing only one animate entity, Pearson et al conducted a second experiment in which each sentence contained two animate entities, as shown in (5) and (6) below:

(5) a. Jason carried Trevor from the pub. AAI
b. Jason drove Trevor to the pub.

(6) a. The club borrowed Peter from Jane. IAA

Animacy of entities	Role Order	Ant. 1st	2nd	3rd	GPS $1^{st} - 3^{rd}$	Statistically Significant Results
AAI	GS	1.94	**4.22**	0.97	+0.97	2nd entity (Goal)
	SG	1.69	**4.50**	1.03	+0.66	
IAA	GS	0.91	**3.31**	**3.41**	-2.50	2nd & 3rd entity (Goal)
	SG	0.34	**2.94**	**3.91**	-3.57	

TABLE 4 Number of Times each Referent was the Subject of the Completions in Animacy Experiment 2. Difference scores (1st minus 3rd) are also shown. [Note: the order of the letters A (animate) and I (inanimate) in column 1 indicate the positions of the animate and inanimate entities in the sentence. **Ant** = Antecedent Position; **GPS** = Goal Preference Score]

b. The club loaned Peter to Jane.

We know from Stevenson et al's (1994) data that when the sentence contains an animate Goal and Source, the Goal is focused. However, we do not know what happens when the Theme is one of the two animate entities. The results are shown in Table 4, in which the entity (or entities) chosen significantly more often than chance are highlighted. Inspection of Table 4 indicates that when there were two animate entities in a sentence and one was the Theme (AAI condition), then the Theme was preferred. If the other animate entity was the 3rd mentioned (IAA condition), then both the Theme and the 3rd mentioned entity were preferred. In this latter condition, there was also a small but significant preference for the Goal.

Finally, Pearson et al examined the choice of subject entity in the completions when all three entities were either animate or inanimate, as shown below:

(7) a. Robert collected Duncan from Bob. AAA
b. Robert sent Duncan to Bob.

(8) a. The club received a letter from the school. III
b. The club sent a letter to the school.

The results are shown in Table 5. Inspection of the table indicates that when all three entities were animate, then the third was preferred, and when all three entities were inanimate, then the Theme was pre-

Animacy of entities	Role Order	Ant. 1st	2nd	3rd	GPS $1^{st}-3^{rd}$	Statistically Significant Results
AAA	GS	2.06	1.69	**3.52**	-1.46	3rd entity (Goal)
	SG	0.97	2.78	**3.72**	-2.75	
III	GS	2.34	**3.25**	1.44	+0.90	2nd entity (Goal)
	SG	0.72	**3.34**	3.00	-2.26	

TABLE 5 Number of Times each Referent was the Subject of the Completions in Animacy Experiment 3. Difference scores (1st minus 3rd) are also shown. [Note: the order of the letters A (animate) and I (inanimate) in column 1 indicate the positions of the animate and inanimate Entities in the sentence. **Ant** = Antecedent Position; **GPS** = Goal Preference Score]

ferred. There was also a preference for the Goal over the Source in both animacy conditions.

We conclude from these results that three different influences affect who is mentioned first after a transfer sentence: animacy, thematic role (Theme and Goal) and recency. Further, both recency and thematic role seem to depend on animacy. First, recency only appeared when the third mentioned entity was animate (IIA in Table 3, IAA in Table 4, and AAA in Table 5). Second, the preference for the Theme only appeared when the Theme was one of two or more animate entities (AAI and IAA in Table 4, AAA in Table 5). Although the Goal preference appeared in all but the AAI condition, it was only above chance level in Stevenson's Experiment in which both Goal and Source were animate (AIA). In an unpublished study at Durham University, Garry also found an effect of animacy in state sentences, this effect over-riding the preference for Stimulus found by Stevenson et al (1994), when both entities are animate.

6.2.4 Implications for Generation Systems

How might the above results be used to inform generation algorithms? What follows is an informal attempt to characterise the findings described above as a series of tests that could be incorporated into a language generation system for deciding which discourse entity to mention first in an utterance. This list is only tentative and should be seen as a first step towards using psycholinguistic data to contribute to the development of natural language generation systems. Gathering further data will significantly enhance this enterprise. There are also difficulties associated with implementing the findings concerning thematic role focusing. It seems likely, for example, that thematic role focusing only occurs in sentences containing implicit causality verbs (McKoon et al, 1993) and determining whether or not a verb exhibits implicit causality is not always straightforward. However, clear cases should not be problematic. In Table 6, I have listed a series of possible tests, in the form of condition-action pairs, that could be employed in a generation system on the basis of the findings described above. I have chosen to couch the actions in terms of a vote for a particular entity, hence suggesting that the entity with the largest number of votes at the end of the tests is the one that is chosen for mention in the current utterance. However, this is for convenience only, and the precise way in which such tests could be implemented will no doubt depend on the precise features of the implementation. For example, the joint effects of competing and converging pressures could be implemented in either a probabilistic rule based system or in an activation based system.

The thematic role results suggest that account needs to be taken of four main things: the presence of an implicit causality verb in U_{n-1}, the type of verb in U_{n-1} event or state, type of event verb - transfer or action, and the coherence relation to be expressed in U_n. The animacy results suggest that each of the three features, animacy, thematic role and recency exerts a pressure for choosing the entity possessing that feature. All of these features are taken into account in Table 6.

6.3 Choice of nominal expression

Centering theory has concentrated on identifying those situations in which a pronoun is preferred to a repeated name in an anaphoric reference. Psycholinguistic studies that have addressed the question of choice of anaphor have also concentrated on pronouns and repeated names. Thus, the discussion in this section will also confine itself to pronouns versus repeated names. There is other work that considers choice of referring expression more widely and that also includes the choice of nominal for introducing a novel entity. For example, Hawkins (1978) identified a range of situations in which indefinite and definite descriptions are used, and Gundel, Hedberg, and Zakarski, (1993) have proposed a referential hierarchy that ranks nominal expressions according to their degree of specificity. Gundel et al propose that choice of a nominal in the hierarchy is a joint function of the information structure of the discourse (that is, whether the discourse entities are "given" or "new" - Clark,

Condition	Action when generating U_n
	Give vote to:
U_n is a new sentence and the last entity in U_{n-1} is animate	Last mentioned entity
U_{n-1} contains one animate entity	The animate entity
U_{n-1} contains an implicit causality transfer verb	Goal
U_{n-1} contains an implicit causality transfer verb and the Theme is one of 2 or more animate entities	Theme
U_{n-1} contains an implicit causality transfer verb and three inanimate entities	Theme
U_n is a Purpose for U_{n-1} and U_{n-1} describes a transfer between two animate participants	Goal
U_{n-1} contains an implicit causality action verb	Patient
U_n is a Result of U_{n-1} and U_n describes an action	Patient
U_n is an Explanation of U_{n-1} and U_n describes an event (action or transfer)	Causal Agent
U_{n-1} contains an implicit causality state verb in which both Experiencer and Stimulus are animate and the coherence relation in U_n is an Explanation	Stimulus
U_{n-1} contains an implicit causality state verb in which both Experiencer and Stimulus are animate and the coherence relation in U_n is a Result	Experiencer

TABLE 6 Proposed tests to determine which nominal to generate in U_n as a function of the salience of the entities in a mental model of U_{n-1} and the intended coherence relation to be expressed in U_n

1977; Prince, 1981; Vallduvi, 1993) and Grice's maxim of quantity. Both of these accounts rely heavily on inferences based on general knowledge, which makes them difficult to implement in a natural language system, particularly a generation system. Consequently, I will not discuss these models further, but will focus on centering theory. In section 2.1, I discuss the role of the **Cb** in centering theory and suggest that, contrary to the implications of centering theory, the **Cb** does not refer to the most salient entity in the preceding utterance. Rather, it refers to the subject of the preceding utterance. In section 2.2, I discuss centering transitions and suggest a way in which topic changes might be introduced into a discourse. Section 2.3. considers the implications of the research reviewed in this section for language generation.

6.3.1 The Role of the Cb in Centering Theory.

In section 1.1, I pointed out that centering theory identified two local discourse centers. The first of these, the **Cf**, was discussed in that section. The second discourse center concerns the way in which coherence is maintained between pairs of utterances. For every utterance except the first in a discourse, there is a preferred site for linking the current utterance to the previous one. This preferred site is known as the backward looking centre or **Cb**.

According to Grosz et al (1995), the **Cb** normally refers to the highest ranked $\mathbf{Cf}(U_{n-1})$ that is realised in U_n and it is realised as a pronoun if there is a pronoun in the sentence. According to Gordon et al (1993), pronominalisation of the **Cb** promotes coherence because finding the referent of a pronoun involves relating it to other aspects of the text. By contrast, a name may contain sufficient information to identify its referent without reference to other aspects of the text. The fact that a name can specify its referent may cause a reader or listener to infer that the utterance in which it occurs is not meant to cohere with the preceding utterance, but rather is the beginning of a new segment. Gordon et al (1993) have further suggested that the **Cb** is typically the grammatical subject of the utterance. Centering theory also posits three constraints, the third of which is relevant for our purposes here. This is that $\mathbf{Cb}(U_n)$ is the highest ranked element of $\mathbf{Cf}(U_{n-1})$ that is realised in U(n). According to Walker et al (1998), the highest ranked element of $\mathbf{Cf}(U_{n-1})$ is the **Cp** and the **Cp** can be used to predict what will be referred to in U_n. From the above, we can infer that wherever possible, the $\mathbf{Cb}(U_n)$ will be realised as a pronoun in subject position and will refer to the **Cp** U_{n-1}.

An increasing number of studies support these claims about the **Cb**. Regarding the site of the **Cb** and its pronominalisation, when a sentence contains an anaphor in subject position that refers to the highest ranked **Cf** of the preceding utterance, subjects judge it to be more coherent when it contains a pronoun than when it contains a repeated name (Hudson-D'Zmura, 1988, Hudson et al, 1986, Hudson-D'Zmura & Tanenhaus, 1998). The same pattern is found when reading times are measured, with faster reading times being associated with a subject pronoun compared to repeated name (Gordon & Chan, 1995; Gordon & Scearce, 1995; Gordon et al., Experiment 4, 1993). However, this "repeated name penalty" does not occur if the anaphor is in non-subject position (Gordon et al, 1994, Experiment 2), unless the referent in subject position is new (Gordon & Chan, 1995, experiment 4). In these circumstances, the repeated name penalty occurs for the direct object of a sentence. Further, the location of the **Cb** is not affected by whether it fills an Agent or a Patient role. Gordon and Chan, (1995, experiments 1-3) used passive sentences and found a repeated name penalty for the surface subject regardless of its thematic role. Taken together, these results suggest that the location of the **Cb** is determined by a hierarchy of grammatical roles, with subject first, and is not influenced by semantic/pragmatic features, such as the thematic role of the **Cb**. A recent study by Chambers and Smyth (1998), however, challenges these claims. They found a repeated name penalty for non-subject anaphors as well as subject anaphors, as long as the antecedent and anaphor occupied parallel grammatical roles. All in all, with the exception of this last mentioned result, the studies support the idea that a subject pronoun in U_n is preferentially used to refer to the highest ranked entity in the $\mathbf{Cf}(U_{n-1})$, where the **Cf** is determined by being the subject and or the first mentioned entity.

However, we saw in section 1.1 that the **Cf** ranking involves thematic role focusing as well as structural focusing based on subjecthood and surface position. We need to determine, therefore, whether or not these factors also affect the choice of a pronoun over a repeated name. Stevenson et al (1994) addressed this issue in their experiments. As well as identifying who was mentioned first in the sentence continuations, they also determined the form of the reference. Contrary to the claims of centering theory, the salience of the antecedent had no effect on the choice of referring expression. Instead, the referring expression depended on the surface grammatical role of the antecedent. The results across all three kinds of verbs (transfers, actions and states) are shown in Table 7.

As can be seen in the table, when the anaphor refers to the first mentioned individual, a pronoun is normally used and when the anaphor refers to the second mentioned individual, then a repeated name is equally, or more, likely to be used. An example of the latter is the fol-

		Position of Antecedent	
		1st	2nd
Referring	Pronoun	6.62	2.73
Expression	Name	0.68	3.40

TABLE 7 Interaction between position of antecedent and choice of referring expression in the subject position of the continuation (from Experiment 3 of Stevenson et al, 1994).

lowing completion to *Terry kicked Nathan. Nathan fell to the ground clutching his knee in pain.*

These results suggest that two different mechanisms are responsible for choosing who or what to refer to and how to refer to them. The choice of *which entity* the subject of U_n refers to depends on the salience of the entities in U_{n-1}, salience being affected by both structural and semantic/pragmatic factors, as discussed in section 1 of this chapter. However, the choice of *how* the reference is made to an entity in the subject position of U_n depends on the entity's grammatical role in U_{n-1}. If the entity is the subject of U_{n-1}, then it will be referred to by a pronoun in the subject position of U_n. If the entity is a non-subject in U_{n-1}, then it is just as likely to be referred to by repeated name in the subject position of U_n. Support for this claim comes from the data shown in Table 7. This latter result also suggests that the repeated name penalty is diagnostic of the **Cb**(U_n) rather than of the salience of entities in the **Cf**(U_{n-1}).

6.3.2 Topic Changes and Transitions between Utterances

Centering theory identifies four types of transition relations between utterances U_n and U_{n-1}, depending on whether or not the **Cb** (U_{n-1}) is maintained in U_n and on whether or not the **Cb** (U_n) is also the **Cp** (U_n) (Walker et al, 1998). Table 8 shows the four transitions as a function of these two dependencies. The most coherent discourse is said to use the continue transition, in which the **Cb** is both the most highly ranked **Cf** (U_{n-1}) and the **Cb** (U_{n-1}).

There is some psycholinguistic evidence to support the idea that a continue transition is more coherent than a rough shift (Gordon & Scearce, 1995, Experiment 1; Gordon et al, 1993, Experiment 4). However, when a smooth shift is used, the results do not support the coherence claim (Gordon et al, 1993, Experiment 5). A further study, using a rough shift, found inconclusive results (Gordon & Scearce, 1995, Experiment 2). Clearly more studies are needed to clarify the psychological

	Cb (U_n)= **Cb** (U_{n-1}) or **Cb** (U_{n-1}) undefined	**Cb** (U_n) =(**Cb** (U_{n-1})
Cb (U_n)= **Cp** (U_n)	Continue	Smooth Shift
Cb (U_n) =(**Cp** (U_n)	Retain	Rough Shift

TABLE 8 Centering transitions

status of the different transitions. Nevertheless, if the **Cb** is normally in subject position and preferentially refers to a preceding subject using a pronoun, we might speculate that the role of the **Cb** is something akin to Sidner's actor focus, and that, furthermore, its role is to track the topic throughout a discourse. Then retain and shift transitions would arise when there is a topic shift. In this section I consider one possible pattern for topic shifting.

A number of researchers have commented that a common pattern in discourse is for a retain to be followed by a smooth shift. Indeed, Brennan et al (1987) have argued that a retain is a signal of an impending shift and that a generation system could use a retain prior to a shift. Kibble (1999) also argues for a pattern of retain followed by a shift and suggests a means of implementing this preference in a generation system. He gives an example from Grosz et al (1995) to illustrate this pattern:

a.	John has had trouble arranging his vacation.	**Cb**=?, **Cp**=John
b.	He cannot find anyone to take over his responsibilities.	**Cb**=John, **Cp**=John
c.	He called up Mike yesterday to work out a plan.	**Cb**=John, **Cp**=John
d.	Mike has annoyed him a lot recently.	**Cb**=John, **Cp**=Mike
e.	He called John at 5 am on Friday last week.	**Cb**=Mike, **Cp**=Mike

The transition from c. to d. above is a retain and the transition from d. to e, is a smooth shift. Brennan (1995) found support for this retain-shift pattern when she analysed a corpus consisting of descriptions of a televised baseball match. She found that when a speaker introduces a new referent, with a definite reference, in object position, it is first referred to again with a definite reference in subject position before being pronominalised in the subject position of the next utterance. We might conclude, therefore, that a good way to change the topic would be to implement this retain-shift pattern.

6.3.3 Implications for Generation

There are two main implications of the above discussion for language generation. One is in the choice of a pronoun versus a repeated name in subject position. If an entity is the subject of U_{n-1}, then a pronoun is most likely to be used in the subject position of U_n to refer to this entity. On the other hand, if the entity is in non-subject position in U_{n-1}, then a repeated name is just as likely to be used in the subject position of U_n to refer to this entity. The second implication is that the choice of a repeated name may be the first step in a topic shift that consists of a retain transition followed by a shift transition. Specifically, a named non-subject entity in U_{n-1} may first be referred to by a repeated name in subject position in U_n before being referred to by a pronoun in U_{n+1}.

6.4 Summary

In this paper, I have proposed that the choice of who to refer to in an utterance depends on the salience of the entity in the speaker's mental model of the preceding utterance. I have also proposed that the choice of how to refer to an entity in the subject position of an utterance depends on the grammatical role of the entity in U_{n-1}. If the subject entity is also the subject of U_{n-1}, then it is realised as a pronoun in U_n. But if subject the entity is a non-subject of U_{n-1}, then it is realised as a repeated name in U_n. In section 1, I identified a number of features that contributed to salience and to the choice of who to mention in the current utterance. These included the thematic role focus evoked by implicit causality verbs, the coherence relation to be expressed in the new utterance, and recency. Animacy was also a potent infuence on salience and it also moderated the effects of verb evoked salience and recency: The most recent entity is only salient when it is animate, and the salience of the Theme or Goal in transfer sentences depends on the precise pattern of animate and inanimate entities in the utterance. Tests for use in a generation system were proposed on the basis of these results. However, the detailed ways in which some features moderate the effects of others still need to be specified more precisely. In section 2, I presented evidence in support of my second proposal and suggested further that the **Cb** may be used to track the topic throughout a discourse. I also suggested that topic shifts may underlie the retain and shift transitions of centering theory. For purposes of generation it was concluded in section 2.3. that a pronoun in subject position would normally refer to the subject of the previous utterance, unless a topic shift was intended. In this latter case, a repeated name would be used in subject position to refer to a named entity in non-subject position in the previous utterance. All in all, psycholinguistic research holds considerable promise for facilitating the development of language generation systems.

Acknowledgements

This work was carried out as part of a project on "Focusing and the representation of events" funded by the Human Communication Research Centre (HCRC) and also as part of the GNOME project (Generating Nominal Expressions), funded by the EPSRC of Great Britain. GNOME is a collaboration between the Information Technology Research Institute in the University of Brighton and the HCRC in the Universities of Edinburgh and Durham. The HCRC was funded by the ESRC of Great Britain. Thanks to two anonymous reviewers for useful comments on an earlier draft of this chapter.

References

Anderson, A., Garrod, S., & Sanford, A.J. (1983). The accessibility of pronominal antecedents as a function of episode shifts in narrative text. *Quarterly Journal of Experimental Psychology, 35*, 427-440

Andrews, A. (1985). The Major Functions of the Noun Phrase. In T. Shopen, (Ed.) *Language Typology and Syntactic Description*, Vol. 1: Clause Structure. Cambridge University Press

Au, T.K-F, (1986). A verb is worth a thousand words: The causes and consequences of interpersonal events implicit in language. *Journal of Memory and Language, 25*, 104-122

Brennan, S.E. (1995). Centering attention in discourse. *Language and Cognitive Processes, 10*, 137-167

Brennan, S.E., M. W. Friedman C.J. Pollard. (1987). A centering approach to pronouns. In *Proceedings of the 25th Annual Meeting of the Association of Computational Linguistics*, pp. 155-162. Stanford

Caramazza , A. Grober, E.H., Garvey, C. and Yates, J.V. (1977). Comprehension of anaphoric pronouns. *Journal of Verbal Learning and Verbal Behaviour, 16*, 601-609

Carroll, J.J. (1958). Process and content in psycholinguistics. In R. Glaser (Ed.), *Current Trends in Description and Analysis of Behaviour*. Pittsburg: University of Pittsburg Press

Chambers, C. & Smyth, R. (1998). Structural parallelism and attentional focus: A test of centering theory. *Journal of Memory and Language, 39*, 593- 609

Clark, H.H. & Begun, J.S. (1971). The semantics of sentence subjects. *Language and Speech, 14*, 34-46

Clark, H.H. (1977). Bridging. In P.N. Johnson-Laird & P.C. Wason (Eds.).

Thinking: Readings in Cognitive Science. London and New York: Cambridge University Press

Ehrlich, K. (1980). Comprehension of pronouns. *Quarterly Journal of Experimental Psychology, 32*, 247-255

Ertel, S. (1977). Where do subjects of sentences come from? In S. Rosenberg, Ed.) *Sentence Production: Developments in Research and Theory.* Hillsdale, NJ: Lawrence Erlbaum Associates

Fillmore, C. (1968). The case of case. In E. Bach & R.T. Harms (Eds.), *Universals in Linguistic Theory.* New York: Holt, Rinehart and Winston

Flores D'Arcais, G.B. (1973), Some perceptual determinants of sentence construction. Report No. EO36-73. Psychological Institute, University of Leiden

Garrod, S., & Sanford, A.J. (1988). Thematic subjecthood and cognitive constraints on discourse structure. *Journal of Pragmatics, 12*, 519- 534.

Garvey, C. & Caramazza, A. (1974). Implicit causality in verbs. *Linguistic Inquiry, 5*, 459-464

Gernsbacher, M.A. (1989) Mechanisms that improve referential access. *Cognition 32*, 99-156

Gernsbacher, M.A. & Hargreaves, D.J. (1989). Accessing sentence participants: the advantage of first mention. *Journal of Memory and Language, 27*, 699- 717

Gordon, P.C. & Chan, D. (1995). Pronouns, passives and discourse coherence. *Journal of Memory and Language, 34*, 216-231. (1995)

Gordon, P.C. & Scearce, K.A. (1995). Pronominalisation and discourse coherence, discourse structure and pronoun interpretation. *Memory and Cognition, 23*, 313-323

Gordon, P.C., Grosz, B.J. & Gilliom, L.A. (1993). Pronouns, names and the centering of attention in discourse. *Cognitive Science, 17*, 311-348

Grosz, B.J., Joshi, A. & Weinstein, S. (1995). Centering: A Framework for Modelling the Local coherence of Discourse. *Computational Linguistics, 21*, 203-225

Gundel, J., Hedberg, N. & Zakarski, R. (1993). Cognitive status and the form of referring expressions in discourse. *Language, 69*, 274-307

Hawkins, J.A. *Definiteness and Indefiniteness.* London: Croom Helm

Hudson D'Zmura, S.B. (1988). The Structure of Discourse and Anaphor Resolution: *The Discourse Center and the Roles of Nouns and Pronouns.* Ph.D. thesis, University of Rochester

Hudson, S. & Tanenhaus, M.K. (1998). Antecedents and ambiguous pronouns. In M.A. Walker, A.K. Joshi & E.F. Prince (Eds.), *Centering Theory in Discourse.* Clarendon Press: Oxford

Hudson, S., Tanenhaus, M.K. & Dell, G. (1986). The effect of the discourse center on the local coherence of a discourse. (1986). In C. Clifton, Jr. (Ed.) *Proceedings of the 12th Annual Conference of the Cognitive Science Society*, pp. 96-101. Erlbaum: Hillsdale, NJ

Jackendoff, R. (1985). The status of thematic relations in linguistic theory. *Linguistic Inquiry, 18*, 369-411

Johnson-Laird, P.N. (1983) *Mental Models*, Harvard University Press, Cambridge, Massachusetts

Johnson-Laird, P.N. & Garnham, A. (1980). Descriptions and discourse models. *Linguistics and Philosophy, 3*, 371-393

Karmiloff-Smith, A. (1980). Psychological processes underlying pronominalisation and nonpronominalisation in children's connected discourse. In J. Kreiman & E. Ojeda (Eds.), *Papers from the Parasession on Pronouns and Anaphora.* Chicago: Chicago Linguistic Society

Kibble, R. (1999). **Cb** or not **Cb**? Centering theory applied to NLG. In *Proceedings of ACL'99 Workshop on Discourse and Reference Structure*, University of Maryland, June 1999

Knott, A. (1996). *A data-driven methodology for motivating a set of coherence relations.* PhD thesis, Department of Artificial Intelligence, University of Edinburgh

Marslen-Wilson, W.D., Tyler, L.K. & Koster, J. (1993). Integrative processes in utterance resolution. *Journal of Memory and Language, 32*, 647-666

McKoon, G., Ward, G., Ratcliff, R. & Sproat. R. (1993). Morphosyntactic and pragmatic factors affecting the accessibility of discourse entities. *Journal of Memory and Language, 32*, 56-75

Moens, M. & Steedman, M.J. (1988). Temporal ontology and temporal reference. *Computational Linguistics, 14*, 15-28

Osgood, C.E. & Bock, K. (1977). Salience and sentencing: some production principles. In S. Rosenberg, Ed.) *Sentence Production: Developments in Research and Theory.* Hillsdale, NJ: Lawrence Erlbaum Associates

Pearson, J., Stevenson, R.J. & Poesio, M. (in preparation). Effects of animacy, thematic role and sentence position on the production of referring expressions

Prince, E.F. (1981). *Toward a taxonomy of given-new information. In P. Cole (Ed.) Radical Pragmatics. New York: Academic Press*

Radford, A. (1988). Transformational Grammar: A First Course. Cambridge University Press, Cambridge

Sanford, A.J., Moar, K. & Garrod. S (1988). Proper names as controllers of discourse focus. *Language and Speech, 33*, 43-56

Sidner, C.L. (1979). *Towards a Computational Theory of Definite Anaphora in English Discourse.* PhD. Thesis, MIT

Stevenson, R.J. & Urbanowicz, A. (1995). Structural focusing, thematic role focusing and the comprehension of pronouns. In *Proceedings of the Seventeenth Annual conference of the Cognitive Science Society.* Erlbaum: Hillsdale, NJ

Stevenson, R.J. & Urbanowicz, A.J. (submitted). Effects of structural and semantic/pragmatic focusing: towards a dynamic model of focus

Stevenson, R.J., Crawley, R.A. & Kleinman, D. (1994). Thematic roles, focus and the representation of actions. *Language and Cognitive Processes, 9*, 519- 548

Stevenson, R.J., Knott, A., Oberlander, J. & McDonald, S. (2000). Interpreting pronouns and connectives: Interactions among focusing, thematic roles and coherence relations. *Language and Cognitive Processes, 15.* 225-262

Tannenbaum, P.H. & Williams, F. (1968). Generation of active and passive sentences as a function of subject and object focus. *Journal of Verbal Learning and Verbal Behaviour, 7*, 246-250

Turner, E.A. & Rommetveit, R. (1968). Focus of attention in active and passive sentences. *Journal of Verbal Learning and Verbal Behaviour, 7*, 543-548

Vallduvi, E. (1993). Information packaging: a survey. Report number HCRC/RP44, Human Communication Research Centre, University of Edinburgh

Walker, M.A., Iida, M., & Cote, S. (1994). Japanese discourse and the process of centering. *Computational Linguistics, 20*, 193-231

M.A. Walker, A.K. Joshi & E.F. Prince (Eds.) (1998). *Centering Theory in Discourse.* Clarendon Press: Oxford

7

Generation of Contextually Appropriate Word Order

IVANA KRUIJFF-KORBAYOVÁ, GEERT-JAN KRUIJFF AND JOHN BATEMAN

7.1 Introduction

In any natural language communication, the content that is being communicated is by nature multi-dimensional (in the sense that conceptual structures are not linear but form complex networks of interacting associations). However, since each participant can only utter the elements in a linear order, linguistic structures of all degrees of complexity need to be projected into one dimension, and the individual elements must be ordered sequentially according to certain rules. The rules and schemes of linear ordering can be studied at different strata of a given language. What we concentrate on in this paper are the rules and schemes pertaining to the linear ordering of elements constituting a clause. The linear ordering of clause elements is usually referred to as **word order** (WO), even though the elements are not only individual words. We consider both the mutual ordering of phrases and groups within a clause, and their ordering with respect to the main verb.

The problem of proper WO treatment is a very important and challenging one in **natural language generation** (NLG), especially when the generation of connected, natural text (spoken or written) is concerned. Without a correct WO any generated text is much less fluent than it should be: even though it might well be syntactically well-formed a contextually wrong WO can even lead to misinterpretation.

Information Sharing: Reference and Presupposition in Language Generation and Interpretation.
Edited by Kees van Deemter and Rodger Kibble.

Well known examples for English include interpretations that assign differing preferred quantifier scopes depending on the order in which the linguistic expressions introducing those quantifiers appear in the surface string; others include controlling preferred sites of prepositional phrase or relative clause attachment by careful ordering. These problems, significant though they are for English, become substantially more important when we consider languages with a higher degree of **word order freedom**, like the Slavonic languages. The issue of WO control for such languages must be addressed in NLG because the various WO variants of a sentence, although *grammatically* well-formed, do not necessarily have the same meaning and are generally not interchangeable in a given context. The following example illustrates this with two versions of a short discourse in Czech: The WOs throughout (2) are bizarre, and do not correspond to the intended meaning. With the exclusion of very particular intonation patterning, this text is even unacceptable and incoherent.[1]

(1) a. Otevřete nový obrázek.
open$_{i2pl}$ new drawing$_{acc}$
"Open a new drawing."

b. Vložte čáru a oblouk.
insert$_{i2pl}$ line$_{acc}$ and arc$_{acc}$
"Insert a line and an arc."

c. Nyní obrázek uložte.
now drawing$_{acc}$ save$_{i2pl}$
"Now save the drawing."

(2) a. Nový obrázek otevřete.
new drawing$_{acc}$ open$_{i2pl}$
"Open the new drawing."

b. Čáru a oblouk vložte.
line$_{acc}$ and arc$_{acc}$ insert$_{i2pl}$
"Insert the line and the arc."

c. Nyní uložte obrázek.
now save$_{i2pl}$ drawing$_{acc}$
"Now save a drawing."

The fact that WO is relatively free in the Slavonic languages, but not arbitrary with respect to a given communicative intention and the current discourse context, brings about two important issues for the process of automatic generation of continuous texts:

- **coverage**: the generator (the grammar) needs to be able to generate all the grammatically well-formed WO variants in a given language.
- **control**: the generator must choose the most appropriate grammatically well-formed WO with respect to the communicative intention and the context.

From a cross-linguistic perspective, or from the viewpoint of building a multilingual NLG system, an additional issue comes in:

[1]Throughout the paper, we assume a neutral intonation pattern in all examples in the Slavonic languages, i.e., the intonation centre coinciding with the last element of a clause. In some cases, the corresponding English sentence may require a marked placement of the intonation center.

- **flexibility**: WO in different languages should be described in uniform terms to enable cross-linguistic generalizations; furthermore, it is desirable to employ a uniform mechanism handling WO, which can be adjusted to a particular language by setting a few parameters, or by providing language-specific preferences.

Our discussion in this paper is anchored within the context of developing a multilingual system for generating software instruction texts in Czech, Bulgarian and Russian. We concentrate on the factors determining WO in these languages, and the corresponding issues of WO control in multilingual generation. Nevertheless, the issues we address and the WO generation approach we propose are also applicable to other languages and are relevant in any register (in (Kruijff *et al.* 2001) we discuss an application to German).

Outline of the paper In Section 7.2 we demonstrate the degree of WO freedom with which one is confronted in Czech, Bulgarian and Russian, by presenting several examples from software instruction texts.

Section 7.3 presents the control issue in more detail. We first give examples supporting the claim that WO in the three Slavonic languages is not arbitrary. Then, we concentrate on the factors restricting WO in any particular case, namely global text organization, information structure, and syntactic structure.

In Section 7.4 we discuss thematic and information structures as a source of WO control. We combine the insights concerning determination of WO in two functionally-oriented approaches: Halliday's (1985) Systemic Functional Grammar framework and the framework of Functional Generative Description (Sgall *et al.* 1986).

In Section 7.5 we present our approach to generating WO; this approach is sufficiently flexible as well as sufficiently constrained, so as to be suitable for languages with varying degrees of WO freedom. We demonstrate the application of our approach with Czech in Section 7.5.2.

Section 7.6 closes the paper with a brief discussion of the overall appropriateness of the proposed approach.

7.2 Word Order Variation

For sentences with a moderate number of syntactic groups there are usually quite a few WO variants in the Slavonic languages that are grammatically well-formed but may differ in the contextual conditions of their use (see Section 7.3). Let us consider the following sentences containing one main verb and two or more nominal groups or prepositional phrases appearing either before or after the verb in different orders.[2]

(3) **Cz** Otevřete soubor příkazem `Open`.
Ru Откройте файл коммандой `Open`.
Bg Отворете файла с командата `Open`.
gloss open$_{i2pl}$ file$_{acc}$ command$_{ins}$ `Open`
En Open a file with the `Open` command.

(4) **Cz** Soubor otevřete příkazem `Open`.
Ru Файл откройте коммандой `Open`.
Bg Файла отворете с командата `Open`.
gloss file$_{acc}$ open$_{i2pl}$ command$_{ins}$ `Open`
En Open the file with the `Open` command.

(5) **Cz** Příkazem `Open` otevřete soubor.
Ru Коммандой `Open` откройте файл.
Bg С командата `Open` отворете файла.
gloss command$_{ins}$ `Open` open$_{i2pl}$ file$_{acc}$
En With the `Open` command, open a file.

(6) **Cz** Příkazem `Open` soubor otevřete.
Ru ? Коммандой `Open` файл откройте.
Bg * С командата `Open` файла отворете.
gloss command$_{ins}$ `Open` file$_{acc}$ open$_{i2pl}$
En With the `Open` command, open the file.

(7) **Cz** Otevřete příkazem `Open` soubor.
Ru ? Откройте коммандой `Open` файл.
Bg * Отворете с командата `Open` файла.
gloss open$_{i2pl}$ command$_{ins}$ `Open` file$_{acc}$
En Open the file with the `Open` command.

(8) **Cz** Soubor příkazem `Open` otevřete.
Ru * Файл коммандой `Open` откройте.
Bg * Файла с командата `Open` отворете.
gloss File$_{acc}$ command$_{ins}$ `Open` open$_{i2pl}$
En Open the file with the `Open` command.

In all three languages, (3,4,5) are grammatical. (6) and (7) are grammatical in Czech, but unnatural in Russian, and ungrammatical in Bulgarian. (8) is grammatical in Czech, but ungrammatical in Russian and Bulgarian. We encountered differences in grammaticality judgements on WO

[2]Note some of the differences between the languages: Czech and Russian have richer morphology, and distinguish seven and six cases, respectively; Bulgarian does not differentiate between cases. In the discussed examples, instrument is expressed by instrumental case in Czech and Russian, but it is expressed using the preposition 'c' in Bulgarian. Another difference concerns articles: whereas in Czech and Russian there is no definite or indefinite article (although demonstrative pronouns can be used as determiners), Bulgarian has a definite suffix, which appears as '-та' in 'командата' in the discussed examples. In spite of these differences, we present just one common gloss in the examples below, for simplicity.

variants in Bulgarian, Czech and Russian also in some other cases (cf. (Adonova *et al.* 1999) for more discussion). However, a more thorough study would be needed to confirm and generalize such observations.

The instructions in (3-8) are expressed by (polite) imperatives (in second person plural). In Czech, it is also possible to formulate instructions in indicative mood with active voice. The Actor in the Subject position can be realized by a zero-pronoun,[3] as in (9). The range of possible WO variation in the indicative mood is the same as in the imperative mood, i.e., all six permutations are grammatically well-formed.

(9) **Cz** Otevřeme soubor příkazem `Open`.
open$_{1pl}$ file$_{acc}$ command$_{ins}$ `Open`
"One opens a file with the `Open` command."

When the Subject is non-pronominal, it undergoes the same ordering mechanisms as other elements in the clause. The Czech sentences in (10,11) thus have twenty four and six WO permutations, respectively, all of which are grammatically well-formed.

(10) **Cz** Uživatel otevírá soubor příkazem `Open`.
user$_{nom}$ open$_{3sg}$ file$_{acc}$ command$_{ins}$ `Open`
"The user opens a file with the `Open` command."

(11) **Cz** Příkaz `Open` otevírá soubor.
command$_{nom}$ `Open` open$_{3sg}$ file$_{acc}$
"The `Open` command opens a file."

Furthermore, all three languages can express instructions by sentences in indicative mood in passive voice, using a reflexive passive construction, as in (12) where we show one WO variant for illustration.

(12) **Cz** Příkazem `Open` se otevírá soubor.
command$_{ins}$ `Open` *refl* open$_{3sg}$ file$_{nom}$
Bg С командата `Open` се отваря файл.
with command$_{def}$ `Open` *refl* open$_{3sg}$ file
Ru Коммандой `Open` откроется файл.
command$_{ins}$ `Open` open$_{refl3sg}$ file$_{nom}$
"With the `Open` command, a file is opened."

The use of the reflexive passive brings about the problem of **clitic placement**, in particular the placement of reflexive particles in Czech and Bulgarian.[4] This is an example of grammatically constrained ordering. In Bulgarian, the particle "се" is placed either after or before

[3]In instruction texts in Czech, first person plural is usually used in indicative mood, less often second person plural. Second person singular can be used only in informal style.

[4]In Russian, reflexive forms are created with the '-ся' suffix attached to the main verb, and hence no particular ordering issue arises.

the main finite verb form in a clause, depending on whether the verb is clause-initial or not, respectively:

(13) **Bg** Отваря се файл.
open$_{3sg}$ *refl* file
"A file opens."

(14) **Bg** Файл се отваря.
file *refl* open$_{3sg}$
"A file opens."

In Czech the situation is more complicated: Czech clitics have to be placed in the so-called **Wackernagel position**, characterized roughly as the position between the first and the second element in a clause.[5] (15-19) show the other grammatically well-formed ordering alternatives corresponding to the Czech sentence in (12).

(15) **Cz** Příkazem `Open` se soubor otevírá.
Command$_{ins}$ `Open` *refl* file$_{nom}$ open$_{3sg}$
"With the `Open` command, the file is opened."

(16) **Cz** Soubor se otevírá příkazem `Open`.
file$_{nom}$ *refl* open$_{3sg}$ command$_{ins}$ `Open`
"The file is opened with the `Open` command."

(17) **Cz** Soubor se příkazem `Open` otevírá.
file$_{nom}$ *refl* command$_{ins}$ `Open` open$_{3sg}$
"The file is opened with the `Open` command."

(18) **Cz** Otevírá se soubor příkazem `Open`.
opens *refl* file$_{nom}$ command$_{ins}$ `Open`
"A file is opened with the `Open` command."

(19) **Cz** Otevírá se příkazem `Open` soubor.
opens *refl* command$_{ins}$ `Open` file$_{nom}$
"A file is opened with the `Open` command."

If there are multiple clitics in a single clause in Czech, then they have to be grouped in a cluster. Their mutual ordering depends on their functions and is constrained by the grammar.

The important conclusion drawn from these comparisons of WO freedom is that in developing a uniform mechanism for handling WO in our multilingual NLG system, we need to allow for a sufficient degree of flexibility such that each grammar can set whatever grammatical constraints are needed in the individual language, while at the same time, leaving grammatically unconstrained ordering to be decided by other appropriate strategies (cf. Section 7.5).

[5]Naturally, this leaves to be defined what "element" means. It is easy to show that "first element" does not equate to "first constituent" in any simple sense, since the element can be of arbitrary complexity. It is also possible to find examples where multiple elements precede the clitic cluster; however, these cases seem to be restricted to cases where all those pre-clitic elements are strongly backgrounded (Oliva and Avgustinova 1995).

7.3 Context and WO

Various factors have been discerned in the language system in general which play an important role in expressing a given content in a specific linear form. The inventory of these factors contains at least the following: information structure, syntactic structure, intonation, rhythm and style. These factors are very general, and can therefore be considered language universals, certainly within the family of Indo-European languages. However, the individual factors may have different importance for the linear ordering in a given language.

For instance, English is an example of a language where WO is strongly constrained by syntactic structure. In such languages, differences in information structure are often reflected by varying the intonation pattern or by the choice of a particular type of grammatical construction. This latter includes, e.g., the use of a definite nominal group to refer anaphorically, and the use of an indefinite nominal group to introduce new entities. In languages with rich cases systems and no definite or indefinite article, such as Czech and Russian, the same effects are achieved by varying WO in accordance to information structure. In contrast, Bulgarian is closer to English in that its WO is more rigid (cf. examples (1) and (2) in Section 7.1).

In order to illustrate the general point that WO selections are related to information structure, let us overview appropriateness judgements for the Czech versions of examples (3-8) presented in Section 7.2, repeated below for convenience. Similar judgments hold in all three languages, although the three languages differ, as we noted in Section 7.2 above, in grammaticality judgments of the sentences.

(20) **Cz** Otevřete příkazem `Open` soubor.
open$_{i2pl}$ command$_{ins}$ `Open` file$_{acc}$
"Open a file with the `Open` command."

The ordering in (20) is neutral with respect to context (cf. 'systemic ordering' in Section 7.4.1, 203). It can be used "out of the blue", or in a context which can be approximated by the question *What should we do?*.[6] Alternatively, (20) could be used in a context characterized by the question *What should we open by the* `Open` *command?*, when the `Open` command is not being contrasted with some other entity.

[6]We use questions to indicate which contexts would be appropriate for uttering sentences with particular WO variants. Such question-answer pairs should be conceived of in terms of the **question test** (Sgall *et al.* 1986) rather than as constituting natural dialogue exchanges.

(21) **Cz** Otevřete soubor příkazem `Open`.
open$_{i2pl}$ file$_{acc}$ command$_{ins}$ `Open`
"Open the file with the `Open` command."

(22) **Cz** Soubor otevřete příkazem `Open`.
file$_{acc}$ open$_{i2pl}$ command$_{ins}$ `Open`
"Open the file with the `Open` command."

Both (21) and (22) are appropriate when some file is salient, for instance when the user is working with a file. That is why we put the definite article into the English translation. The action of opening can, but does not have to, be salient, too. The contexts in which (21) and (22) can be appropriately used can be characterized by the questions *What should we do with the file?* or *How should we open the file?*. Unlike (21), (22) can also be used if 'soubor' (file) is contrasted with another entity.

(23) **Cz** Příkazem `Open` otevřete soubor.
command$_{ins}$ `Open` open$_{i2pl}$ file$_{acc}$
"With the `Open` command, open a file."

(24) **Cz** Příkazem `Open` soubor otevřete.
command$_{ins}$ `Open` file$_{acc}$ open$_{i2pl}$
"With the `Open` command, open the file."

The contexts in which (23) can be used are characterized by *What should we do with the* `Open` *command?*. While (23) does not refer to a specific file, in (24) a salient file is presumed. (24) is appropriate in contexts characterized by *What should we do to the file with the* `Open` *command?*.

It is also possible to use (23) in a context characterized by *What should we do?*, and (24) in a context characterized by *What should we do to the file?*, if it is presumed that we are talking about using various commands (or various means or instruments) to do various things. In the latter type of context, the `Open` command does not have to be salient.

(25) **Cz** Soubor příkazem `Open` otevřete.
file$_{acc}$ command$_{ins}$ `Open` open$_{i2pl}$
"Open the file with the `Open` command."

Example (25) is appropriate when both a file and the `Open` command are salient. The contexts in which (25) can be appropriately used can be characterized by *What should we do to the file with the* `Open` *command?*.

Analogous judgements concerning contextual appropriateness apply to the variants of these instructions in indicative mood, both in active voice and in the reflexive passive, cf. (9-19) in Section 7.2. The orders in which the verb is first do not presume the salience of either a file or a command. The orders in which 'file' precedes the verb appears to presume the salience of a file, the order in which 'command' precedes the verb appear to presume the salience of a command. When both 'file' and 'command' precede the verb, the salience of both a file and a command appears to be presumed.

These judgements show that differences in WO very often correspond to differences in informative status of the entities and processes that the text concerns: in particular, whether they are already familiar or not, and whether they are assumed to be salient. Note that in English, a definite vs. indefinite nominal expression, i.e. 'a|the file', is used in the individual WO variants.

The extent to which WO reflects information structure is constrained by the degree of WO freedom in a given language (cf. (Kruijff 2001) for a detailed cross-linguistic discussion). In Czech and Russian, as expected, WO reflects information structure in most cases (cf. (Adonova *et al.* 1999) for exceptions observed in Russian). Bulgarian resembles English in its preference for a single element preceding the main verb of a clause. On the other hand, the ordering of the elements following the verb has a higher degree of freedom, at least in some configurations. We hypothesize that the Bulgarian WO follows information structure in this case.

To summarize so far: Since sentences which differ only in WO (and not in syntactic realizations of constituents) are not freely interchangable in a given context, we have to be able to generate contextually appropriate WO. In order to achieve this, we need to be able to capture not only the structural restrictions specific for the individual languages, but also the information status of the entities being referred to.

7.4 Sources for Contextual Control of Word Order

In the Praguian linguistic tradition, **information structure** has always been considered the main factor determining the linear ordering within a sentence (cf. the works of Mathesius (1939), the Prague School (Sgall *et al.* 1973; Sgall *et al.* 1986; Hajičová and Sgall 1987; Hajičová 1993); or Firbas (1992)).

Although "information structure" can be used as a general term for various notions employed in contemporary theories of the syntax-semantics interface—notions that reflect how the conveyed content is distributed over a sentence, and how it is thereby structured or "perspectivized"[7]—we also need it to become sufficiently focused so as to support an implemented generation system. This task is complicated by the fact

[7] The term information structure has been coined by Halliday (1967), and is explicitly used for example by Steedman (1994; 1996; 2000a; 2000b). Consider also Chafe's *information packaging* as used by Vallduví (1992), *topic-focus articulation* within the Modern Prague School (Sgall *et al.* 1986), or Firbas' (1992) *functional sentence perspective*.

that many terminological frameworks have been proposed in the literature, but it is in general unclear to what extent these varying accounts are mutually compatible (see (Steedman and Kruijff-Korbayová 2001) for an overview). Comparison and use is further complicated by the fact that similar terms are also often used (not always knowingly) to refer to quite different theoretical entities. For example, in every approach to information structure, the clause is considered to consist of (at least) two parts: The often used dichotomies are, e.g. *Theme-Rheme* (Sgall *et al.* 1973; Halliday 1985; Daneš 1985; Firbas 1992; Steedman 2000a), *Topic-Focus* (Sgall *et al.* 1986), *Background-Focus* (Krifka 1992), *Ground-Focus* (Vallduví 1992).[8] But there are substantial differences between the individual usage of particular researchers.

In order to provide constraints for WO decisions within our generation architecture, we require mechanisms through which particular patterns of information structuring can appropriately influence the choice among the WO variants available. These patterns are provided by our text planning component. We have found two complementary approaches to the relationship between aspects of information structuring and WO to be ripe for application in the generation of extended texts. In this section, we briefly introduce them and show their application.

In order to clarify the 'complementary' nature of the approaches that we have adopted, it is necessary first to distinguish between two dimensions of organization that are often confused or whose difference is contested: in his Systemic Functional Grammar (SFG), Halliday (1970;1985) distinguishes between the **thematic structure** of a clause and its **information structure**.

The thematic structure and information structure of a clause are closely related but not the same. Whereas the **Theme** "is the starting point for the message, it is the ground from which the clause is taking off" (Halliday 1985: p.38), the information structure concerns the distinction between the **Given** as "what is presented as being already known to the listener" (Halliday 1985: p.59), and the **New** as "what the listener is being invited to attend to as new, or unexpected, or important" (*ibid*).

7.4.1 Information Structure and Ordering

In Halliday's original approach, the root assumption for English is that ordering, when not grammatically constrained, is iconic with respect to "newsworthiness"—which is part of the information structure and hence concerns Given/New. So under the scale from Given to New, the

[8]Within the scope and aim of the present paper, we have to refrain from a more in-depth discussion of the various approaches to information structure (see, e.g., (Hajičová and Kruijff-Korbayová 1999)).

"newer" elements would come towards the end of the information unit; the "newest" element would be the bearer of nuclear stress. This approach relies on the possibility of giving a complete ordering of all elements in the context with respect to their salience or newsworthiness. But, to our knowledge, this approach has not yet been applied in a complete NLG system. (Although Steedman's (1996) approach to information structure, for example, has been applied to generation of spoken English (Prevost and Steedman 1994; Prevost 1995), the main concern of that work was to assign contextually appropriate intonation to answers in a dialogue system. The ordering of clause elements was fully determined by syntactic structure.)

The notion of ordering by newsworthiness in Halliday's approach is parallel to the notion of **communicative dynamism** (CD) introduced in the early works of Firbas (for a recent formulation see (Firbas 1992)) and used also within the Functional Generative Description (FGD, Sgall *et al.* 1986). In this view, too, the prototypical ordering of clause elements from left to right respects newsworthiness: in prototypical cases, WO corresponds to CD. However, textually motivated thematization or grammatical constraints may force WO to diverge from CD.

The FGD approach differs from Halliday's in that, in addition to CD, it works with a default (canonical) ordering, called **systemic ordering** (SO). SO is a *language specific* ordering of complements, i.e. "arguments" and "adjuncts", of verbs, nouns, adjectives or adverbs which corresponds to the canonical ("neutral") WO. SO is considered constant within a given language. SO has been studied in most detail for Czech (Sgall *et al.* 1980; Sgall *et al.* 1986; Hajičová and Sgall 1987; Petkevič 1995); for SO in English see (Hajičová *et al.* 1995), for SO in German see (Sgall *et al.* 1995). Similar ideas for Japanese have been developed for instance by Kuno (1972). The SOs for Russian and Bulgarian have not yet been studied in general. We follow Sgall *et al.* (1986) in considering the SOs for the main types of complementations in Russian and Bulgarian to be similar to the Czech one, though there can be slight differences (cf. the observations reported in (Adonova *et al.* 1999)).

For our current purpose we concentrate on the SO for a subset of the complement types discerned in FGD. The initial versions of the SO we work with are shown below:[9]

[9]The labels we use for the various types of complements are a mixture of FGD and SFG terminology. We unfortunately do not have the space to describe the complement types here or to present out a detailed comparison between the complements types distinguished in FGD and the Participants and Circumstances distinguished in SFG (cf. (Panevová 1974; Halliday 1985; Sgall *et al.* 1986; Petkevič 1995; Kruijff 2001). For an illustration, see examples (28-42).

(26) SO for Czech, Russian, Bulgarian:
Actor < TemporalLocative < Purpose < SpaceLocative < Means < Addressee < Patient < Source < Destination

(27) SO for English:
Actor < Addressee < Patient < SpaceLocative < TemporalLocative < Means < Source < Destination < Purpose-dependent

The SO for the Slavonic languages is based on that for Czech presented by Sgall *et al.* (1986); the only difference is that we have placed Patient before Source ('from where'). The SO for English combines the suggestions made by Sgall *et al.* (1986) and the ordering defaults of the NIGEL grammar of English (cf. Section 7.5.2).

Informational prominence (in the negative and positive sense) is established through deviation of CD from the SO background. This leads us to the distinction FGD makes between **contextually bound** (CB) and **contextually non-bound** (NB) items in a sentence (Sgall *et al.* 1986): A CB item is assumed to convey some content that bears a contextual relationship to the discourse context. Such an item may refer to an entity already explicitly referred to in the discourse, or an "implicitly evoked" entity (Hajičová 1993). At each level of syntactic structure, CB items are ranked lower than NB items in the CD ordering. The motivation behind and the meaning of the CB/NB distinction in FGD corresponds to those underlying the Given/New dichotomy in SFG.

Contextual boundness is a local feature, i.e., a complex CB item can contain "locally" NB items, and vice versa (Petkevič 1987). For instance, constituents within clauses in a complex sentence are discerned as locally CB vs. NB. Also within a complex nominal group which is, e.g., NB as a whole, some parts can be CB (a straightforward example of this kind of nominal group is an NB noun modified by a CB possessive pronoun). In (32) below, both 'soubor' (file) and 'editor' (editor) are locally CB.

The following examples illustrate the relation between WO, CD, SO and CB/NB. The types of arguments and adjuncts, as well as the CB/NB assignment, are indicated in superscripts. The WO in the Czech versions respects CD, while in the English versions the WO diverges from CD due to grammatical constraints. Note also that there are differences in ordering due to the difference in SO between Czech and English; e.g., Means precedes Patient in the SO in Czech, but follows it in English.

(28) Přeneseme myší ikonu z plochy do editoru.
drag_{1pl} $\text{mouse}^{Means/NB}_{ins}$ $\text{icon}^{Patient/NB}_{acc}$ from $\text{surface}^{Source/NB}_{gen}$ into $\text{editor}^{Destin/NB}_{gen}$
"We drag the icon with the mouse from the desktop to the editor."

(29) Ikonu přeneseme myší z plochy do editoru.
icon$_{acc}^{Patient/CB}$ drag$_{1pl}$ mouse$_{ins}^{Means/NB}$ from desktop$_{gen}^{Source/NB}$ into editor$_{gen}^{Destin/NB}$

"The icon we drag with the mouse from the desktop to the editor."

(30) Myší z plochy do editoru přeneseme ikonu.
mouse$_{ins}^{Means/CB}$ from desktop$_{gen}^{Source/CB}$ into editor$_{gen}^{Destin/CB}$ drag$_{1pl}$ icon$_{acc}^{Patient/NB}$

"With the mouse we drag the icon from the desktop to the editor."

(31) Ikonu myší do editoru přeneseme z plochy.
icon$_{acc}^{Patient/CB}$ mouse$_{ins}^{Means/CB}$ into editor$_{gen}^{Destin/CB}$ drag$_{1pl}$ from desktop$_{gen}^{Source/NB}$

"The icon we drag with the mouse to the editor from the desktop."

(32) Pro otevření souboru ikonu souboru přeneseme myší z pracovní plochy do okna editoru.
(For opening file$_{gen}$)$^{Purpose/CB}$ (icon$_{acc}$ file$_{gen}$)$^{Patient/CB}$ drag$_{1pl}$ mouse$_{ins}^{Means/NB}$ (from work$_{adj}$ desktop$_{gen}$)$^{Source/NB}$ (into window$_{gen}$ editor$_{gen}$)$^{Destin/NB}$

"In order to open the file, we drag the file's icon with the mouse from the desktop to the editor window."

From a generation point of view, the ordering variants illustrated above are fully determined by the CB/NB assignment, the SO and the principles of ordering CB elements before NB ones and placing the verb between the CB and the NB elements. Although WO is generally much more restricted in English than in Czech, it is interesting to observe that there are differences as well as parallels in ordering between the Czech and English sentences.

(28) shows the basic case where the only CB element is the Actor (realized by the implicit (dropped) Subject in Czech), all other elements are NB, and their ordering follows the SO. In (29), which should be seen as an answer to *What do we do with the icon using the mouse?*, both Czech and English allow ordering the CB element 'icon' before the verb. In (30), which should be seen as an answer to *What do we drag from the desktop to the editor using the mouse?*, and in (31), which should be seen as an answer to the question *From where do we drag the icon to the editor using the mouse?*, Czech but not English allows ordering all the CB elements before the verb.

The final example (32) is an extension of (29), with an additional CB element, namely Purpose, and with more complex constituents. The latter are enclosed in round brackets for clarity. For simplicity, we do not mark local CB/NB, because it is not relevant for the discussion in this paper. We can again observe the CB/NB motivated WO in Czech, and a difference in ordering between Czech and English.

Note that the CB/NB distinction enables us to explain and motivate the difference in ordering between the English version of (29) and (31), following the discussion of similar examples in (Sgall *et al.* 1986):

(33) a. They flew from Chicago to Boston.
b. They flew to Boston from Chicago.

(34) a. They went by car to a river.
b. They went to a river by car.

In (33a) and (34a), the ordering of the circumstantial modifiers after the verb is in accordance with the SO (cf. p. 203): Source and Means precede Destination, respectively, while in (33b) and (34b) this is not the case. Sgall *et al.* attribute the difference in WO to information structure: both circumstantial modifiers in (33a) and in (34a) are NB, and therefore their order respects the SO. On the other hand, the Source in (33b) and the Means in (34b) are CB, and therefore they are ordered before the Destination which remains NB in both cases (under neutral intonation).

Likewise, the CB/NB distinction enables us to explain and motivate the difference in ordering between (35) and (36).

(35) He picked up the pen. (36) He picked the pen up.

Such **particle movement** constructions are discussed, for example by Gries (1999). Within a cognitive approach, he attributes the difference in ordering to the degree of effort needed to "process" the direct object. Our explanation in terms of CB/NB is as follows: We treat the particle as expressing the Destination (which is ranked higher on the SO scale than the Patient, cf. p. 203). It can be either CB or NB.[10] (35) is then an ordering corresponding to 'up' being CB and 'pen' being NB, e.g., in an answer to *What did he pick up?*. (36) is an ordering corresponding to one of three possible situations: (i) 'pen' is CB and 'up' is NB, e.g. in an answer to *What did he do with the pen?*, (ii) both 'pen' and 'up' being NB, e.g. in an answer to *What did he do?*, (iii) both 'pen' and 'up' being

[10]For a "phrasal verb", it is quite likely that the particle's CB/NB assignment follows the CB/NB assignment of the verb. In order to pursue this line further, we would first have to be more specific regarding the treatment of CB/NB for verbs and complex verb forms, and its influence on CD and consequently on WO. Such discussion is, however, beyond the scope of the present paper.

CB, e.g. in an answer to *Who picked the pen up?*, and with a marked intonation stressing 'he'.

In FGD, the CB/NB distinction is also held responsible for the so-called **dative shift** in English. Whereas (37) is considered to be neutral, for (38) it is said that 'Christmas cards' are understood as CB–presuming the neutral intonation patterns with the intonation center on the last sentence element (Sgall *et al.* 1986: p.201):

(37) A young linguist sent a few colleagues Christmas cards.

(38) A young linguist sent Christmas cards to a few colleagues.

The view that the ordering of the Participants corresponding to the Actor, Patient and Addressee is constrained by information structure in the same way as the ordering of Circumstances, is natural for Czech, where the Participants are realized by nominal groups in different morphological cases and their order is free.

Adopting such an account also for English would mean that information structure would determine the grammar's choice between (i) realizing both the Patient and the Addressee by a nominal group in the oblique case, or (ii) realizing the Patient as a direct complement and the Addressee as a prepositional phrase. Such an approach, however, may need to be refined. For example, Steele (1978) has argued that there is a difference in meaning between (39) and (40):

(39) Mary threw John the ball. (40) Mary threw the ball to John.

Steele argues that in (39) John has to be actively participating in the act, whereas in (40) he need not. Hence, she considers (39′) semantically awkward, while (40′) would be fine.

(39′) # Mary threw John the ball but he wasn't looking.

(40′) Mary threw the ball to John, but he wasn't looking.

We therefore leave it open at this moment whether dative shift should be attributed solely to information structure or also to a meaning difference (see also (Oehrle 1975), (Kunze 1991)).

Also Czech WO is subject to grammatical restrictions, although to a lesser degree than English WO. Besides the ordering of clitics (Section 7.2, p. 198) there is also a preference for **verb second placement**. This is what explains the difference in WO between (31) and (41):

(41) Ikonu přeneseme myší do editoru z plochy.
$\text{icon}_{acc}^{Patient/CB}$ drag_{1pl} $\text{mouse}_{ins}^{Means/CB}$ into $\text{editor}_{gen}^{Destin/CB}$ from $\text{desktop}_{gen}^{Source/NB}$
"The icon we drag with the mouse to the editor from the desktop."

Both in English and Czech, there are also orders we cannot explain solely on the basis of the CB/NB distinction along with SO and grammatical constraints. On the one hand, it has been claimed that the ordering of CB elements follows CD rather than SO, and that CD is determined by contextual factors (Sgall *et al.* 1986). On the other hand, cases where an NB element appears at the beginning of a clause are far from rare. While we currently do not have more to add to the former issue, we will discuss the latter issue in the next section. For illustration, consider (42) used as the first step in a sequence of instructions for editing an existing file. The context can thus be illustrated by the question *What is to be done with the file?*.

(42) **Cz** Myší přeneseme ikonu z plochy
Mouse$^{Means/NB}_{ins}$ drag$_{1pl}$ icon$^{Patient/CB}_{acc}$ from surface$^{Source/NB}_{gen}$
do editoru.
into editor$^{Destin/NB}_{gen}$
En "Using the mouse, we drag the icon from the desktop to the editor."

For the sake of argument, we can consider 'icon' as CB (making such a decision in the course of text planning would be justified by the fact that the icon of a file can be assumed to be known to the reader of the instruction text). The placement of this CB element after rather than before the verb in the Czech version of (42) can be explained by verb secondness. However, how do we explain the placement of 'mouse' at the beginning of the sentence?

In the Prague School tradition, it has always been acknowledged that WO can diverge from the prototypical ordering proceeding left-to-right from CB (Given) to NB (New) elements. By inverting the order, and presenting the NB (New) elements first, one obtains what has been called the **subjective order** (Firbas 1992). Example (30′) illustrates the subjective-order variant of (30), which could be used to answer the same question, i.e., *What do we drag from the desktop to the editor using the mouse?*,

(30′) Ikonu přeneseme myší z plochy do
icon$^{Patient/NB}_{acc}$ drag$_{1pl}$ mouse$^{Means/CB}_{ins}$ from desktop$^{Source/CB}_{gen}$ into
editoru.
editor$^{Destin/CB}_{gen}$
"The icon we drag with the mouse from the desktop to the editor."

The speaker has the choice of answering the question using the unmarked prototypical order or the marked subjective order. Note that the subjective order needs to be accompanied with a marked intonation pattern stressing 'icon' (in both Czech and English). It is probably due to its close coupling to intonation that the subjective order is more common in spoken language than in writing. We did not encounter any occurrences of the subjective order in our corpus of written instructions. Therefore, we do not consider it further in the present account.

However, even subjective order does not enable us to explain the WO in (42). First of all, in line with all other examples, (42) is intended to be pronounced with unmarked intonation, i.e. with the intonation center on 'editor'. Moreover, if subjective order were used, then all NB elements should occur before the CB ones, which is not the case in (42). So, we conclude that we cannot motivate the WO in (42) on the basis of information structure (alone).

7.4.2 Theme and Textual Organization

Central to Halliday's approach is the notion that many languages *grammaticize* a very particular textual function: that of signposting the intended development or "scaffolding" that a writer employs for structuring an extended text. In the grammar of English this textual function is realized in the first position in the clause and Halliday calls this textual function 'Theme': "The Theme is the element which serves as the point of departure of the message; it is that with which the message is concerned. [...] and the [thematic] structure is expressed by the order - whatever is chosen as the Theme is put first" (Halliday 1985: p.37).

Halliday's use of the term 'Theme', which we henceforth refer to as **Theme**$_{SFG}$, can only be understood in relation to the thematic structure. The specialized textual role of Theme$_{SFG}$ was originally identified empirically in the work of Fries (1981) and has since been applied in many analyses of extended texts (e.g., (Halliday 1993; Matthiessen 1995; Ventola 1995)). Although the claim of this special role for the first position in the clause has been questioned or rejected in various works (Lyons 1977; Huddleston 1988; Bolinger 1989; Steedman 1996, 2000b), these critiques miss the point that it is the larger **textual organization** to which Theme$_{SFG}$ contributes, not the local sentence-by-sentence organization found in dialogue or as highlighted by question tests. For instance, Steedman's notion of 'Theme', which we henceforth abbreviate as **Theme**$_{is}$ diverges from Theme$_{SFG}$ as follows:[11] (i) Theme$_{is}$ does not need to be sentence-initial, it can be ordered before or after Rheme$_{is}$; (ii) Theme$_{is}$ can contain multiple experiential elements (for example, multiple circumstantial modifiers, but also multiple participants, as well as the main verb), and (iii) disjoint parts of a sentence might belong to Theme$_{is}$ (Steedman 2000b: p.7). It is an unfortunate terminological confusion that most non-Hallidayan uses of 'Theme' refer instead to

[11]Similar comments apply to the Theme$_{is}$ counterparts in other approaches to information structure, e.g., Topic (Sgall *et al.* 1980, 1986) or Ground (Vallduví 1992).

properties that Halliday attributes to information structure.

Theme_{SFG} is thus concerned primarily with textual organization. For example, it is a matter of such global text organization strategy that a biography can be organized along the dates when or the places where important events in one's life happened. These dates or places are not "given" information individually, but they are nevertheless broadly "predictable" from the knowledge of the text type. Such strategies then guide the choice of Theme_{SFG}.

Similar textual organization strategies are also at play in the written instructions for software products. For example, consider (44) which demonstrates a kind of thematization appearing repeatedly in the English, Czech, Bulgarian and Russian versions of the AutoCAD user guide. This particular occurrence was preceded only by the respective language counterpart of (43).

(43) First open the Multiline styles dialog box using one of the following methods.

(44) **Cz** Z menu `Data` vyberte `Multiline Style`.
Ru В меню `Data` выберите `Multiline Style`
Bu От менюто `Data` изберете `Multiline Style`
En "From the `Data` menu choose the `Multiline Style`."

The preceding context does not refer to the `Data` menu or make it salient in any way. Working only with the notion of information structure discerning CB (Given) and NB (New) elements, one is thus unable to explain the WO. The notion of Theme_{SFG} as a reflex of a global text organization strategy makes such explanation possible for (44) as well as for (42) in the preceding section, p. 208.

In the software instructions we analyzed, we encountered regular thematization of (i) the location where actions are performed (44,45), (ii) the particular action that the user is instructed to perform (46), or (iii) the goal that the user wants to achieve (47).[12]

(45) **Cz** Z menu `File` vyberte `Save` pro uložení souboru.
from menu_{gen} `File` choose_{i2pl} `Save` for saving_{acc} file_{gen}
"From the `File` menu, choose `Save` to save the file."

(46) **Cz** Vyberte `Save` z menu `File` pro uložení souboru.
choose_{i2pl} `Save` from menu_{gen} `File` for saving_{acc} file_{gen}
"Choose `Save` from the `File` menu to save the file."

(47) **Cz** Pro uložení souboru vyberte `Save` z menu `File`.
for saving_{acc} file_{gen} choose_{i2pl} `Save` from menu_{gen} `File`
"To save the file, choose `Save` from the `File` menu."

[12]The same variation of thematic structure is available also in Bulgarian and Russian.

If we cannot avail ourselves of Theme_{SFG}, then rather more of the WO decisions in an extended text appear unmotivated than need be; this has also been shown with respect to examples drawn from extended narrative texts in, for example, (Martin 1995). For a text generation system this would be particularly unfortunate; the rather straightforward selection of initial constituents in many text types would not be available. It is for this role that we maintain the use of Theme_{SFG} for text generation.

Conversely, we also certainly do not want to deprive ourselves of the constraining power for the *rest* of the clause offered by information structure. The position we advance, therefore, is to distinguish between information structure and the textually determined thematic structure, and employ *both* of them as orthogonally applying sources of WO constraint. By this, we follow the original suggestion made by Halliday (1967).

7.5 Word Order Control in Generation

Our approach to handling WO fits within the standard pipeline architecture of a NLG system (Reiter and Dale 1997), with the addition that our approach is also applicable in a multiligual NLG system. Such a system takes as an input user-defined (language-independent) content specifications. These are first processed by a text and sentence planner (strategic generation), yielding, in our case, a list of **sentence planning language** (SPL) formulae (Kasper 1989). These SPL formulae are then processed by the grammar(s) generating the individual sentences in each target language (tactical generation).

It is in this setting, in which individual sentences are specified and generated that ultimately make up a text, that the issue of generating contextually appropriate sentences arises. For only in this way can a smooth flow of text be assured.

7.5.1 Flexible Word Order Algorithm

As we have discussed, constraints from various sources need to be combined in order to determine grammatically well-formed and contextually appropriate WO. We propose to ensure this as follows:

- The grammar imposes structural constraints, such as the ordering of connectives, placement of sentential clitics and possibly verb secondness.
- The text planner can choose a particular textual organization and determine the element which should become the Theme. If no particular element is chosen as the Theme, the grammar chooses the least communicatively dynamic element as the Theme. The Theme is then placed at the beginning of the clause, although not neces-

sarily at the very first position, as this might be occupied, e.g., by a connective. The placement of the Theme can also be resolved by the grammar.

- The text and sentence planner determine information structure, in particular, contextual boundness or non-boundness of each item. During text planning, a discourse model is maintained which records the use of pieces of content. Whenever the sentence planner encounters a piece of content that the discourse model notes as previously used, it marks the corresponding item in the SPL formula as CB.
- Contextual boundness is then used to constrain WO (at the clause level) as follows:
  - The CB elements (if there are any) precede the NB elements in the prototypical cases, that is, leaving the subjective order aside.
  - The mutual ordering of multiple CB items in a clause corresponds to communicative dynamism, and the mutual ordering of multiple NB items in a clause follows the systemic ordering (with the exceptions required by grammatically constrained ordering as described below). The default for communicative dynamism is systemic ordering.
  - The main verb of a clause is ordered at the boundary between the CB elements and the NB elements, unless the grammar specifies otherwise (verb secondness).

We combine the following two phases in which information structure (CB/NB) is taken into account during tactical generation:

- information structure can determine particular realization choices made in the grammar; for example, when inserting and placing the particle of a phrasal verb, when inserting and ordering the Source and Destination for a motion process (cf. Section 7.4.1, p. 206), and possibly also when ordering elements at lower structural levels, e.g., within nominal groups, etc.
- information structure can determine the ordering of elements whose placement has not been sufficiently constrained by the grammar.

This also enables each language within multilingual resources to establish its own balance between the two phases. To show our approach in a nutshell, we present an abstract WO algorithm in Figure 1.

The ordering constraints posed by the grammar have the highest priority. Note that this includes the ordering of the textually determined Theme. Then, any elements which are not ordered by the grammar, are

FIGURE 1 Abstract ordering algorithm

```
Given:
    a set GC of ordering constraints imposed by the grammar
    a list L1 of constituents that are to be ordered,
    a list D giving ordering of CB constituents (default is SO)

Create two lists LC and LN of default orders:

    Create empty lists LC (for CB items) and LN (for NB items)
    Repeat for each element E in L1
            if E is CB,
                then add E into LC,
                else add E into LN.
    Order all elements in LC according to D
    Order all elements in LN according to SO
    if the Verb is yet unordered then
        Order the Verb at the beginning of LN

Order the elements of L1
    if GC is not empty then
         use the contraints in GC, and
         if the contraints in GC are insufficient,
            apply first the default orders in LC and then those in LN
```

subject to the ordering according to information structure, i.e. systemic ordering in combination with the CB/NB distinction. The ordering of the NB elements (i) is restricted by the syntactic structure or (ii) follows SO. The ordering of the CB elements can be (i) specified on the basis of the context, (ii) restricted by the syntactic structure, (iii) follow SO. The verb is placed between the last CB and the first NB element, unless its placement has been determined by the grammar, e.g. if it itself is the Theme or due to verb secondness.

The ordering algorithm as such is language independent, and could be usefully applied in the generation of any language. What differs across languages is first of all the extent to which the grammar of a particular language constrains ordering, i.e. which elements are subject to ordering requirements posed by the syntactic structure, and which elements can be ordered according to information structure. Secondly, individual languages may differ in their SO (cf. Section 7.4.1, p. 203).

7.5.2 Algorithm Application

The algorithm described above has been implemented and used in the process of tactical generation of Czech and English. The Czech grammar resources used at this stage in generation have been built up along with the Bulgarian and Russian grammar resources as described by Kruijff *et al.* (2000). The NIGEL grammar for English was re-used for this purpose.

The original NIGEL grammar itself already combines the specification of ordering constraints in the grammar with the application of defaults. If any ordering is underspecified in the grammar, the defaults are applied. The defaults are "static", i.e. specified once and for all. The algorithm we have described can be used to replace these "static" defaults with a "dynamic" construction of default ordering constraints. Two separate sets of "dynamic" defaults are computed on the basis of the SO for the CB and the NB elements in each sentence/clause.

We use the SO specified in (26) for Czech and the SO specified in (27) for English (cf. Section 7.4.1, p.204). For each element in the input SPL we specify whether it is CB (:contextual-boundness yes) or NB (:contextual-boundness no); in addition, we can specify the textual Theme in the SPL (theme <id>). The SPL in Figure 2 illustrates this (the corresponding generated output in shown in (53)).

The CB/NB assignments can be varied to obtain different WO variants (cf. Section 7.4.1). The examples below list some of the CB/NB assignment combinations and the outputs generated using the Czech and English grammars.

(48)

user	choose	Open	menu	mouse	open file
Actor/NB		Patient/NB	SpaceLoc./NB	Means/NB	Purpose/NB

Uživatel	vybere	pro otevření	souboru	v menu	myší	Open.
user$_{nom}$	choose$_{3sg}$	for opening$_{gen}$	file$_{gen}$	in menu$_{loc}$	mouse$_{ins}$	Open

"The user chooses Open in the menu with the mouse to open a file."

(49)

user	choose	Open	menu	mouse	open file
Actor/CB		Patient/NB	SpaceLoc./CB	Means/NB	Purpose/NB

Uživatel	v menu	vybere	pro otevření	souboru	myší	Open.
user$_{nom}$	in menu$_{loc}$	choose$_{3sg}$	for opening$_{gen}$	file$_{gen}$	mouse$_{ins}$	Save

"The user chooses Open in the menu with the mouse to open a file."

(50)

user	choose	Open	menu	mouse	open file
Actor/CB		Patient/NB	SpaceLoc./CB	Means/CB	Purpose/CB

Pro otevření	souboru	uživatel	v menu	myší	vybere	Open.
for opening$_{gen}$	file$_{gen}$	user$_{nom}$	in menu$_{loc}$	mouse$_{ins}$	choose$_{3sg}$	Open

"To open a file the user chooses Open in the menu with the mouse."

As we said above, we preserve the notion of textual Theme. An SPL can contain a specification of a theme, and the corresponding element is then ordered at the front of the sentence, as determined by the grammar. The WO of the rest of the sentence is determined as before. The following examples of generated output illustrate this.

FIGURE 2 The input SPL for both the English and the Czech version of (53)

```
(R / RST-purpose
    :speechact assertion
    :DOMAIN (ch / DM::choose
        :actor (a1 / DM::user
                  :identifiability-q identifiable
                  :contextual-boundness yes)
        :actee (a2 / object :name gui-open
                  :identifiability-q identifiable
                  :contextual-boundness no)
        :instrumental (mea / DM::mouse
                  :identifiability-q identifiable
                  :contextual-boundness no)
        :spatial-locating (loc / DM::menu
                  :identifiability-q identifiable
                  :contextual-boundness yes
                  :class-ascription (label / object :name gui-file))
      :RANGE (open / DM::open
                :contextual-boundness no
                :actee (f / DM::file :contextual-boundness no)))
      :theme open)
```

(51) user choose `Open` menu mouse open file
Actor/NB Patient/NB SpaceLoc/NB Means/NB Purpose/theme

Pro otevření souboru uživatel vybere v menu myší `Open`.
for opening$_{gen}$ file$_{gen}$ user$_{nom}$ choose$_{3sg}$ in menu$_{loc}$ mouse$_{ins}$ `Open`

"To open a file, the user chooses `Open` in the menu with the mouse."

(52) user choose `Open` menu mouse open file
Actor/CB Patient/NB SpaceLoc/CB Means/CB Purpose/CB

Pro otevření souboru uživatel v menu myší vybere `Open`.
for opening$_{gen}$ file$_{gen}$ user$_{nom}$ in menu$_{loc}$ mouse$_{ins}$ choose$_{3sg}$ `Open`

"To open a file, the user chooses `Open` in the menu with the mouse."

(53) user choose `Open` menu mouse open file
Actor/CB Patient/NB SpaceLoc/CB Means/NB Purpose/theme

Pro otevření souboru uživatel v menu vybere myší `Open`.
for opening$_{gen}$ file$_{gen}$ user$_{nom}$ in menu$_{loc}$ choose$_{3sg}$ mouse$_{ins}$ `Open`

"To open a file, the user chooses `Open` in the menu with the mouse."

In both the English and Czech grammars we are using, there are already several decision points whose control naturally calls for access to information structure. These include the particle placement and dative shift in English (mentioned in Section 7.4.1, p. 206), as well as components of the active/passive and pronominalization decisions. Given the functional orientation of our grammars, it would be a natural move to take the CB/NB distinction into account when making these choices.

Our last note concerns handling clitics in Czech. There are essentially two options for the implementation: (i) to introduce a specially handled category for clitics in the ordering algorithm, (ii) to order clitics explicitly in the grammar. In the current version of the Czech grammar we opt for the latter. Using $<$ for linear precedence, the ordering we implemented for simple clauses can be schematized as follows:

```
Theme < Clitics < Rest-CB < Verb < Rest-NB
```

If no Theme has been determined by the text planner, then the Czech grammar takes the CB element with the lowest SO degree as the Theme; if there is no CB element, then the verb becomes the Theme. The examples of generated Czech output below illustrate this.

(54)

choose	`Open`	menu	mouse	open file
	Patient/NB	SpaceLoc/NB	Means/NB	Purpose/NB

Vybere	se	pro	otevření	souboru	v	menu	myší	`Open`.
choose$_{3sg}$	*refl*	for	opening$_{gen}$	file$_{gen}$	in	menu$_{loc}$	mouse$_{ins}$	`Open`

"One chooses `Open` in the menu with the mouse to open a file."

(55)

choose	`Open`	menu	mouse	open file
	Patient/NB	SpaceLoc/CB	Means/NB	Purpose/NB

V	menu	se	vybere	pro	otevření	souboru	myší	`Open`.
in	menu$_{loc}$	*refl*	choose$_{3sg}$	for	opening$_{gen}$	file$_{gen}$	mouse$_{ins}$	`Save`

"One chooses `Open` in the menu with the mouse to open a file."

(56)

choose	`Open`	menu	mouse	open file
	Patient/NB	SpaceLoc/CB	Means/CB	Purpose/theme

Pro	otevření	souboru	se	v	menu	myší	vybere	`Open`.
for	opening$_{gen}$	file$_{gen}$	*refl*	in	menu$_{loc}$	mouse$_{ins}$	choose$_{3sg}$	`Open`

"To open a file one chooses `Open` in the menu with the mouse."

Thus, our approach combines WO constraints imposed by syntactic structure, thematic structure and information structure. Information structure is determined by the CB/NB assignments in the input SPL. The language-specific SO is employed as a source of ordering defaults.

7.6 Concluding Remarks and Further Research

In this contribution we have addressed the issue of how to generate contextually appropriate word order – even though a particular word order may be syntactically well-formed, it need not give rise to the right interpretation in a given discourse context. We argued that there are several factors determining contextual appropriateness, focusing thereby on Halliday's thematic structure and the Praguian conception of information structure. We substantiated our arguments linguistically by numerous examples from Bulgarian, Czech, and Russian.

Subsequently, we showed how this approach can be integrated into the general pipeline architecture of NLG systems. We paid special attention to multilinguality: The approach we propose is -arguably- capable of generating contextually appropriate word order in languages with a varying degree of word order freedom, ranging from English, over German, to Bulgarian, Czech and Russian. Precisely because our approach is grounded on solid linguistic insights, we are able to give a principled account that deals with the issues of generation control and coverage in a flexible manner.

We believe that the discussion we have provided raises some general issues concerning system modularity and architecture. The focus of the workshop where an earlier version of this paper was presented was on the generation of nominal expressions. In this respect, there is the question of what should be considered as the task of nominal expression generation. Although a first approximation to nominal expression generation might posit a 'nominal expression generation module' whose responsibility it is to map chunks of semantic/conceptual representation into appropriate nominal expressions, our discussion in this paper demonstrates that the boundaries in semantic responsibility within an NLG architecture are far from clear. Given such a module, the ordering of clause elements might seem to lie outside rather than inside the module as such. However, factors that play a role in determining word order in Slavonic languages are often precisely the same factors that play a role in determining certain syntactic, morphological or phonological features of/within nominal expressions in other languages. It would seem that some subset of the decisions that have been proposed for generating nominal expressions may instead be better considered as decisions concerning *clause* generation. This may also occur when we consider other components of the generation process. Therefore, architectural decisions made on the basis of surface syntactico-morphological behaviour of any individual language may well turn out not to be appropriately general when other languages come to be considered.

Acknowledgements The paper builds on work we have carried out in relation to the AGILE project (Automatic Generation of Instructions in Languages of Eastern Europe) supported by the European Commission grant No. PL961104. The overall aim of AGILE was to develop a multilingual system for generating continuous instructional texts in Bulgarian, Czech and Russian (Adonova *et al.* 1999). We would like to thank Elke Teich, Tony Hartley, Eva Hajičová and two anonymous reviewers of earlier versions of this paper for their comments; Serge Sharoff and Lena Sokolova contributed examples and judgments for Russian, Danail Dochev and Kamenka Staykova for Bulgarian.

References

Adonova et al. 1999. E. Adonova, J. Bateman, N. Gromova, A. Hartley, G. J. M. Kruijff, I. Kruijff-Korbayová, S. Sharoff, H. Skoumalová, L. Sokolova, K. Staykova, and E. Teich: Formal specification of extended grammar models. AGILE project deliverable. Technical Report. ITRI, University of Brighton, UK.

Bolinger 1989. D. Bolinger. *Intonation and its Uses.* Stanford University Press.

Daneš 1985. F. Daneš. *Věta a text [A sentence and a text]*, volume 21 of *Studie a práce lingvistické.* Academia, Prague, Czech Republic.

Firbas 1992. J. Firbas. *Functional Sentence Perspective in Written and Spoken Communication.* Studies in English Language. Cambridge University Press.

Fries 1981. P. H. Fries. On the status of theme in English: Arguments from discourse. *Forum Linguisticum*, 6(1):1 – 38.

Gries 1999. S. T. Gries. Particle movement: a cognitive and functional approach. *Cognitive Linguistics*, 10(2):105–146.

Hajičová 1993. E. Hajičová. *Issues of sentence structure and discourse patterns*, volume 2 of *Theoretical and computational linguistics.* Charles University, Prague, Czech Republic.

Hajičová and Kruijff-Korbayová 1999. E. Hajičová, and I. Kruijff-Korbayová. On the notion of topic. In *Prague Linguistic Circle Papers.* John Benjamins Publishers, Amsterdam, the Netherlands.

Hajičová and Sgall 1987. E. Hajičová, and P. Sgall. The ordering principle. *Journal of Pragmatics*, 11(4):435–454.

Hajičová et al. 1995. E. Hajičová, P. Sgall, and H. Skoumalová. An automatic procedure for topic-focus identification. *Computational linguistics*, 21(1):81–94, 1995.

Halliday 1967/8. M. A. K. Halliday. Notes on transitivity and theme in English. *Journal of Linguistics*, 3(1):37–81, 3(2):199–244, 4(2):179–215.

Halliday 1993. M. A. K. Halliday. The construction of knowledge and value in the grammar of scientific discourse: Charles Darwin's *The Origin of the Species.* In M. A. K. Halliday and J. R. Martin, editors, *Writing Science: literacy and discoursive power*, pages 86–105. The Falmer Press, London.

Halliday 1970 . M. A. K. Halliday. *A Course in Spoken English: Intonation.* Oxford Uniersity Press, Oxford.

Halliday 1985. M. A. K. Halliday. *Introduction to Functional Grammar.* Edward Arnold, London, U.K.

Hudleston 1988. R. D. Huddleston. Constituency, multi-functionality and grammaticalization in Halliday's Functional Grammar. *Journal of Linguistics*, 24.

Kasper 1989. R. Kasper. A flexible interface for linking applications to PENMAN's sentence generator. In *Proceedings of the DARPA Workshop on Speech and Natural Language.*

Krifka 1992. M. Krifka. A compositional semantics for multiple focus constructions. In J. Jacobs, editor, *Informationsstruktur und Grammatik,* Linguistische Berichte, Sonderheft 4.

Kruijff et al. 2000. G. J. M. Kruijff, E. Teich, J. Bateman, I. Kruijff-Korbayová, H. Skoumalová, S. Sharoff, L. Sokolova, A. Hartley, K. Staykova, and J. Hana. A multilingual system for text generation in three slavic languages. In *Proceedings of the 18th Conference on Computational Linguistics (COLING'2000), July 31 - August 4 2000*, pages 474–480. Universität des Saarlandes, Saarbrücken, Germany.

Kruijff et al. 2001. G. J. M. Kruijff, I. Kruijff-Korbayová, J. Bateman and E. Teich. Linear Order as higher-level decision: Information Structure in strategic and tactical generation. In *Proceedings of the 8th European Workshop on Natural Language Generation, July 6–7 2001*, pages 74–83. CNRS - Institute de Recherche en Informatique de Toulouse, and Université des Sciences Sociales, Toulouse, France.

Kruijff 2001. G. J. M. Kruijff. *A Categorial-Modal Logical Architecture of Informativity: Dependency Grammar Logic & Information Structure.* PhD thesis, Faculty of Mathematics and Physics, Charles University, Prague, Czech Republic.

Kuno 1972. S. Kuno. Functional sentence perspective. *Linguistic Inquiry*, 3:269–320.

Kunze 1991. J. Kunze. *Kasusrelationen und semantische Emphase.* Studia Grammatica XXXII. Akademie Verlag, Berlin.

Lyons 1977. J. Lyons. *Semantics*, volume II. Cambridge University Press.

Martin 1995. J. R. Martin. More than what the message is about: English theme. In Mohsen Ghadessy, editor, *Thematic development in English texts*, pages 223–258. Pinter, London.

Mathesius 1939. V. Mathesius. On information bearing structure of the sentence. In S. Kuno, editor, *Harvard studies in syntax and semantics.* Harvard University Press. 1975.

Mathiessen 1995. C. M. I. M. Matthiessen. Theme as an enabling resource in ideational 'knowledge' construction. In M. Ghadessy, editor, *Thematic development in English texts*, pages 20–54. Pinter Publishers, London.

Oehrle 1975. R. T. Oehrle. *The Grammatical Status of the English Dative Alternation.* PhD thesis, M.I.T.

Oliva and Avgustinova 1995. K. Oliva, and T. Avgustinova. Wackernagel position and related phenomena in Czech. In *Wiener Slavistiches Jahrbuch*, pages 21–42. Verlag der Österreichischen Akademie der Wissenschaften, Wien.

Panevová 1974. J. Panevová. On verbal frames in functional generative description I. *Prague Bulletin of Mathematical Linguistics*, 22:3–40.

Petkevič 1987. V. Petkevič. A new dependency based specification of underlying representations of sentences. *Theoretical linguistics*, 14:143–172. Walter de Gruyter, Berlin, Germany.

Petkevič 1995. V. Petkevič. A new formal specification of underlying structures. *Theoretical linguistics*, 21(1):7–61. Walter de Gruyter, Berlin, Germany.

Prevost 1995. S. Prevost. *A Semantics of Contrast and Information Structure for Specifying Intonation in Spoken Language Generation.* Ph.d. dissertation, IRCS TR 96-01, University of Pennsylvania, Philadelphia.

Prevost and Steedman 1994. S. Prevost, and M. Steedman. Specifying intonation from context for speech synthesis. *Speech Communication*, 15:139–153.

Reiter and Dale 1997. E. Reiter and R. Dale. Building applied natural language generation systems. *Journal of Natural Language Engineering*, 3:57–87.

Sgall et al. 1973. P. Sgall, E. Hajičová, and E. Benešová. *Topic, focus and generative semantics.* Kronberg, Taunus.

Sgall et al 1980. P. Sgall, E. Hajičová, and E. Buráňová. *Aktuální členění věty v češtině (Topic-focus articulation of the Czech sentence).* Academia, Prague, Czech Republic.

Sgall et al. 1986. P. Sgall, E. Hajičová, and J. Panevová. *The meaning of the sentence in its semantic and pragmatic aspects.* Reidel, Dordrecht, The Netherlands.

Sgall et al. 1995. P. Sgall, O. Pfeiffer, W. U. Dressler, and M. Půček. Experimental research on systemic ordering. *Theoretical Linguistics*, 21:197–239.

Steedman 1994. M. Steedman. The grammar of intonation and focus. In Paul Dekker and Martin Stokhof, editors, *Proceedings of the 9th Amsterdam Colloquium.* Institute of logic, language and computation, Department of Philosophy, Universiteit van Amsterdam.

Steedman 1996. M. Steedman. *Surface Structure and Interpretation.* M.I.T. Press.

Steedman 2000a. M. Steedman. *The Syntactic Process.* M.I.T. Press.

Steedman 2000b. M. Steedman. Information structure and the syntax-phonology interface. *Linguistic Inquiry*, 31(4):649–689.

Steedman and Kruijff-Korbayová 2001. M. Steedman and I. Kruijff-Korbayová. Introduction: Two Dimensions of Information Structure in Relation to Discourse Semantics and Discourse Structure. In *Proceedings of the ESSLLI Workshop on Information Structure, Discourse Structure and Discourse Semantics, August 20–24 2001*, pages 1–6. ESSLLI'2001, The University of Helsinki, Finland.

Steele 1978. S. Steele. Word order variation: A typological study. In Joseph H. Greenberg, editor, *Universals of Language. Volume 4: Syntax*, pages 585–624. Stanford University Press.

Vallduví 1992. E. Vallduví. *The Informational Component.* Garland, New York.

Ventola 1995. E. Ventola. Thematic development and translation. In M. Ghadessy, editor, *Thematic development in English texts*, pages 85–104. Pinter Publishers, London.

8

Efficient Context-Sensitive Generation of Referring Expressions

EMIEL KRAHMER AND MARIËT THEUNE

8.1 Introduction

In their interesting 1995 paper, Dale & Reiter present various algorithms they developed alone or in tandem to determine the content of a *distinguishing description*. That is: a definite description which is an accurate characterization of the object being referred to, but not of any other object in the current 'context set'. They argue that their *Incremental Algorithm*, discussed in more detail below, is the best one from a computational point of view (it has a low complexity and is fast) as well as from a psychological point of view (humans appear to do it in a similar way).

Even though Dale & Reiter (1995) primarily aimed at investigating the computational implications of obeying the Gricean maxims,[1] the Incremental Algorithm has become more or less accepted as the state of the art for generating descriptions. However, due to their original motivation, various other aspects of the generation of definites remained somewhat underdeveloped. In this chapter, we flesh out a number of these aspects, *without losing sight of the attractive properties of the original algorithm* (speed, complexity, psychological plausibility). In particular, we focus on the role of context-sensitivity for referring expression generation.

The basic idea we want to pursue is that a definite description refers

[1]For a discussion of this aspect of their work, see Oberlander (1998).

Information Sharing: Reference and Presupposition in Language Generation and Interpretation.
Edited by Kees van Deemter and Rodger Kibble.

to the *most salient* element satisfying the descriptive content (Lewis 1979: 348-350, see Krahmer 1998 for a formalization in dynamic semantics). Lewis mentions the following example (due to McCawley):

(1) The dog got in a fight with another dog.

Lewis notes that this statement can only be true in a domain which contains at least two dogs, which entails that *the dog* cannot be a distinguishing description. According to Lewis, (1) means that the most salient dog got in a fight with some less salient dog. Lewis does not mention descriptions which refer to 'unique' objects, but it is readily seen that they can also be understood in terms of salience: if there is only one object with the relevant properties, it *has* to be the most salient one. Arguably, a notion of salience is implicit in Dale & Reiter's usage of context sets, and also extensions such as Horacek (1997:210) and Stone & Webber (1998:183) explicitly remark that some form of salience is important. None, however, specify how salience should be determined nor which repercussions the inclusion of a notion of salience has for the generation algorithm.

In this chapter we show that it is possible to integrate an explicit notion of salience into Dale & Reiter's Incremental Algorithm and that this paves the way for efficient context-sensitive generation of referring expressions.[2] This is done in a number of stepwise refinements of Dale & Reiter's original Incremental Algorithm. In the first step we describe a generalized version of the Incremental Algorithm which incorporates a notion of salience. This provides us with a way of modelling salience differences between objects: some objects can be more prominent in the linguistic context than others. We argue that the modified algorithm only needs to distinguish the intended referent from those objects which are equally or more salient. As we shall see, this means that in those cases the modified algorithm typically outputs shorter descriptions, which are not 'distinguishing' in the sense of Dale and Reiter, but which are ana-

[2]Horacek (1997) and Stone & Webber (1998) are closely related in spirit to the current work. Horacek (1997) makes various interesting observations about the limitations of the Incremental Algorithm and its ilk and proposes a new algorithm with 'flexible interfaces' to other modules. Many of the issues discussed by Horacek are also addressed in this chapter, and some of his suggestions are taken over, in particular the integration of linguistic constraints during generation. This integration is also a central ingredient of Stone & Webber (1998), who go one step further and argue for the simultaneous inclusion of semantic and pragmatic information as well. While both approaches look promising, it is difficult to make a precise judgement of their respective performance and predictions since central components (e.g., selection of properties, salience determination) are left unspecified. As a consequence, the computational properties of their algorithms are not clear (see Horacek 1997:212 and Stone & Webber 1998:186).

phoric to previous references to the intended referent and thus are only distinguishing in context. If we make the (unrealistic) assumption that all objects in the domain are equally salient, then the generalized algorithm produces the same output as the Incremental Algorithm, albeit in a slightly different way. We also propose a number of extensions required for embedding the algorithm in a general data-to-speech system (i.e., a system which converts structured, non-linguistic data into spoken language). For this purpose, we follow Horacek (1997) and extend the algorithm with a check on the expressibility of properties and a procedure to build a natural language expression within the algorithm. In addition, it is directly checked whether properties are contrastive or not, which is relevant for prosody computation in speech generation.

Of course, it only makes sense to integrate a notion of salience in the Incremental Algorithm if there is a method to assign salience weights in a principled way. Fortunately, a number of such methods exist. We discuss and compare two of those, selected more or less at random; one is based on the hierarchical focusing constraints of Hajičová (1993), the other on the constraints of Centering Theory (Grosz *et al.* 1995). The advantages and disadvantages of both methods are discussed and a synthesis of the two is proposed. While this synthesis is certainly open for further refinements, it provides us with a workable salience function which can be used in tandem with the modified Incremental Algorithm.

The proposed modified algorithm and method for salience weight assignment have been implemented and integrated in a data-to-speech system called D2S. In addition, we carried out an experiment verifying some of the basic assumptions underlying the modified algorithm. In this experiment it was investigated whether subjects prefer the reduced and generalized descriptions that the modified algorithm generates over the full distinguishing descriptions that Dale & Reiter's Incremental Algorithm gives rise to. This was indeed the case, although there was, as we shall see, one somewhat surprising finding: subjects only prefer more general descriptions if these have the same head noun as their antecedent. Thus, once an object has been introduced as a mastiff, people prefer subsequent references to have the same head noun and not a more general one, such as 'dog'. The modified algorithm will be extended to take this finding into account.

A number of further extensions of the modified Incremental Algorithm can be made. First, a conservative pronominalization decision can be taken within the algorithm; a pronoun can be used to refer to the single most salient object in the domain. Second, and more substantially, it is shown how a slight modification of the modified algorithm enables the generation of relational descriptions, that is, descriptions which describe an object in terms of its relation to another object (called the relatum). This has various useful consequences. In particular, the method of determining the best values for certain attributes used in the Incremental Algorithm carries over in an interesting way to the relational algorithm in that now also the best values of *relations* between objects can be determined.[3] Finally, it is argued that an algorithm which can generate pronouns and relational descriptions, can in principle also generate bridging descriptions. From the current perspective, a bridging description is treated as a relational description with a highly salient relatum.

This chapter is structured as follows. In section 8.2 we briefly describe Dale & Reiter's (1995) original Incremental Algorithm. Then, in section 8.3 we describe the modified version of the Incremental Algorithm using salience weights. In section 8.4, the two aforementioned ways of assigning salience weights to objects are discussed and compared, and a synthesis is offered. Section 8.5 describes the experiment that was carried out to verify some of the basic assumptions underlying the modified Incremental Algorithm. In section 8.6 a number of extensions of the modified Incremental Algorithm are sketched, which can generate pronouns (section 8.6.1), relational descriptions (section 8.6.2) and, finally, bridging descriptions (8.6.3). In the concluding section we briefly discuss the implementation of the modified algorithm and its integration in a data-to-speech system, and mention some lines for future research.

8.2 The Incremental Algorithm (Dale & Reiter 1995)

The Incremental Algorithm (and the extensions that are discussed in the rest of this chapter) can be used in any domain which meets the following criteria (Dale & Reiter 1995:254): (*i*) each object in the domain is characterized by a list of attribute value pairs, or *properties*, (*ii*) each object has at least an attribute *type* and (*iii*) there may be a subsumption hierarchy on the values of certain attributes. Some of the values in such a hierarchy are the *basic level values* (e.g., Rosch 1978) for a certain attribute. Basic levels are the first levels which children learn to understand and use. Additionally, and most relevant for current purposes, basic levels are normally used in neutral contexts. Lakoff (1987:46): "*For example,* There's a dog on the porch *can be used in a neutral context, whereas special contexts are needed for* There's a mammal on the porch *or* There's a wire-haired terrier on the porch. (See Cruse (1977))." From the perspective of generation, the basic level values might not only be viewed as context-dependent (cf. Rosch 1978:42)

[3] A version of the relational extension of the modified algorithm has recently been implemented, but is not integrated yet in D2S.

but also as user-dependent (Dale, p.c.). For instance, it seems likely that for a professional dog-breeder the 'basic level' is below 'dog' in the subsumption hierarchy. Here, the basic levels are simply treated as given.

Dale & Reiter (1995) use a dogs and cats domain to illustrate the workings of the Incremental Algorithm. Although this domain may not be an obvious choice for language generation applications, it is suitable for illustrative purposes, as it fits the above criteria very well: cats and dogs are familiar physical entities with easily perceivable properties, and at least one of their attributes ('type') can be organised in a subsumption hierarchy. We therefore follow Dale & Reiter and stick to the cats and dogs domain throughout this chapter.

Suppose, for the sake of illustration, that we have a domain D_1 consisting of the following four objects $d_1 - d_4$.

d_1 $\langle$ type, chihuahua $\rangle$, $\langle$ size, small $\rangle$, $\langle$ colour, black $\rangle$
d_2 $\langle$ type, chihuahua $\rangle$, $\langle$ size, large $\rangle$, $\langle$ colour, white $\rangle$
d_3 $\langle$ type, siamese cat $\rangle$, $\langle$ size, small $\rangle$, $\langle$ colour, black $\rangle$
d_4 $\langle$ type, poodle $\rangle$, $\langle$ size, small$\rangle$, $\langle$ colour, white $\rangle$

Assume that there is a subsumption hierarchy for the attribute 'type': 'dog' subsumes 'chihuahua' and 'poodle', 'cat' subsumes 'siamese cat', and 'animal' in its turn subsumes 'dog' and 'cat'. Following Dale & Reiter, the basic level values for 'type' are taken to be 'dog' and 'cat' respectively.

The input for the Incremental Algorithm is an object r, a *context set* C consisting of alternative objects from which r has to be distinguished (the *distractors*), and, crucially, a list of preferred attributes. This list contains, in order of preference, the attributes that human speakers and hearers prefer for a particular domain. For instance, it seems likely that a human speaker would first try to describe an animal by its 'type' (is it a dog? is it a cat?), and if that does not help attributes like 'colour' and 'size' may be used. It is reasonable to assume that speakers have a general preference for *absolute* properties such as 'colour', which are easily observed without taking the other objects into account, over *relative* properties such as 'size', which are less easily observed and always require inspection of the distractors.[4] Thus let us assume that the list of preferred attributes for the example domain is $\langle$ type, colour, size $\rangle$. Essentially, the Incremental Algorithm goes through the list of preferred attributes, and for each attribute it encounters it looks for the *best value* of this property. The best value of a property is the value closest to

[4]The literature on perception contains a wealth of empirical evidence for such general orderings, see, for instance, Pechmann (1989), Levelt (1989) and, more recently, Beun & Cremers (1998).

the basic level value such that there is no *more specific* value that rules out *more* distractors. If adding this best value to the already selected properties has the effect of ruling out any of the remaining distractors, it is included in the list of properties to be used in the generation of the distinguishing description. The algorithm stops when the end of the list of preferred attributes is reached (failure), or when the set of distractors is empty (success). In the latter case, it is checked whether the 'type' property was included, and if not, its basic value is added to the selected list of properties.

Dale & Reiter (1995:247) argue that this algorithm has a polynomial complexity and that the theoretical run time can be characterized as $n_d n_l$: the run time depends solely on the number of distractors n_d and the number of iterations (i.e., selected properties) n_l. This means that the Incremental Algorithm is the fastest algorithm discussed in Dale & Reiter (1995). One of the central features of the Incremental Algorithm is that there is no backtracking (hence the term 'incremental'): once a property p has been selected, it will be realised in the final description, even if a property which is added later would render the inclusion of p redundant with hindsight. This aspect is partly responsible for the efficiency of the algorithm, but Dale & Reiter additionally claim that this property is 'psychologically realistic' since human speakers also often include redundant modifiers in their referring expressions (see e.g., Pechmann 1989).[5]

8.3 A Modification of the Algorithm Based on Salience

8.3.1 Motivation: Determining the Context Set

The contents of the descriptions generated by the Incremental Algorithm are to a large extent determined by the context set. Nevertheless, Dale

[5]Dale & Reiter (1995:248): "*For example, in a typical experiment a participant is shown a picture containing a white bird, a black cup, and a white cup and is asked to identify the white bird; in such cases, participants generally produce the referring expression* the white bird, *even though the simpler form* the bird *would have been sufficient*." Yet, it seems to us that the Incremental Algorithm would produce the description *the bird* in this situation: if we make the natural assumption that 'type' is the most preferred attribute, the property 'bird' will be the first one selected and immediately rules out the black and the white cup. In general, it should be noted that Pechmann's notion of incrementality refers to *speech production*; the fact that speakers, when describing an object, start uttering properties of that object without making sure whether these are actually distinctive or not. Dale & Reiter's incrementality refers to the lack of backtracking in property selection, but the order in which properties are selected is not related to the order in which properties are realized in speech. It is worth noting that full incrementality in the latter sense (each property is uttered as soon as it is selected), cannot be obtained without taking a certain amount of lookahead into account (Levelt 1989).

and Reiter do not address the question how such context sets are constructed nor how their contents can be updated during the generation process. They only write:

> We define the context set to be the set of entities that the hearer is currently assumed to be attending to; this is similar to the set of entities in the focus spaces of the discourse focus stack in Grosz and Sidner's (1986) theory of discourse structure. (Dale & Reiter 1995:236)

Dale (1992:192-193) is somewhat more explicit and briefly describes a full and a partial order on focus spaces. However, he concludes that:

> [i]n the present domain [recipes, K&T], since the number of entities we are dealing with is relatively small, it is adequate to take the global working set to be the context.

(The 'working set' refers to the set of "identifiable distinct entities in the domain at any point in time," Dale 1992:56.) Our aim is to be explicit about the continuously changing contents of context sets and the repercussions this has for the Incremental Algorithm. It is instructive at this point to look at some of the options we have at our disposal. We assume that there always has to be a domain of discourse D: the total set of objects which can be referred to (in a data-to-speech system this set is given as part of the data). Some people have suggested that a context set may be a proper subset of D, containing those objects of D which have been referred to before (or which are prominent for some other reason). This should make it possible to generate reduced anaphoric descriptions, because the intended referent only has to be distinguished from the members of the context set, and not from all domain objects. However, there appear to be some problems with this approach. We illustrate this using the following example.

Suppose the domain of discourse consists of all dogs that are present at a dog show, and thus contains hundreds of dogs of all kinds, sizes, and colours. We assume that initially, the context set equals the domain of discourse, since at the beginning of the discourse all objects in the domain are equally prominent (or, in terms of Grosz & Sidner 1986, the focus space is still empty).[6] If, in this situation, we wish to generate a distinguishing description for one of these dogs, say d_{45}, this description will necessarily include many of its properties, e.g., *the large black long-haired sausage dog*. After d_{45} has been referred to, it seems an obvious

[6]This is a simplification, which has no influence on the arguments presented here. In reality, it will often be the case that some objects in the domain are initially more salient than others, for instance because they are (physically) closer to the conversational situation.

move to restrict the context set so that it only includes d_{45}, as the hearer's attention has now been directed to this object (in other words, d_{45} is now added to the focus space). If we now wish to generate a second reference to d_{45}, the reduced context set allows us to generate the anaphoric description *the dog*. After all, in this situation d_{45} has no distractors. If we would not restrict the context set, but would re-refer to d_{45} with respect to the entire domain, this would cause a repetition of the initial description *the large black long-haired sausage dog*, which is clearly undesirable. On the other hand, if instead of generating a second reference to d_{45} we wish to refer to another object from the domain, say d_{53} (which happens to be a small grey pygmy poodle with a perm wave), it becomes clear that the context set cannot be restricted to contain only d_{45}, because then describing d_{53} as *the grey dog* would be sufficient to distinguish d_{53} from d_{45}, its only distractor. Obviously, the introduction of d_{53} to the discourse requires a description which is distinguishing relative to the entire domain, and not only relative to d_{45}. This means that the context set cannot be restricted to d_{45}, even though d_{45} is the only dog that has been mentioned so far.

In sum, restricting the context set to a proper subset of the domain, and then generating all distinguishing descriptions relative to this set does not always produce the desired results. Apparently, different context sets should be used depending on the object to be described. For instance, an object that is being newly introduced to the discourse must be distinguished from all other objects in the domain, whereas an object that has been previously mentioned can have a reduced description. Our proposed solution to this problem is to structure the domain by marking certain objects as more prominent than others. As our metric of prominence we shall use *salience weights.*

8.3.2 Preliminaries

The underlying idea of our modifications is the following:

> A definite description 'the $\overline{\text{N}}$' is a suitable description of an object d in a state s iff d is the most salient object with the property expressed by $\overline{\text{N}}$ in state s

Since the denotation of the $\overline{\text{N}}$ is an important factor, we use the notion of a *value set*. Let L be the list of properties expressed by some $\overline{\text{N}}$. The value set of L in some domain D (notation: $\mathsf{Val}_D(L)$) is the set of objects $d \in D$ which have the properties expressed by L.[7] More formally:

[7]The use of value sets marks a minor deviation from Dale & Reiter. Whereas they use a function RulesOut which determines the objects which do *not* have a certain property p, we check which objects *do* have this property. This difference is akin to

Definition 1 (Value sets)

1. $\mathsf{Val}_D(\langle A, V\rangle) = \{d \in D \mid d$ has the property expressed by $\langle A, V\rangle\}$,
2. $\mathsf{Val}_D(\{p_1, \ldots, p_n\}) = \mathsf{Val}_D(p_1) \cap \ldots \cap \mathsf{Val}_D(p_n)$,
   where $p_i = \langle A_i, V_i\rangle (1 \leq i \leq n)$.

Thus, as an example: $\mathsf{Val}_{D_1}(\{\langle \text{colour, white}\rangle, \langle \text{type, chihuahua}\rangle\})$ amounts to $\mathsf{Val}_{D_1}(\langle \text{colour, white}\rangle) \cap \mathsf{Val}_{D_1}(\langle \text{type, chihuahua}\rangle) = \{d_2, d_4\} \cap \{d_1, d_2\} = \{d_2\}$. The domain subscript and the attributes are omitted when this does not lead to confusion; e.g., we write $\mathsf{Val}(\text{small, chihuahua})$. By definition, the value set of the empty list of properties is the entire domain ($\mathsf{Val}_D(\{\}) = D$). Following common practice, we use $|S|$ to denote the cardinality of a set S.

How can we model the salience of an object? For that purpose we use a function variable sw (salience weight) which per state represents a function mapping elements in the domain to a natural number.[8] For the sake of simplicity, we shall assume that in the initial state (s_0), say the beginning of the generation process, all objects are minimally salient (represented as a zero salience level). Formally, $\forall d \in D : sw(s_0, d) = 0$. Below, in section 8.4, we discuss and compare two methods for salience weight assignment and offer a useful synthesis of the two. For the time being we simply assume that the salience weights are given. So let sw be the function assigning salience weights, then we can define that an object r is the most salient object having certain properties L in a state s (notation: $\mathsf{MostSalient}(r, L, s)$) if, and only if, every object in $\mathsf{Val}(L)$ different from r has a lower salience weight in s than r itself.[9]

Definition 2 (Salience condition)
$\mathsf{MostSalient}(r, L, s) \Leftrightarrow \forall d \in \mathsf{Val}(L)(d \neq r \rightarrow sw(s, d) < sw(s, r))$

8.3.3 Outline of the Modified Algorithm

Figures 1 and 2 contain our proposal for a modified algorithm in pseudocode. We have stuck as closely as possible to the algorithm from Dale & Reiter (1995:257) to ease comparison. Below, we illustrate it with a

the difference between a cup which is half full and one which is half empty. We find the use of value sets somewhat more intuitive from a semantic point of view.

[8] It is also possible to assign salience weights to *groups* of objects (such as focus spaces). Notice that the point-wise assignment can be mapped onto a group-wise assignment, but not vice versa. The additional information that point-wise assignments have is potentially useful for the sake of pronominalization. We do not believe, however, that there is a knock-down argument for either of the alternatives. For that the two are too similar.

[9] A computationally more efficient version would intersect the value set of L with the set of objects which are equally or more salient than the referent r (that is $\{d \in D \mid sw(s, r) \leq sw(s, d)\}$). See Theune (2000).

MakeReferringExpression (r, P, s)

$L \leftarrow \{\}$, *tree* $\leftarrow$ nil, *contrast* $\leftarrow$ **false**
for each member A_i of list P **do**
  $V \leftarrow$ FindBestValue $(r, A_i, \text{BasicLevelValue}(r, A_i), s)$
  contrast $\leftarrow$ Contrastive(r, A_i, V)
  tree' $\leftarrow$ UpdateTree (*tree*, V, *contrast*))
  if $(|\text{Val}(L \cup \{\langle A_i, V\rangle\})| < |\text{Val}(L)| \vee A_i = \text{type}) \wedge$ *tree'* $\neq$ nil
  then $L \leftarrow L \cup \{\langle A_i, V\rangle\}$
    tree $\leftarrow$ *tree'*
  endif
  if MostSalient $(r, L, s) =$ **true**
  then *tree* $\leftarrow$ AddDefDet (*tree*)
    return *tree*
  endif
return failure

FIGURE 1 Sketch of the main function of the modified algorithm.

number of examples. First, we give a general overview.

The algorithm is called by MakeReferringExpression (r, P, s) (figure 1); that is, we try to generate a definite description for a referent r given some pre-defined list P of *preferred attributes* in a state s. L is the list of properties which have been selected for inclusion in the expression generated and is initialized as the empty list. The variable *tree* contains the syntactic tree for the NP under construction which corresponds with the current list of properties L. Finally, *contrast* is a boolean variable which indicates whether the property under consideration is contrastive or not. As in the original version of the algorithm, the main loop iterates through the list P of preferred attributes. For each attribute A on this list, the best value V is sought (essentially in the same way as done in the Incremental Algorithm, using the function FindBestValue, see figure 2). Once the best value V is found, the algorithm immediately checks whether the property is contrastive or not (using the function Contrastive, figure 2), and attempts to incorporate V in the NP under construction (using the function UpdateTree). The property $\langle A, V\rangle$ is actually included in the description if it 'shrinks' the value set (and thus rules out one or more distractors) or if the attribute A is 'type',[10] pro-

[10]This latter option marks a minor deviation from Dale & Reiter. They always include the 'type', but only *check* whether it was included after a distinguishing

FindBestValuc$(r, A, \textit{initial-value}, s)$

if UserKnows$(r, \langle A, \textit{initial-value}\rangle) =$ **true**
then $\textit{value} \leftarrow \textit{initial-value}$
else $\textit{value} \leftarrow$ novalue
endif
if MostSalient$(r, \{\langle A, \textit{value}\rangle\}, s) =$ **false** $\wedge$
  $(\textit{msv} \leftarrow$ MoreSpecificValue$(r, A, \textit{value})) \neq$ novalue $\wedge$
  $(\textit{new-value} \leftarrow$ FindBestValue $(r, A, \textit{msv}, s)) \neq$ novalue $\wedge$
  $|\mathsf{Val}(\{\langle A, \textit{new-value}\rangle\})| < |\mathsf{Val}(\{\langle A, \textit{value}\rangle\})|$
then $\textit{value} \leftarrow \textit{new-value}$
endif
return $\textit{value}$

MostSalient(r, L, s)

if $\forall d \in \mathsf{Val}(L)(d \neq r \Rightarrow sw(s, d) < sw(s, r))$
then return true
else return false
endif

Contrastive(r, A, V)

$LC \leftarrow \{d \in \mathsf{DR}(\mathsf{PrevS} \cup \mathsf{CurrS}) \mid d \neq r \wedge$
  $\mathsf{Parent}(\mathsf{BasicLevelValue}(d, \mathrm{type})) =$
  $\mathsf{Parent}(\mathsf{BasicLevelValue}(r, \mathrm{type}))\}$
if $\exists d \in LC : \mathsf{Value}(d, A) \neq V$
then return true
else return false
endif

FIGURE 2 Sketch of auxiliary functions of the modified algorithm.

vided that the function UpdateTree was successful. If this is not the case (i.e., the lexical or syntactic restrictions of the generation module make it impossible to express the property), V is rejected. After that it is checked whether the intended referent r is the most salient object in the current state of the discourse which satisfies L (using the function Most-Salient (r, L, s), see figure 2). If so, the function AddDefDet inserts the determiner *the* to produce a full definite description and the algorithm succeeds.

The function Contrastive (r, A, V) checks whether the property under consideration is contrastive, i.e., if it serves to distinguish the object r in some linguistic context LC. LC is defined as the set of objects/discourse referents (DRs) which are referred to in the previous sentence (PrevS) or in the sentence currently being generated (CurrS), and of which the basic level value of the attribute 'type' has the same parent as that of r. A property $\langle A, V \rangle$ of r is considered to be contrastive if there is an element $c \in LC$ which has a different value for the current attribute. Thus, loosely speaking, the adjective *large* in the NP *the large dog* is marked as contrastive in the context of *a small cat* but not in the context of *a small car.*[11]

In contrast with the rest of the algorithm, the function UpdateTree is largely domain and language dependent. Since this function is not the focus of our work, we do not provide a detailed specification of it here, but restrict ourselves to a broad sketch based on a few rather simplified assumptions. Roughly, UpdateTree works as follows: starting from a prototypical NP structure, the function attempts to integrate each new value V in the syntactic tree constructed so far. We assume that the value of the 'type' attribute (and no other value) is always realised as the head noun, and therefore can always be included in the tree under construction.[12] Unary properties are added as prenominal AP modifiers to designated slots in the tree.[13] Relations (discussed in

---

description has been generated. The result will be the same in all cases where 'type' is first on the list of preferred attributes.

[11]This treatment of contrast is closely related to the proposal of Prevost (1996), who presents an algorithm for deciding which properties should receive contrastive accent in a manner which, incidentally, is somewhat similar to the Incremental Algorithm. See Theune (1997, 2000) for some further discussion on Prevost's approach to contrast.

[12]This is a simplification, as has been pointed out by Horacek (1995) among others, which we make following Dale & Reiter (1995). In fact, we believe that the decision to include type information depends on the kind of domain and on the list of preferred attributes. For example, in a domain where all objects are basically of the same type, type information is unnecessary and should thus not be included at all; see van der Sluis & Krahmer (2001).

[13]For a discussion of adjective orderings, see Dale 1992:127-130, and the references

section 8.6.2) may be realized as postnominal PPs or relative clauses. Following Horacek (1997), we allow each available slot in the prototypical NP structure to be filled only once. If this implies that the current property cannot be added to the tree under construction, UpdateTree returns nil. Below we assume that UpdateTree always succeeds unless noted otherwise. If *contrast* is **true**, the expression of the value V is marked by a [+c] feature, which can be taken into account during the computation of prosody in a spoken language generation system. No lexical selection takes place: we assume that each attribute-value pair is associated with a fixed lexicalized tree; e.g., $[_{AP}$ *small*] for $\langle$ size, small $\rangle$.

8.3.4 Examples

First example: non-anaphoric description Reconsider our example domain D_1, and suppose that we start generating a monologue in the initial state s_0. Thus, by assumption, all elements of the domain are equally salient. Now we want to generate an expression for d_2. MakeReferringExpression (d_2, P, s_0) is called, assuming that P is $\langle$ type, colour, size $\rangle$. The list of properties L is initialized as $\{\}$, *tree* as nil and *contrast* as **false**. We consider the first property of d_2, $\langle$ type, chihuahua $\rangle$. The best value for this attribute is 'chihuahua', since $|\mathsf{Val}(\text{chihuahua})| = 2 < |\mathsf{Val}(\text{dog})| = 3$. The property 'type' is always included, but note that it is also informative in that it rules out two distractors: $|\mathsf{Val}(\text{chihuahua})| = 2 < |\mathsf{Val}(\{\})| = 4$. After one iteration, the description under construction is tree (I) from figure 3. The value of L is now $\{\langle$ type, chihuahua $\rangle\}$. MostSalient$(d_2, \text{chihuahua}, s_0)$ fails because d_1 is also a chihuahua, and d_1 and d_2 are both minimally salient by assumption. So we proceed by taking the second property of d_2, $\langle$ colour, white $\rangle$. Now $|\mathsf{Val}(\text{white, chihuahua})| < |\mathsf{Val}(\text{chihuahua})|$; this property is discriminating and thus included. After adding the property 'white' to the current NP tree, the tree looks as in (II, figure 3). Now, the condition MostSalient$(d_2, \{\text{white, chihuahua}\}, s_0)$ *is* true: d_2 is the only white chihuahua in the domain, so it is by definition the most salient one. The definite article is added, and the resulting tree (III, figure 3) is returned. When the description is conveyed, d_2 increases in salience, becoming more salient than the other objects in the domain.

Notice that when we assume that all objects in the domain are always equally salient (thus sw represents the constant function mapping each $d \in D$ to some n), the modified algorithm selects exactly the same properties as the original Incremental Algorithm. In other words, our version truly generalizes the original, which brings us to the next example.

---

cited therein. For an alternative, data-oriented approach, see Malouf (2000).

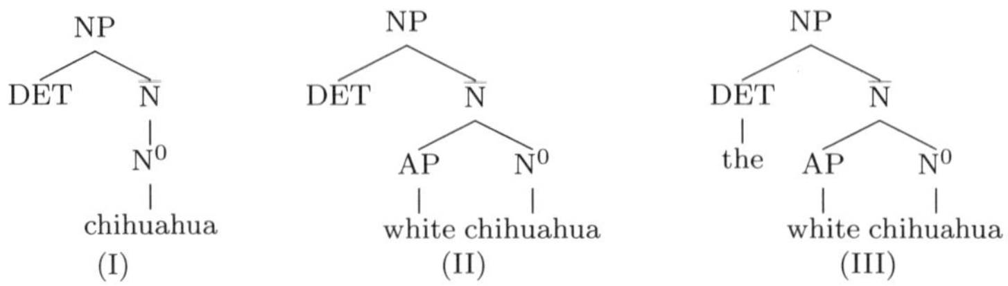

FIGURE 3 The three stages of generating the first example description.

Second example: anaphoric description An anaphoric description generally contains less information than its antecedent. This may be reflected by the omission of properties, by the use of a more general head noun, or by both, as this example shows. Suppose we want to refer to d_2 in a situation s' where d_2 is more salient than the other animals in the domain (e.g., because d_2 was referred to in the previous sentence). The BasicLevelValue for d_2 with attribute 'type' is 'dog', and since d_2 is currently the most salient dog in the domain, the modified Incremental Algorithm immediately succeeds and returns a tree for *the dog.*[14]

Third example: contrast Now suppose that the preceding sentence referred to both d_1 and d_2 (e.g., '*the black chihuahua and the white chihuahua* ...') and that we call MakeReferringExpression (d_2, P, s). Then the first property added to the description under construction will be 'chihuahua' (as the reader may check for herself). The second property, 'white' is also added to the description, since it distinguishes d_2 from d_1. Moreover, this property is *contrastive*, since d_1 and d_2 have the same basic level value for the 'type' attribute and different values for the 'colour' attribute. The result is '*the white*$^{[+c]}$ *chihuahua*' (where [+c] is a feature indicating a contrastive relation).

8.3.5 Discussion

We have described a generalization of the Incremental Algorithm which extends the original in a number of ways. First and foremost, it explicitly takes the discourse context into account by treating context sets as a combination of a discourse domain with a salience function. This generalization entails that creating a referring expression for one object (here d_2 of domain D_1) can result in e.g., *the white chihuahua* (in the initial state), *the dog* (in a context like *the white chihuahua* ...), *the dog*$^{[+c]}$ (sample context: *the white chihuahua and the cat*) and *the white*$^{[+c]}$

[14] As we will see, the experiment in section 8.5 shows that it is not always a good idea to use more general head nouns. Below the algorithm will be improved with respect to this issue.

chihuahua (context: *the black chihuahua and the white chihuahua* ...). This does not make the algorithm more complex: it still has a polynomial complexity, and a similar theoretical run time as the original algorithm $(n_d n_l)$.[15]

8.4 Determining Salience Weights

So far we did not discuss how salience weights are computed. The literature contains various methods to do so, such as Alshawi (1987), Hajičová (1993), Lappin & Leass (1994), and Grosz *et al.* (1995). The basic idea underlying these methods is the same: objects that have (recently) been mentioned are more salient than objects that have not been mentioned. This basic idea is worked out differently for each method, for instance in the way that factors like syntactic position or discourse function are taken into account. As a consequence, the choice for a specific method of salience weight assignment may influence the outcome of the algorithm. As an illustrative example, we discuss and compare the hierarchical focusing constraints of Hajičová (1993) and the Centering approach of Grosz *et al.* (1995). Throughout this section we let sw be a total function mapping the objects in a domain D to the set $\{0, \ldots, 10\}$, with the intuition that 0 represents complete non-salience and 10 maximal salience.[16] We continue assuming that in the initial situation s_0 all objects in the domain are equally (not) salient: $sw(s_0, d) = 0$ for all $d \in D$.

8.4.1 Hajičová: Hierarchical Focus Constraints

Salience weight assignment in the Praguian approach is based on the notions *topic* and *focus* (see e.g., Sgall *et al.* 1986 for precise definitions of these notions). Informally speaking, the topic of utterance U is what U is about (generally this corresponds to the grammatical subject), while the focus[17] of U is what the sentence says about its topic (the rest of the sentence). Informally, the Praguian approach says that objects which have been referred to in the focus part of a sentence have maximal salience; they constitute new information that is assumed to be in the centre of attention. Objects which have been referred to in the topic have a lower salience weight than those referred to in the focus.

[15]To see this, observe that the modified algorithm still requires as much iterations as properties realized in the description (n_l) and in each of the iterations has to inspect the set of distractors (n_d).

[16]We are not committed to an 11-point scale of salience *per se*. Any finite subset of the integers will do. In general, it may well be that more than 11 objects are referred to in a particular sentence, but this poses no problems for an 11-point scale because not every object needs to be assigned a unique salience weight.

[17]Notice that the notion of focus used here is very different from that used in e.g., Grosz & Sidner (1986) and Grosz *et al.* (1995).

Their exact weight is determined by the form of the referring expression that has been used: if a non-pronominal NP has been used, the highest-but-one salience weight is assigned, and if a pronoun has been used, the object's salience weight does not change. If an object has not been referred to in a sentence (i.e., it is part of neither focus nor topic) then its salience weight decreases. The salience weight of objects that have been previously referred to in the topic part of a sentence decreases at a slower rate than that of objects that have been previously referred to in the focus. Formally:

Definition 3 (Salience weight assignment based on Hajičová (1993)) *Let U_i be a sentence uttered in state s_i, and let $\mathsf{topic}(U_i) \subseteq D$ and $\mathsf{focus}(U_i) \subseteq D$ be the sets of objects which are referred to in the topic and the focus part of U_i respectively. Then the salience weight of objects in s_{i+1} is determined as follows:*

$$sw(s_{i+1}, d) = \begin{cases} 10 & \text{if } d \in \mathsf{focus}(U_i) \\ 9 & \text{if } d \in \mathsf{topic}(U_i), \\ & \quad \text{and } d \text{ is referred to by a definite NP} \\ sw(s_i, d) & \text{if } d \in \mathsf{topic}(U_i), \\ & \quad \text{and } d \text{ is referred to by a pronoun} \\ \mathsf{max}(0, sw(s_i, d) - 1) & \text{if } d \notin \mathsf{topic}(U_i) \cup \mathsf{focus}(U_i), \\ & \quad \text{and } d \in \mathsf{topic}(U_j), j < i \\ \mathsf{max}(0, sw(s_i, d) - 2) & \text{if } d \notin \mathsf{topic}(U_i) \cup \mathsf{focus}(U_i), \\ & \quad \text{and } d \in \mathsf{focus}(U_j), j < i \end{cases}$$

The salience function given in definition 3 above closely corresponds to the rules given by Hajičová (1993), except that in our version objects are mapped to a *higher* number as they become more salient, with a maximum of 10, whereas in Hajičová (1993) objects are assigned a *lower* number as they become more salient, maximal salience being indicated by 0. As a consequence, the Praguian approach allows for an infinite decrease in salience weight, keeping track of objects which have faded from the discourse long ago. We do not think this is psychologically realistic, so we assume there is not only a maximal but also a minimal salience level: in our version, the salience weight of an object cannot decrease below zero.

8.4.2 Grosz *et al.*: Centering

An alternative definition of salience weight assignment can be based on the ranking of the so-called *forward looking centers* (C_f) of an utterance. According to Centering Theory (Grosz *et al.* 1995), the set of forward looking centers of an utterance contains the objects referred to in that utterance. This set is partially ordered to reflect the relative prominence of the referring expressions within the utterance. Grammatical roles are a major factor here, so that *subject* > *object* > *other*.

Definition 4 (Salience weight assignment based on Centering Theory) *Let U_i be a sentence uttered in state s_i, in which reference is made to $\{d_1, \ldots, d_n\} \subseteq D$. Let $C_f(U_i)$ (the forward looking centers of U_i) be a partial order defined over $\{d_1, \ldots, d_n\} \subseteq D$. Then the salience weight of objects in s_{i+1} is determined as follows:*

$$sw(s_{i+1}, d) = \begin{cases} 0 & \text{if } d \notin C_f(U_i) \\ n & \text{otherwise, where } n = \mathsf{level}(d, C_f(U_i)) \end{cases}$$

Here, $\mathsf{level}(d, C_f(U_i))$ refers to the level of the occurrence of d in the ordering $C_f(U_i)$, defined in such a way that the highest element(s) on the ordering are mapped to 10, the element(s) immediately below are mapped to 9, etc. Thus, $\mathsf{level}(d_i, \langle d_1, \ldots, d_n\rangle) = \mathsf{max}(0, 11 - i)$, where $\langle d_1, \ldots, d_n\rangle$ is the partially ordered set of forward looking centers of the relevant utterance.

8.4.3 Examples, Predictions and Comparison

Here we discuss two illustrative examples in some detail, emphasizing the repercussions of choosing either way of assigning salience weights for the generation of referring expressions. We use sw^h to indicate the salience weights as assigned by the Hajičová-based approach (definition 3), while sw^c gives the salience weights as based on the Centering approach (definition 4). Indices on words refer to objects in the domain. In the example sentences, the Praguian topic always coincides with the syntactic subject. Suppose the domain of discourse is D_1, and consider the following example.

(2) a. The$_2$ white chihuahua was angry.
$sw^h(s_1, d_2) = 9$
$sw^c(s_1, d_2) = 10$

b. It$_2$ viciously attacked the$_1$ black chihuahua.
$sw^h(s_2, d_1) = 10$ $\quad sw^h(s_2, d_2) = 9$
$sw^c(s_2, d_1) = 9$ $\quad sw^c(s_2, d_2) = 10$

c. { The$_1$ dog (H)/The$_1$ black dog (C) } barked loudly.
$sw^h(s_3, d_1) = 9$ $\quad sw^h(s_3, d_2) = 8$
$sw^c(s_3, d_1) = 10$ $\quad sw^c(s_3, d_2) = 0$

First we take the Praguian point of view, using sw^h as defined above. In (2)a the modified algorithm produces the description *the white chihuahua* to refer to d_2. Thereby, d_2 becomes the most salient object, with the highest-but-one degree of salience, as it is introduced in the topic of the sentence. In (2)b a new object, d_1, is introduced to the discourse using the description *the black chihuahua*. Since this is done in the focus of the sentence, d_1 rises to maximal salience. Object d_2 is referred to by a pronoun occurring in the topic of the sentence, so its salience weight remains the same.[18] In (2)c, d_1 is referred to for the second time, and as it is currently the most salient dog, the modified algorithm generates the description *the dog*. This result, though marginally acceptable, is not what we want. A simple solution to this problem is to ignore small differences in activation degree between competitors (see also Kruijff-Korbayová & Hajičová 1997:41).

Let us now discuss example (2) from the Centering perspective. After the first sentence has been uttered, we find that C_f ((2)a) is the singleton set containing d_2, and as a result this object is now the most salient object. In (2)b we refer to both d_2 and d_1, and C_f ((2)b) therefore contains both d_1 and d_2. Since d_2 is referred to in subject position, it is ranked higher than d_1. Consequently, to refer to d_1 in (2)c the modified Incremental Algorithm correctly produces *the black dog*.

Now consider the following discourse, based on the dog show example from section 8.3.1. Suppose Joe went to the dog show and bought the dogs d_{45} and d_{53}.

(3) a. Joe bought the$_{45}$ large black long-haired sausage dog and the$_{53}$ small grey pygmy poodle with the perm wave.
$sw^h(s_1, joe) = 9$ $\quad sw^h(s_1, d_{45}) = 10$ $\quad sw^h(s_1, d_{53}) = 10$
$sw^c(s_1, joe) = 10$ $\quad sw^c(s_1, d_{45}) = 9$ $\quad sw^c(s_1, d_{53}) = 9$

b. The$_{45}$ sausage dog was a bargain.
$sw^h(s_2, joe) = 8$ $\quad sw^h(s_2, d_{45}) = 9$ $\quad sw^h(s_2, d_{53}) = 8$
$sw^c(s_2, joe) = 0$ $\quad sw^c(s_2, d_{45}) = 10$ $\quad sw^c(s_2, d_{53}) = 0$

c. { The$_{53}$ poodle (H) / The$_{53}$ small grey pygmy poodle with the perm wave (C) } was very expensive though.
$sw^h(s_3, joe) = 7$ $\quad sw^h(s_3, d_{45}) = 8$ $\quad sw^h(s_3, d_{53}) = 9$
$sw^c(s_3, joe) = 0$ $\quad sw^c(s_3, d_{45}) = 0$ $\quad sw^c(s_3, d_{53}) = 10$

[18] We address the problem of pronoun generation in section 8.6.1 below.

Comparing the two different salience weight assignments in this example presents the following picture. After generation of the first sentence, both approaches assign high salience weights to *joe* and the dogs d_{45} and d_{53}. The second sentence only contains a reference to d_{45} (*the sausage dog*). Using the Centering approach, this reduces the salience weight of *joe* and d_{53} to zero as they are not mentioned in (3)b, whereas using the Hajičová approach entails that the salience weights of *joe* and d_{53} are reduced much less. The difference in salience weight reduction for d_{53} greatly influences its description in (3)c. Seen from a Praguian perspective, d_{53} is still the most salient poodle at this stage, and the generated description is *the poodle.* However, from the Centering perspective, d_{53} is not salient at all and the modified Incremental Algorithm again produces the description *the small grey pygmy poodle with the perm wave*, just as it did for the first-mention of this dog in (3)a. In our opinion, this shows that the Centering assumption that only objects mentioned in the previous sentence can have a non-zero salience weight, is too strong from the perspective of definite descriptions. Again, there is an obvious way to remedy this shortcoming: we can take the structure of the discourse into account (see e.g., Walker 1998 for a proposal to this effect).

8.4.4 Discussion and Synthesis

There are several principled ways to determine salience weights that can be used in the modified algorithm. Here, we have discussed and compared two of them: one is based on the hierarchical focusing constraints of Hajičová (1993) and the other on the Centering approach of Grosz *et al.* (1995). Probably the most important distinctions between the two are (*i*) the Praguian assumption that information introduced in the focus of an utterance has a somewhat higher salience weight than information introduced in the topic, as opposed to the Centering assumption that information referred to in subject position is more salient than information referred to in object position,[19] and (*ii*) the Centering assumption that only objects mentioned in the previous sentence can have a non-zero salience weight, while in the Praguian approach the determination of salience weights is not restricted to the previous sentence.

We have discussed two examples illustrating the differences between the two approaches. In the first case, the Centering approach yields better results, while in the second case, it is the Hajičová way of determining salience weights which pays off. These examples suggest that the Centering ordering of salience is preferable over the Praguian topic/focus

[19]In most cases, but not always, the subject of a sentence refers to topical information. In those cases, the approaches we have discussed make different predictions.

ordering, but that a gradual decrease in salience of non-mentioned objects gives better results than an abrupt loss of salience. An obvious step is therefore to combine the Centering definition of salience with a mechanism for gradual decrease. Here, we opt for the most simple form of decrease, where the salience of all discourse objects that have not been mentioned in the current sentence decreases by one. (This simplification of the Praguian approach is sufficient for current purposes.) Thus, we arrive at definition 5:

Definition 5 (Revised salience weight assignment)
Let U_i be a sentence uttered in state s_i, in which reference is made to $\{d_1, \ldots, d_n\} \subseteq D$. Let $C_f(U_i)$ (the forward looking centers of U_i) be a partial order defined over $\{d_1, \ldots, d_n\} \subseteq D$. Then the salience weight of objects in s_{i+1} is determined as follows:

$$sw(s_{i+1}, d) = \begin{cases} \mathsf{level}(d, C_f(U_i)) & \text{if } d \in C_f(U_i) \\ \mathsf{max}(0, sw(s_i, d) - 1) & \text{if } d \notin C_f(U_i) \text{ and } d \in \mathrm{C}_f(U_j), j < i \end{cases}$$

Using the above definition, the modified algorithm produces the intuitively correct results for the examples discussed so far (as the reader may check). We certainly do not consider definition 5 as the ultimate way of salience weight assignment. It probably needs to be refined to account for salience fluctuations in more complicated examples, e.g., containing complex grammatical constructions. In this respect it would be highly interesting to fine-tune definition 5 using results from more recent, corpus-based approaches to salience (Lappin & Leass 1994, Popescu-Belis *et al.* 1998, Poesio & Viera 1998, and McCoy & Strube 1999). For the time being, definition 5 provides us with a workable salience function to be used in the modified algorithm and at least shows that it is possible to assign salience weights in a principled manner.

For the generation of reduced anaphoric descriptions, it is very important to have some form of salience weight assignment, ensuring that objects which have been recently mentioned are regarded as being (much) more salient than the other objects in the domain. Without such a mechanism, the MakeReferringExpression algorithm would generate a full description of an object at every mention of this object, using the same description throughout the output text. For the generation of reduced definite descriptions, in most cases it seems sufficient to only keep track of large differences in salience weight (e.g., between mentioned versus unmentioned entities); small differences (e.g., between entities that have been mentioned in different positions in the same sentence) appear to be mainly relevant for pronominalization (discussed in section 8.6.1). So far, we have set our 'salience threshold' to one: a referent r counts as being more salient than other objects in the domain if its salience weight is at least one point higher than that of those other objects (in other words, only those objects that are at least equally salient as r count as its distractors). However, to stay on the safe side we might set the threshold higher. A consequence of such a measure would be the generation of fewer reduced descriptions, which reduces the risk of ambiguity but also reduces coherence of the generated texts. In general, the choice between fewer or more reduced anaphoric descriptions involves a trade-off between incoherence and ambiguity. Less ambiguity (due to fewer reduced descriptions) entails more incoherence, and vice versa. The desired ratio between the two might depend (among other things) on text genre (Reiter p.c.). For instance, in legal texts coherence is far less important than unambiguous reference, as observed by Maes (1991).

Finally, a word on the computational consequences of adding a salience function to the algorithm. In general, the determination of salience adds little computational overhead. To compute a new salience function only the weights of the objects mentioned in the current clause and the objects with a non-zero salience weight have to be updated. Even for huge domains, the latter set is highly restricted, containing only the objects mentioned in the last few sentences.

8.5 Experimental Evaluation

Some of the hypotheses underlying the modified Incremental Algorithm have been experimentally tested using a forced choice experiment. In this experiment, the subjects had to indicate for a number of texts which of two versions of these texts they found most natural. The two versions differed only with respect to the description of one item. In this section, the experiment is described and its results are discussed.

8.5.1 Hypotheses and Assumptions

The following hypotheses were tested in the experiment:

> **Hypothesis I**: People prefer anaphoric descriptions that contain fewer properties than their antecedents.
>
> **Hypothesis II**: People prefer anaphoric descriptions that express attribute values which are closer to the basic level value than those expressed in their antecedents.

Hypothesis III: If an anaphoric expression can refer to only one object, people prefer the anaphor to be pronominalized.

Hypothesis IV: Hypotheses I and II apply also if there is an intervening sentence between the anaphor and its closest antecedent. (This hypothesis is divided into two parts: IVa relates to hypothesis I, and IVb relates to hypothesis II.)

By testing the first three hypotheses, we intended to find out if people really prefer the reduced, generalized or pronominalized descriptions (see section 8.6.1) generated by the modified algorithm over the full descriptions that would be generated if the effects of salience were not taken into account. The fourth hypothesis was added to test if a discourse object still remains salient after it has not been mentioned for one sentence (the gradual decrease in salience discussed in section 8.4).

8.5.2 Method

The modified algorithm is meant to generate referring expressions which will be preferred by human hearers, rather than to reproduce the variety of referring expressions which human speakers produce in various contexts. Therefore a forced-choice experiment was used to test the hypotheses presented above, rather than a production experiment. In the experiment, the subjects had to indicate their preference for one of two alternative referring expressions.

The experiment was performed by 51 naive subjects. All subjects were native speakers of Dutch, except one, whose mother tongue was English. The subjects (of different ages and backgrounds) were presented with 32 texts in Dutch, displayed in two versions on a computer screen. For each text, they had to indicate which of its two versions they found most natural. The texts were presented in a random order. The experiment was self-paced.

8.5.3 Materials

The texts used in the experiment were constructed to test the hypotheses presented above. There were eight texts per hypothesis. (In the case of hypothesis IV, four of these texts were associated with IVa and four texts were associated with IVb.) The texts were written in Dutch and consisted of two or three sentences. Each text had two versions, A and B, that were the same except for the description of one discourse item (the grammatical subject in the final sentence). The description in the A version was in line with the hypothesis associated with the modified algorithm, whereas the description in the B version was overspecified

Hypothesis I: omission of properties

De poedel en de grote terrier maakten ruzie over een bot.
{ *De terrier* / *De grote terrier* } *ging er met het bot vandoor.*

The poodle and the large terrier had a fight over a bone.
{ The terrier / The large terrier } ran off with the bone.

Hypothesis II: more basic values

De poedel en de kat woonden op de boerderij.
{ *De hond* / *De poedel* } *waakte over de kippen.*

The poodle and the cat were living at the farm.
{ The dog / The poodle } guarded the chickens.

Hypothesis III: pronominalization

De zwarte siamese kat had honger.
{ *Hij* / *De kat* } *ging op zoek naar een visje in de keuken.*

The black siamese cat was hungry.
{ It / The cat } went to the kitchen to look for a fish.

Hypothesis IVa: intervening sentences (I)

John kocht een grote witte chihuahua en een poedel in het asiel.
De poedel was een koopje.
{ *De chihuahua* / *De grote witte chihuahua* } *was iets duurder.*

John bought a large white chihuahua and a poodle at the asylum.
The poodle was a bargain.
{ The chihuahua / The large white chihuahua } was a bit more expensive.

Hypothesis IVb: intervening sentences (II)

De bruine rottweiler en de zwarte rottweiler lagen in de tuin te slapen.
Plots begonnen twee grijze katten te vechten in de tuin.
{ *De bruine hond* / *De bruine rottweiler* } *werd wakker door het lawaai.*

The brown rottweiler and the black rottweiler were sleeping in the garden.
Suddenly, two grey cats started fighting in the garden.
{ The brown dog / The brown rottweiler } was awakened by the noise.

FIGURE 4 Examples of texts associated with hypotheses I to IV.

	Significant preference for A	Significant preference for B	No significant preference
Hypothesis I	8^a	0	0
Hypothesis II	2^b	5^c	1^d
Hypothesis III	8^a	0	0
Hypothesis IV	4^a	3^a	1^e

a: $p < 0,001$
b: for one text, $p < 0,005$ and for the other text $p < 0,001$
c: for one text, $p < 0,01$ and for the other four $p < 0,001$
d: non-significant preference for A $(0,1 < p < 0,25)$
e: non-significant preference for B $(0,25 < p < 0,5)$

TABLE 1 The number of texts for each hypothesis, for which (*i*) a significant number of subjects preferred version A; (*ii*) a significant number of subjects preferred version B; (*iii*) there was no significant preference for either version.

according to the same hypothesis. Both descriptions were distinguishing. Figure 4 shows an example text for each of the hypotheses. To save space, we do not show both versions of each text. Instead, we show only one text with the pair of differing descriptions in the last line. The first description of each pair is the description that is in line with the corresponding hypothesis, and the second one is the overspecified description.

8.5.4 Results

Table 1 shows the results of the experiment. For each hypothesis, it shows the number of texts for which (*i*) a significant number of subjects preferred version A; (*ii*) a significant number of subjects preferred version B; (*iii*) there was no significant preference for either version. Significance was computed using the χ^2 test.

The results of the experiment can be summed up as follows. For all texts associated with hypotheses I and III, a highly significant number of subjects ($p <$ 0,001) preferred version A, containing a description in line with the associated hypothesis. However, for only two of the texts associated with hypothesis II, the subjects had a significant preference for version A. For five of the texts associated with this hypothesis, there was a significant preference for version B. Hypothesis IV also showed mixed results: for half of the texts, version A was significantly preferred, and for three other texts, B was significantly preferred. This difference in preference corresponds closely to the division of hypothesis IV into parts IVa and IVb. As shown in Table 2, for the texts associated with hypothesis IVa the A version is significantly preferred in three of the four cases, whereas for the texts associated with hypothesis IVb it is the

B version which is significantly preferred in three of the four cases.

	Significant preference for A	Significant preference for B	No significant preference
Hypothesis IVa	3^a	0	1^b
Hypothesis IVb	1^a	3^a	0

a: $p < 0,001$
b: non-significant preference for B $(0,25 < p < 0,5)$

TABLE 2 The results for hypothesis IV, divided into two groups of text pairs corresponding to hypothesis I and hypothesis II respectively.

8.5.5 Discussion

The experimental results confirm hypotheses I and III: the subjects in the experiment showed a significant preference for anaphoric descriptions that contained fewer properties than the antecedent, or that were pronominalized. A plausible explanation for this preference is that the reduced descriptions increased the coherence of the example texts, without giving rise to ambiguity. The findings for hypothesis III are in line with the experimental results of Gordon *et al.* (1993), who found that utterances are more difficult to read if they contain a definite description or a proper name where a pronoun could have been used.

Hypothesis II was not confirmed: for only two of the eight texts, a significant number of subjects preferred the version containing a description with a more basic head noun than the antecedent. For five texts, a significant number of subjects preferred the version that did *not* contain a description with a more basic head noun. If we look at the three[20] texts for which a more basic head noun was preferred (in line with hypothesis II), we see that in all three cases, the head noun in the anaphor is a substring of the more specific head noun of the antecedent, e.g., *siamese cat* → *cat*. In the other five texts, this is not the case; here the more basic head noun is completely different from the more specific one. An example is *poodle* → *dog*. These observations suggest that the preference for repeating the same head noun, observed in five of the eight texts associated with hypothesis II, should be seen as a preference for using the same *wording* in both anaphor and antecedent. This is similar to the 'priming' effect that has been found in dialogues: speakers tend to use the same literal expressions as their interlocutors (see e.g., Levelt & Kelter 1982 and Clark & Wilkes-Gibbs 1986). Presumably, holding on to the same wording (both within and among speakers) should be

[20]This includes one text for which a non-significant majority of the subjects preferred version A; see Table 1.

seen as another method for maintaining the coherence of a discourse. When the more basic head noun is lexicalized as a substring of the more specific one (*cat* versus *siamese cat*), then there is no "switch" to a different wording. In such cases, the use of the more basic head noun is preferred.[21]

Like hypothesis II, hypothesis IVb was not supported by the experimental results. This hypothesis was constructed to test if hypothesis II holds if there is an intervening sentence between anaphor and antecedent. For three of the four texts associated with IVb, the B version was preferred. This may be explained through the fact that the A versions of these three texts contained a head noun with a different wording than the antecedent. As discussed above, hypothesis II does not hold for such head nouns. For the fourth text, the A version was preferred. In this text, the more basic head noun used in the anaphor had the same wording as the antecedent. Thus, for hypothesis IVb we see exactly the same picture as for hypothesis II. On the other hand, for three of the four texts associated with hypothesis IVa (constructed to test if hypothesis I holds if there is an intervening sentence), version A was preferred. This is in line with the results for hypothesis I.

The conclusions we can draw from the experiment are the following. People prefer anaphoric descriptions that contain fewer properties than the antecedent (provided that the referent is the most salient object with the included properties); this holds even if there is an intervening sentence between anaphor and antecedent. So, the strategy of not including non-discriminating properties is correct, as is the gradual decrease of salience argued for in section 8.4. In addition, people prefer pronominalized anaphoric descriptions over non-pronominalized ones (provided that the referent is the single most salient discourse object). This justifies the extension of the modified algorithm to generate pronouns, discussed in section 8.6.1.

Finally, people prefer to use a more basic head noun in the anaphor only if the wording is similar to that of the antecedent; otherwise, they prefer to repeat the same head noun even if this leads to overspecification. Apparently, using the same wording in both antecedent and anaphor leads to a higher degree of perceived coherence than reducing overspecification through the use of a more general head noun. This finding suggests that an additional check should be made in the FindBestValue function of the modified algorithm (see Figure 5). This check should only apply to anaphoric descriptions (referring to the most salient

[21]Possibly, the subjects perceived these cases as the omission of a property (hypothesis I) rather than the use of a different head noun (hypothesis II).

```
FindBestValue(r, A, initial-value, s)

if UserKnows(r, ⟨A, initial-value⟩) = true
then value ← initial-value
else value ← novalue
endif
if (msv ← MoreSpecificValue(r, A, value)) ≠ novalue ∧
   (new-value ← FindBestValue (r, A, msv, s)) ≠ novalue ∧
     [(MostSalient(r, {⟨A, value⟩}, s) = false ∧
     |Val({⟨A, new-value⟩})| < |Val({⟨A, value⟩})|) ∨
     BetterMatch (r, ⟨ A, new-value ⟩, ⟨ A, value ⟩) = true ]
then value ← new-value
endif
return value
```

```
BetterMatch(r, ⟨ A, new-value ⟩, ⟨ A, value ⟩)

if ∃c : Antecedent(c, r) ∧
   SameWording (⟨A, value ⟩, c) = false ∧
   SameWording (⟨A, new-value ⟩, c) = true
then return true
else return false
endif
```

FIGURE 5 FindBestValue extended with a check on wording.

object with the relevant property). In that case, a more specific value (*new-value*) should be chosen only if its words are 'better matching' than those expressing the more general value. Otherwise, the value is chosen that has the smallest value set. The BetterMatch function returns true if the intended referent r has an antecedent c, and *value* has a different wording than the corresponding value expressed in c while *new-value* does not. To check this, a function SameWording is used which takes as input the antecedent c and an attribute value pair $\langle A, V\rangle$ and returns false if the linguistic realization of $\langle A, V\rangle$ is not a substring of the corresponding expression in c. In the experiment, hypothesis II was only tested for the 'type' attribute, as this attribute is generally expressed as the head noun in a description. However, we assume that the effect of wording also holds for other attributes such as 'colour', so that for instance a cat that has been previously described as *the chestnut cat* will not be anaphorically referred to as *the brown cat.*

We end with a brief example to illustrate the effect of the proposed extension. Reconsider domain D_1, and suppose that d_2 is currently the most salient object in the domain (context: *The white chihuahua ...*). This corresponds with the second example from section 8.3.4. Now we want to generate a second reference to the chihuahua. When determining the best value for its 'type' attribute, we consider the values 'dog' (*value*) and 'chihuahua' (*new-value*). Since d_2 is currently the most salient dog, the first disjunct of the condition is false. However, the *new-value* 'chihuahua' provides a better match with the antecedent and is therefore selected. The resulting description is *the chihuahua*, and not *the dog* as our first proposal would have it. As a second example, consider the situation in which we have a persian cat, a siamese cat and a poodle, where the siamese cat is the most salient one (having been described as *the siamese cat*). When generating a second description for this object we consider the values 'cat' (*value*) and 'siamese cat' (*new-value*). In this case, the MostSalientCondition is **true** for 'cat' (after all, the siamese is the most salient cat in this example domain), hence the first disjunct is false. The second disjunct is also false, since *cat* is a substring of *siamese cat* and SameWording returns true for both comparisons. As a consequence, FindBestValue returns 'cat' (the value of *value*).

8.6 Three Sketches of Further Extensions

So far, we have shown in some detail how the modified Incremental Algorithm can generate reduced definite descriptions which are only distinguishing in context. In addition, we think that the modified algorithm can serve very well as a basis for the generation of other kinds of referring expressions, such as pronouns, and relational and bridging descriptions. In this section we outline three further extensions of the modified Incremental Algorithm. In section 8.6.1 a simple form of pronominalization within the modified algorithm is discussed, in section 8.6.2 it is shown how relational descriptions can be generated by slightly modifying the algorithm and in section 8.6.3 it is outlined how the combination of the two preceding extensions paves the way for the generation of bridging descriptions.

8.6.1 Pronominalization

Reiter & Dale (1997:81) point out that a simple but surprisingly effective strategy for pronominalization is to "use a pronoun to refer to an object if the entity was mentioned in the previous clause, and there is no other entity in the previous clause that the pronoun could possibly refer to". This is a fairly conservative strategy, which has the advantage that it will not often produce incorrect pronominalizations. On the other hand, it has been claimed that a pronoun should be used whenever this is possible.[22] The presence of salience weights in the modified algorithm makes it possible to employ a somewhat less conservative strategy, taking the pronominalization decision *within* the algorithm. The basic idea is as follows: if r is the single most salient object in the domain (thus: r is the most salient object with respect to the empty list of properties) and there is an antecedent for this object in the direct linguistic context, then r can be referred to using a pronoun.

MakeReferringExpression (r, P, s)

$L \leftarrow \{\}$, *tree* $\leftarrow$ nil, *contrast* $\leftarrow$ **false**
if MostSalient $(r, \{\}, s) =$ **true** $\wedge\ \exists c$: Antecedent(c, r)
then *tree* $\leftarrow$ Pronominalize (*tree*, r) $\wedge$
    return *tree*
else for each member A_i of list P **do**
⋮

FIGURE 6 Pronominalization within MakeReferringExpression. The remainder of the algorithm is as given in figures 1 and 2.

We certainly do not offer this as the final answer to the problem of generating pronouns. One obvious limitation is that it does not take the role of semantics and common sense into account (see e.g., Kameyama 1996, Passonneau 1996). The current approach is only concerned with the default approach to pronoun generation, which is purely syntactically motivated, and does not address how semantic or pragmatic information can override the default. The success of this strategy depends fully on the adequacy of the underlying model of salience weight determination, but we contend that the approaches discussed in the previous section could serve as a starting point. Suppose, for example, that we determine salience weights as in definition 4 (based on Centering Theory). If sentence (4)a has been uttered at the onset of a discourse, object d_2 is more salient than object d_3. If the modified algorithm subsequently generates a referring expression for d_2, it will produce *it*, while a subsequent reference to d_3 will yield a full, anaphoric description. This is intuitively right, in the sense that most people would interpret *it* as referring to the white chihuahua.[23]

[22]This is a specific instance of the DOAP principle from Williams (1997): "Don't Overlook Anaphoric Possibilities."

[23]This intuition has been experimentally confirmed by Gordon *et al.* (1993), Walker *et al.* (1994) (for Japanese), Hudson-D'Zmura & Tanenhaus (1998), and others.

(4) a. The$_2$ white chihuahua was chasing the$_3$ cat.
b. {It$_2$/The$_3$ cat} ran fast.

In pronominalization, the notion of a 'salience threshold' and the trade-off between incoherence and ambiguity are particularly relevant, because pronouns are even more likely to give rise to ambiguities than reduced definite descriptions. For instance, the pronoun *it* in the above example is ambiguous in the sense that it is most likely to refer to d_2, but it could also be interpreted as referring to d_3. This ambiguity can be avoided by raising the salience threshold so that d_2 no longer counts as the single most salient object in the domain. Given the increased salience threshold, d_3 now counts as a distractor from which d_2 has to be distinguished, and this results in the non-ambiguous description of d_2 as *the chihuahua*.

8.6.2 Relational Descriptions

Dale & Haddock (1991) offer an algorithm for the generation of relational descriptions, which is couched in terms of the "Greedy Heuristics algorithm" (Dale 1992). The basic claim we want to make here is that it is possible to generate relational descriptions using a slightly adapted version of the modified Incremental Algorithm and that this has some interesting consequences. Sticking to our continuing cats and dogs theme, let us consider the following situation:

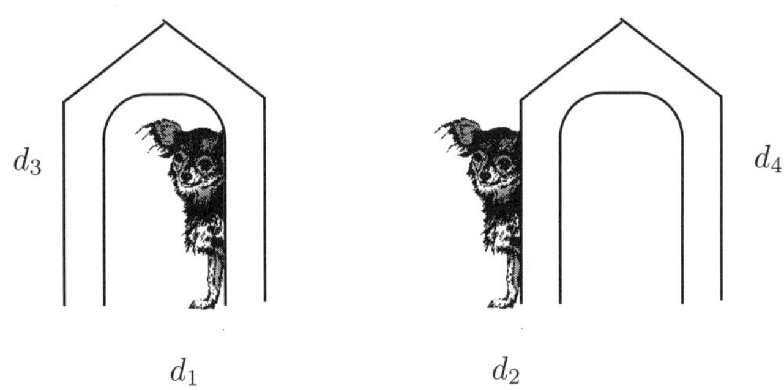

In addition to the usual properties (type, colour, size), this new domain, which we denote as D_2, now also includes spatial relations. In particular, d_1 can be found in d_3 and d_2 to the left of d_4. We denote these relations as $\langle$ spatial, in (d_1, d_3) $\rangle$ and $\langle$ spatial, left of (d_2, d_4) $\rangle$ respectively.[24]

[24]Of course, d_1 is also located to the left of d_2. However, to keep matters relatively simple, we assume that only spatial relations between objects that are physically close to each other are represented (cf. Horacek 1997:208). The problem of deciding which objects are 'close' may be likened to the problem of deciding which objects are 'large'. In a realistic database, both size and spatial distances would be given in absolute

When an object a is the intended referent and stands in a relation R to some object b, then —following Levelt (1989)— b is referred to as the *relatum* of a.

In addition, we assume that there is a subsumption hierarchy on certain relations. Figure 7 shows a relevant portion of such a subsumption hierarchy for spatial relations. We assume that 'in', 'next to' and 'on top of' are basic level values; the subsuming σ can be thought of as the underspecified spatial relation ("there is some spatial relation between these objects"). The value stored for relations in the domain is the most specific one, just as for the animal types. The advantages of having subsumption hierarchies for relations are discussed below.

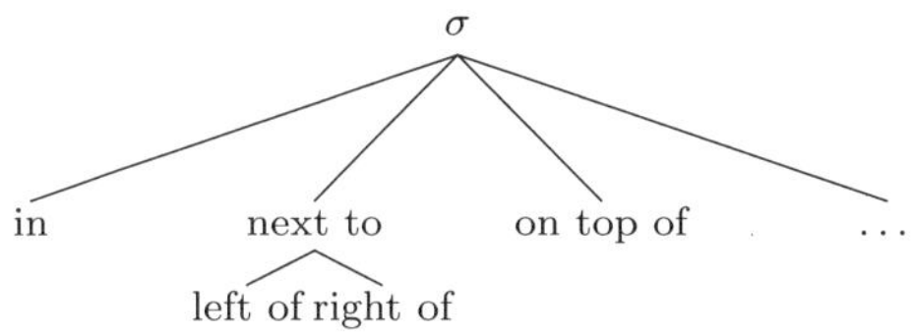

FIGURE 7 Part of the subsumption hierarchy on spatial relations.

It is interesting to note that most of the work on categorization in cognitive science has been concerned with physical objects, and not with relations. A notable exception is Case study 2 in Lakoff (1987). Here Lakoff studies the interrelations between various senses of the preposition *over*, which leads – on a lower level – to a similar structure as shown in Figure 7. However, to the best of our knowledge the notion of basic level values for certain classes of relations has not been studied, and we certainly do not intend to claim psychological reality for our assumptions here.

Before we show how the MakeReferringExpression algorithm can be extended to include relations in the description of objects, we need to reflect on the ordering of relations and properties. It seems an acceptable assumption that people prefer to describe an object in terms of simple properties, and only shift to relations when properties do not suffice (i.e., properties stand to relations as absolute properties stand to relative properties). This follows from the omnipresent *principle of least effort* (e.g., Zipf 1949, Clark & Wilkes-Gibbs 1986): it takes less effort to consider and describe only one object. How the different kinds of relations

measures (cm/in/pt) and a reasoning component would have to determine which objects are indeed large or nearby. It may be that this kind of (spatial) reasoning in its general form is rather complex and computationally expensive (see e.g., Lemon & Pratt 1997).

(spatial, possessive, etc.) should be ordered is somewhat less obvious; however, it seems likely that people have a preference for relations that are easily perceivable, as is the case with properties. From this it follows that spatial and part-of relations will be preferred over relations that are (usually) less easy to perceive, such as possessive relations. Reasonable as such assumptions seem, we are not aware of any psycholinguistic research into these issues. In the current section, we simply assume that properties are preferred over relations and that spatial relations are preferred over other kinds of relations. Thus, for our example domain D_2, we simply assume that $P = \langle$ type, colour, size, spatial $\rangle$.

A final preliminary modification that needs to be made is the definition of value sets. A minor complication is that we now have to keep track of the object whose value set we want to determine (either the first or the second argument of a relation); therefore the intended referent is included as a subscript.

Definition 6 (Value sets (modified))
$\mathsf{Val}_{a,D}(\langle A, V\rangle) = \{d \in D \mid d \text{ has the property expressed by } \langle A, V\rangle\}$
$\mathsf{Val}_{a,D}(\langle A, R(a,b)\rangle) = \{d \in D \mid \exists d' \in D : \langle d, d'\rangle \text{ stand in relation } R\}$
$\mathsf{Val}_{a,D}(\langle A, R(b,a)\rangle) = \{d \in D \mid \exists d' \in D : \langle d', d\rangle \text{ stand in relation } R\}$
$\mathsf{Val}_{a,D}(\{p_1, \ldots, p_n\}) = \mathsf{Val}_{a,D}(p_1) \cap \ldots \cap \mathsf{Val}_{a,D}(p_n)$.

For example: $\mathsf{Val}_{d_3,D_2}(\{\langle \text{ spatial, in } (d_1, d_3) \rangle\}) = \{d \in D_2 \mid \exists d' \in D_2 : d'$ is contained in $d\}$ (the set of objects which contain something) $= \{d_3\}$.[25]

Figure 8 shows a version of the modified Incremental Algorithm which is suited for the generation of relational descriptions.[26] The chief novelty is that the algorithm now allows for recursion: as soon as a relation R is included, the MakeReferringExpression function is called again with as parameters the relatum, the list of preferred attributes, the relation (which already provides some information about the relatum!), and the current state. This recursive call yields a description for the relatum which is later included in the main description currently being generated. To enable this recursive call of MakeReferringExpression, the variable L has been promoted to the level of parameters.

[25] In certain situations the selected properties of the relatum (L_b) are also of interest. So a more general definition of the value set of a relation would be $\mathsf{Val}_{a,D}(\langle A, R(a,b)\rangle) = \{d \in D \mid \exists d' \in \mathsf{Val}_{b,D}(L_b) : \langle d, d'\rangle \text{ stand in relation } R\}$. For expository reasons, we stick to the simpler definition in the main text.

[26] It has to be kept in mind that the functions FindBestValue, BasicLevelValue and Contrastive are polymorphic here, in that the A_i argument can be either a property or a relation. See Theune (2000) for a version of this algorithm which makes the difference between properties and relations explicit in this respect.

```
MakeReferringExpression (r, P, L, s)
tree ← nil, contrast ← false
for each member A_i of list P do
    V ← FindBestValue (r, A_i, BasicLevelValue(r, A_i), s)
    contrast ← Contrastive(r, A_i, V) ∧
    tree' ← UpdateTree (tree, V, contrast))
    if (|Val(L ∪ {⟨A_i, V⟩})| < |Val(L)| ∨ A_i = type)∧ tree' ≠ nil
    then L ← L ∪ {⟨A_i, V⟩}
            tree ← tree'
            if V expresses a relation between r and r'                          *
            then t2 ← MakeReferringExpression (r', P, {⟨A_i, V⟩}, s)            *
                    tree ← AddTree (tree, t2)                                    *
            endif                                                                *
    endif
    if MostSalient (r, L, s) = true
    then tree ← AddDefDet (tree)
            return tree
    endif
return failure
```

FIGURE 8 Extension of the modified Incremental Algorithm which incorporates relational descriptions. Other functions as in Figure 2. The main differences with the previous version of the MakeReferringExpression algorithm are marked by a *.

Let us discuss an example: suppose we want to generate a description for object d_1 of example domain D_2 in the initial situation s_0 (all objects are equally non-salient). We call the function MakeReferringExpression $(d_1, P, \{\}, s_0)$, where $P = \langle$ type, colour, size, spatial $\rangle$ and $\{\}$ is the empty set (of properties of d_1 which have so far been included). As before, we iterate through P. The first property we encounter is $\langle$ type, chihuahua $\rangle$. The best value is 'dog', and including this property rules out the two doghouses. This property is realized as the N^0 in the NP tree under construction. The MostSalient condition is not true: d_2 is a dog as well. The second and third attributes ('colour' and 'size') fail to distinguish d_1 from d_2. Then the algorithm encounters the fourth element of P (spatial), and consequently considers the relation $\langle$ spatial, in $(d_1, d_3)\rangle$. This *does* rule out d_2, which is not inside something. This item is included in the tree under construction as the head of a PP. The resulting tree (I) is given in Figure 9. Now we enter the recursion: the function MakeReferringExpression is called with as parameters d_3 (the relatum), the list of preferred attributes, the one property of d_3 already included (namely that it contains d_1) and the state s_0. The first element on the list of preferred attributes is 'type'. The type of d_3 is 'doghouse'. This property is automatically included. Now, MostSalient $(d_3, \{\langle$ type, doghouse $\rangle, \langle$ spatial, in $(d_1, d_3)\rangle\}, s_0)$ is true: d_3 is the most salient non-empty doghouse in this situation. The function AddDefDet inserts a definite determiner into the NP and this finalizes the generation of a description referring to the relatum (*the doghouse*). The resulting tree is returned and the initial call of MakeReferringExpression continues. At this point, the description generated for the relatum is added to the description currently being generated for d_1, which results in (II) in figure 9. At this point, the selected properties of d_1 are $L_{d_1} = \{\langle$ type, dog $\rangle$, $\langle$ spatial, in (d_1, d_3) $\rangle$ $\}$. MostSalient (d_1, L_{d_1}, s_0) is true. To wrap things up AddDefDet inserts a definite article into the main NP and the final tree is returned. Thus, the algorithm outputs *the dog in the doghouse*. The interesting thing about this description is that it is distinguishing, while neither *the dog* nor *the doghouse* in isolation are.

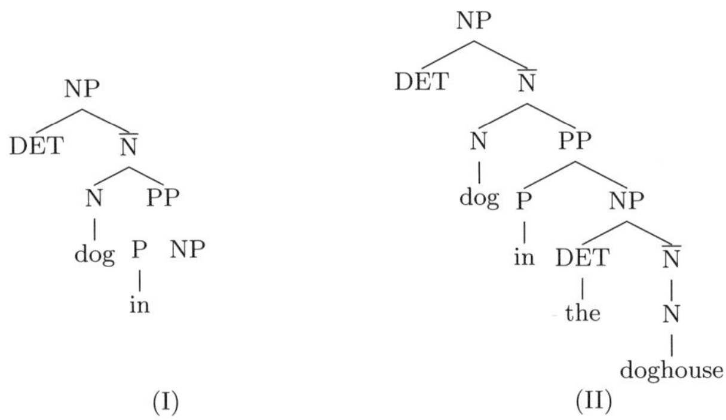

FIGURE 9 Two crucial stages in the generation of *the dog in the doghouse*.

In order to show why it is useful to determine the best value for a relation, let us briefly discuss another example: the generation of a description for object d_2 in domain D_2, again in state s_0. For the first part, the algorithm proceeds as in the previous example. The property $\langle$ type, dog $\rangle$ is selected and an expression for it is incorporated in the tree for d_2. Again, colour and size do not help to distinguish d_2 from d_1, so the algorithm goes on to check the relations in which d_2 is involved and finds ⟨ spatial, left of (d_2, d_4) ⟩. When trying to find the best value, it turns out that this is the basic level value *next to*. The more specific value 'left of' is not the best value since it fails to rule out more distractors than 'next to': both have the same value set. Therefore, the more general value of the two is selected, which is 'next to'. The rest of the generation procedure is similar to the previous example, resulting in the description of d_2 as *the dog next to the doghouse*. Simply expressing the 'type' value stored in the database, instead of searching for the best value, would have resulted in the description *the dog left of the doghouse*. This description is overly specific, since the information that d_2 is located to the *left* of doghouse d_4 is irrelevant in the current domain. However, as the reader may check, the addition to the domain of a dog which is located to the right of a doghouse *would* lead to the description of d_2 as *the dog left of the doghouse*.

Let us take stock. We have shown that some simple modifications to the modified Incremental Algorithm suffice for the generation of descriptions involving relations. In contrast with e.g., Horacek (1997) and Stone & Webber (1998), this algorithm is fully explicit about which properties should be tried in which order. The use of subsumption hierarchies on relations seems to offer an attractive and plausible means of obtaining some of the required flexibility. Moreover, this exercise shows how insights of Dale & Haddock (1991) can be incorporated in Dale & Reiter's Incremental Algorithm, which is more efficient than the Greedy Heuristics strategy used by Dale & Haddock. Unfortunately, by including recursion in the way we have done here the algorithm is no longer polynomial. The problem is that, as the algorithm stands, it may make the wrong choice of relatum. Interestingly, Beun and Cremers (1998) show that humans only select *salient* objects as relata. This can be incorporated in the algorithm by always choosing the most salient member of the set of potential relata (see van der Sluis & Krahmer 2001). This increases the chance of finding a solution in polynomial time.

A somewhat related problem of the extension proposed here is that it predicts that generating relations is incremental as well. Suppose that the first relation the algorithm selects fails to rule out all the remaining distractors. Then the algorithm will select a further relation and continue recursively from there. The incrementality assumption implies that the first relation will always be realised, even if adding further relations would render it redundant with hindsight. It would seem rather far-fetched to claim psychological reality for this kind of incrementality. It is unlikely that someone would describe an object as *the dog next to the tree in front of the garage* in a situation where *the dog in front of the garage* would suffice. In Krahmer *et al.* (2001), this problem of 'forced incrementality' is addressed in more detail and a general solution is offered.

8.6.3 Bridging Descriptions

Finally, we would like to point out that the two extensions of the modified Incremental Algorithm described above and displayed in figures 6 and 8 respectively can be combined in a straightforward way, and that this combination paves the way for the generation of bridging descriptions. Bridging descriptions are very complex from an interpretation perspective, because the 'bridge' which an interpreter needs to construct between antecedent and anaphor is left implicit. Things are somewhat easier from a generation perspective, provided that the 'bridge' is part of the input data. In our approach, a bridging description is just a relational description with a highly salient relatum. To illustrate this, consider a domain of discourse which contains three objects d_1, d_2 and d_3: d_1 is a man, while d_2 and d_3 are chihuahua's of the same size and colour, the former being in the possession of d_1, the latter being a stray dog. Suppose that the man has just been mentioned ('A man is walking in the park') and thus is maximally salient. Now we attempt to generate a description referring to d_2. To begin with, the type ('dog') is included. The attributes 'size' and 'colour' are not included in the description since they fail to rule out the other chihuahua. Finally, the possessive relation is encountered: the fact that d_2 is in the possession of d_1 is included as this does rule out the stray chihuahua. At this point, the algorithm enters the recursion. Since d_1 is the single most salient object in the domain, we can pronominalize the reference to d_1 and a suitable pronoun is inserted in the current tree. Normally, this would result in (a tree for) *dog of him*, but following common practice (see e.g., Geurts 1995, Krahmer & van Deemter 1998) the function UpdateTree rewrites such descriptions using a possessive pronoun as determiner, with *his dog* as the net-result. As a rule of thumb, we assume that this happens only if the relatum is animate. Thus, if a particular car c is highly salient and we want to refer to the motor of c, the resulting NP will not be *its motor* but *the motor*. It should be noted that this distinction is highly language dependent. In French, for example, it is common to refer to someone's hand as *la main* instead of *sa main*.

8.7 Concluding remarks

We have discussed a generalization of Dale & Reiter's Incremental Algorithm which extends the original algorithm in a number of respects. To begin with, we have made the notion of context sets more precise by adding salience weights. This makes it possible to generate descriptions in a fully context sensitive manner, without jeopardizing the attractive properties of the original algorithm. Additionally, the algorithm now immediately attempts to incorporate selected properties in the NP tree under construction and marks contrastive properties as such. An experimental evaluation confirmed most of the hypotheses underlying these modifications. In particular, humans prefer reduced and pronominalized anaphoric references. They do not, in general, prefer a more general phrasing if this leads to a different lexical phrasing from the antecedent. A slight modification of the proposed algorithm captures this finding.

Three related extensions of the modified algorithm have been outlined. First, a simple pronominalization decision within the algorithm was discussed. Second, we have shown that some modifications of the modified Incremental Algorithm allow for the generation of relational descriptions. Finally, the combination of these two extensions enables the generation of bridging descriptions.

The modified Incremental Algorithm has been fully implemented and integrated in a data-to-speech system called D2S (see e.g., Van Deemter & Odijk 1997, Theune 2000 and Theune *et al.* 2001). One of the side-effects of this integration is that the generated descriptions are automatically converted to enriched text, that is: they are dressed up with prosodic annotations indicating where prosodic boundaries should be placed and which words should receive a pitch accent (due to newness or contrastiveness, the latter being marked by the modified Incremental Algorithm using the [+c] feature). For example, suppose that D2S generated the following mini-discourse (where the modified Incremental Algorithm is responsible for the definite descriptions).

(5) The white poodle won the hair contest.
The gray poodle came first in the obedience contest.

In the context of the first sentence, the accentuation of the second sentence is determined as follows: the modified Incremental Algorithm assigns contrast [+c] features to *gray* and *obedience*, and consequently these words are assigned a pitch accent. Newness (and its counterpart, givenness) are not determined by the MakeReferringExpression algorithm, but these are accounted for by D2S: the phrases *poodle*, *contest* and *came first* are deaccented since they express concepts that were mentioned in the previous sentence. Determiners and prepositions are only accented when they are contrastive, so the resulting accentuation pattern is as follows (where small capital letters mark pitch accents):

(6) The GRAY poodle came first in the OBEDIENCE contest.

For more details on the implementation of the modified algorithm and the embedding in D2S we refer to Theune (2000).

In this chapter we have primarily been concerned with the context-sensitive generation of descriptions, and we have stuck as close as possible to Dale & Reiter's original Incremental Algorithm. This implies that the algorithms discussed here inherit the limitations of the Incremental Algorithm which are not related to context-issues. For example, as noted in Horacek (1995), the Incremental Algorithm does not take prominence of *properties* into account, and neither does our modified version. This issue is dealt with in Horacek (1995, 1997) by always including a prominent property of the intended referent, even if it does not rule out any distractors (an example might be including the colour when describing a pink elephant in a group of flamingoes). The work of Beun & Cremers (1998), however, indicates that humans do not always systematically include inherently salient properties. Nevertheless, it would be interesting to see whether it is possible to combine Horacek's notion of (property-)salience with the notion of (object-)salience studied here. In fact, van der Sluis and Krahmer (2001) treat salience as a three-dimensional notion, including linguistic salience, but also inherent property-salience and focus-of-attention salience. Another limitation of the Incremental Algorithm which we inherit is the treatment of relative attribute values. Dale & Reiter treat all attribute values as if they are absolute, assuming that relative attribute values such as 'big' are simply given in the domain database. Van Deemter (2000) has offered a novel treatment of such relative properties. The combination of this treatment with the proposals made here should be straightforward. Similarly, neither the Incremental Algorithm nor our extension of it has anything to say about plurals. Stone (2000) presents a treatment which allows for the generation of set descriptions. The combination and integration of such extensions with the proposals made in this chapter is facilitated by the meta-algorithmic approach of Krahmer *et al.* (2001).

One other important open question which we hope to address in future work concerns the coverage of the algorithms proposed in this chapter. It seems safe to conclude that this coverage is considerably larger than that of the Incremental Algorithm, which only generates distinguishing descriptions without taking context into account. Still, it is an open question what the coverage would be with respect to a collection of corpora. One way to answer this question might be to remove all definite NPs (probably with the exclusion of proper names) from a given corpus and ask the modified algorithm to fill the gaps. However, this could not work unless we have access to the underlying domain information: how could the algorithm otherwise decide which properties to include? In general, it is certain that data-oriented approaches to generation will become increasingly important for natural language generation. However, for many natural language generation tasks —and certainly for the generation of referring expressions— both rule-based and statistical techniques will be necessary. One of the main tasks for the future will be finding meaningful combinations of the two.

Acknowledgments

The work described in this paper was carried out at IPO, the Center for User-System Interaction at the Eindhoven University of Technology. The authors are mentioned in alphabetical order. Theune was supported by the Priority Programme Language and Speech Technology, sponsored by the Netherlands Organization for Scientific Research (NWO). The modified algorithm was implemented and integrated in D2S by John-Pierre Verhagen, who also helped carrying out the experiment described in section 8.5. A version of the relational extension of the modified algorithm was implemented by Sebastiaan van Erk and André Verleg. Many thanks to all three of them. Earlier versions of this work have been presented at ICSLP'98 (Sydney), the Semantics Colloquium (Nijmegen, May '99), the ESSLLI workshop on the Generation of Nominals (Utrecht, August '99) and the ITRI seminar (Brighton, December '99). Thanks are due to the audiences at these occasions as well as to Kees van Deemter, Janet Hitzeman, Jan Landsbergen, Jon Oberlander, Massimo Poesio, Ehud Reiter, Petr Sgall, Ielka van der Sluis, Matthew Stone, Marc Swerts, Jacques Terken and three anonymous referees for useful comments. We have greatly benefitted from Robert Dale's constructive and detailed comments on a previous version of this chapter.

References

Alshawi, H. (1987), *Memory and Context for Language Interpretation.* Cambridge University Press, Cambridge, UK.

Beun, R.-J. and A. Cremers (1998), Object Reference in a Shared Domain of Conversation, *Pragmatics & Cognition* **6**(1/2): 121-152.

Clark, H. & D. Wilkes-Gibbs (1986), Referring as a Collaborative Process, *Cognition* **22**: 1-39.

Cruse, D. (1977), The Pragmatics of Lexical Specificity, *Journal of Linguistics* **13**: 153-164.

Dale, R. (1992), *Generating Referring Expressions: Constructing Descriptions in a Domain of Objects and Processes*, MIT Press, Cambridge, MA.

Dale, R. & N. Haddock (1991), Generating Referring Expressions Involving Relations, *Proceedings of the 5th EACL*, Berlin, 161-166.

Dale, R. & E. Reiter (1995), Computational Interpretations of the Gricean Maxims in the Generation of Referring Expressions, *Cognitive Science* **18**: 233-263.

van Deemter, K. (2000), Generating Vague Descriptions, *Proceedings of the First International Natural Language Generation Conference*, Mitzpe Ramon, Israel.

van Deemter, K. & J. Odijk (1997), Context Modelling and the Generation of Spoken Discourse, *Speech Communication* **21**(1/2): 101-121.

Geurts, B. (1995), *Presupposing*, Ph.D. dissertation, University of Osnabrück.

Gordon, P., B. Grosz & L. Gilliom (1993), Pronouns, Names, and the Centering of Attention in Discourse, *Cognitive Science* **17**: 311-347.

Grosz, B., A. Joshi & S. Weinstein (1995), Centering: A Framework for Modeling the Local Coherence of Discourse, *Computational Linguistics* **21**(2): 203-225.

Grosz, B. & C. Sidner (1986), Attention, Intentions and the Structure of Discourse, *Computational Linguistics* **12**: 175-204.

Hajičová, E. (1993), Issues of Sentence Structure and Discourse Patterns. *Theoretical and Computational Linguistics*, Vol 2, Charles University, Prague.

Horacek, H. (1995), More on Generating Referring Expressions, *Proceedings of the Fifth European Workshop on Natural Language Generation*, Leiden, The Netherlands, 43-85.

Horacek, H. (1997), An Algorithm for Generating Referential Descriptions with Flexible Interfaces, *Proceedings of the 35th ACL/EACL*, Madrid, 206-213.

Hudson-D'Zmura, S. & M. Tanenhaus (1998), Assigning Antecedent to Ambiguous Pronouns: The Role of Center Attention as the Default Assignment, in: *Centering in Discourse*, M. Walker, A. Joshi, and E. Prince (eds.), Oxford University Press, New York, 199-226.

Kameyama, M. (1996), Indefeasible Semantics and Defeasible Pragmatics, in: *Quantifiers, Deduction and Context*, M. Kanazawa, C. Piñon, and H. de Swart (eds.), CSLI Publications, Stanford, 111-138.

Klabbers, E., E. Krahmer, & M. Theune (1998), A Generic Algorithm for Generating Spoken Monologues, *Proceedings of ICSLP'98*, Sydney, Australia, 2759-2862.

Krahmer, E. (1998), *Presupposition and Anaphora*, CSLI Publications, Stanford.

Krahmer, E. & K. van Deemter (1998), On the Interpretation of Anaphoric

Noun Phrases, *Journal of Semantics* **15**(3/4): 355-392.

Krahmer, E., S. van Erk & A. Verleg (2001), A Meta-Algorithm for the Generation of Referring Expressions, *Proceedings of the 9th European Workshop for Natural Language Generation*, Toulouse.

Kruijff-Korbayová, I. & Hajičová, E. (1997), Topics and Centers: A Comparison of the Salience-based Approach and the Centering Theory, *Prague Bulletin of Mathematical Linguistics* **67**: 25-50.

Lakoff, G. (1987), *Women, Fire, and Dangerous Things: What Categories Reveal about the Mind*, The University of Chicago Press, Chicago.

Lappin, S. & H. Leass (1994), An Algorithm for Pronominal Anaphora Resolution, *Computational Linguistics* **20**(4): 535-561.

Lemon, O. & I. Pratt (1997), Spatial Logic and the Complexity of Diagrammatic Reasoning, *Machine Graphics & Vision*, **6**(1): 89-108.

Levelt, P. & S. Kelter (1982), Surface Form and Memory in Question-Answering, *Cognitive Psychology* **14**: 78-106.

Levelt, W. (1989), *Speaking, from Intention to Articulation*, MIT Press, Cambridge, MA.

Lewis, D. (1979), Scorekeeping in a Language Game, *Journal of Philosophical Logic* **8**: 339-359.

Maes, A. (1991), *Nominal Anaphors and the Coherence of Discourse*, Ph.D. dissertation, Tilburg University.

Malouf, R. (2000), The Order of Prenominal Adjectives in Natural Language Generation, *Proceedings of the 38th ACL*, Hong Kong, 85-92.

McCoy, K. & M. Strube (1999), Generating Anaphoric Expressions: Pronoun or Definite Description?, *Proceedings of the Workshop on the Relation of Discourse/Dialogue Structure and Reference, held in conjunction with the 37th ACL*, Maryland, 63-71.

Oberlander, J. (1998), Do the Right Thing, *Computational Linguistics*, **24**(3): 501-507.

Passonneau, R. (1996), Using Centering to Relax Gricean Informational Constraints on Discourse Anaphoric Noun Phrases, *Language and Speech* **39**(2/3): 229-264.

Pechmann, T. (1989), Incremental Speech Production and Referential Overspecification, *Linguistics* **27**: 98-110.

Poesio, M. & R. Vieira (1998), A Corpus-Based Investigation of Definite Description Use, *Computational Linguistics* **24**(2): 183-216.

Popescu-Belis, A., I. Robba & G. Sabah (1998), Reference Resolution Beyond Coreference: a Conceptual Frame and its Application. *Proceedings of COLING-ACL'98*, Montreal, 1046-1052.

Prevost, S. (1996), An Information Structural Approach to Spoken Language Generation, *Proceedings of the 34th ACL*, Santa Cruz, 294-301.

Reiter, E. & R. Dale (1997), Building Applied Natural Language Generation Systems, *Natural Language Engineering* **3**(1): 57-87.

Rosch, E. (1978), Principles of Categorization, *Cognition and Categorization*, E. Rosch and B. Lloyd (eds.), Erlbaum, Hillsdale NJ, 27-48.

Sgall, P., E. Hajičová & J. Panevová (1986), *The Meaning of the Sentence in its Pragmatic Aspects.* Reidel, Dordrecht.

van der Sluis, I. & E. Krahmer (2001), Generating Referring Expressions in a Multimodal Context: An Empirical Approach, *Proceedings of CLIN XI*, W. Daelemans *et al.* (eds.), Rodopi, Amsterdam/Atlanta.

Stone, M. & B. Webber (1998), Textual Economy Through Close Coupling of Syntax and Semantics, *Proceedings of the Ninth International Workshop on Natural Language Generation*, Montreal, 178-187.

Theune, M. (1997), Contrastive Accent in a Data-to-Speech System, *Proceedings of the 35th ACL/EACL*, Madrid, 519-521.

Theune, M. (2000), *From Data to Speech: Language Generation in Context*, Ph.D. dissertation, Eindhoven University of Technology.

Theune, M., E. Klabbers, J.R. de Pijper, E. Krahmer & J. Odijk (2001), From Data to Speech: A General Approach, *Natural Language Engineering* **7**(1): 47-86.

Walker, M. (1998), Centering, Anaphora Resolution and Discourse Structure, in: *Centering in Discourse*, M. Walker, A. Joshi and E. Prince (eds.), Oxford University Press, New York, 401-435.

Walker, M., M. Iida & S. Cote (1994), Japanese Discourse and the Process of Centering, *Computational Linguistics* **20**(2): 193-232.

Williams, E. (1997), Blocking and Anaphora, *Linguistic Inquiry* **28**: 577-628.

Zipf, G.K. (1949), *Human Behavior and the Principle of Least Effort*, Addison-Wesley, Cambridge, MA.

9

Generating Descriptions Containing Quantifiers: Aggregation and Search

NORMAN CREANEY

9.1 Introduction

A good deal of attention has been paid to the treatment of quantifiers in the context of natural language understanding (Alshawi 1990, Creaney 1999, Grosz et al. 1987, Hobbs and Shieber 1987, Park 1995, Saint-Dizier 1984). Only relatively recently, however, has attention been paid to their treatment in the context of language generation (Shaw & McKeown 2000, Creaney 1996, Creaney 1999, Stone 2000). The problem is of both linguistic and practical interest. From a linguistic point of view, there is the possibility that the new (generation) perspective may shed light on an old problem. From a practical point of view, it is clear that many areas of potential application for natural language generation, require the use of quantification. For instance the MAGIC system (Shaw & McKeown 2000), and almost any application that you might imagine where summaries or descriptions are to be generated from database tables.

This paper does not deal with a particular application or domain but, instead, focuses on the domain independent aspects of the problem. It extends the work in (Creaney 1999), and describes a general purpose, domain independent algorithm for generating descriptions, involving quantification, of finite models, in which groups of individuals are related in various ways. While the algorithm is intended to be domain independent, there are aspects of the quantifier generation problem that

Information Sharing: Reference and Presupposition in Language Generation and Interpretation.
Edited by Kees van Deemter and Rodger Kibble.

are clearly domain dependent. While these aspects are not dealt with in detail, the points in the algorithm where domain dependent knowledge might be exploited are clearly identified. The algorithm takes the following input.

- A *contextual model*: this is a hierarchically organised taxonomy of properties, together with a collection of individuals – each categorised according to the taxonomy. The contextual model is assumed to be available to both speaker and listener.
- A *target relation*: this is a single relation between individuals from the contextual model. It is assumed to be new information, which is available only to the speaker, and which is to be communicated to the listener.

The output of the algorithm is a collection of logical forms for sentences that describe the *target relation* against the background of the *contextual model*. The processing involves a kind of *aggregation*, in which a description such as "*Two men ate a banana*" is arrived at by aggregating the information in the assertions, "*Fred ate a banana*" and "*Barney ate a banana*". The aggregation process also produces logical forms for sentences with compound noun phrases, such as the following.

Two men and three women ate a banana.
Each man ate two bananas or three oranges.

It is normal in natural language generation for compound noun phrases, such as those above, to be arrived at by a process of aggregation, in which logical forms are merged. In the approach that is taken in this paper, *all* quantified descriptions result from a process of aggregation. For instance, a sentence such as "*Three men ate a banana*" is derived by aggregating structures that assert that, "*one man ate a banana*", and "*two (different) men ate a banana*".

One of the most striking characteristics of the quantifier generation problem is its non-determinism. A great many alternative descriptions are generally possible for any given target relation: even if the form of the description is pre-determined, up to the assignment of individual quantifiers to fixed positions. Each alternative description emphasises some aspects of the model over others but none of them describe the model completely – some information is always left out. For example, the sentences "*Every representative saw a sample*", "*Three representatives saw at least two samples*" and "*Exactly one representative saw exactly three samples*" might all be generated to describe the same model, but they each convey slightly different information. This raises the issue of what it means for a sentence, containing quantifiers, to describe a model.

A minimal criterion is that the sentence should be true in the model, but beyond this it is a question of pragmatics – some descriptions are better than others because: they are more informative; they are more succinct; or, they are better tailored to the individual reader. The list of potential criteria is open ended, and most of them are domain and context dependent.

In this paper we will concentrate on discriminating between descriptions on the basis of informativeness. For example, in a context in which they are both true, the sentence, "*At least four representatives saw every sample*", makes a stronger claim than the sentence, "*At least three representatives saw every sample*". We say that the former is *stronger* or *more informative* than the latter. Informativeness is a relatively domain and context independent criterion. Related to the problem of discriminating between descriptions is the issue of search: quantifier generation has the potential for exponential search. A heuristic approach is presented that promotes stronger descriptions over weaker ones, while also drastically reducing the search space. Although heuristics are proposed that choose a single description for the model, the algorithm leaves open the possibility that a domain specific component can intervene in this choice; and stages where this is possible are clearly identified.

It is assumed that the quantifier generation component sits between a strategic planning component and a realisation component. The function of the strategic planning component is to determine a target relation from some larger body of information to be communicated. The function of the realisation component is to generate a sentence from a logical form supplied by the quantifier generation component. The design of planning and realisation components have been widely discussed elsewhere (Shieber et al. 1990, Dale 1990, Elhadad 1996, Lavoie & Rambow 1997) and are not directly addressed in this paper.

9.2 Models and dependency functions

A quantifier generation problem consists of a contextual model and a target relation. The combination of these is referred to simply as a model, and is represented textually as in (1) below, where the target relation is in **bold**.

(1)	sub(rep,man)	man(r1)	table(s1)	**saw(r1,s1)**	**saw(r4,s3)**
	sub(rep,woman)	woman(r2)	table(s2)	**saw(r2,s2)**	**saw(r4,s4)**
	sub(sample,table)	woman(r3)	chair(s3)	**saw(r3,s3)**	**saw(r5,s3)**
	sub(sample,chair)	woman(r4)	chair(s4)	**saw(r3,s4)**	**saw(r5,s4)**
		woman(r5)	chair(s5)		**saw(r5,s5)**

Model (1) asserts that *man* and *woman* are subclasses of *rep* (representative) and that *table* and *chair* are subclasses of *sample.* It also states that there is one man, {r1}; four women, {r2,r3,r4,r5}; two tables, {s1,s2}; and three chairs, {r3,r4,r5}. In addition to this *shared* information, it also specifies some *new* information, which is to known only to the speaker, and is to be communicated to the listener – namely the particular pattern of seeing that took place between the representatives and the samples. Of course, the pattern of seeing that took place cannot be described fully by a quantified description – some aspects will be emphasised, and others ignored.

The first stage in the generation process is the construction of a dependency function from the target relation. This requires that a scoping configuration is chosen – this will be the scoping configuration of the logical form that is to be generated. Creaney (Creaney 1995, 1999) discusses the issues relating to quantifier scoping more fully. The possibilities in this example are:

- the first argument of saw has scope over the second – R>S;
- the second argument of saw has scope over the first – S>R.

If R>S is chosen then dependency function (2^a) is constructed; and if S>R is chosen, dependency function (2^b) is constructed

(2) a saw: {r1,r2,r3,r4,r5} → power({s1,s2,s3,s4,s5})
r1 →{ s1 }
r2 →{ s2 }
r3 →{ s3, s4 }
r4 →{ s3, s4 }
r5 →{ s3, s4, s5 }

b saw: {s1,s2,s3,s4,s5} → power({r1,r2,r3,r4,r5})
s1 → { r1 }
s2 → { r2 }
s3 → { r3, r4, r5 }
s4 → { r3, r4,r5 }
s5 → { r5 }

By inspecting a dependency function such as (2^a) it is not difficult to verify the truth (or otherwise) of sentences such as those in (3) below.

(3) a Every representative saw at least one sample.
b Exactly two women saw exactly two chairs.
c Each woman saw at least one sample.
d The man saw exactly one sample.

Verifying the truth of a sentence, however, is not the same thing as generating it. It will be shown that, by applying a process of aggregation to a dependency function, it can be transformed into a structure from which logical forms for sentences such as those in (3) may be generated, by the kinds of realisation components that are commonly used for natural language generation.

9.3 Aggregation

Since the kinds of descriptions that are to be generated do not mention individuals by name, the dependency function is first rewritten in such a way that it does not mention individuals by name – only quantity and taxonomic properties are relevant. Hence (2^a) is rewritten as (4).

(4) saw(5:rep → 5:samp)
    1:man → 1:table
    1:woman → 1:table
    1:woman → 2:chair
    1:woman→ 2:chair
    1:woman → 3:chair

Note that, where two or more taxonomic properties are applicable, the most specific one is chosen. Hence *man* and *woman* are used, rather than *rep*. Structures such as (4) are referred to as *anonymous dependency functions* (ADF), and it is ADFs that are subject to aggregation. For example: sentence (3^a) results from aggregating the information from all of the mappings in (4); sentence (3^b) results from aggregating the information from the third and fourth mappings; sentence (3^c) results from aggregating the information from the final four mappings in (4); and, sentence (3^d) results from the first mapping only.

The necessary aggregation is carried out by merging subsets of mappings in the ADF, in a way that respects their semantics. In order to do this it is necessary first to enrich the notation that is used. In particular, consider merging the final two mappings of (4). Taken individually they mean, respectively:

- there is a woman who saw two chairs; and,
- there is a (different) woman who saw three chairs.

In aggregate, however, they imply, *there are two women who each saw either 2 chairs or 3 chairs*. In order to express this, the following notational convention is introduced:

$$\text{2:woman} \rightarrow \text{(2:chair)}\vee\text{(3:chair)}$$

Similarly, consider merging the information in the second and third mappings. Taken in aggregate, they imply, *there are two women who each saw one table or two chairs*:

$$2\text{:woman} \rightarrow (1\text{:table}) \vee (2\text{:chair})$$

or, alternatively, *there are two women who each saw between one and two (inclusive) samples*:

$$2\text{:woman} \rightarrow [1,2]\text{:sample}$$

In replacing a disjunction by a numerical interval in this way, some information is generally lost. This is justified, however, by the fact that the interval based notation maps more directly to natural language quantifiers.

It is convenient to be able to refer to individual components of a mapping and so the following terminology will be used. The *restriction* of a mapping is the component to the left of the arrow, while its *scope* is the component to the right. The restriction consists of a *quantity* and a *restricting property*, while the scope consists of an *interval* and a *scopal property*. For example, the quantity, restricting property, interval and scopal property of the mapping, $N{:}P \rightarrow M{:}Q$, are respectively N, P, M and Q.

The aggregation process is not confined to merging pairs of mappings from the initial ADF. It is an iterative process that may involve mappings, such as those above, that are themselves the result of merging. The merging operation can be viewed as a kind of inference, and it is convenient to describe it in terms of a collection of inference schemas.

(5) $$\frac{\begin{array}{l}\mathsf{N1{:}P1} \rightarrow \mathsf{M1{:}Q1}\\ \mathsf{N2{:}P2} \rightarrow \mathsf{M2{:}Q2}\end{array}}{(\mathsf{N1{:}P1}) \wedge (\mathsf{N2{:}P2}) \rightarrow (\mathsf{M1{:}Q1}) \vee (\mathsf{M2{:}Q2})}$$

(6) $$\frac{(\mathsf{N1{:}P1}) \wedge (\mathsf{N2{:}P2}) \rightarrow \mathsf{X}}{(\mathsf{N1+N2}){:}\mathsf{lub(P1,P2)} \rightarrow \mathsf{X}}$$

(7) $$\frac{\mathsf{X} \rightarrow (\mathsf{M1{:}Q1}) \vee (\mathsf{M2{:}Q2})}{\mathsf{X} \rightarrow \mathsf{int(M1,M2){:}lub(Q1,Q2)}}$$

The *lub* function in (6,7) is the *least upper bound* function, which returns the least general taxonomic class that subsumes both arguments. For example:

$$\text{lub(table,chair)=sample} \qquad \text{lub(man,man)=man}$$

The *int* function in (7) constructs an interval from its arguments. The arguments may be either integers or intervals, and the value that is returned is the smallest interval that contains both arguments. For example.

$$\text{int}(1,3)=\text{int}(3,1)=[1,3] \qquad \text{int}([1,5],7)=\text{int}(7,[1,5])=[1,7]$$

int([1,3],[5,7])=int([5,7],[1,3])=[1,7]   int(2,2)=2

Schema (5) is very general: it describes the space of possible mergers, and gives details of how to perform them. Schemas (6,7) have the effect of simplifying the resulting mappings for certain specific cases. Example (8) below illustrates the use of inference schemas (5-7).

(8) a saw(5:rep → 5:samp) — the initial ADF
    1:man → 1:table
    1:woman → 1:table
    1:woman → 2:chair
    1:woman → 2:chair
    1:woman → 3:chair

b saw(5:rep → 5:samp) — by schema (5)
    1:man → 1:table
    1:woman → 1:table
    (1:woman)∧(1:woman) →(2:chair)∨(2:chair)
    1:woman → 3:chair

c saw(5:rep → 5:samp) — by schema (6)
    1:man → 1:table
    1:woman → 1:table
    2:woman → (2:chair)∨(2:chair)
    1:woman → 3:chair

d saw(5:rep → 5:samp) — by schema (7)
    1:man → 1:table
    1:woman → 1:table
    2:woman → 2:chair
    1:woman → 3:chair

e saw(5:rep → 5:samp) — by schema (5)
    1:man → 1:table
    1:woman → 1:table
    (2:woman)∧(1:woman)→(2:chair)∨(3:chair)

f saw(5:rep → 5:samp) — by schemas (6,7)
    1:man → 1:table
    1:woman → 1:table
    3:woman →[2,3]:chair

At this point, (8^f) might be passed to a realisation component to generate the sentence, "*Exactly three women saw at least two samples*". In this case, the third mapping in (8^f) is the one on which realisation was based. The mapping on which realisation is to be based will be referred to as the *distinguished mapping*. Aggregation need not stop at this point;

instead it might continue as follows.

(9) a saw(5:rep → 5:samp) from (8^f)
1:man → 1:table
1:woman → 1:table
3:woman → [2,3]:chair

b saw(5:rep → 5:samp) by schema (5)
1:man → 1:table
(3:woman)∧(1:woman) → ([2,3]:chair)∨(1:table)

c saw(5:rep → 5:samp) by schemas (6,7)
1:man → 1:table
4:woman → [1,3]:sample

d saw(5:rep → 5:samp) by schema (5)
(4:woman)∧(1:man) →([1,3]:sample)∨(1:table)

e saw(5:rep → 5:samp) by schemas (6,7)
5:rep → [1,3]:sample

At this point no more aggregation is possible, and (9^e) might be selected as the basis of generation – to give, for example, "*Each representative saw at least one sample*". The examples above illustrate the broad thrust of the algorithm, however a number of issues need to be dealt with in more detail. In particular:

- **Interface with realisation**. The interface with realisation is via the logical form. This structure, which is the output of the algorithm, contains natural language determiners, such as "*each*", "*most*", "*the*" or "*both*", that express quantification. It will be demonstrated that such determiners can be generated from an ADF using simple lookup tables. These determiners, together with taxonomic and relational information from the model, can then easily be assembled into the kinds of logical forms that are needed.
- **Search**: It is evident from examples (8,9) that the aggregation process is underconstrained and may involve a good deal of search. In particular, nothing has been said about choosing which mappings to be merged; the order in which they should be merged; or, when the aggregation process should terminate. To rectify this, it will be demonstrated that a number of linguistically plausible heuristics can be used to control the search.

9.4 Interface with realisation

Generating a logical form (LF) from an aggregated dependency function is a two-stage process. Firstly, a *pre logical form* (preLF) is generated from the ADF; then an LF is generated from the preLF. For example, taking the distinguished mapping in (9^e) as the starting point, the following preLF can be generated:

saw(<exactly 5, of the 5, rep> → <at least 1, of the 5, sample>)

This, in turn, can be used to generate the following LF:

saw(<each, rep> → <a, sample>)

which can, in turn, be used to generate the sentence, "*Each representative saw a sample*". The process is, of course, non-deterministic at each stage – these are not the only preLFs and LFs that can be generated from (9^e). A more detailed discussion of the processing is given below.

9.4.1 Generating the pre-logical form

A preLF is a structure of the following form, in which: R is the predicate symbol of the target relation; P & Q are taxonomic properties; and N, Nt, M & Mt are integers.

R(< at least N, of the Np, P > → < at most M, of the Mp, Q >)

A preLF may be expressed in terms of "*at least N*", "*at most N*" or "*exactly N*", so that the following are all valid preLFs.

R(< at least N, of the Np, P > → < exactly M, of the Mp, Q >)
R(< exactly N, of the Np, P > → < at least M, of the Mp, Q >)
R(< exactly N, of the Np, P > → < exactly M, of the Mp, Q >)

In some cases, the arrow in a preLF may point from right to left, to indicate the alternative scoping configuration. We will not consider any such examples, but note that they do not present any particular difficulty.

The relationship between an ADF and any preLFs that may be generated from it, is specified in *Table 1* below. This relationship, however, depends on the following assumption. In the next section it will be demonstrated that this assumption is always satisfied before the stage at which a preLF is to be generated.

Definition 7 Distinct mapping assumption
If an aggregated dependency function contains two mapping of the form:

- X1 → M1:Q1
- X2 → M2:Q2

then M1 and M2 must be distinct, in the sense that, $M1 \cap M2 = \emptyset$

The distinct mapping assumption forbids functions such as the following ones, which might *otherwise* be constructed from model (1).

saw(5:rep → 5:samp) saw(5:rep → 5:samp)

1:woman → 2:table
3:woman → [2,3]:chair

1:woman → [2,3]:table
3:woman → [2,3]:chair

ADF	**preLF**
R(Nt:P → Mt:Q) ... N:P1 → [M_1,M_2]:Q1 X → Y...	R(< at least N, of the n(P1), P1 > → < at least M_1 , of the n(Q1),Q1>) R(<at most n(P1)-N, of the n(P1), P1> → <at least M_2+1, of the n(Q1), Q1>)
R(Nt:P → Mt:Q) X → Y... N:P1 → [M_1,M_2]:Q1 ...	R(< at least N, of the n(P1), P1 > → < at most M_2 , of the n(Q1),Q1>) R(<at most n(P1)-N, of the n(P1), P1> → <at most M_1-1, of the n(Q1), Q1>)
R(Nt:P → Mt:Q) ... N:P1 → [M_1,M_2]:Q1	R(< exactly N, of the n(P1), P1 > → < at least M_1 , of the n(Q1),Q1>)
R(Nt:P → Mt:Q) N:P1 → [M_1,M_2]:Q1 ...	R(< exactly N, of the n(P1), P1 > → < at most M_2 , of the n(Q1),Q1>)
R(Nt:P → Mt:Q) ... N:P1 → M:Q1 ...	R(< exactly N, of the n(P1), P1 > → < exactly M_1 , of the n(Q1),Q1>)

Note that: '...' denotes zero or more unspecified mappings; 'X→Y...' denotes one or more unspecified mapping; and n(P) denotes the number of individuals in the contextual model, that satisfy P.

TABLE 1 Relating PreLfs to ADFs

Table 1 defines the possible preLFs, in cases, depending on the form of the aggregated dependency function. For example (first row), the preLF:

R(<at least N, of the Nt, P1> → <at least M_1, of the Mt, Q1>)

is only possible if the distinguished mapping is not the last one in the ADF. Similarly (row 2), the preLF:

R(<at least N, of the Nt, P1> → <at most M_2, of the Mt, Q1>)

is only possible if the distinguished mapping is not the first one in the ADF.

This demonstrates how preLFs are generated from ADFs using a simple lookup table. Note that in the case of the first row of *Table 1*, more than one preLF may be generated (the same is true of the second row). This is a reflection of the fact that the process is non-deterministic.

9.4.2 Generating the logical form

An LF is a structure of the following form, where D1 & D2 are natural language determiners, and P & Q are taxonomic properties.

$$R(<D1, P> \rightarrow <D2, Q>)$$

Consequently, generating the LF, from a preLF, amounts to generating the linguistic determiners.

An assumption behind the algorithm is that a large and significant class of natural language determiners that express quantification, can be characterised in terms of three components. For example, "*most*" may be characterised as:

at least N   of the M $N \geq \frac{1}{2}M$

The respective components will be referred to as the *focal* component, the *contextual component* and the *relational* component.

- The *focal* component is so called because it describes, in general, only a subset of the individuals in the current context. This component is always of one of the forms *at least N*, *at most N* or *exactly N*. These correspond (respectively) to, what are known in the generalised quantifier literature as: *monotonically increasing*, *cardinal* and *monotonically decreasing* quantifiers.
- The *contextual* component is so called because it refers to all the individuals in the current context. This component is always of the form *of the M*.
- The *relational* component is so called because it imposes a relational constraint on the other two components.

A sample collection of determiners are described in terms of their three components in *Table 2* below.

Note that, while a focal component is always required, the contextual and relational components are often *unspecified* – as in the case of the determiner "*a*".

Determiners are generated using this table together with information from a preLF. In particular focal and contextual components are matched against the corresponding information from the preLF, and the relational component is checked for consistency. For example:

$$R(< \text{at least } 1, \text{ of the } 10, P > \rightarrow < \text{at least } 4, \text{ of the } 6, Q >)$$

Determiner	Focal component	Contextual component	Relational component
a	at least 1		
some (singular)	at least 1		
some (plural)	at least 2		
the (singular)	at least 1	of the 1	
the (plural)	at least N	of the N	
at least two	at least 2		
exactly five	exactly 5		
both	at least 2	of the 2	
all ten	at least 10	of the 10	
most	at least N	of the M	$N \geq \frac{1}{2}M$
all	at least N	of the N	
neither	at most 0	of the 2	
no	at most 0		
less than half of	at most N	of the M	$N \leq \frac{1}{2}M$

TABLE 2 Determiner components

may be used to generate the following logical forms.

$$R(< a, P > \rightarrow < most, Q >) \qquad R(< some, P > \rightarrow < most, Q >)$$

This demonstrates how LFs are generated from preLFs using a simple lookup table. The fact that more than one LF can be generated from the same preLF is a reflection of the fact that the process is non-deterministic.

9.5 Search

There are two sides to the search issue. Firstly, we are interested in reducing the amount of computation, and secondly we are interested in discriminating between descriptions on the basis of informativeness. Moreover, we are interested in achieving both of these simultaneously.

In a context where both sentences are true, "*At least four women saw a sample*" makes a stronger claim than "*At least two women saw a sample*". We say that the former is a stronger description, or a more informative description, than the latter. The distinction between strong and weak descriptions is relatively clear cut in this example, and similar examples have been discussed by Grice (1975) and others. However, it is not always so easy to make such distinctions. Consider the following two sentences, in a context in which they are both true.

Exactly three representatives saw at least six samples

Exactly five representatives saw at least four samples

It is not clear which makes the stronger claim: the former includes information about more of the samples, while the latter includes information about more of the representatives. In cases such as these there is a trade-off between the two quantifiers, and it is not possible to choose reliably without some quantitative understanding of the concept of strength or informativeness. One can imagine a quantitative approach to informativeness that involves counting all the possible models that are consistent with a given description, and choosing the one with the fewest models – on the basis that it does a better job of picking out the intended model. It is not clear, however, that there would be much linguistic plausibility to such an approach – it seems far more likely that, in choosing between the two sentences above, domain and context specific factors dominate. The approach that is taken in this paper is: to distinguish between alternative descriptions using an informativeness criterion, to the extent that this seems linguistically plausible; and to leave further distinctions to be made using domain and context specific methods. To this end the following generalisations, regarding informativeness, are offered:

- **Maximum quantity preference**. Everything else being equal, a mapping with a big *quantity* component will result in a more informative description than a mapping with a small *quantity* component. For example, in a context where they are both true, "*Five boys ate a mango*" is more informative than "*Three boys ate a mango*".
- **Singleton interval preference**. Everything else being equal, a mapping with a singleton *interval* will result in a more informative description than a mapping with a non-singleton *interval*. For example, in a context where they are both true, "*Each boy ate exactly two mangos*" is more informative than "*Each boy ate at least two mangos*".
- **Low maximum preference**. Everything else being equal a mapping whose *interval* has a low maximum will give a more informative description than a mapping whose *interval* has a high maximum. For example, in a context where they are both true, "*Some boys ate at most two mangos*" is more informative than "*Some boys ate at most four mangos*".
- **High minimum preference**. Everything else being equal a mapping whose *interval* has a high minimum will give a more informative description than a mapping whose *interval* has a low minimum. For example, in a context where they are both true, "*Some boys ate at least four mangos*" is more informative than "*Some*

boys ate at least two mangos".

These might be (collectively) roughly paraphrased as, **maximise the *quantity* and minimise the *interval*** (i.e. singleton interval, low maximum and high minimum preferences all have the effect of minimising the interval). Of course, it is generally impossible to do both of these things at the same time – as the *quantity* increases (with aggregation), so does the *interval*. The problem becomes one of trading one off against the other in a linguistically plausible way. An algorithm is developed that does just this.

9.5.1 Maximum quantity preference

Inspection of dependency function (2) reveals that the mappings were sorted according to the size of their interval components. Inspection of the aggregation process used in examples (8,9) will reveal that merging was only ever applied to adjacent mappings. These two facts are not accidental: they amount to a powerful strategy for reducing the amount of search. Furthermore, from a linguistic point of view, the strategy makes sense because it partially implements the maximum quantity preference. For example, mapping (10^a) results from merging the 2nd and 5th mappings in (8^a) – and sentence (10^b) would ultimately be generated (using Tables 1 & 2, and an appropriate realiser).

(10) a 2:woman → [1,3]:sample
b At least two women saw at least one sample.

Sentence (10^b) is true in the model, but it is weaker than it need be. In particular, it is weaker than sentence (11^b), which might be generated if mappings 2nd, 3rd, 4th & 5th were merged.

(11) a 4:woman → [1,3]:sample
b At least four women saw at least one sample.

The requirement to sort the dependency function and forbid the merging of non-adjacent mappings partially implements the maximum quantity preference, ensuring that unnecessarily weak output such as (10^b) is avoided.

9.5.2 High minimum preference

Any of the sentences ($12^{bi,ci,di}$), below, might be generated from (12^a) using the approach that has been outlined so far. They result from ADFs ($12^{bii,cii,dii}$) respectively. While all are true, not all are equally good descriptions. In particular (12^{bi}) performs poorly with respect to the high minimum preference and is unduly weak. The descriptions in ($12^{ci,di}$), on the other hand, perform better with respect to this preference. In the present example, however, there is clearly a line to between (12^b)

and (12^c), rather than between (12^c) and (12^d). This is because (12^b) significantly reduces the interval minimum, relative to (12^c), but only increases the quantity a little.

(12) a saw(4:woman → 12:chair)
1:woman → 1:chair
1:woman → 10:chair
1:woman → 11:chair
1:woman → 12:chair

b i Four women saw at least one chair
ii saw(4:woman → 12:chair)
4:woman →[1,12]:chair

c i Three women saw at least ten chairs
ii saw(4:woman → 12:chair)
1:woman → 1:chair
3:woman →[10,12]:chair

d i Two women saw at least eleven chairs
ii saw(4:woman → 12:chair)
1:woman → 1:chair
1:woman → 10:chair
2:woman → [11,12]:chair

To illustrate this further, consider the following example.

(13) saw(8:woman → 12:chair)
1:woman → 1:chair
1:woman → 2:chair
1:woman → 3:chair
1:woman → 4:chair
1:woman → 8:chair
1:woman → 9:chair
1:woman → 10:chair
1:woman → 11:chair

We could choose to merge the final two mappings and generate the description, "*Exactly two women saw at least ten chairs*". Alternatively we could choose to merge the final three mappings and generate the description, "*Exactly three women saw at least nine chairs*". Our preferences give conflicting advice regarding which of these (or other) options to choose: the *maximum quantity preference* urges us to choose the second alternative; while the high minimum preferences urges us to choose the first. It might, however, be argued (heuristically) that there is little to choose between these alternatives, but that there is some merit in choosing another alternative – to merge the final *four* mappings to generate "*Exactly four women saw at least eight chairs*". The rationale for this is that it involves merging a collection of mappings that are separated from the others by a jump in the interval minimum. A similar argument can be applied to the interval maximum, to suggest that "*Exactly four women saw at most four chairs*" is preferable to both "*Exactly three women saw at most three chairs*" and "*Exactly five women saw at most eight chairs*". This will be referred to as the *jump heuristic* – it is a method for balancing conflicting advice that may be given by the maximum quantity preference and the low maximum/high minimum preferences. To understand how this heuristic is implemented, the following definitions are needed.

Definition 8 Difference between two mappings
Assuming, without loss of generality, that $Max_1 > Max_2$, in the following two mappings.

- X1 → [Min_1, Max_1]:Q1
- X2 → [Min_2, Max_2]:Q2

The **upper difference** is defined to be, Max_1-Max_2; the **lower difference** is defined to be, Min_1-Min_2; and, the **difference** is defined to be the smaller of the upper and lower differences.

For mappings that contain con/disjunction, the difference is computed by applying *Definition 2* to the corresponding con/disjunction free mappings. For example, the difference between the following pair of mappings:

1:man → 1:table 3:woman → ([2,3]:chair)∨(4:table)

is the same as the difference between the following pair:

1:man → 1:table 3:woman → [2,4]:sample

which is min(4-1,2-1) = min(3,1) = 1.

Definition 9 Merging mappings
A pair of mappings are merged by a single application of schema (5).

It is convenient to temporarily exclude from consideration, some steps in the aggregation process. This is achieved by subjecting the merging operation to the following constraint, which governs the application of schemas (6,7), as follows:

Constraint 1: Application of schemas (6,7)
Schemas (6,7) are applied immediately when any pair of mappings, in which the corresponding properties are identical, are merged. They are only applied in these circumstances.

Constraint 1 allows us to ignore ($8^{b,c,e}$) because they are immediately subject to schemas (6,7); and to exclude ($9^{c,e}$) because they would never be produced. One desirable effect of *Constraint 1* is to render the application of schemas (6,7) entirely deterministic, in the sense that, in any situation where they can be applied, they must be applied. Hence schema (5) is now the sole source of non-determinism in the aggregation process – i.e. the choice of which mappings to merge at each stage in the process. *Constraint 1* will be relaxed at a later stage in processing so that potentially valid descriptions are not lost.

Definition 10 Aggregation sequence, aggregation, direct aggregation
A sequence of ADFs in which each ADF is constructed from its predecessor by merging a single adjacent pair of mappings, is called an **aggregation sequence**. If A_i precedes A_j in an aggregation sequence, A_j is called an **aggregation** of A_i. If A_i directly precedes A_j in an aggregation sequence, A_j is called a **direct aggregation** of A_i.

For example, (8^a), (8^d), (8^f) is an aggregation sequence – ($8^b, c, e$) are not part of the sequence since they simplify the mappings but do not merge any. ADF (8^f) is an aggregation of (8^a), and direct aggregation of (8^d).

Definition 11 Level k aggregation of, levelled ADF
If A_n and A_m are two ADFs, A_m is said to be a **level k aggregation of** A_n if and only if there is an aggregation sequence, $A_n, \ldots, A_m$ - in which:

- for each i (n$\geq$ i >m), A_{i+1} is derived from A_i by merging a single pair of mappings whose distance apart is less than or equal to k;
- A_m contains no pairs of mappings whose distance apart is less than or equal to k.

For example: (14^b) is a level 0 aggregation of (14^a); (14^d) is a level 1 aggregation of (14^b), and (14^e) is a level 3 aggregation of (14^d). Note that not all ADFs are levelled.

Definition 12 Levelled aggregation sequence
A sequence of ADFs, $A_0, \ldots, A_n$, is a **levelled aggregation sequence** if and only if, for each i (n$\geq$ i >0), A_i is a level i-1 aggregation of A_0.

For example, ($14^{a,b,d,e}$) form a levelled aggregation sequence – (14^c) is not a part of the levelled sequence because its final two mappings are a distance of 1 apart.

(14) a saw(7:woman → 10:chair) initial ADF
1:woman → 1:chair
1:woman → 1:chair

1:woman → 2:chair
1:woman → 4:chair
1:woman → 5:chair
1:woman → 7:chair
1:woman → 8:chair

b saw(7:woman → 10:chair) level 0 aggregation of (14^a)
2:woman → 1:chair
1:woman → 2:chair
1:woman → 4:chair
1:woman → 5:chair
1:woman → 7:chair
1:woman → 8:chair

c saw(7:woman → 10:chair)
3:woman → [1,2]:chair
2:woman → [4,5]:chair
1:woman → 7:chair
1:woman → 8:chair

d saw(7:woman → 10:chair) level 1 aggregation of (14^a)
3:woman → [1,2]:chair also a level 2 aggregation of (14^a)
2:woman → [4,5]:chair
2:woman → [7,8]:chair

e saw(7:woman → 10:chair) level 3 aggregation of (14^a)
7:woman → [1,8]:chair

The linguistic significance of the concept of a levelled aggregation sequence is that it suggests a method for implementing the jump heuristic. In particular, levelled ADFs are precisely the ones in which collections of mappings are merged if and only if they are separated from other mappings by a jump in the interval minimum or maximum. Consequently, only levelled ADFs need be considered as the source for quantifier generation. Consider, for example, the levelled aggregation sequence (15^{a-c}) below.

(15) a saw(8:woman → 12:chair) initial ADF
1:woman → 1:chair
1:woman → 2:chair
1:woman → 3:chair
1:woman → 4:chair
1:woman → 8:chair
1:woman → 9:chair
1:woman → 10:chair
1:woman → 11:chair

b saw(8:woman → 12:chair) — level 1 aggregation of (15^a)
4:woman → [1,4]:chair — also level 2, 3, 4, 5
4:woman → [8,11]:chair — & 6 aggregation of (15^a)

c saw(7:woman → 12:chair) — level 7 aggregation of (15^a)
8:woman → [1,11]:chair

d i Exactly four women saw at most four chairs
ii Exactly four women saw at least eight chairs
iii Each woman saw at least one chair

e i Exactly three women saw at most three chairs
ii Exactly two women saw at most two chairs
iii Exactly three women saw at least nine chairs
iii Exactly two women saw at least ten chairs

If generation is only to be based on levelled ADFs, there are only three possible mappings to be considered – i.e. the ones in ($15^{b,c}$). Consequently, the sentences in (15^d) might be generated. The sentences in (15^e), while true, will not be generated, because they are not generated from a *levelled* ADF.

The computational significance of the concept of a levelled aggregation sequence is this – while there are, in general, many alternative aggregation sequences starting with a given initial ADF, there is only one levelled aggregation sequence. In this sense levelled aggregation sequences represent islands of determinism in a highly non-deterministic search space. Furthermore, a levelled aggregation sequence is typically much shorter than a corresponding aggregation sequence – in the worst case the relationship between their lengths is $O(n^{\frac{1}{2}})$. Clearly, restricting attention to levelled ADFs only, avoids an enormous amount of search. The following algorithm computes the levelled aggregation sequence from a given initial ADF. The computation is entirely deterministic.

Algorithm 1: Generate levelled sequence

```
Input: STACK1        % A stack of mappings representing the input
   % ADF - has operations POP1 & PUSH1.
Output: STACK3       % A stack of stacks of mappings representing
   % the output levelled sequence - has operations POP3 & PUSH3.
Local: STACK2        % A stack of mappings used as temporary
   % storage. The current ADF is decanted between STACK1 and
   % STACK2 as it is processsed - has operations POP2 & PUSH2.
Local: DISTANCE      % A loop variable. ADFs are merged if their
   % distance is =< DISTANCE. This avoids merging ADFs that
   % are separated by a jump
Begin
```

```
DISTANCE := 0; STACK2 := NIL; STACK3 := NIL
repeat                            % construct the next levelled ADF
   repeat                 % merge next 2 mappings if sufficiently close
      THISMAPPING := POP1; NEXTMAPPING := POP1
      if the distance between
      THISMAPPING and NEXTMAPPING =< DISTANCE
      then PUSH1(MERGE(THISMAPPING,NEXTMAPPING))
      else PUSH2(THISMAPPING); PUSH1(NEXTMAPPING)
   until STACK1 contains a single mapping
   PUSH2( POP1 )              % STACK2 now contains a levelled ADF
   DISTANCE := DISTANCE + 1
   PUSH3( STACK2 )               % add the levelled ADF to STACK3
   STACK1 := REVERSE( STACK2 ); STACK2 := NIL
until STACK1 contains a single mapping
PUSH3( POP2 )  % STACK3 now contains levelled sequence of ADFs
End Generate levelled sequence
```

The search space has been drastically reduced by the approach that has been developed, but some search still remains. In particular, a single distinguished mapping must be chosen from one of the ADFs in the levelled aggregation sequence. For the time being no method of choosing is specified, but we will return to this point later.

9.5.3 Taxonomic properties

The above discussion focused on structuring the search space to facilitate discriminating between alternative descriptions on the basis of their quantitative content (quantity and interval). However, there are cases in which taxonomic information should also influence the process. Consider the descriptions in (16^b), which might be generated from the levelled aggregation sequence in (16^a). These descriptions are perfectly acceptable. However, the descriptions in (16^d) are also perfectly acceptable – and in some cases preferable – but these ones cannot be generated from the levelled aggregation sequence.

(16) a i saw(6:rep → 15:chair) — initial ADF, also level 0 aggregation of itself

- 1:woman → 1:chair
- 1:woman → 2:chair
- 1:woman → 5:chair
- 1:man → 6:chair
- 1:man → 7:chair
- 1:man → 8:chair

ii saw(6:rep → 15:chair) — level 1 aggregation of (16ai), also level 2, 3,

- 2:woman → [1,2]:chair

4:rep → [5,8]:chair   4 & 5 of (16ai)

iii saw(6:rep → 15:chair)   level 6 aggregation of (16ai)
6:rep → [1,8]:chair

b i Exactly two women saw at most two chairs
ii Exactly four representatives saw at least five chairs
iii Each representative saw at least one chair
iv Each representative saw at most eight chairs

c saw(6:rep → 15:chair)
3:woman → [1,5]:chair
3:man→ [6,8]:chair

d i Exactly three women saw at most five chairs
ii Exactly three men saw at least six chairs

In particular, the descriptions in (16^d) require ADF (16^c) and, while (16^c) is certainly an aggregation of the initial ADF, it is not a *levelled* aggregation. Consequently, the descriptions in (16^d) are not generated by the approach that has been presented so far. The difficulty arises because, quantity considerations (*at most five* vs. *at most two*) lead the aggregation process down one path (i.e. the levelled sequence); while property considerations (*man*, *woman* vs. *rep*) lead it down a different path (i.e. (16^c)).

The key to generating the descriptions in (16^d) without losing the advantages gained by the use of levelled aggregation sequences, lies in noting that they are only appropriate because the *man*, *woman* distinction partitions the initial ADF into non-interleaved sub-functions. The solution is to split (16^a) into two separate ADFs – the initial one and the two new ones are now each processed in the normal way to give a collection of possible descriptions that includes (16^b) and (16^d). This is illustrated in ($17^{a,b}$) below.

(17) a i saw(3:woman → 5:chair)   initial ADF, after splitting
1:woman → 1:chair
1:woman → 2:chair
1:woman → 5:chair

ii saw(3:woman → 5:chair)   level 1
2:woman → [1,2]:chair
1:woman → 5:chair

ii saw(3:woman → 5:chair)   level 3
3:woman → [1,5]:chair

iii Exactly three women saw at most five chairs

b i saw(3:man → 10:chair) initial ADF, after splitting
1:man → 6:chair
1:man → 7:chair
1:man → 8:chair

ii saw(6:rep → 10:chair) level 1
3:man → [6,8]:chair

iii Exactly three men saw at least six chairs

A similar tactic can be used when the ADF is partitioned by the scopal property, as in (18^a) below. In this case, the descriptions in (18^b) are generated from the un-split ADF, while those in (18^c) are generated from the sub-functions.

(18) a saw(6:rep → 15:sample)
1:rep → 1:chair
1:rep → 2:chair
1:rep → 5:chair
1:rep → 6:table
1:rep → 7:table
1:rep → 8:table

b i Exactly two representatives saw at most two chairs
ii Exactly four representatives saw at least five samples

c i Exactly three representatives saw at most five chairs
ii Exactly three representatives saw at least six chairs

The result of this strategy is to produce a collection of aggregation sequences: one based on quantity alone (e.g. 15); a collection based on any partitions derived from the restricting properties (e.g. $16^{a,c}$); and a collection based on any partitions derived from the scopal properties (e.g. 17). Note that, the increase in the search space is not significant because the additional aggregation sequences are typically much shorter than the main one.

9.5.4 Generating compound noun phrases

As a result of *Constraint 1*, all non-trivial con/disjunctions are left in place in during the aggregation process (trivial ones are those where the corresponding properties are identical). If there are many con/disjuncts, the resulting sentences are likely to be unwieldy. At this stage it is appropriate to relax *Constraint 1* and allow schemas (6,7) to be used to simplify the con/disjunctions. The problem, of course, lies in deciding, for particular cases, whether it is better to simplify (remove) any con/disjunction, or to leave it in place. This choice is largely a matter of style and pragmatics, so no definitive method of choosing should be expected. However, the following generalisations are offered.

- A description, such as "*Four men and three women saw three chairs or four tables*", that uses *both* conjunctive and disjunctive noun phrases is awkward and difficult to understand. Such descriptions should be avoided.
- A description that uses a conjunctive noun phrase is generally more informative that the corresponding description in which the conjunctive information has been aggregated. For example, "*Three men and four women saw a sample*" is more informative than "*Seven representatives saw every sample*".
- A description that uses a disjunctive noun phrase is more informative than the corresponding description in which the disjunctive information has been aggregated. For example, on the basis of, *6:rep*$\rightarrow$*([1,3]:chair)*$\vee$*([6,8]:table)*, the description "*Each representative saw at most three chairs or at least six tables*" is more informative than "*Each representative saw at least one sample*".
- A description that uses a disjunctive noun phrase has more potential for ambiguity than one that does not. For example "*Each representative saw at most three chairs or at least six tables*" has an interpretation that might be paraphrased as, *either each representative saw at most three chairs, or each representative saw at least six tables*. The intended interpretation can, of course, be made explicit if the realisation component is sensitive to the issue. For example, the description "*Each representative saw either; at most three chairs, or at least six tables*" might be generated.
- Disjunction and conjunction both increase the length of a description and so make it a little more difficult to understand.

Taken together these suggest the heuristic approach to conjunctive and disjunctive noun phrases that is detailed in *Algorithm 2* and *Algorithm 3*, below.

Algorithm 2: Generate description
Input: % *A contextual model and target relation*
Output: % *LF ready to be passed to a realiser*
Begin
1. Construct ADF from target relation
2. Construct the levelled aggregation sequence according to **Algorithm 1**, subject to Constraint 1.
3. Choose the ADF on which realisation is to be based.
4. Choose the distinguished mapping from the chosen ADF.
5. Process the distinguished mapping according to **Algorithm 3**.

6. Choose the preLF by Table 1.
7. Choose the LF by Table 2.
End Generate description

Note that no method of making the choices in steps 3 and 4 has yet been specified.

Algorithm 3: Process distinguished mapping

Input: % *A distinguished mapping containing*
% *dis/conjunction.*

Output: % *A corresponding distinguished mapping*
% *with reduced dis/conjunction.*

Begin
1. If the distinguished mapping contains both conjunction and disjunction then eliminate the disjunction using schema (7).
2. If the distinguished mapping contains only disjunction then eliminate the disjunction using schema (7) unless the realiser can make the intended interpretation explicit.
3. Eliminate enough of the remaining disjunction/conjunction using schemas (6,7) so that the resulting description is not unwieldy.

End Process distinguished mapping

Some discussion of step 3 is needed. In the examples that have been considered so far, each mapping has had at must two conjuncts (disjuncts). This was due to the fact that there were only two taxonomic alternatives for each noun phrase (i.e. *man* vs. *woman*, *chair* vs. *table*). In general, though, there may be any number of alternatives and consequently any number of conjuncts (disjuncts). Step 3 in *Algorithm 3* is intended to reduce these to a number that is consistent with natural text. For example,

$$(6{:}\mathrm{rep})\wedge(2{:}\mathrm{manager})\wedge(5{:}\mathrm{secretary})\wedge(1{:}\mathrm{typist})\wedge(1{:}\mathrm{programmer}) \rightarrow \mathrm{X}$$

might be realised as "*Six representatives, two managers, five secretaries, one typist and one programmer ...* ". In many contexts this might be thought to be unwieldy, and less natural than, say, "*Six representatives, five secretaries and four other employees*". The latter might be generated by selectively combining conjuncts, to give:

$$(6{:}\mathrm{rep})\wedge(5{:}\mathrm{secretary})\wedge(4{:}\mathrm{employee}) \rightarrow \mathrm{X}$$

It is difficult to be precise about which conjuncts should be combined, as it is highly dependent on the purpose to which the description is put. We will return to this issue in the next section.

9.5.5 Unresolved choices

There remain the following occasions when choices need to be made by the algorithm, but where no method has been given.

- choice of ADF on which to base realisation (Algorithm 2, step 3);
- choice of distinguished mapping from the chosen ADF (Algorithm 2, step 4);
- choice of con/disjuncts to be combined within a distinguished mapping (Algorithm 3, step 3);
- choice of preLF and LF (Algorithm 2, steps 6 & 7).

It is difficult to say anything domain and context independent about any of these. It is, however, possible to suggest heuristics that give reasonable results.

Choice of preLF and LF

In many cases this choice may be made on the basis that cardinal quantifiers (of the form, *exactly N*) are more informative than monotonic ones (of the form, *at least N, at most N*), which are in turn more informative than comparative ones (such as *most*). This does not help when a choice has to be made between two monotonic quantifiers, but in such cases context dependent methods are probably more appropriate. For example, in choosing between, "*At least three representatives saw a sample*" and "*At most two representatives saw a sample*", pragmatic factors are likely to dominate.

Choice of con/disjuncts

This is highly context dependent, but reasonable results are obtained by combining all con/disjuncts that collectively account for less than 1/3 of the total number of individuals.

Choice of distinguished mapping

It is not clear how to proceed in this case – indeed, the the preferences that have been proposed (*Maximum quantity preference, Low maximum preference, etc.*) typically give conflicting advice. One possible solution is based on the observation that it is not absolutely necessary to base realisation on a single mapping. It is also acceptable to use all of the mappings in the chosen ADF. For example, (15^b) might lead to the description "*Exactly four women saw at most four chairs and exactly four women saw at least eight chairs*". In some cases there may be too many mappings in the ADF to produce a single sentence description – in such cases multiple sentences might be used. Reasonable results can be obtained by including a mapping only if it is indicated by one of the four preferences, which results in a maximum of four mappings.

Choice of ADF

Part of the motivation for the use of the levelled aggregation sequence was to make explicit those points in the aggregation process where the interval difference took a jump. The intuition was that we should be reluctant to merge mappings across a jump because it results in a weaker description. Pursuing this line of reasoning further, it may be better to choose the ADF that occurs at the biggest jump. For example, in (15) this would result in choosing (15^b), and in (14) it would result in (14^d). Indeed, this approach does seem to give very acceptable results.

Domain and context specific knowledge

These heuristics are simply offered as reasonable strategies that can easily be incorporated into the algorithm. However, a more satisfactory approach would allow for the intervention of a domain and context specific filter to make the choices. Since this paper is concerned with domain independent methods, this issue is not pursued – except to note that the points in the algorithm where such intervention is possible have been clearly identified.

9.6 Related work

Reape and Mellish (Reape & Mellish 1999) propose a classification of aggregation into six types: conceptual aggregation, discourse aggregation, semantic aggregation, syntactic aggregation, lexical aggregation and referential aggregation. Although the aggregation process that has been described in this paper is a simple and uniform process, it does not fit neatly into their classification, but has characteristics of referential, semantic and conceptual aggregation types. Dalianis and Shaw (Dalianis 1999, Shaw 1998) also discuss a variety of types of aggregation, including their position within a typical natural language generation architecture. It is not clear that there is much to be gained by pursuing parallels between the aggregation process described this paper, and the work of Reape and Mellish, Shaw, Dalianis and others. It is likely that the term *aggregation* does not describe a single linguistic phenomenon: rather, it is used to describe a range of different and distinct processes – each with their own distinct characteristics.

Shaw and McKeown (2000) describe quantifier generation in the MAGIC system, which generates multimedia briefings to describe the post-operative status of coronary patients. Their system deals with a more restricted range of quantifiers than those that are dealt with in this paper. Their work is also more concerned with the domain specific aspects of the problem, whereas this paper has emphasised the development of a domain independent algorithm.

Stone (1999, 2000) describes an approach to describing sets that characterises the problem as constraint satisfaction. He emphasises cover semantics as the theoretical underpinning of his work and as a natural way to accommodate both collective and distributive interpretations.

None of the above work addresses the issues of informativeness and search that are addressed in detail in this paper. This paper extends the work reported in (Creaney 1996, 1999) in: its use of the levelled aggregation sequence to control search and avoid unduly weak output; its ability to generate descriptions that use conjunctive or disjunctive noun phrases; and its use of taxonomic information.

Conclusion

A domain independent approach to quantifier generation has been described, which views the processing as a kind of aggregation. An algorithm was presented that generates logical forms for expressions of the form, *Q1 men love Q2 women* – where *Q1* and *Q2* are natural language quantifiers. It also generates structures involving conjunction and disjunction, such as, *Q1 men and Q2 women saw Q3 samples*, and *Q1 representatives saw Q2 chairs or Q3 tables.*

It was demonstrated that many alternative descriptions might be generated for the same model; and argued that it was not possible to select a single best description on the basis of domain and context independent information alone. It was noted, however, that one area in which domain independent methods might usefully be applied, is in filtering out weaker, less informative descriptions. The *jump heuristic* was presented as a way of doing this. With this heuristic, the description "*At least three men arrived*", for example, would never be generated in a context in which a stronger one such as "*At least four men arrived*" could be used.

It was demonstrated that the jump heuristic could be implemented using the concept of a *levelled aggregation sequence.* This technique avoids the generation of unduly weak descriptions whilst also reducing the complexity of the computation. There remain choice points, within the algorithm, where no definitive method of choosing has been specified. It was argued that these remaining choices were largely a domain and context dependent matter, and that the most a domain independent algorithm should do is to clearly identify their location within the algorithm.

It has been suggested that it might sometimes be preferable to generate descriptions that list named individuals as an alternative to quantifiers: for example: "*John, Paul, George and Ringo ate a peach*" as an alternative to "*Four boys ate a peach*". The algorithm that has been described can be adapted to do this without much trouble. All that is needed is that: all mappings are annotated with the lists of corresponding individuals; schemas (5,6,7) are changed to accommodate the lists; and, some method of deciding whether to generate a list or a quantifier is specified.

References

Barwise & Cooper 1981. J.Barwise and R.Cooper: Generalised Quantifiers and Natural Language, Linguistics and Philosophy, 4, 159-219.

Creaney 1999. N.Creaney: Generating Quantified LFs from Raw Data, Proceedings ESSLLI-99 Workshop on The Generation of Nominal Expressions, Utrecht, August 1999

Creaney 1996. N.Creaney: An Algorithm for Generating Quantifiers, Proceedings of 8th International Workshop on Natural Language Generation, INLG'96, Herstmonceux, Brighton.

Creaney 1995. N.Creaney: Implementing Scope and Dependency Constrains in a Typed Attribute Logic, Proceedings of 5th International Workshop on Natural Language Understanding and Logic Programming, NLULP'95, Lisbon.

Dale 1990. R.Dale: Generating Recipes: An Overview of Epicure, in Dale, Mellish & Zock (1990).

Dale & Haddock 1991a. R.Dale and N.Haddock: Content Determination in the Generation of Referring Expressions, Computational Intelligence, 1991.

Dale & Haddock 1991b. R.Dale and N.Haddock: Generating Referring Expressions Involving Relations. Proc. 5th Conf. Of European ACL, Berlin, 1991.

Dale, Mellish & Zock 1990. R.Dale, C.Mellish and M.Zock: Current Research in Natural Language Generation, Academic Press, 1990.

Dalianis 1999. H.Dalianis: Aggregation in Language Generation, Computational Intelligence, Volume 15, Number 4, 1999.

Elhadad & Robin 1996. M.Elhadad and J.Robbin: An Overview of SURGE: a reusable comprehensive syntactic realization component, Proc 8th Int. Natural Language Generation Workshop INLG96.

Gailly 1988. PJ. Gailly: Expressing Quantifier Scope in French Generation, COLING 1988.

Grice 1975. HP.Grice: Logic and Conversation, in *Cole & Morgan, (Eds.), Syntax and Semantics: Vol 3, Speech Acts*, Academic Press.

Hobbs & Shieber 1987. JR.Hobbs and SM.Shieber: An Algorithm for Generating Quantifier Scopings, Computational Linguistics, Vol.3, No.1, 47-63.

Lavoie & Rambow 1997. B.Lavoie and O.Rambow: A Fast and Portable Realizer for Text Generation Systems, Proc. 5th Conf. Applied NLP ANLP97, pp. 265-268.

Reape & Mellish 1999. M.Reape and C.Mellish: What is Aggregation Anyway?, Proc. of the 7th European Workshop on Natural Language Generation. Toulouse, France

Saint-Dizier 1984. P.Saint-Dizier: Handling Quantifier Scoping Ambiguities in a Semantic Representation of Natural Language Sentences. in Dahl & Saint-Dizier 1984.

Shaw 1998. J.Shaw: Segregatory Coordination and Ellipsis in Text Generation, COLING-ACL'98, pp. 1220-1226

Shaw & McKeown 2000. J.Shaw and K.McKeown: Generating Referring Quantified Expressions, INLG-2000, Mitzpe Ramon.

Stone 2000. M.Stone: On Identifying Sets, INLG-2000, Mitzpe Ramon.

Stone 1999. M.Stone: Describing Sets with Covers and Sets of Ordinary Assignments, Proceedings ESSLLI-99 Workshop on The Generation of Nominal Expressions, Utrecht, August 1999

10

Contextual Influences on Attribute Selection for Repeated Descriptions

PAMELA W. JORDAN

10.1 Introduction

In an extended discourse, speakers often redescribe objects that were introduced earlier in order to say something more about the object or the event in which it participates. As an object is described, the hearer and speaker create a discourse entity to relate the information about the object in the utterance to the appropriate mental representation of the object (Karttunen 1976, Webber 1978, Heim 1983, Kamp 1993, Passonneau 1996). The main goal when redescribing an entity is generating an expression that will efficiently and effectively re-evoke the appropriate discourse entity.

However, a goal-directed view of sentence generation suggests that speakers can attempt to satisfy multiple goals with each utterance (Appelt 1985) and that a single linguistic form can opportunistically contribute to the satisfaction of multiple goals (Stone and Webber 1998). The possibilities that goals besides identification could influence the content of a nominal expression and that an identification goal could be satisfied by more than a nominal expression have not yet been addressed in computational work on generating discourse anaphoric expressions.

The many-one mapping of goals to linguistic forms is more generally referred to as *overloading intentions* (Pollack 1991). Overloading can involve tradeoff across linguistic levels. For example, an intention which is achieved by complicating a form at the semantic level may al-

Information Sharing: Reference and Presupposition in Language Generation and Interpretation.
Edited by Kees van Deemter and Rodger Kibble.

low the speaker to simplify at the syntactic level by omitting important information (Stone and Webber 1998).

Although we have learned that overloading is natural and perhaps even necessary, we have no well supported account of what degree of overloading is reasonable and what forms can more readily address multiple goals in dialogue. Without such an account, we have no principled way to deploy overloading in the automatic generation of natural language. Without well supported constraints on overloading, we are liable to create overloads in unnatural ways which will actually impede effective communication. For instance, we may produce descriptions and utterances that are too densely packed to be readily comprehensible by the hearer.

To begin an exploration of overloading, we analyzed a corpus of computer-mediated design dialogues which contain a large proportion of redescriptions that appear to be overspecified (Passonneau 1996, Vonk et al. 1992, O'Donnell et al. 1998). We define a *redescription*, in this work, as anything syntactically realized within an utterance that is mutually known and could be used to re-evoke a discourse entity. This includes nominal and pronominal expressions as well as adjectives within copulas, but excludes any information about a discourse entity that is new to the hearer (e.g. my desk chair is maple, it is maple). Overspecified redescriptions are those that provide more information about the discourse entity than is needed for identification purposes.

First we will describe the corpus we used in our analyses and then show that there are a large proportion of overspecified redescriptions in this corpus using an estimation procedure similar to that of (Passonneau 1996). Having a large proportion of overspecified redescriptions ensures that something besides identification is influencing the redescriptions in the corpus. We expect that the influences on redescriptions will vary with the type of task that is the topic of the dialogue and the communications setting and that there could be tasks and settings in which identification is the only prevalent influence on the descriptions (e.g. the tangram task (Clark and Schaefer 1989, Brennan 1990)).

Next we will describe five communication and problem solving inferences that could influence the choice of attributes used in redescriptions. We will describe their theoretical motivations and give examples from the corpus. In general they are motivated by the functions of repetition at the utterance or propositional level (Walker 1993, Johnstone 1994) and the inferences and implicit knowledge that bind natural language utterances together to form a coherent discourse (Grice 1975). Our main hypothesis is that attribute selections will be influenced by the contexts or situations in which we can expect inferences about joint commitments, changes to problem solving constraints, motivations for a proposal, closing a subtask and achieving understanding of task entity descriptions. The low-level definitions of the contexts in which we expect these inferences to occur are particular to the task addressed in the dialogues and the particular inference involved and are derived from sets of features annotated in the corpus. We will describe the features and how the contexts are recognized from the feature sets. We expect the types of inference we are considering to extend to other corpora, but that the applicability of each inference type will depend on the underlying task and communications setting of a corpus.

Finally, we will describe a two-part analysis of the corpus that explores our hypotheses about influences on redescriptions. The first part of the analysis examines the correlations between utterance and dialogue features that are indicative of when particular inferences are expected and the attributes expressed in redescriptions. The second part of the analysis utilizes computer simulations of attribute selection strategies. The data input to the selection strategies are the discourse entities evoked in the corpus and the contexts in which they occur. We measure the performance of a selection strategy by comparing the attributes it selects to those expressed in the corpus. We then compare the performances of two attribute selection strategies that consider only the identification goal with that of a selection strategy that considers both the identification goal and the inference contexts we described.

Within each selection strategy, parameters direct how supporting calculations for each strategy are made (e.g. how a distractor or context set is determined). Although these low-level adjustments in the strategies partially fit the selections to the corpus, our goal in this analysis is not to produce a general attribute selection algorithm for the domain of our corpus or any other corpus but to extract the best possible performance from each strategy before comparing them to one another. Our goal is to find out whether overloading applies to redescriptions and if so what general types of inferences or other communicative goals could potentially be overloaded in redescriptions.

The results of the two part analysis indicate that the first four of the five inference contexts we listed above have merit as possible influences on attribute selection for redescriptions. Neither analysis indicated that an inference involving understanding would influence the content of a redescription in our corpus.

10.2 The COCONUT Corpus

Our analysis is based on the COCONUT corpus (Di Eugenio et al. 2000). This corpus contains 24 computer-mediated dialogues and we used 13 of these dialogues to test our hypotheses.[1] On average each dialogue in this subset of 13 contained 42 utterances, 25 discourse entities, 12 redescriptions and 6 utterances between redescriptions.

In each dialogue, two people collaborate on a simple design task; buying furniture for two rooms of a house. The information needed to complete the design task is divided between the two designers in such a way that a good design cannot be achieved without collaboration. With this task, the designers typically describe the furniture items that they believe are relevant to the current subtask and design constraints. It is characteristic of design tasks that designers often adjust their problem solving constraints in order to arrive at an agreeable solution (Lottaz and Smith 1997, Lyons 1995).

10.2.1 Task Description

The COCONUT task is related to those described in (Walker 1993, Whittaker et al. 1993) but differs in the emphasis and complexity of the task.[2] Each of the two participants in the task is given a separate budget and inventory of furniture that lists the quantities, colors, and prices for each item in that inventory.[3] Neither participant knows what is in the other's inventory or the money that the other has. The participants have the same types of knowledge but different instantiations of it. By sharing information, the participants can combine their budgets and can select furniture from each other's inventories. Purchasing decisions are joint; they must be mutually known and approved. The participants are equals in that there is no master-slave or expert-client relationship. Both participants have been briefed on the task goals, incentives and the tools and have had no prior contact.

The participants' main goal is to negotiate the purchases; the items of highest priority are a sofa for the living room and a table and four chairs for the dining room. The participants also have specific secondary goals which further complicate the problem solving task. Participants are instructed to try to meet as many of these goals as possible, and

[1]The remaining dialogues have not been fully annotated.

[2]Walker's similar task is performed by two artificial agents whereas our task and that in Whittaker et.al. is performed by two humans. Whittaker et.al.'s dialogues are spoken whereas ours are written.

[3]In Walker's task this information is committed to memory but in our task the participants have this information in written form.

are motivated to do so by associating points with satisfied goals.[4] The secondary goals are: 1) Match colors within a room, 2) Buy as much furniture as you can, 3) Spend all your money.

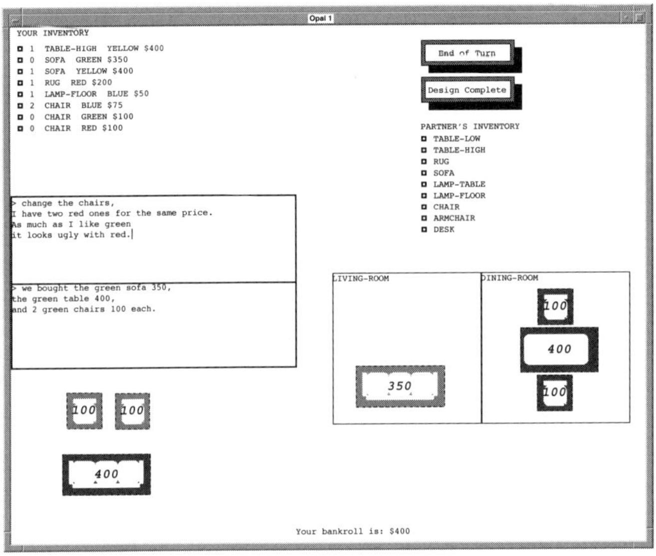

FIGURE 1 A View of the COCONUT Interface

10.2.2 Communications Setting

The participants are in separate rooms and can communicate via the computer interface only. They are asked to maintain private graphical representations of their discussions and incremental agreements. The participants share dialogue windows but the inventories, budgets and updated floor plans are private and appear only on the owner's color display. Figure 1 shows the interface as it looks in the middle of a design session.

The buttons in the upper right corner of Figure 1, "End of Turn" and "Design Complete", enforce turn-taking and initiate incremental recording of the conversation and the graphics updates. No interruption of the partner's turn is allowed. Also note that only the participants' current turns are available, i.e., the sender's current turn in the top dialogue box and the partner's previous turn in the bottom one.

During an incremental recording, the most recently transmitted message is recorded as well as the state of the sender's graphics display. The

[4]In Whittaker et.al.'s task the incentives and goals are simpler.

graphics display record is a description of the furniture icons in the two rooms as well as those that have been created but not assigned to any room. The participants incrementally update the floor plan by placing the furniture icons in meaningful locations. Whenever possible we have used this private information in our corpus analysis as partial evidence of what the speaker's utterance meant and what the hearer understood. However, the primary purpose of the graphics display is as a memory aid for the participants and is only intended secondarily to help clarify possible sources of misunderstanding during analysis.

Note that since a participant does not know what furniture his partner has available, there is a menu (see the mid-right section of the display in Figure 1) that allows a participant to define furniture icons that represent what he understands his partner to have as his partner shares this information with him. There is nothing to prevent the participant from creating an icon for a piece of furniture the partner does not actually have since the menu is general. An icon for a non-existent item could result from either a misunderstanding of his partner's item description or an error in selecting feature values for the item. At minimum the participant must know the type of the furniture item (e.g. chair, table). If the participant does not know or is uncertain about any of the other feature values of the furniture item, he can leave that feature unspecified (i.e. color and purchase price).

The participants first worked through a trial problem to familiarize themselves with the task and the communications setting. During this time they could ask for guidance on using the interface and clarification of the goals and incentives. The participants then solved 1-3 scenarios where the inventories and budgets vary. The problem scenarios ranged from ones where items are inexpensive and the budget is relatively large to ones where the items are expensive and the budget relatively small.

Nothing intrinsic to this task should result in unusual redescriptions. It is reasonable to assume that design tasks, and the COCONUT task in particular, should not affect the number of redescriptions. While we will see evidence that this specific task does lead to the inclusion of identificationally unnecessary attributes in redescriptions, we expect that this interaction should hold for a wide range of tasks where many object attributes are relevant to the problem solving task and where the definition of success is also negotiable. However, because of the non-interruptible setting of the dialogues, attentional limits may also cause redescriptions to be longer than they would otherwise be (Garrod and Anderson 1987, Issacs and Clark 1987, Oviatt and Cohen 1991).

10.2.3 Estimating Overspecified Redescriptions

In our preliminary investigations of the COCONUT corpus, we noticed that there seemed to be a large number of overspecified redescriptions of furniture items. As we noted earlier, a redescription includes any explicit information in an utterance that could describe a discourse entity and that is mutually known. For example, if a shared discourse entity for a chair is mutually known to have the color *red*, then including *red* in the utterance, as with "My chair is red" makes it part of the redescription and if there is only one chair then it is also overspecified.[5] But if *red* is not a mutually known attribute then the redescription is defined as expressing only the type attribute *chair* and the owner attribute *self*.

We confirmed our initial impressions by first determining for each description what other furniture discourse entities might be salient for the dialogue participants. Following the terminology of (Dale 1992), we call these salient, mutually known entities, the distractors. Different definitions for a distractor set are suggested in the literature (Dale 1992, Passonneau 1996, Grosz and Sidner 1986, Levelt 1989, Krahmer and Theune 2002). Since it is not yet clear what definition of the distractor set is correct, we tried several plausible definitions that relate to current theories in computational linguistics and psycholinguistics. Using several definitions of the distractor set, we were able to see how many overspecified redescriptions resulted under each definition. Since there was a large proportion of overspecified redescriptions no matter what distractor set definition we used, we reasoned that the COCONUT corpus would be useful for studying our hypotheses. Below we give the details of how we identified overspecified redescriptions and of the distractor set definitions we tried. Finally we report the number of overspecified redescriptions we found.

To identify overspecified redescriptions we followed Passonneau's procedures for identifying overspecified noun phrases (Passonneau 1996). She used a distractor set that is the union of all the discourse entities (indicated by noun phrases only) in the current discourse segment (as indicated in (Grosz and Sidner 1986)) and all the entities in the last segment that most recently evoked the entity to be described. To be conservative, she assumes that if the most recent segment to evoke the target entity is not the same as the current segment then it is a resumption and the intervening focus spaces should not be included in the distractor set. The descriptive content that is needed to avoid ambiguity and the size of the distractor set are positively correlated. So

[5] Note that this example is also an informationally redundant utterance (Walker 1993).

Passonneau's model, which minimizes the distractors, will also provide a conservative measure of the number of overspecifications in a corpus. We will call this distractor set definition **SEG**.

Similarly to Passonneau, we first identified all the redescriptions that were potentially overspecified by selecting those that used more mutually known attributes than in their previous description. We then filtered this set of redescriptions using the **SEG** distractor set definition. With the first step, we found that 51% (84 of 166) of the redescriptions in the COCONUT corpus were potentially overspecified. And after filtering these with **SEG**, we found that 46% (76 of 166) of all the redescriptions were overspecified. This seems to confirm our initial impressions.

Because it is possible that **SEG** is not the best distractor set definition for all genres, we also tested for overspecification using some other cognitively motivated distractor set definitions. We followed the same methodology as above but we substituted the following distractor set definitions for **SEG**;

- **ALL**: all discourse entities previously mentioned in the discourse.
- **1UTT**: all discourse entities mentioned in the previous utterance.
- **SEG+**: all discourse entities in the current discourse segment and all the entities currently in the solution set
- **5UTT**: all discourse entities mentioned in the previous 5 utterances.

ALL and **1UTT** are two simple and rather implausible definitions for the distractor set and have been included to determine what happens at the extremes. Actually, there is some theoretical merit to **ALL**. (Poesio 1993) indicates that the distractor set should be a combination of the perceptual focus space and the discourse focus space. In the COCONUT setting, the designers often created graphics icons to help them remember the items their partner had described to them and which items they had presented to their partner. These graphical representations could behave as a perceptual focus space for the speaker. However, in view of the evidence discussed in (Clark and Marshall 1981), the participants would have to assume they are both keeping such a record (i.e. the representations would need to be part of their common ground) in order for the dialogue to proceed successfully.

1UTT, while extreme, also represents a focus space similar to that used in computational research on centering (Walker et al. 1997) to determine acceptability conditions for anaphoric reference.

SEG+ assumes that items that have been selected already as part of the solution will remain in focus during the rest of problem solving. The reasoning task provides a rationale for this definition since these

	degree of redundancy	average distractor set size
SEG	46% (76)	5
ALL	39% (64)	19
1UTT	46% (76)	2
SEG+	46% (76)	4
5UTT	44% (73)	4

TABLE 1 Degree of redundancy under different distractor set definitions

items serve to limit the money that is left to spend and may be applicable for determining color match constraints. Finally, **5UTT** is a simple approximation of recency in the discourse.

Table 1 shows the percentage of overspecified redescriptions under each distractor set definition. The degree of overspecification runs as low as 39% with the **ALL** distractor set definition and as high as 46% with the **SEG**, **1UTT** and **SEG+** definitions. No matter which of these distractor set definitions we use, there is still a high degree of overspecification in the COCONUT corpus.

10.3 Potential influences on redescriptions

Now we turn to the question of what else in addition to the identification goal could intentionally influence attribute selection for redescriptions. Our hypotheses reflect non-identification goals that are motivated by the functions of repetition at the utterance or propositional level (Walker 1993, Johnstone 1994) and the inferences that relate utterances to one another and make a discourse coherent (e.g. changes to the color match constraint that are not directly communicated by the dialogue participants).

The first type of task-related inference we considered is motivated by the observation that participants in task-oriented dialogues appear to be able to coordinate on the relaxation of particular task constraints without needing to discuss it. For example, the participants may decide it is impossible to achieve the optional task goal of matching furniture colors within a room. In the COCONUT dialogues, in 38% of the cases where optional goals were abandoned, the participants appeared to agree to abandon the goal without explicit discussion.[6] Our hypothesis is that this inference can also be cued by the content of a redescription when it realizes attributes of a domain object that are not needed to iden-

[6]In (2) there is some explicit discussion about the color match goal.

tify which object is under discussion. For example, in (1)[7] A specifies both the color and price for both the sofa and the lamp even though the price attributes alone would adequately identify each item. By specifying the color, one can easily infer that the color match constraint has been dropped in the proposal. A has eliminated having to explicitly communicate this information (Walker 1993) but has reduced the risk of the hearer missing the inference (Carletta 1992).

(1) S: <...> if we do that i have 400 blue sofa and a 350 yellow sofa, and i have a 250 blue floor lamp or a 150 yellow rug. <...>
A: <...> so now we have 600 left for the living room. if we get *your 350 yellow sofa* and *your 250 blue floor lamp*, that sounds good to me because I don't have anything better in my inventory.

DOMAIN CONSTRAINT CHANGES HYPOTHESIS: Attributes related to constraint changes are expressed in a context where the change is to be inferred by the hearer.

The second task related inference is based on previous research that suggests that discourse relations between utterances, such as *motivation*, can influence the content and form of utterances (Mann and Thompson 1987, McKeown 1985, Moser and Moore 1995). It seems plausible that the speaker can cue these same inferences via redescriptions. For example, in (2) one can infer from O's last utterance and the redescription *mine for 150* that his motivation for proposing his rug is its better price.

(2) U: i have a blue rug for 250. that would leave us with 50 or any other options you may have for us.
O: ok lets take the blue rug for 250, my rug would not match which is yellow for 150.
U: we don't have to match...
O: well then lets use *mine for 150*.

PERSUASION HYPOTHESIS: Attributes that are relevant to getting the hearer to agree with the speaker's proposed action may be expressed in the context of a goal to propose that action.

The next two types of inference are based on the idea that if a speaker repeats an utterance and provides no new information, this can show that a stage of the interaction is complete (Whittaker and Stenton 1988, Jordan and Di Eugenio 1997). Repeating attributes for a recently evoked item could show that the current stage has just been completed while doing so for an older item could indicate that a higher level subproblem

[7] All of the COCONUT excerpts appear verbatim except that we italicize redescriptions and omit parts of turns when they are unrelated to the point of the example. We indicate omissions with <...>.

has been completed. In (3), S's second utterance appears to end a stage in the interaction, in this case the end of the agreement process for a *select sofa* action (Di Eugenio et al. 2000).

(3) S: <...> I have a $300 yellow sofa <...>
G: My sofa's are more expensive so buy *your $300 yellow sofa.* Also <...>
S: <...> *I* will go ahead and buy *the $300 yellow sofa.*

COMMITMENT HYPOTHESIS: In the context of a joint commitment to a proposal, all the attributes expressed in the proposal will be repeated.

The second case in which a higher level subproblem was completed is illustrated by the summary in (4). Note that D summarizes both living room (as requested) and dining room items. Summaries differ from commitments in that they are delayed redescriptions. The action associated with the object was completed and the participants had moved on to a new part of the task.

(4) G: I got the rug. What do you have in the living room and what are the prices of the items
D: the green sofa in the living room 350. dining room—> *3 yellow chairs 75 each, 1 high-table yellow, 1 yellow rug*

SUMMARIZATION HYPOTHESIS: In the context of a previously completed problem or subproblem, all the mutually known attributes for an item will be repeated.

The final type of inference we considered is when a speaker repeats an utterance to show that it was understood (Clark and Schaefer 1989, Brennan 1990, Walker 1992,1993). In the COCONUT corpus, the hearer sometimes repeats the description in the turn immediately following. For example, in (3) G repeats S's description of the sofa, although the sofa was introduced by S. We claim that this type of redescription could help verify that the attribute information was correctly understood.

VERIFICATION HYPOTHESIS: In the context of a newly introduced entity, all the attributes expressed will be repeated by the hearer in his/her next turn.

10.4 Analyzing the Corpus

To verify our hypotheses, we undertook a two part corpus investigation. First, we did correlational studies of the corpus using factors derived from annotation features related to the agreement process as described in (Di Eugenio et al. 2000), other discourse features, discourse entities and the problem solving state. However, since one cannot infer causality merely from correlational studies, in the second part of our investigation we analyzed the performance of parameterized attribute selection strategies which used the annotated corpus as input and output test data.

For both parts of the investigation, we needed to define the inference contexts we described in the hypotheses in terms of the annotated features and other easily extractable features of the corpus (e.g. the utterance speaker and the proximity of a redescription to its last mention). As part of recognizing the contexts, we used the following agreement process definitions[8] which were presented and supported in (Di Eugenio et al. 2000):

- propose: The speaker offers the item and unconditionally commits to using it and the offer makes the mutual solution state determinate.
- partner decidable option: The speaker offers an item and conditionally commits to using it but the offer leaves the mutual solution state indeterminate.
- unconditional commit: The speaker indicates his unconditional commitment to using the item
- unendorsed option: The speaker offers an item but does not show any commitment to using it when the mutual solution state is already determinate.

The annotation features that comprise these definitions were all found to have good intercoder reliability (Di Eugenio et al. 1998).

10.4.1 Annotation Scheme

We developed two additional types of corpus annotation features to support our study: (1) discourse entity level annotations that capture (a) the definitions and updates for discourse entities as a dialogue progresses and (b) the attributes selected to describe discourse entities, and (2) utterances that capture problem solving and discourse features.

Features of type (1) are needed to supply information about the furniture entities evoked in the dialogue. The main objective was to identify the entity being communicated and how the information about that entity was communicated. Both initial and subsequent references were annotated so that we could capture how the description of a single discourse entity developed during the course of the dialogue. By tracking the discourse entities in the dialogue we could tell when a subsequent

[8]The definitions presented here are abbreviated. There is also an aspect that relates to the problem solving architecture which distinguishes them from speech acts.

reference to an entity might also add new information about the entity or correct erroneous information. For example in, "I have a $200 table. It is green.", entity_1 from the first utterance is ((type table)(owner A)(price 200)). The pronoun "it" in the next utterance corefers to entity_1 but the utterance also adds to it new information about the color of the object. The entity description then gets updated to ((type table)(color green)(owner A)(price 200)). These entity descriptions serve as input to the attribute selection strategies. However, the strategies cannot choose to use attributes that are new to an entity (i.e. not mutually known) to corefer. In comparing a strategy's selections with those made by the human, choices about whether to describe a new attribute are not considered.

For the furniture entities, we asked annotators to indicate the attribute-value pair information for each discourse entity in an utterance, and the sources for this information (e.g. from the utterance, the NP or locally inferred). Annotators were also asked to indicate whether the discourse entity was new or a coreference to a previous discourse entity and to what other discourse entities the current entity might be related. Here, some of the relevant relations include set, part-of, and class relations. Finally, we also asked the annotators to indicate the action in which the discourse entity was an argument.

In addition to the agreement process components we described earlier, we also needed other problem solving and discourse features at the utterance level to test our hypotheses. First, we needed to know what constraint changes were communicated, and whether these changes were communicated explicitly or implicitly. We assumed a set of initial constraint settings that would maximize the number of points earned. In general, these initial settings held true for all of our participants since the task instructions that explained the scoring for solutions was the only common ground that the participants had at the start of the problem solving trials. Annotators were instructed to pick an appropriate constraint description from a given list whenever there was a change to that constraint from its previous setting.

Finally, we also needed to identify the task structure and the discourse segments. We used a change to a different domain action as a cue for the non-linguistic task structure (Terken 1985). Each domain action provides a discourse segment purpose so that each utterance that relates to a different domain action or set of domain actions defines a new segment.

We assumed that there were at least three and at most five component actions to be discussed (distinguished by furniture type and room): selecting four chairs for the dining room, selecting a table for the dining room, selecting a sofa for the living room, and selecting a set of optional items for the living room and dining room. We instructed the annotators to determine the actions addressed in each utterance by considering whether any furniture items or furniture templates (e.g. "do you have a red sofa?") being discussed in the utterance could unambiguously be related to one of these actions. Annotators were also asked to distinguish between when an action was first addressed and when the utterance continued the discussion. If the relation of the furniture item or template to actions was ambiguous, the annotators were instructed to indicate the highest level action that was unambiguous (e.g. select items for the dining room). Contiguous utterances that discussed a particular action were taken to define a discourse segment. Utterances that introduced or restarted action discussions while also continuing active discussions of other actions, were interpreted as starts of embedded discourse segments.

To develop and validate the annotation scheme, we conducted intercoder reliability studies using a balanced subset of the corpus. 30% of the corpus was annotated by two annotators for the purpose of determining intercoder reliability.[9] We use the Kappa coefficient of agreement (Krippendorff 1980, Carletta 1996) to assess intercoder reliability; this measure factors out chance agreement between coders. The discourse processing community uses Krippendorff's scale (Krippendorff 1980) to interpret and apply the Kappa coefficient, which varies between 0 and 1. Krippendorff's scale discounts any variable with $K < .67$, allows tentative conclusions when $.67 < K < .8$, and definite conclusions when $K \geq .8$. Table 2, which shows the intercoder reliability results after two development iterations and one reconciliation meeting that identified omissions, suggests that all of the features are defined clearly enough so that they can be reliably annotated and used in studies. After establishing the intercoder reliability, additional dialogues were annotated by one annotator. The overlap between the dialogues that were annotated for this study and those annotated by the COCONUT project for the agreement structure resulted in 13 fully annotated dialogues which we used for testing our hypotheses about attribute selection in redescriptions.

10.5 Results of the Correlational Analysis

We used chi-square and the Fisher exact test[10] to check for correlations between factors in the corpus. The factors are all derived from the annotated features we described earlier. Although these tests assume

[9]One annotator's area of expertise is linguistics; the other is the author of this paper.

[10]We use the Fisher exact test when $N < 20$ or an expected cell frequency is ≤ 5.

Actions & Constraints	Introduce Actions	Continue Actions	Change Constraints	
	.897	.857	.881	
Discourse Entities	Reference Coreference	Discourse Relations	Attributes	Entities to Actions
	.863	.819	.861	.857

TABLE 2 Kappa values for the Annotation Scheme

independence, we feel we can violate this assumption given that the dependencies in a discourse aren't direct and obvious. In all of the contingency tables we will present, the counts are restricted to utterances that contain redescriptions. Finally the counts were all done automatically using software that interpreted the annotation features since the contextual factors generally involved multiple annotation features.

Domain Constraint Changes Hypothesis

For this hypothesis we test whether there is a difference in attribute usage when a constraint change is communicated implicitly or explicitly. Recall that COCONUT is directly annotated with features indicating (1) whether a constraint change was communicated and whether this was accomplished implicitly or explicitly (2) which attributes were included in the redescriptions.

Changes	Related Attributes
Room Color Limit	color
Price Upper Limit	price
Price Evaluator	price
Attribute Limit	color, price

TABLE 3 Associated Attributes and Changes

We only counted attributes that relate to constraints. For example, we only looked at the usage of the color attribute for the color match constraint or price for placing price limits. In Table 3, we list each of the constraint types that we examined and the attribute that we expected would be useful for inferring that change.[11] Our expectations derive from the instructions given to the COCONUT dialogue participants.

Table 4 shows that in the context of an implicit constraint change,

[11]The relevant attribute for the attribute limit constraint is indicated in the annotation for the constraint change.

	Attribute Used	Attribute not Used
Implicit change	9	0
Explicit change	2	11

TABLE 4 Contingencies for Domain Constraint Changes Hypothesis

attributes related to the change are more likely to be used in the description than when the change is explicit (Fisher Exact Test, $p < 0.0002$).

Persuasion Hypothesis

For the Persuasion hypothesis, we wish to test whether expressing an attribute in a redescription is related to whether the expressed attribute makes the redescribed item more desirable as a solution for an action than the alternatives. For example, the cost of the item being redescribed might be lower than any of the alternatives that have been discussed so far.

A persuasion context exists when a proposal is to be made and alternate solutions exist and there is a contrast between the colors or prices that make the proposed item clearly a better choice. Given the analysis of the agreement process in (Di Eugenio 2000), we first look for either a propose utterance, or an unconditional commitment utterance where the previous state is a partner decidable option, an unendorsed option or a list of options in which the speaker intentions are unclear.

For each of the unconditional commitment cases, we present examples. First, in (5), A's partner decidable option is followed by B's unconditional commitment.

(5) A: I have a blue sofa for $200.

B: I have a yellow sofa for $250. Let's go with your $200 sofa.

In (6), B does not endorse the option he presents but A overrides his objection with an unconditional commitment to it.

(6) A: We have $100 left. I still have that $50 blue chair.

B: I have a rug for $100, but it is yellow.

A: We don't need to match. Let's get your $100 rug.

Finally, in (7), A lists all of the items he has available. From the perspective of the agreement structure, lists such as this have no action intention associated with them. However, the items do become part of the dialogue participants shared knowledge allowing all the items to be considered during problem solving so that they can become alternative options for the actions they are implicitly associated with. Because of this, B's second utterance is annotated as an unconditional commitment because he was in a position to deliberate.[12] In this case there are two possibilities for what sofa to select and so a persuasion context arises.

(7) A: I only have 2 red tables for $200, 1 green table for $350 and 4 $50 blue chairs. I don't have any rugs or lamps but I have 1 yellow sofa for $200.

B: I have yellow rug for $75 and a blue sofa for $200. Let's buy your yellow sofa and my rug.

Once we have identified possible proposals, we need to check for contrasts with alternatives. The alternatives are approximated by accumulating a list of the items evoked for each action. After a propose or unconditional commitment, all the items in the list for an action get flushed before starting over with the proposed item. The list must still be maintained after a proposal in case a counterproposal arises.

Contrast	Related Attribute
Matches room but not alternatives	color
Cheaper than alternatives	price
More expensive than alternatives (near end of problem)	price

TABLE 5 Associated Attributes and Contrasts

Next we check for contrasts between the item being proposed and the alternatives.[13] The contrast possibilities are shown in table 5 and arise from the COCONUT problem description. We were unable to accurately model the goal of buying as many items as possible with the annotations available. For color we compare the color of the proposed item to those items already selected for the room and the alternative items. If the proposed item matches items already selected for the room while none of the alternatives do, then a persuasion context exists. For prices there are two possibilities that depend on whether or not the end of the problem solving effort is nearing. An item may be a better choice 1) when the price of the proposed item is greater than that of each alternative (i.e. it may be helping to spend out the budget) or 2) when the price of the proposed item is less than that of each alternative (i.e. the cheaper item

[12] This requirement for unconditional commitment is related to the problem solving architecture and is justified in (Di Eugenio 2000).

[13] (Krahmer and Theune 2002) also check for contrastive attributes in spoken dialogue applications.

may be preferred since it leaves some money for other purchases).

	Attribute Not Used	Attribute Used
no contrast	18	9
contrast	13	24

TABLE 6 Contingencies for Persuasion Hypothesis

Table 6 indicates that in contexts where a contrast is predicted, the contrastive attribute is more likely to be included in a redescription ($\chi^2 = 5, p < .05, df = 1$).

Commitment Hypothesis

Here we test whether in the context of a joint commitment to a proposed action all the attributes expressed in the proposal are more likely to be repeated. A joint commitment context exists when either 1) there is a previous proposal or unconditional commitment for the action involving the entity in the immediately previous turn and no other items have been discussed for the action in the interim or 2) a speaker unconditionally commits again after doing so in his previous turn.

When determining repeated attributes, we discount the type and owner attributes. The type attribute is excluded because it involves pronominalization and zero anaphora; issues we are not addressing in this research. We exclude the owner attribute because its only function is identification in this domain.

	Not Repeat Attributes	Repeat Attributes
No Commitment	7	8
Commitment	2	20

TABLE 7 Contingencies for Commitment Hypothesis

Table 7 indicates that in contexts where a joint commitment is predicted, all mutually known attributes are more likely to be included in redescriptions (Fisher Exact Test, $p < .0171$).

Summarization Hypothesis

Here we test if the previous completion of a problem or subproblem is related to the expression of all the mutually known attributes in a redescription. First, we must isolate redescriptions that occur after an agreement has been reached for the action.

A summarization context exists when an agreement has been reached for the action without the action being readdressed between the agreement and the current turn. The achievement of an agreement state is approximated when either 1) a propose or partner decidable option was the last state for the action and it happened more than two turns ago or 2) an unconditional commit was the last state and it happened two or more turns ago. In the first case, the agreement must be inferred and in the other the agreement is more explicit.

For the agreement state under condition 1), we require more than two turns to intervene because we want to allow for the cases where the partner left the decision pending by moving on to a dependent action (e.g. a final table decision may be left pending until the chair options are explored). We are estimating that if the action is not revisited after three turns, then it was not put on hold pending work on another action and that the partner agreed by moving on to another independent action.[14] This test for agreement takes into consideration that the initiation of the relevant next contribution shows evidence of understanding (Clark and Schaefer 1987) and possibly joint commitment. For condition 2), we require that there be an intervening turn so that the partner is able to show that he has moved on to some other problem.

	All Mutual Attributes Used	Not All Mutual Attributes Used
Not End of Agreement Process	54	117
End of Agreement Process	8	8

TABLE 8 Contingencies for Summarization Hypothesis

As with the commitment hypothesis, the type and owner attributes are excluded when determining whether mutually known attributes are repeated.

Table 8 indicates there is no correlation between a summarization context as we have characterized it and whether all the mutually known attributes that relate to decisions get repeated ($\chi^2 = 1.49, df = 1$, NS).

	Attributes Not All Repeated	Attributes All Repeated
initial not in previous turn	1	0
initial in previous turn	44	2

TABLE 9 Contingencies for Verification Hypothesis

Verification Hypothesis

With this hypothesis we test whether the repetition of all the attributes presented in a previous description correlate with a context in which the entity was just introduced. In this case we collect all the attributes that were presented in the turn where the item was first described and check whether this mention of the item was in the immediately previous turn or further back in the dialogue. As with the commitment and summarization hypotheses, the type and owner attributes are excluded when determining whether attributes are repeated. Table 9 shows no correlation between the verification context and the choice of attributes ($\chi^2 = .06, df = 1$, NS).

10.6 Comparing Redescription Strategies

The first part of our study shows which of the contexts that predict communicative goals are more likely to influence redescriptions—the inference contexts and attribute choices indicated in our hypotheses positively correlated for all but Verification and Summarization. In what follows, we will describe our experimental comparisons of selection strategies for redescribing objects—two identification-only strategies and a strategy that incorporates identification and responds to the contexts indicated in our hypotheses.

We analyzed how well computer simulated selections for the COCONUT corpus matched human selections. We reasoned that if our hypotheses were valid then a selection strategy that incorporates them should match the selections made by humans at least as well as an identification-only selection strategy. We anticipated that the degree of match to humans could be similar between the selection strategies since there may be many allowable ways to express a description for identification purposes and the selections intended to cue the inferences could intersect some of these allowable ways.

[14] In the initial version of the annotation scheme, there was a feature for indicating dependent actions but it was dropped because of poor intercoder reliability.

We used the human generated descriptions in the COCONUT corpus to evaluate the descriptions created by the selection strategies we wished to test. We simulated selections for the COCONUT dialogues by using annotations about the discourse entities to be evoked and the contexts in which they appeared as input to the selection strategies. To compare the performance of a selection strategy to that of humans, we used a measure of the degree of match between the human's and the parameterized strategy's selection of attributes for the same discourse entity in the same dialogue context. Inclusion and exclusion of an attribute both count in the degree of match. A perfect match means that the strategy included or excluded the same attributes as the human did for a particular entity. The measure, X/N, ranges between 0 and 1 inclusive, where X is the number of attribute inclusions and exclusions that agree with the human data and N is the number of attributes that can be expressed for an entity. This response variable is called *match* in the experiments that follow.

To determine the best internal parameter settings for each strategy and to compare strategies we first did an analysis of variance (MathSoft Inc. 1998) on the results of the experiments. The analysis of variance indicates whether there were any significant differences in the performance as we varied the parameter settings or redescription strategy. To determine where and how large any performance differences are, we then did either multiple pairwise comparisons (MCA) (Hsu 1996) or multiple comparisons with a control (MCC) (Dunnett 1964).[15] We display the results of the multiple comparisons as 95% confidence intervals, (e.g. as in Figure 2), and they are always of the form:

$$\text{(estimate)} \pm \text{(critical point)} \times \text{(standard error of estimate)}$$

The critical point in the above calculation depends on the multiple comparison method used (e.g. Tukey, Dunnett, LSD). We chose the method that created the smallest critical point and the selected method is indicated in each graph.[16]

Intervals in the graphs that exclude zero indicate statistically significant performance differences. The labels on the y axis indicate the two levels or experimental factors that were compared and represent the differences in performance. If the interval is to the right of zero then the first member of the label pair performed better and if the interval is to the left then the second member of the pair performed better.

[15] We used S-plus' multicomp function to perform the multiple comparisons (MathSoft Inc. 1998).

[16] S-plus' multicomp function can optionally consider all the the valid methods to find the smallest critical point.

It doesn't follow automatically that performance is identical when there are no significant differences. We will discuss non-significant differences in terms of performance trends in making judgement calls about equality of performance. If the center point of an interval is to the right of zero then we will say that the first member of the label pair has a trend towards performing better, and vice versa if the center point is to the left of zero.

10.6.1 Defining the Attribute Selection Strategies

There are a variety of strategies suggested in the literature for satisfying the identification goal but many aspects of the strategies or the information they depend upon are vague. We will examine two different strategies for choosing attributes to satisfy the identification goal. The first strategy is the incremental algorithm (**INC**) described in (Dale and Reiter 1995). **INC** incrementally builds a description by checking an ordered list of attribute types and selects an attribute only when it rules out any remaining distractors. As distractors are ruled out, they no longer influence the selection process. The initial set of distractors are computed according to what is expected to be in focus for the speaker and the hearer based on the intentional structure of the dialogue.

The second strategy we examined for satisfying the identification goal is based on the gestalt search template (**gestalt**) described in (Levelt 1989). In this strategy, the template is overspecified in a way that makes the search for the referent easier. Following (Levelt 1989), we identified which static attribute template would maximize the number of redescriptions matched in the corpus and used it to create the base description for any entity that is to be re-evoked. We then supplemented the description using **INC** to rule out any remaining distractors.

These two selection strategies are parameterized for many lower level calculations which are not yet well specified by any theories but here we will only discuss determining the best distractor set definition to use within each selection strategy. The distractor set is used to assess whether a description will uniquely select the target object from its set of potential distractors.[17]

We will compare the performance of these two identification only selection strategies to each other and to a parameterized selection strategy called *intentional influences* (**IINF**). **IINF** tests for the inference contexts described in our hypotheses and selects appropriate attributes for each context that it finds in the corpus for the discourse entity that is to be redescribed. Afterwards, **IINF** then incrementally selects additional

[17](Krahmer and Theune 2002), in this volume, provide a more detailed specification of the distractor set. Our future experiments will incorporate their findings.

attributes as needed to rule out any remaining distractors. The identification strategy used when none of the inference contexts applies is parameterized so that we can incorporate the best identification strategy into **IINF**. **IINF** is also parameterized for which contexts are allowed to influence attribute selection so that we can determine which combinations of our hypotheses result in the best match to human descriptions.

10.6.2 Determining Internal Parameter Settings for the Selection Strategies

To find the best distractor set definition for both of the identification only strategies we varied only the discourse partitioning approach. There are many theories for partitioning the discourse but no empirical studies that conclusively support one over another. We will use the distractor set definitions we introduced earlier when estimating the degree of redundancy in the COCONUT redescriptions. Recall that we described two interpretations of partitioning that are based on the discourse segment purpose (Grosz and Sidner 1986), **SEG** and **SEG+**, and three extremes that assume no partitioning of the discourse other than recency, **5UTT**, **1UTT** and **ALL**.

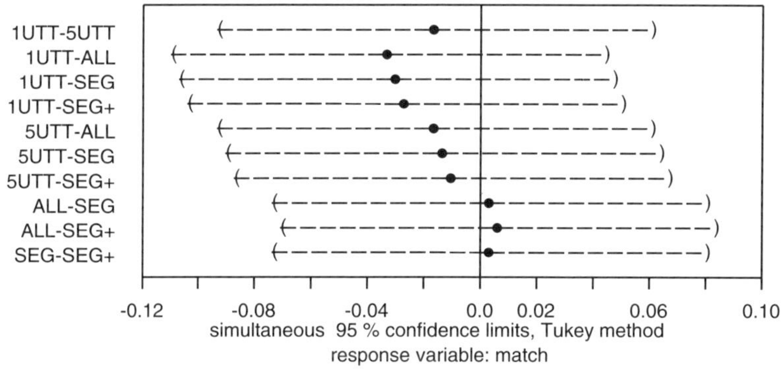

FIGURE 2 Comparing Distractor Set Definitions for INC

We found that while there were no significant differences between these definitions for **INC**, **ALL** was the better choice as shown in Figure 2. Likewise there were no significant differences between the definitions for **gestalt** but the more widely assumed and more restrictive definition, **SEG**, worked better as shown in Figure 3.

We found that when using the best distractor set definitions for each redescription strategy, the **gestalt** strategy, while not significantly bet-

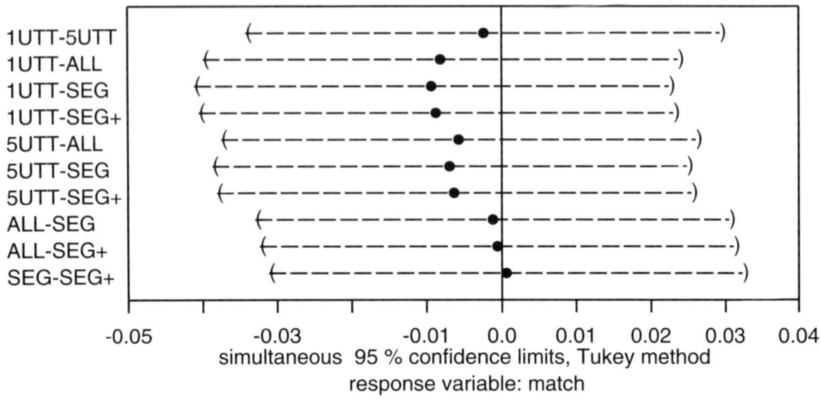

FIGURE 3 Comparing Distractor Set Definitions for Gestalt

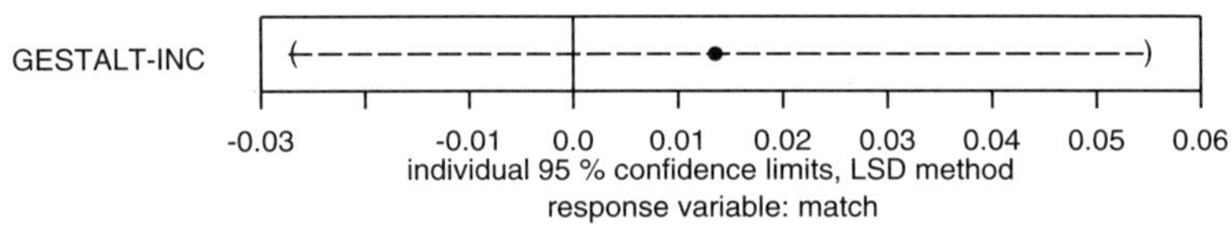

FIGURE 4 Comparing Identification Strategies

ter, had a trend towards better performance than the well known **INC** strategy as shown by the confidence interval in Figure 4. The main conceptual difference between the best versions of **gestalt** and **INC** was the gestalt search template. **INC** always includes the "type" attribute whereas the best **gestalt** setting was to always include both "type" and "color" attributes.[18] This means the main difference was that **gestalt** always included "color" in every redescription.

These results indicate that including "type" and "color" and not just "type" as with **INC** was a better strategy since it both performed slightly better and agreed with a standardly accepted way of partitioning a discourse (i.e. partitioning according to discourse segment purpose as with (Grosz and Sidner 1986)). Perhaps **INC** may have needed a reason to include "color" and a large distractor set would be more likely to justify the inclusion.

After establishing the best internal parameter settings for the two

[18]Experiments to determine the best search template for **gestalt** are reported in (Jordan 2000).

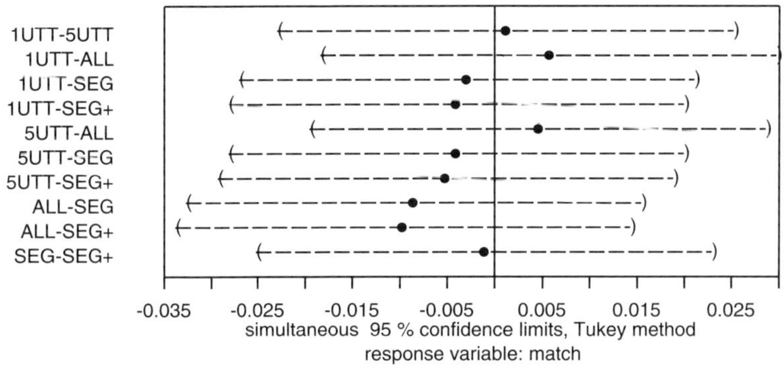

FIGURE 5 Comparing Distractor Sets for INC within IINF

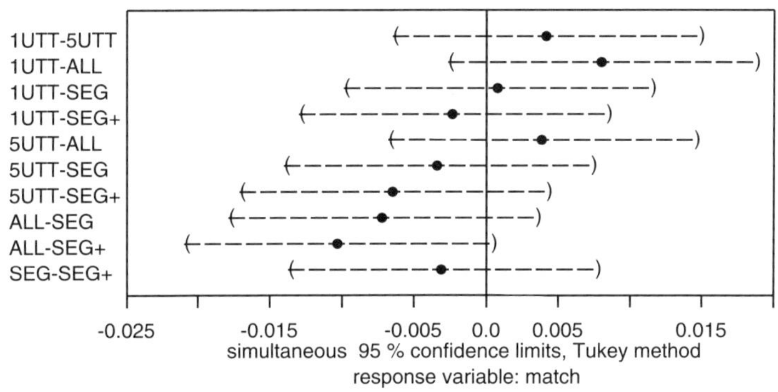

FIGURE 6 Comparing Distractor Sets for gestalt within IINF

identification strategies, we next did the same for **IINF**. It was parameterized for which contexts to check and for which identification strategy to incorporate. However, we did not want to assume that we should use the same settings when an identification strategy was embedded within **intentional influences** as when it was a stand-alone strategy that ignored other influences. Looking again at the distractor set definition when identification was one of many possible goals that could influence attribute choices, we found that there were no significant performance differences for embedded **INC** or **gestalt**. But we can see from Figures 5 and 6 there is now a trend for the more restrictive **SEG+** to be the best setting for both.

Finally, we compared versions of **intentional influences** using the

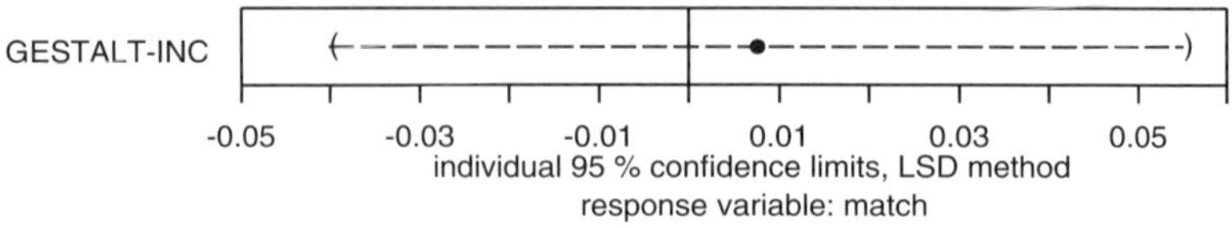

FIGURE 7 Comparing Identification Strategies within IINF

newly determined settings for the incorporated identification strategy. There were no significant differences in performance, as shown in Figure 7, but there was still a trend towards better performance when **gestalt** was the embedded identification strategy. However, we can also see from this that when we are able to include other influences in addition to identification, the performance of the more widely used **INC** strategy tends to improve. This lends some additional credibility to our claim that there are multiple influences because, when we account for these influences, the standard theories and approaches tend to make choices more like that of humans.

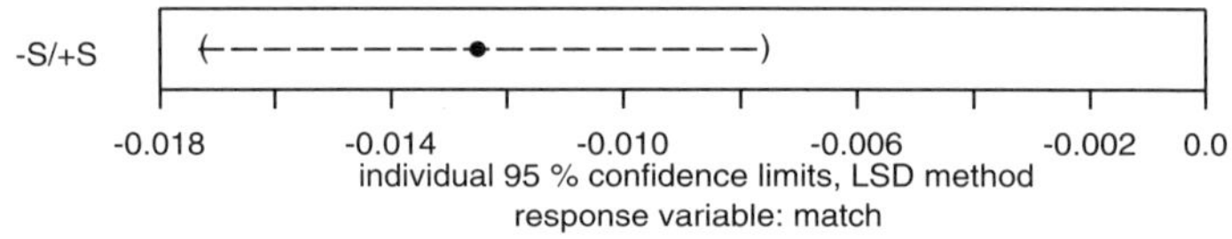

FIGURE 8 Comparing Summarization for IINF

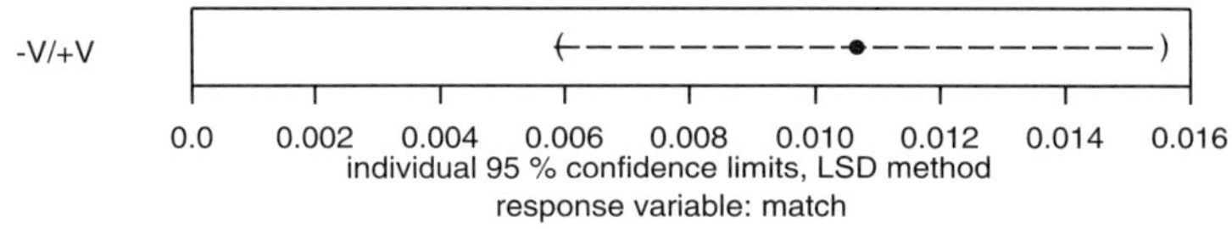

FIGURE 9 Comparing Verification for IINF

Finally, by parameterizing the inference contexts that were considered by **intentional influences**, we were able to see which of our hypothesized contexts affected the performance of the **intentional influences** strategy. We accepted the positive correlational results from the first part of our study and only skeptically tested the negative ones. We found that Summarization had a clear positive influence while Verification had a clear negative one. For Summarization there is a significant difference in performance ($F = 25.71, p < .0000004$) and the MCA comparison shown in Figure 8 indicates that it is better to include the summarization hypothesis. For Verification there is also a significant difference in performance ($F = 18.71, p < .00002$) but Figure 9 indicates it is better not to consider Verification.

In the case of the Summarization hypothesis, the results of our two part analysis may mean that our definition of the summarization context needs refinement. But with the Verification hypothesis, the results confirm it is not a valid influence for our corpus.

10.6.3 Comparing the Selection Strategies for Redescriptions

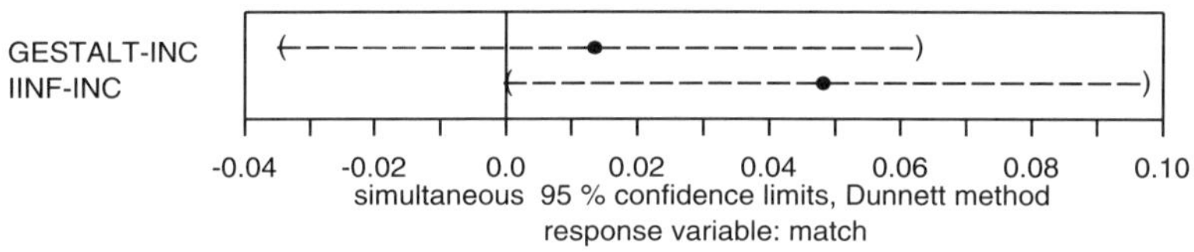

FIGURE 10 Comparing Redescription Strategies

Overall, we found that while the **intentional influences** strategy was not significantly better ($F = 2.58, p < .08$), it had a trend towards better performance compared to the stand-alone identification strategies, as shown by the MCC confidence intervals in Figure 10. The **intentional influences** strategy indirectly allows domain and discourse goals to override the pre-ordered list of attributes that represent attribute saliency in **INC**. For example, when a Persuasion context exists, it can allow attributes such as price to sometimes become more salient than color which is usually considered highly salient.

Although we do not have enough data to determine which, if any, of the contexts in our hypotheses is most influential for attribute selection, we can show in Table 10 the relative contributions of each of these contexts and the contribution of the identification goal within the **intentional influences** strategy. This gives us an informal view of the relative contributions without considering the frequency with which a particular context arises. The contribution made by the identification goal includes both the cases in which identification was the only predicted goal and the cases in which additional attributes had to be added to ensure unique identifiability after the initial selections made by the

Hypothesis	Percentage Contribution to Descriptions
Identification	29.33%
Commitment	26%
Summarization	22.67%
Persuasion	16.67%
Domain constraint changes	5.33%

TABLE 10 Contributions of Goal Contexts to Redescriptions

context checks. Although the contribution is smaller than one might expect, this does not mean that the identification goal was invalid for some redescriptions. Instead it indicates that the problem of identification was addressed already by the attributes that had been selected by the inference contexts. This reflects the economy that can be achieved with goal overloading.

10.7 Discussion

In comparing the performance of the **intentional influences** strategy to that of the two identification-only strategies, it is clear that there is a trend towards better performance especially in comparison to the incremental algorithm **INC**. We expected that the performance measures from the computer simulations could be statistically similar because there may be multiple allowable ways of redescribing some of the objects and the identification-only and **intentional influences** selection strategies could both be intersecting similar sized subsets of the actual expressions in the corpus.

An interesting question that arises in using human performance as the ideal measure is how well humans would agree with one another if asked to describe a particular entity in the context given in the corpus. (Yeh and Mellish 1997) found evidence that there are multiple possible solutions when deciding whether to use a zero anaphor, pronominal, full nominal, or nominal with just the head noun to redescribe entities. There was low agreement between human subjects about which form to use in a set of test texts (Kappa of .41). Although we examined a subset of this issue, it is reasonable to expect that we would obtain similar results.

If we look at the actual mean matches of the strategies in Table 11 $(F = 26, p < 0)$[19], they fall far below the ideal. To give a bound on poor performance, we included the **RANDOM** strategy which loops over the number of attribute choices possible and randomly selects an attribute

[19] Recall that to agree with a human, $match = 1$.

value to include.

Strategy	Mean Match
IINF	.6958
gestalt	.6611
INC	.6476
RANDOM	.4970

TABLE 11 Mean Strategy Performances

The argument for multiple solutions could mean that we have topped out on the performance measure. There could be speaker preferences with respect to the degree and type of overloading attempted. If this is true, we would also expect these preferences to change as the partners get acquainted and adapt to one another given the principle of LEAST COLLABORATIVE EFFORT (Clark and Wilkes-Gibbs 1986). Preferences and adaptation imply that we would always fall short of perfect agreement since we are looking at data from more than one speaker pair in our measures. In that case, we may be as close in agreement with the humans represented in the COCONUT corpus as other humans would be. If we are near the top line for performance, then we would not expect to see significant performance differences.

10.8 Conclusions

We have found evidence through corpus analysis and computer simulations that redescriptions do get overloaded with more than just the identification goal. We expect the types of inferences we have considered here to apply to other corpora but that the extent to which they apply depends on the underlying task and the communications setting. For example, there may be no problem solving constraints in the task that can be changed and so the selection strategy would never encounter a context in which this inference would be expected. Likewise, there may be inferences that are relevant for other corpora that did not appear in the one we analyzed. For instance, we would expect that something like the verification inference might be more applicable in a face to face dialogue where information is more likely to be misheard or missed.

Clearly the extent to which we can study inferential influences on redescriptions will be limited by the complexity of the task that is the topic of the corpus. For example, it may be difficult to enumerate and annotate all the features that would signal that a particular inference is expected. However in a generation application in which we have access to the problem solving state there would not be the same problem and we could instead evaluate the comprehension effects of allowing different types of overloading in redescriptions. The results of our experiments should provide guidance as to what types of overloading would be most fruitful to try in applications that interact with users.

References

Appelt 1985. D. E. Appelt: Planning English referring expressions. *Artificial Intelligence* 26(1), pp.1-33.

Brennan 1990. S. E. Brennan: *Seeking and Providing Evidence for Mutual Understanding.* PhD thesis, Stanford University Psychology Dept., Unpublished Manuscript.

Carletta 1992. J. C. Carletta: *Risk Taking and Recovery in Task-Oriented Dialogue.* PhD thesis, Edinburgh University.

Carletta 1996. J. C. Carletta: Assessing agreement on classification tasks: the kappa statistic. *Computational Linguistics*, 22(2), pp.249-254.

Clark and Marshall 1981. H. H. Clark and C. R. Marshall: Definite reference and mutual knowledge. In A. Joshi, B. Webber, and I. Sag, editors, *Linguistics Structure and Discourse Setting.* Cambridge University Press, Cambridge, England, pp.10-63.

Clark and Schaefer 1987. H. H. Clark and E. F. Schaefer: Collaborating on contributions to conversations. *Language and Cognitive Processes* 2, pp.19-41.

Clark and Schaefer 1989. H. H. Clark and E. F. Schaefer: Contributing to discourse. *Cognitive Science* 13, pp.259-294.

Clark and Wilkes-Gibbs 1986. H. H. Clark and D. Wilkes-Gibbs: Referring as a collaborative process. *Cognition* 22, pp.1-39.

Dale 1992. R. Dale: *Generating Referring Expressions.* ACL-MIT Series in Natural Language Processing. The MIT Press.

Dale and Reiter 1995. R. Dale and E. Reiter: Computational interpretations of the Gricean maxims in the generation of referring expressions. *Cognitive Science* 19(2), pp.233-263.

Di Eugenio et al. 1998. B. Di Eugenio, P. W. Jordan, J. D. Moore, and R. H. Thomason: An empirical investigation of collaborative dialogues. In *ACL-COLING98, Proceedings of the Thirty-sixth Conference of the Association for Computational Linguistics*, Montreal, Canada.

Di Eugenio et al. 2000. B. Di Eugenio, P. W. Jordan, R. H. Thomason, and J. D. Moore: The agreement process: An empirical investigation of human-human computer-mediated collaborative dialogues. *International Journal of Human-Computer Studies* 53(6), pp.1017-1076.

Dunnett 1964. C. Dunnett: New table for multiple comparisons with a control. *Biometrics* 20, pp.482-491.

Garrod and Anderson 1987. S. Garrod and A. Anderson: Saying what you mean in dialogue: A study in conceptual and semantic co-ordination. *Cognition* 27, pp.181-218.

Grice 1975. H. Grice: Logic and conversation. In P. Cole and J. Morgan, editors, *Syntax and Semantics III - Speech Acts*, Academic Press, New York, pp.41-58.

Grosz and Sidner 1986. B. J. Grosz and C. L. Sidner: Attentions, intentions and the structure of discourse. *Computational Linguistics* 12, pp.175-204.

Heim 1983. I. Heim: File change semantics and the theory of definiteness. In R. Bauerle, C. Schwarze and A. von Stechow, editors, *Meaning, Use, and the Interpretation of Language*. Walter de Gruyter, Berlin.

Hsu 1996. J. C. Hsu.: *Multiple Comparisons: Theory and Methods*. Chapman and Hall, London.

Issacs and Clark 1987. E. A. Issacs and H. H. Clark: References in conversation between experts and novices. *Journal of Experimental Psychology: General* 116, pp.26-37.

Johnstone 1994. B. Johnstone: Repetition in discourse: A dialogue. In B. Johnstone, editor, *Repetition in Discourse: Interdisciplinary Perspectives, Volume 1*, volume XLVII of *Advances in Discourse Processes*, chapter 1. Ablex.

Jordan 2000. P. W. Jordan: *Intentional Influences on Object Redescriptions in Dialogue: Evidence from an Empirical Study*. PhD thesis, Intelligent

Systems Program, University of Pittsburgh.

Jordan and Di Eugenio 1997. P. W. Jordan and B. Di Eugenio: Control and initiative in collaborative problem solving dialogues. In *Computational Models for Mixed Initiative Interaction. Papers from the 1997 AAAI Spring Symposium. Technical Report SS-97-04*, The AAAI Press, pp.81-84.

Kamp 1993. H. Kamp: *From Discourse to Logic; Introduction to Modeltheoretic Semantics of Natural Language, Formal Logic and Discourse Representation Theory.* Kluwer Academic Publishers, Dordrecht Holland.

Karttunen 1976. L. Karttunen: Discourse referents. In McCawley, J., editor, *Syntax and Semantics*, volume 7. Academic Press.

Krahmer and Theune 2002. E. Krahmer and M. Theune: Efficient context-sensitive generation of referring expressions. In K. van Deemter and R. Kibble, editors, *Information Sharing* (eds). CSLI Publications.

Krippendorff 1980. K. Krippendorff: *Content Analysis: an Introduction to its Methodology.* Beverly Hills: Sage Publications.

Levelt 1989. W. J. M. Levelt: *Speaking: From Intention to Articulation.* MIT Press.

Lottaz and Smith 1997. C. Lottaz and I. Smith: Collaborative design using constraint solving. From Swiss Workshop on Collaborative and Distributed Systems, Lausanne Switzerland.

Lyons 1995. K. W. Lyons: Collaborative design for assembly of complex electromechanical products. Presentation abstract for NCMS Manufacturing Technical Conference.

Mann and Thompson 1987. W. Mann and S. Thompson: Rhetorical Structure Theory: A Framework for the Analysis of Texts. Technical Report RS-87-190, USC/Information Sciences Institute.

MathSoft Inc 1998. MathSoft Inc.: *S-Plus 5 for Unix Guide to Statistics.* MathSoft, Inc., Seattle, Washington.

McKeown 1985. K. R. McKeown: *Text Generation. Using Discourse Strategies and Focus Constraints to Generate Natural Language Text.* Cambridge University Press.

Moser and Moore 1995. M. Moser and J. D. Moore: Investigating cue placement and selection in tutorial discourse. In *Proceedings of 33rd Annual Meeting of the Association for Computational Linguistics*, pp.130-135.

O'Donnell et al. 1998. M. O'Donnell, H. Cheng and J. Hitzeman: Integrating referring and informing in NP planning. In *COLING-ACL'98, Workshop on Computational Treatment of Nominals.*

Oviatt and Cohen 1991. S. L. Oviatt and P. R. Cohen: Discourse structure and performance: Efficiency in interactive and non-interactive spoken modalities. *Computer Speech and Language*, pp.297-326.

Passonneau 1996. R. J. Passonneau: Using centering to relax Gricean informational constraints on discourse anaphoric noun phrases. *Language and Speech* 39(2-3), pp.229-264.

Poesio 1993. M. Poesio: A situation-theoretic formalization of definite description interpretation in plan elaboration dialogues. In P. Aczel, D. Israel, Y. Katgiri, and S. Peters, editors, *Situation Theory and its Applications*, volume 3, pp.339-374. CSLI Publications.

Pollack 1991. M. E. Pollack: Overloading intentions for efficient practical reasoning. *Noûs* 25, pp.513-536.

Stone and Webber 1998. M. Stone and B. Webber: Textual economy through close coupling of syntax and semantics. In *Proceedings of 1998 International Workshop on Natural Language Generation*, Niagara-on-the-Lake, Canada.

Terken 1985. J. M. B. Terken: *Use and Function of Accentuation: Some Experiments.* PhD thesis, Institute for Perception Research, Eindhoven, The Netherlands.

Vonk et al. 1992. W. Vonk, L. G. M. M. Hustinx and W. H. G. Simons: The use of referential expressions in structuring discourse. *Language and Cognitive Processes* 7(3-4), pp.301-333.

Walker et al. 1997. M. Walker, A. Joshi, and E. Prince: Centering in naturally occurring discourse: An overview. In M. Walker, A. Joshi, and E. Prince, editors, *Centering Theory in Discourse*, Oxford University Press, Oxford. pp.1-28.

Walker 1992. M. A. Walker: Redundancy in collaborative dialogue. In *Fourteenth International Conference on Computational Linguistics*, pp.345-351.

Walker 1993. M. A. Walker: *Informational Redundancy and Resource Bounds in Dialogue.* PhD thesis, University of Pennsylvania.

Webber 1978. B. L. Webber: *A Formal Approach to Discourse Anaphora.* PhD thesis, Harvard University. Garland Press.

Whittaker et al. 1993. S. Whittaker, E. Geelhoed and E. Robinson: Shared workspaces: How do they work and when are they useful? *International Journal of Man-Machine Studies* 39, pp.813-842.

Whittaker and Stenton 1988. S. Whittaker and P. Stenton: Cues and control in expert client dialogues. In *Proc. 26th Annual Meeting of the ACL, Association of Computational Linguistics*, pp.123-130.

Yeh and Mellish 1997. C. L. Yeh and C. Mellish: An empirical study on the generation of anaphora in Chinese. *Computational Linguistics* 23(1), pp.169-190.

11

Towards the Generation of Document-Deictic References

Ivandré Paraboni and Kees van Deemter

11.1 Introduction

Consider a written document dealing with a certain domain of discourse. Typically, most referring expressions in the document will refer to entities in this domain. The words in medical patient information leaflets, for example, refer to the medicine and the patient, as well as such more abstract entities as actions (e.g., taking a pill) and side effects (e.g., headache). But, in addition to this, the leaflets contain expressions referring to entities of a very different kind: sections, paragraphs, pictures, etc., which do not 'live' in the domain of discourse. Instead, they are parts of the document itself. Examples include the following (cf. ABPI 1997).

1a. *This booklet* gives you information about (MEDICINE)
1b. Read *section F* before using your medicine.
1c. The side effects mentioned *above* should disappear after a few days.
1d. Stick the patch onto your skin as shown in *the picture.*

Documents may of course refer to *other* documents. For example, a scholarly publication usually refers to a number of other publications. We will discuss the phenomenon of documents referring to their own parts. Moreover, we will limit ourselves to physically *continuous* document parts, which are not interrupted by other parts of the document. (For exam-

Information Sharing: Reference and Presupposition in Language Generation and Interpretation.
Edited by Kees van Deemter and Rodger Kibble.

ple, we exclude the part of the paper which contains all footnotes, unless these are printed as a separate section.) With the partial exception of work on *cross-media* references in multimedia generation (McKeown et al 1992; André & Rist 1994), this phenomenon has received little attention, and no generally accepted terminology appears to be in usage.

Expressions like 'the previous section' are deictic, in the sense that they involve an implicit or explicit reference to the immediate situation of the reader ('the section before the one you're reading now'). It is worth noting the difference with *anaphoric* expressions, which do not refer to parts of the document but to ordinary domain entities, albeit with help from their antecedents (van Deemter and Kibble 2000). Consistent with this view, Lyons (1977) defines the expressions which refer to, but are *not co-referential with* any preceding linguistic form, as 'textual deixis'. 'Impure' textual deixis, according to Lyons, is the case where the reference is to abstract entities such as facts, and ideas, as in 'This idea was first put forward by Aristotle', where the subject refers to the idea expressed by some previous text, rather than the text itself. Impure textual deixis has also been dubbed 'discourse deixis' and this phenomenon has recently received a fair amount of attention (Levinson 1983; Webber 1991; Asher 1993; Eckert & Strube 1999). Many of the phenomena we are interested in could be subsumed under Lyons' textual deixis, but we will avoid this term since it suggests an unnecessary limitation to references to text excluding references to pictures and other graphical components of documents. Therefore, we use the term *document deixis* (DDX) to refer to references to document parts, paralleling the use of the term 'discourse deixis' (Webber 1991; Paraboni & van Deemter 1999).

The goal of this paper is twofold. First, we intend to discuss this little-known linguistic phenomenon, discuss how it differs from a such related phenomena as anaphora and discourse deixis, and introduce some of its main incarnations. Second, we will try to shed more light on the phenomenon by asking how document-deictic expressions may be produced by a natural language generation (NLG) programme of a particular kind. This NLG perspective will allow us to ask when it is proper to use a document-deictic expression and what is its proper form in a given situation.

In section 11.2, we introduce the phenomenon of document deixis. In section 11.3, we formulate assumptions about the type of natural language generation system under which we intend to generate DDX. Sections 11.3 and 11.4 explore how the semantic content and the surface realisation of DDX can be generated. Section 11.4.3 describes some of the consequences of DDX generation for the architecture of an NLG program. The final section (11.5) summarizes and draws some conclusions.

11.2 The phenomenon of Document Deixis

At the heart of the issue of document deixis lies an ontological distinction, between what we will call *domain entities* (e.g., pills, patients, side effects), which lead a life independently of the document, and *document entities* (e.g., sections, paragraphs, lists, sentences), which are only created by the author during the writing process. Accordingly, one can distinguish between Noun Phrases referring to document entities (NP_{dom}) and Noun Phrases referring to domain entities (NP_{doc}). Interestingly, however, both types of NPs can contain NPs of the other type as a constituent. For example, an NP_{dom} can contain an NP_{doc} (e.g., 'the side effects described in section 4'); the reverse is also possible (e.g., 'the section$_{doc}$ that warns against side effects'). In principle, such embeddings can get very complex, e.g.

> [The advice given in [the section that warns against [the side effect described in [section 5]]]].

In fact, such embeddings can be arbitrarily deep:

$$\ldots\ldots\ {}_{NPdom}[\cdots\ {}_{NPdoc}[\cdots\ {}_{NPdom}[\cdots\ {}_{NPdoc}[\cdots\ {}_{NPdom}[\ldots\ldots]\ \ldots]\ \ldots]\ \ldots]\ \ldots]\ \ldots\ldots$$

(The innermost NP can be an NP_{dom} or an NP_{doc}, and the same is true for the outermost NP.) Our study of existing corpora, however, suggests that most of these embeddings are extremely infrequent. Henceforth, we will limit attention to unembedded DDX and embeddings of the form $NP_{dom}[..NP_{doc}[..]..]$. Let us look at these two types in turn.

First, the unembedded kind. This most pure form of DDX is frequent in the introductory parts of scientific papers, for example, where they announce which issues are treated in which section. For instance,

> 2. In *the previous section* we have introduced the phenomenon of document deixis

Sentences containing such DDX tend to be semantically redundant, making explicit something which is true of the document itself. As a result, they are one of the most common instantiations of self-reference (Barwise & Etchemendy 1987, Hofstadter 1985). Self-reference, as is well known, can cause a sentence to be *self-affirming* ('This sentence contains five words'), *self-defeating* ('This sentence contains exactly five words'), or *paradoxical* ('This sentence is false'). Each of these complications can arise from document deixis: If a text contains meta-level DDX then this causes the text as a whole to become self-referential, leading to the logical peculiarities just mentioned. For example, consider a document D containing the example sentence (2). There are two possibilities: either the indicated section describes the side effects or it does not. In the first case, the truth of (2) can be inferred by reading the remainder of the document (in particular the next section); hence, (2) becomes analytical; in the second case, (2) makes the document self-defeating.

DDX that are used in this way will be called *meta-level* DDX and we will distinguish them from another type, which we will call *object-level* DDX. Object-level DDX are usually part of a larger constituent (e.g. 'the pills described under the header 'Your medicine' ') which refers to a domain entity. The domain entity in question may be concrete (e.g., a medicine, as in 3a) or abstract (e.g., a problem, as in 3b), in which case we are dealing with discourse deixis (Webber 1991).

> 3a. The pills described under the header 'Your medicine' are best swallowed with water.
> 3b. The problems described in section 5 need to be discussed with your doctor.

Since *object*-level DDX have as their primary purpose to refer to a domain entity, *via* the reference to a document entity, they are typically part of a statement that adds to the logical content of the document. Having said this, object-level DDX can, just like any other type of referring expressions, contain logically superfluous material (e.g. (Dale & Reiter 1995), section 2.4); in particular, the DDX itself can be superfluous (i.e., not necessary for the identification of the intended referent). Consider, for example, the following sentence, written in a context where the deictic part of the description (i.e., 'in section 5') is non-restrictive because we assume that side effects are mentioned in one section only.

> 4. Consider (...) the side effects mentioned in *section 5*,

On the one hand, the deictic description *'section 5'* is instrumental in the reference to a particular class of side effects (which may be most easily identified by looking them up in section 5); on the other hand, the deictic description might also be motivated by the need to point the reader to some information, also contained in section 5, *about* these side effects.

Similar complications arise in relation to meta-level DDX. The *core* function of a meta-level DDX is not to add to the logical content of the document (i.e., to make claims about the domain) but to increase its readability, for example by pointing the reader to a part of the document that the author deems instructive for some reason. Having said this, meta-level DDX *can* add logical content. A slight variant of sentence (1a), for example, uses a meta-level DDX to make the novel point that the information in the leaflet is important.[1]

1a. This booklet gives you information about (name of medicine)
1a′. This booklet gives you important information about (name of medicine)

To sum up, object-level DDX are primarily used as a part of a statement that makes a document more informative (but nonrestrictive properties may serve to make the statement more accessible); meta-level DDX, by contrast, are primarily employed to make a document more accessible (but they sometimes add information about the domain as well).

11.3 Generating Document Deixis

We now turn to questions of natural language generation. Firstly, we will introduce a class of NLG systems, one of whose tasks it is to find out under what circumstances a document-deictic expression is called for, as well as to determine its proper form (section 11.3.1). Since document-deictic references are referring expressions, it will be useful to make some preliminary remarks about existing algorithms in this area (section 11.3.2) before we turn to the generation of document-deictic reference in section 11.4.

11.3.1 Language Generation for Document Authoring

NLG systems may serve different purposes, and the nature of the texts that they produce can vary greatly. In this paper, we will be focusing primarily on a class of NLG systems whose purpose is the authoring of complex documents. Systems of this kind have a user who is trying to create a document, assisted by the system. The user, or *author*, specifies the content (and sometimes some aspects of the form) of the document, whereupon the system has to convert this specification into a coherent document in a given target language. Document authoring systems try to make the creation of documents – possibly in a number of languages at the same time – easier by taking away from the author much of the responsibility over the linguistic form of the document. In its most extreme form, the user of this type of system is no longer a *writer*, but just a specifier of content (Power and Scott 1998).

[1]In some cases, a meta-level DDX may even be employed to clarify reference. For example, in *"The red 30mg pills are best swallowed with water. (See the text under the header 'Your medicine' to be sure you're taking the right pills.)"*, the text in brackets involves a meta-level DDX whose purpose is to add information about the reference of the NP 'The red 30mg pills'.

In actual practice, the degree to which the author is still involved in decisions about the form of a document can vary. Document-authoring software can, for example, allow an author to ask for a text without semi-colons, to avoid certain types of overly complex texts (Bouayad-Agha et al. 2000). Even these systems, however, take away low-level details such as lexical choice, and the construction of referring expressions, from the author. For example, the author may specify that a certain person a has a certain property F. Whether a is referred to using a proper name, a pronoun, or some lengthy description – possibly involving an object-level DDX – is up to the system, and analogously for the way in which the property F is designated. Before we turn to the question how DDX can be generated by a system of this kind, let us briefly sketch how 'ordinary' referring expressions are generated.

11.3.2 Referring Expressions Generation Algorithm

Generation of referring expressions is a key component of NLG programs. Two types of algorithms are used in this area, one of which deals with NPs that stand in an anaphoric relationship with an earlier-generated NP and where the main problem is to determine what type of NP is most appropriate: a description, a proper name, a pronoun, or a demonstrative for example (Passonneau 1998; McCoy & Strube 1999). The other type of algorithm usually disregards linguistic context (see Krahmer & Theune (1999) for an exception) and focuses, primarily, on the problem of finding a set L of properties which pick out a given unique individual from among a set of distractors. Since the starting point for much work in this area is Dale & Reiter (1995), we will start by summarizing their algorithm, also known as the Incremental Algorithm or simply D&R.

The *properties* which form the basis of the algorithm are formalized as pairs of the form ⟨Attibute,Value⟩. Attributes are ordered in a list P to reflect their degree of 'preference' (see below). Suppose r is the individual to be singled out, and C is the set of elements from which r is to be selected. Simplifying considerably, what happens is the following: the algorithm iterates through the list of attributes A; for each attribute, it checks whether it has a value that rules out at least one member of C that has not already been ruled out; if so, the attribute is added to L, with a suitable value. Members that are ruled out are removed from C. The process of expanding L and contracting C continues until $C = \{r\}$. The properties in L can be used by a linguistic realisation module to produce NPs such as 'the white pill', 'the white pills for your heart condition', etc. The algorithm is *incremental* because properties are only *added* to L: there is no backtracking. As a result, L may contain semantically redundant properties. According to Dale and Reiter, this has two advantages: it keeps the algorithm polynomial; and if the right preference order of attributes is chosen (reflected by the order of the attributes in P), the algorithm produces descriptions that are not unlike those uttered by humans. (See Krahmer & Theune (this volume), for criticism.)

It is worth elaborating on the function `FindBestValue` that chooses a value once an attribute has been selected. This function operates on a tree of values, where a daughter is more specific than (i.e., extensionally subsumed by) its parent. The function starts by considering the 'Basic-level' value of the attribute which, for simplicity, we can assume to be the most general value of the attribute (i.e., a value whose extension is a superset of all other values of the attribute) and moving to more specific values only if that value removes more distractors. This function balances a preference for more generic values with a preference for values that remove more distractors: the number of distractors is crucial, but genericity decides in case of a tie. The following schema summarizes the algorithm. ($\boldsymbol{A}$ is the list of attributes, $[[\boldsymbol{V_i}]]$ is the denotation of $\boldsymbol{V_i}$.)

> $\boldsymbol{L} := \oslash$ $\{\boldsymbol{L}$ is initialized to the empty set$\}$
>
> For each $\boldsymbol{A_i} \in \boldsymbol{A}$ do
>
> > $\boldsymbol{V_i}$:= FindBestValue$(\boldsymbol{r}, \boldsymbol{A_i}, \boldsymbol{BasicLevel}(\boldsymbol{A_i}))$
> >
> > If $\boldsymbol{r} \in [[\boldsymbol{V_i}]]$ & $\boldsymbol{C} \not\subseteq [[\boldsymbol{V_i}]]$ $\{\boldsymbol{V_i}$ removes distractors but not $\boldsymbol{r}\}$ then do
> >
> > > $\boldsymbol{L} := \boldsymbol{L} \cup \{\langle \boldsymbol{A_i}, \boldsymbol{V_i} \rangle\}$ { Property of $\boldsymbol{V_i}$ is added to $\boldsymbol{L}$ }
> > >
> > > $\boldsymbol{C} := \boldsymbol{C} \cap [[\boldsymbol{V_i}]]$ { Elements outside $\boldsymbol{V_i}$ are removed from $\boldsymbol{C}$ }
> > >
> > > If $\boldsymbol{C} = \{\boldsymbol{r}\}$ then Return $\boldsymbol{L}$ {*Success*}
>
> Return *Failure* { All attributes have been tested, yet $\boldsymbol{C} \neq \{\boldsymbol{r}\}$ }

Even if a given object can be characterized uniquely, Dale and Reiter's algorithm does not always find a characterization (van Deemter 2002). A limitation that will be of specific relevance when DDX are generated arises when a given Attribute can have two values, say V_1 and V_2, which *overlap* in the sense that $V_1 \not\subseteq V_2$ and $V_2 \not\subseteq V_1$. This issue will be discussed in the section 11.4.1.

11.4 Generating DDX in a Document Authoring System

Suppose our document authoring system is of the kind where it is up to the system to decide *whether* a DDX is called for and, if so, *which document entity* it should refer to, and *what form* it should take. We will analyse the different tasks that face a system of this kind. Section 11.4.1 will focus on the first two questions, while section 11.4.2 addresses the third question. Section 11.4.3 describes architectural issues. Throughout the discussion, the distinction between object-level and meta-level DDX will be crucial.

11.4.1 Determining the content of a description

In the context of DDX generation, when we say *content determination*, we mean the process of determining, at a given point during the generation of a text, whether a DDX is called for and, if so, what document entity it should refer to. Whether the generated DDX is of object-level or meta-level, an important source of information is what we will call the *document description base*, which contains a record of the information conveyed by each relevant document entity.

The document description base

Documents contain document parts (e.g., sections, subsections, paragraphs, lists and pictures) each of which serves to express particular chunks of information. When the document has been produced by an NLG system, it is possible to find out what information is expressed by each document part. In particular, it is not necessary to parse and interpret the document, since the pairing between document parts and domain entities is retrievable from the generation process. The data structure in which this pairing is stored is called the document description base. In this section, we will sketch what type of information the document description base might contain and how the document description base may be constructed.

The document description base records, for referable document entities, what they are 'about'. Aboutness, however, is not a trivial concept. For example, if a section s makes a passing reference to a topic t that is treated much more fully in section s', then the link between s and t is less relevant than that between s' and t. If, for example, an object-level DDX is employed as a means of referring to a domain entity ('the side effects discussed in section 5'), then this is unlikely to help the reader much unless the section in question is associated strongly with the domain entity (i.e., if section 5 is the main repository of information about the side effects in question). We will simplify by not distinguishing the different ways in which a document entity may refer to a domain entity; for example, it will not matter whether the document entity 'discusses', 'introduces', 'enumerates' (or even 'denies the existence of') the domain entity: all are modelled through what we call the `describe` relation.

First of all, we represent the relations between document entities and the domain entities they realise in the form of 'describe' relations. For example, if a section (s) describes the side effects (sfx1) of a medicine, we represent this relation as `describe(s, sfx1)`. Consider, for example, the following paragraph,

> *Estraderm MX patches contain a substance called oestradiol. Oestradiol is a form of oestrogen and belongs to a group of medicines known as Hormone Replacement Therapy (HRT).* (ABPI 1997)

Suppose this paragraph is generated from a structure containing the following chunks of information:

1. Estraderm MX patches contain Oestradiol
2. Oestradiol is an oestrogen
3. Oestradiol is a Hormone Replacement Therapy

This suggests that, at a semantic level, Oestradiol has been described three times whereas each of Estraderm MX patches, oestrogen and Hormone Replacement Therapy has been described only once. This information may be simplified using a variety of methods. One extremely simple quantitative method, for example, might discard all objects except the one most often referred to in each given paragraph:

Document Description Base:
`describe(s, Oestradiol)`

In addition to quantitative methods of this kind, which are familiar from work on *text summarization*, a more direct approach is possible in those systems whose input draws a distinction between central and peripheral information. For example, if the input to the generator uses *rhetorical structures* (Mann & Thompson 1987), which organize texts in hierarchical structures most nodes of which have one *nucleus* and one *satellite*, then this can be taken into account, for example, by allowing the document description base to limit itself to domain entities described by the most nuclear constituent of any given paragraph. Applied to the example, it seems clear that the first sentence corresponds with the most nuclear information expressed in the paragraph, and hence this method suggests that both Estraderm and Oestradiol deserve a place in the document description base:

Document Description Base:
```
describe(s, Oestradiol)
describe(s, Estraderm)
```

Let us assume that a document description base can be built up during generation and move on to the question of how it can be exploited during content determination. Both main types of DDX will be discussed but the main focus of our proposal will involve object-level DDX.

Meta-level Document Deixis

A recent paper has sketched the outlines of a system for the authoring of newspapers, focusing on what happens when articles 'go over the page' (Bateman et al. 2000). In newspapers, this does not always mean that the remainder of the paper follows on the next page, which is why a highly specific document-deictic reference is called for to facilitate reading, which says *'Continued on page x'* or something equivalent to it. The authors analyse this as a mismatch between rhetorical structure (i.e., the structure of the document in terms of rhetorical relations cf. Mann & Thompson 1987) and layout structure, and sketch how such mismatches give rise to 'navigational' pointers.

From our current perspective, the following observations may be made. Firstly, the navigational pointers in question are meta-level DDX aimed at making the newspaper more accessible without changing its truthconditional content. Secondly, the pointers in question do not require the generator to take into account what the remainder of the article is *about*: it suffices to know where it is located. Thirdly, Bateman et al. were able to assume that the system knows in advance where the article is continued. (Some newspapers, for example, invariably put the remainder of any front-page article on the back page.) This makes the generation of DDX considerably easier since it allows them to disregard the architectural problems that are a consequence of the unpredictability of physical realisation (section 11.4.3).

Unfortunately, meta-level DDX are not always so easily finessed. They appear to be motivated by a wide variety of reasons, of which clashes between rhetorical and layout structure are only one. Moreover, the references often do require the generator to know what the document entity in question is 'about'. The point may be illustrated by comparing

> 5a. The final section contains a discussion of our experimental results.
> 5b. The final section compares our results with those of Simon (1970).

In some genres, where experimental results are routinely discussed in the final section, (5a) may be generated using canned text. This, however, is different for (5b), in the absence of similar conventions concerning the place where specific papers are discussed. The generation of (5b) would require the generator to 'know' *which section* has made a comparison with Simon (1970), which is where the document description base comes in.

Of particular relevance in the domain of patient information leaflets is the case where meta-level DDX are generated because semantically or rhetorically related items of information happen to have been separated in the document. One type of case is especially frequent in instructional domains, of which patient information leaflets are an example. To illustrate, suppose a part of the document expresses the information that an effect ('Goal') may be achieved via some procedure ('Method'):

```
Goal: Clean your inhaler
Method: Step 1: Take the inhaler apart
        Step 2: Rinse its components in cold water
        Step 3: Let the components dry in the air
        Step 4: Reassemble the inhaler
```

Suppose, furthermore, that this relation between `Goal` and `Method` is expressed in section x, while some other section y discusses the `Goal` *without* specifying the `Method`. (For example, section y explains that the inhaler must always be cleaned before use, and so on.) Then it is highly natural for this instruction to be accompanied by a reference to section x ('see section x'), since it may be instructive to read section x.

Similar triggers for meta-level DDX include the existence of a gap in the user's vocabulary (Feiner & McKeown 1990). For example, if the generator makes use of a term which is unknown to the reader, and which is discussed in another part of the document defined by a document entity, a reference to this other document part may be added:

'(...) reset your insulin pen to position A (see section 3)'

where section 3 describes how to reset an insulin pen. References of the kinds discussed here appear to be especially useful if x and y are not on the same page and

(a) y occurs in a section of the document that is likely to be skipped, *or*
(b) the document does not have a fixed left-to-right reading order, *or*
(c) x precedes y by a large number of pages.

Differences in style and genre exist, even within a given application domain. In some patient information leaflets, for example, such references are produced whenever the unknown term is used, (sometimes several times within the same section), whereas others use them on first mention only; yet others do not use them at all. Given the function that meta-level DDX have – namely, to make the document more easily accessible – such diversity is to be expected, since different authors can entertain different assumptions about their readership.

Object-level Document Deixis

Object-level DDX versus anaphora. We have seen in section 11.2 that there is more to object-level DDX than reference only. But, if we limit ourselves to restrictive uses of document-deictic information then one can view object-level DDX as abbreviation devices not unlike discourse anaphora: they are employed as a means of avoiding the repetition of a long description which has already been introduced in the discourse. For example, given the antecedent 'a medicine for yellow fever type B', a subsequent reference to the same domain entity can be realised via object-level DDX (e.g., 'the medicine mentioned in chapter 1').

Interestingly, object-level DDX as such appear to be immune from many of the known constraints on discourse anaphora. For example, if a list of pathological symptoms has occurred somewhere in the document but no name has been attached to them, *recency* constraints (e.g., Ariel 1990) prohibit the use of anaphora (e.g., 'they', 'the symptoms', or 'these symptoms') if these symptoms become relevant at a much later place in the document. In such a case, a DDX can be used as an indirect way of referring to the symptoms, *via* the document part that describes them: e.g., 'the symptoms described in Section 1.1'. Note that the specific form of the DDX *can* be constrained by various factors. A DDX of the form 'the symptoms mentioned above', or 'the just-mentioned symptoms' for example, is only felicitous if its 'antecedent' has occurred fairly recently.

In what follows we will assume that the choice between an anaphoric reference and a full, Dale and Reiter-type description has already been made (McCoy & Strube 1999; Krahmer & Theune 1999) and explore how a full description involving document-deictic properties may be made.

Object-level DDX as Dale & Reiter-type descriptions. The semantic function of a restrictive object-level DDX does not differ from that of 'ordinary' referring expressions, namely to single out an object. One obvious approach is to assume that object-level document deictic expressions are constructed in the same way as ordinary referring expressions (see section 11.3.2). Document entities can be viewed as document deictic properties of some of the domain entities they describe, e.g., a domain entity realised as a picture may have, besides all its domain properties, the DDX property 'being described by' the picture, and this property can be used in referring expressions just like any domain property. Thus, we will assume there to be an attribute `DescribedBy` which can have any document entity as its value. The relation with the `describe` relation in the document description base is obvious:

> The domain entity `dom-ent` has the Value `doc-ent` for the Attribute `DescribedBy` iff `describes(doc-ent,dom-ent)` holds in the document description base.

Continuing to assume that the parts of a document are sections ordered in a tree, the permitted values for a given document may be arranged in the form of a tree according to their place in the document. Properties

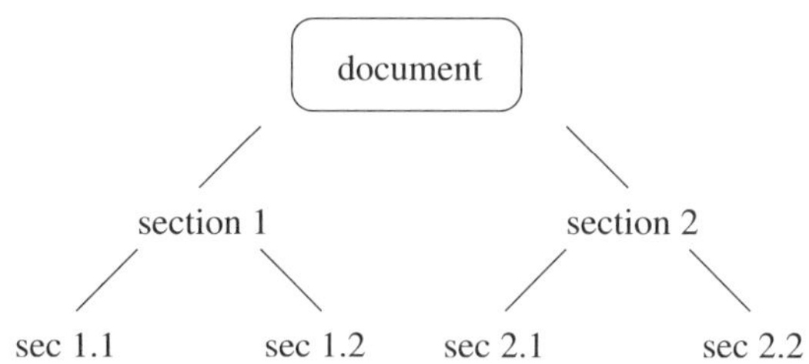

like 'x is described by section 2.1' (where x is a domain entity) will be called *document-related* properties, as opposed to the ordinary, domain-related properties. To appreciate the analogy, suppose the document deals with medicines, for example, then the description 'the tablet *mentioned in section 1.2*' may distinguish one tablet from all others, analogous to an 'ordinary' description like 'the *white* tablet'. As a result, the improved generation algorithm could produce both ordinary descriptions and ones that combine ordinary descriptions with a property consisting of the attribute `DescribedBy` and one of its permitted values.

The problem of overlapping values. There is one problem, however: the tree of values just described instantiates the problem of *overlapping values* (In fact, the problem of overlapping values first occurred to us in the present context.) Suppose sections 1 and 2 describe some of the same medicines, while a is the target object:

> DescribedBy: section 1 ($\{a, b, e\}$), section 2 ($\{a, c, d, f\}$),
> Colour: Brown ($\{a, b\}$), Yellow ($\{c, d\}$)

The Value 'section 1' (being the BestValue of DescribedBy, since it removes more distractors than 'section 2') is chosen first, reducing the initial set C to $\{a, b, e\}$. Now, the algorithm is doomed to end in `Failure`, since the different Values of colour are unable to remove the unwanted b without sacrificing a. None of this can be corrected, since the algorithm does not use backtracking. Note that a uniquely identifying description of a would have been possible if 'section 2' had been chosen instead of 'section 1', leading to a description like 'the brown medicine described in section 2'. In other words, the algorithm fails in a situation where `Success` was perfectly achievable.

A number of possible solutions to this problem are proposed in van Deemter (2002), of which the following seems most appropriate under the present circumstances: a limited kind of backtracking is added to the algorithm, which "remembers" where the algorithm has encountered overlapping Values and, when it results in `Failure`, goes back to the last-encountered situation where it has made a choice between overlapping Values; if this does not lead to `Success`, the algorithm tracks back to the previous choice situation, and so on until no more choice situations are left (`Failure`) or a distinguishing description has been reached. As a result of this modification, the incremental algorithm is guaranteed to find a distinguishing description (possibly involving document-related properties) if one exists.

The choice of basic-level Values. It is interesting to explore the consequences of this approach, which uses the algorithm proposed by Dale and Reiter more or less unamended. In particular, the approach predicts (through the `FindBestValue` attribute) that whenever a section and one of its subsections remove the same number of distractors, the larger section will be chosen, because 'being described by section 1' is more general than 'being described by section 1.2', for example. In many cases, the strategy of favouring less specific properties may be correct, but in the case of document-related properties it would be misguided. To see why, imagine that the object-level document deictic expression serves to identify a particular side effect of a medicine. It is unlikely that the reader keeps in mind exactly which sections discuss which side effects. It is much likelier that she will use the ddx to *look up* where in the leaflet the side effect is described. Clearly, this is easier when the *most* specific (sub)section is mentioned, rather than the *least* specific section.

This means that an alternative approach is called for, which favours the most specific values of the 'described by' attribute. This can be done in two different ways: one possibility is to adapt the algorithm to favour the most specific values of this particular attribute (while still favouring the *least* specific values of all other attributes). A more uniform account is obtained, however, if the DESCRIBEDBY attribute is modelled as having the most specific subsections (i.e., the leaves of the document tree) as its only values, while the algorithm for selecting values is left unchanged:

> `DescribedBy`:
> sec 1.1 ($\{a, b\}$), sec 1.2 ($\{a, e\}$),
> sec 2.1 ($\{a\}$), sec 2.2 ($\{c, d, f\}$)

With this second modification in place, the algorithm will generate references that are easier to interpret than would otherwise have been the case.

When to use document-related properties? It will be convenient to think of this variant of the algorithm (let us call it D&R$_{ddx}$) as separate from one that makes use of domain-related properties only (D&R). Whether to choose the first (and obtain an NP containing a DDX) or the latter (and obtain an ordinary description) is a choice that can be made in different ways, depending on application domain and document genre.

In some genres, the decision for the generation of object-level DDX is linked directly to the layout decisions made during document generation. Papers in linguistics, for instance, make use of enumerated linguistic examples to facilitate reference (e.g., 'see example 17'), and when this happens, object-level DDX appears to be the method of choice. This observation may be incorporated into the Dale & Reiter algorithm by assigning different priorities to document-related properties depending on layout: document-related Attributes that are made salient as a result of layout decisions (e.g., numbering the example sentences) receive higher priority than any other property. The algorithm itself can be used unamended.

In other cases, however, document-related properties are probably better viewed as a repair strategy: ordinary descriptions (i.e., those not using any document-related properties) are the method of choice. In these cases, document-related properties are used to avoid overly long, or otherwise awkward descriptions, reflecting a Gricean-style brevity maxim (Grice 1975). Suppose, for example, the generator has to refer to a particular side effect, discussed in the body of a leaflet (i.e., not marked by numbers, headers, or other layout devices). Suppose, furthermore, that the description produced by D&R – i.e., the one without document-related properties – contains the following long list of properties:

> L = { associated with medicine 1, associated with medicine 2, long-term }

whereas the side effect in question is also the only one to be described in section 1. In a case like this, the length of L might be sufficient reason to use the document-related leading to a description like 'The side effects described in section 1', rather than 'The long-term side effects that are associated with both medicine 1 and medicine 2'. This suggests an algorithm of the following form. ('Output' delivers the output of an algorithm; 'Length' counts the number of properties in a list.)

> $L :=$ Output(D&R)
>
> If Length(L) $> x$ Then
>
> > $L' :=$ Output($D\&R_{ddx}$)
> > If Length(L') $\leq x$ Then $L := L'$

Note that $D\&R_{ddx}$ is only calculated if 'standard' D&R leads to an excessively lengthy description. The best way to measure the length of a description (and the best value for x) has yet to be determined. We conclude this section by listing some remaining problems which have to be addressed:

1. The choice for a particular referent may be influenced by the distance between the DDX and its referent, or by a particular preference order among referent types.
2. Issues of aggregation are to be taken into account. For example, if a particular type of domain entity is described through all subsections of a document section, we may either list the subsections (e.g., 'the symptoms described in section 3.1 and 3.2') or only the main section as a whole (e.g., 'the symptoms described in section 3').
3. The algorithms described so far work as if document-related properties were always completely precise. A more sophisticated version of the algorithm would take vague references like 'above', 'below', 'earlier', etc. into account.

11.4.2 How to refer to a document entity

In this section, we turn to issues of surface realisation, focussing on NPs referring to document entities.[2] As in the case of ordinary referring expressions, linguistic realisation of DDX poses nontrivial problems. Consider a DDX *Re* that refers to the document entity *Rt*. The surface realisation of *Re* can vary between, for example,

'this section',
'section 2',
'the section printed in boldface',
'the section starting on page 5', etc.

We have seen that realisation is, to some extent, genre-dependent. For example, in some genres, pictures are most often referred to by their spatial position on the page (e.g., 'the left-most picture'), but in scientific papers they tend to be referred to via numbers (e.g., 'picture 3.2.'). In the discussion that follows, we will concentrate on references to document entities that are constituents of a hierarchically-organised document such as sections, subsections, pictures, items, etc. References to parts of the document that lie outside such a hierarchy (e.g., pages), although very relevant in some genres (magazines, newspapers, etc.), are virtually non-existent in patient information leaflets and computational linguistics papers and also, of course, in most web-based documents. The following is an example of a hierarchical document made up of sections and enumerated items (A, B, and A). DDX is a special case of

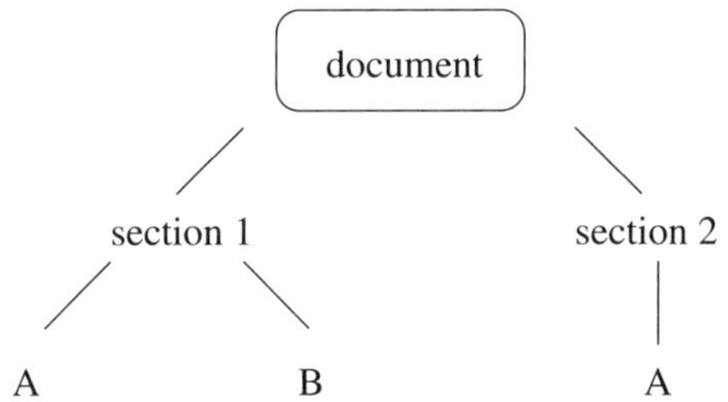

reference, so one might expect to see another application of a Dale and Reiter-style algorithm, perhaps with appropriate modifications (cf. sections 11.3.2 and 11.4.1), applied to a domain of discourse whose elements

[2] Object-level DDX involve referring expressions at two different levels: if the DDX has the syntactic structure $[\ldots [\ldots]_{NP_2} \ldots]_{NP_1}$ then both NP_1 and NP_2 are referring expressions whose generation gives rise to similar (but distinct) questions. Generation of NP_1 was the topic of section 11.4.1; generation of NP_2 is presently under discussion. For a discussion of surface realisation of NPs referring to domain entities, see Shaw & Hatzivassiloglou (1999).

are document entities and whose properties are document-related. There are reasons, however, to use a different approach.

Firstly, when characterizing a document entity, we will disregard domain properties, using layout properties only. Layout properties are of the form ⟨ Attribute,Value ⟩, where Attribute is a layout attribute (e.g., *section number, section title, item number, picture number*). Layout properties must be used in such a way that the hierarchical structure of the document is taken into account, allowing us to distinguish between, for example, picture 5 *of section 1* and picture 5 *of section 2*.

Secondly, and perhaps more interestingly, finding a distinguishing description is sometimes not enough. This issue at hand is akin to what Dale and Reiter called Navigational information (Dale & Reiter 1995). Navigational information is often disregarded, but in the present setting, where we are dealing with domains that are potentially huge, it becomes vital: a felicitous DDX also has to provide information on how to *locate* the referent in the document taking into account the reader's search strategy. In recent experimental work, we found that document-deictic references in hierarchically organised documents are consistent with the assumption that writers seek to minimize the amount of search that readers need to perform to find the referent of the DDX. We assume that readers will initially search for referents locally (e.g., within the subtree representing the section where the referring expression is found) and in case the referent cannot be found, taking into account progressively higher subtrees. This assumption makes possible short descriptions of entities near the referring expression that are not unique with respect to the whole document (e.g., the description "item C" refers to the nearest item labelled as "C"). Note that there are situations in which the reader may be wrongfooted. For example, if the local section (section 1) contains two subsections A and B, and the distinguishing description "subsection C" refers to a subsection in another part (section 2) of the document, the reader may find it difficult to decide to which section the referent (i.e., the subsection) belongs, since the existing document structure suggest it could have been part of the local section: For this reason, our algorithm will sometimes make use of structural information (relating to the hierarchical structure of the document) even in cases where this is not needed for unique identification of a document entity. For example, suppose an item of the document has been assigned the label 'B'. The *Re* 'item B' on its own may be infelicitous if the distance between *Re* and *Rt* is large, even if there is only one item B in the entire document, because the description offers little help in finding the

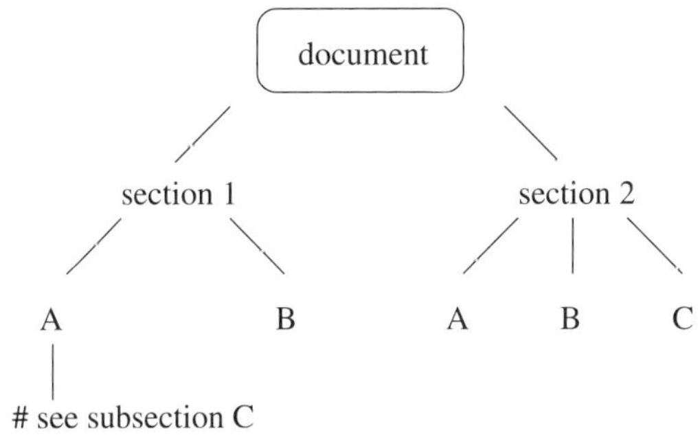

intended referent, which could be located literally *anywhere* in the document. Let us sketch how this idea is formalized.

We will assume that the generator knows, for each layout attribute what its 'scope' is. For example, it can look up whether picture numbers are assigned at the level of the document itself, at one of its main sections, etc. If an attribute is assigned at a document entity x then its values are uniquely distinguishing within x (and possibly in a larger part of the document). In our example, the scope of the layout attribute 'item label', for document entity marked *Rt*, is the subtree rooted in section 1, since items are assigned labels A, B, etc. *per section*.

> Let d be a document tree containing a node n, and let A be a layout Attribute associated with n. Then the *scope* of A with respect to d and n is that ancestor of n where the values of A are assigned.

The notion of scope is utilised as follows (Paraboni 2000):

1. Select the first document entity to be referred to and call it *Rt*.
2. Generate a description of *Rt* making use of an attribute A that distinguishes *Rt* from each of its sibling nodes.
3. If the scope of A includes *Re* then stop.
4. Otherwise, select an ancestor node of *Rt* (typically, its parent node), call this node *Rt* and go back to step 2.

Thus, references are added to the resulting description in hierarchical order, from lowest to highest level. The crucial part of the algorithm is step 3, which states that the reference is complete when the scope subtree of the latest reference includes *Re*. Let us illustrate the procedure, once again assuming a document structure made up of sections 1 and 2 containing enumerated items A and B (as depicted above). Now a reference in section 2 to item B in the previous section has to include information about the section which contains the referent, even though "item B" is a distinguishing description within the entire document: One

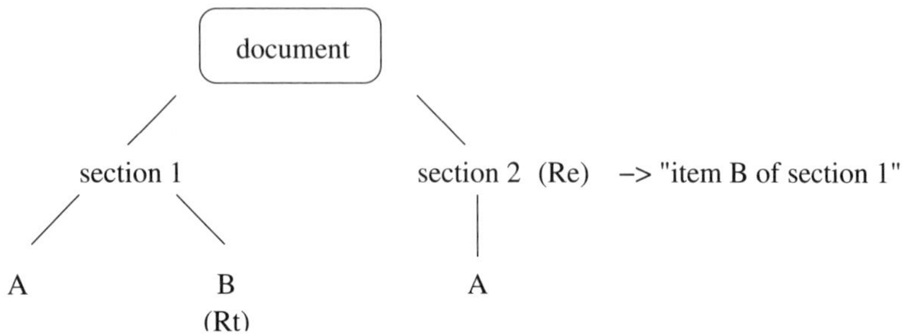

way to see why hierarchical information is required for the description of Rt is that, although this is not necessary for the unique identification of Rt itself, hierarchical information *would* be necessary to identify Rt's sibling ('part A of section 1').

Navigational issues are not confined to document-deictic references. In fact, it appears that issues analogous to the ones discussed here arise in relation to all other hierarchically structured domains. Consider, for example, a speaker located in a building b_1 of a University campus, who refers to a room in another building b_2 of the same campus: even if b_2 is the only building with as many as 6 floors, it is more helpful (and therefore more felicitous) to refer to it as 'room 603 *of building* b_2' than simply as 'room 603'. Making utterances *easy to interpret* (e.g., making it easy to find the referents of referring expressions) is an important issue which, we believe, deserves to be taken into account much more widely in Natural Language Generation.

This concludes our discussion of the algorithm for referring to document entities. The account can be extended to many other kinds of attributes, such as spatial relations (e.g., "above", "below" etc.) which cannot, however, be discussed here.

11.4.3 Architectural Issues

The issues discussed so far, although most crucial in an NLG context are also at least indirectly relevant for interpretation. If a text says 'item B of the list in section 4.3.2', for example, a reader will normally understand that 4.3.2 is not the present section.[3] Something similar is true to

[3] For a discussion of the connection between Gricean maxims and the interpretation of referring expressions, see Dale & Reiter (1995).

the issues discussed in what follows: they are most directly relevant to NLG, but there are obvious ramifications for *incremental interpretation* (e.g., Kempson et al. 2000).

One potential issue in this area concerns meta-level DDX, which pose the question where they come from, given that they do not add to the truthconditional content of the text (section 11.2). If, for example, the input to the generator is based on Rhetorical Structure Theory, then the most obvious approach is to let Rhetorical Structure distinguish between a document with and without a given DDX. (In the first case, the content of the sentence containing the DDX might, for example, stand in an ELABORATE relation to that of some other text span.) But if this is the case, then the generator's autonomous decision to generate a DDX involves changing its own input. The alternative is to make DDX a lower-level decision which does not affect Rhetorical Structure, in which case there appear to be no architectural consequences.

A more general problem, which can arise in connection with both types of DDX, concerns the order in which the several subtasks of the generation process are to be carried out. For example, in the pipelined NLG architecture that is often applied in NLG (Reiter 1994), linguistic realisation has to wait until late in the generation process. Normally – unless a DDX has somehow been anticipated – this will mean that the document description base (cf. section 11.4.1) is not available when DDX are generated. More precisely, if a document entity has not been 'created' (or specified in sufficient detail) by the time the NLG system has to refer to it, the document description base cannot be produced and, therefore, neither meta-level nor object-level DDX can be generated. For example,

1. *Dependency between surface realisation and* DDX*:* the realisation of references to the text (e.g., 'Read the section entitled "how to use your medicine"') may not be possible if the referred text has not been realised yet. For example, if realisations operates from left to right, then forward-referencing DDX (where *Rt* occurs to the right of *Re*) become problematic. This is analogous to problems with the interpretation and generation of *kataphoric* (i.e., forward-anaphoric) references (van Deemter 1990). The following two problems appear to be specific to DDX generation.

2. *Dependency between layout and* DDX*:* the realisation of references making use of layout properties (e.g., 'Read section *B*') may not be possible if the referred layout property has not been generated yet.

3. *Dependency between page model and* DDX*:* since the text of the referring expression is part of the same document which contains the referent, the surface realisation of a DDX containing a page number may move the intended referent to the next page of the document, causing the DDX to point to the wrong place.

It is interesting to see how similar problems in the area of multimedia document generation have been tackled in McKeown et al. (1992). Among other things, the COMET system generates descriptions like 'the old holding battery shown in a separate picture', where the problem is to let the Referring Expressions Generation module know that the battery happens to be shown in a separate picture, reflecting a decision by the Realisation module. McKeown et al. tackled the problem by using logical forms as the basis of the different components of a multimedia generator, the subformulas of which are annotated with information about media choice. By using the logical forms in this way, they play the role of a *blackboard* onto which the multimedia generator can write what combination of media is employed to express certain things, and from which the generator can read information of the same type. In the case of COMET, media choice appears to be the only kind of annotation employed, but this idea may be generalized to include the fact that something is expressed in the second picture occurring in section 3, for example. A solution along these lines is compatible with the use of a document description base, but it would be a radical departure from pipelined architectures and a stark generalization of the work on COMET as well. The alternative would be a two-phase generator whose first phase generates a document containing preliminary DDX expressions; in a revision phase, the DDX are adjusted so as to correspond to the actual realisation of the document.[4]

We have seen that document-deictic expressions can be dependent on subtle layout features of the document. Accordingly, some layout features of the document seem to be specifically chosen to facilitate DDX. A case in point is the use of numbered examples in scientific papers, which allow the use of references like 'Example 1.2.1. shows that...' etc. But, of course, authors may change their minds. Ideally, therefore, a document authoring system allows authors to jump back and forth through a document, for example, adding layout features to facilitate document-deictic reference. Issues of this kind do not concern the architecture of an NLG system proper, but they are crucial to the architecture of a document

[4]Compare Inui et al. (1992) for a different motivation for a two-phase generation architecture.

authoring system (Power & Scott 1998).

11.5 Conclusion

Having introduced the phenomenon of document deixis and having discussed briefly how it differs from other types of context-sensitive referring expressions, such as anaphora and discourse deixis, we have explored how the two main kinds of document deictic expression, object-level and meta-level DDX, may be produced by a Natural Language Generation program. Efforts at implementing the ideas in this paper are underway. An algorithm for generating references to document parts (see section 11.4.2), for example, has been described in Paraboni (2000).

Although meta-level and object-level DDX raise partly different issues for a generator, there are also important commonalities between them. Both, for example, can make use of what we have called a Document Description base, an information source which is generated as a side effect of the generated document (Section 2.1), and both pose some difficult problems for traditional NLG architectures, mainly with respect to the dependency between document content and layout (Section 4.4).

We have devoted most of our attention in this paper to object-level DDX, which make use of a combination of domain-related and document-related properties to characterize a domain entity. The fact that the document-related properties of which object-level DDX make use (e.g., 'being described in section 3.2') refer to the inhabitants of a secondary, potentially huge, and spatially structured domain (namely the document itself) makes the generation of object-level DDX an intriguing area for investigation of various aspects of reference.

Firstly, we have argued that the spatial nature of this secondary domain poses a challenge to traditional referring expressions generation algorithms such as presented in Dale & Reiter (1995) because it highlights the problems that arise when the Values of an Attribute overlap, and we have shown how this limitation may be removed.

Secondly, we have argued that the hierarchical structure of the domain (i.e., the document itself), tends to make the problem of finding a uniquely distinguishing description relatively easy, whereas the potentially great size of the domain tends to make navigational issues of paramount importance. This issue has come up in two different guises.

a. It is often necessary to include additional properties into a description, over and above the ones that uniquely distinguish a document entity. For example, even when a document contains only one item labelled as 'B', it is normally necessary when referring to the item, to add in which part of the document (e.g., in which section) the item occurs.

b. Consider a situation in which it is useful (either for ensuring uniqueness or to make the reference easier to interpret) to include a document-related property. Then the usual assumption, that general properties are better than specific ones is not always valid. For example, if an object was described in section 2 only once, namely in section 2.3.1, then it is better to refer to it as being 'described in section 2.3.1' than as 'described in section 2'.

Finally, we have discussed a number of ways in which the generation of document deixis poses an architectural challenge to existing NLG (and document authoring) systems. Some of these challenge the assumption that NLG systems follow a pipeline model (Reiter 1994); others challenge the assumption that generation of a text operates basically from left to right. Space has not allowed us to discuss questions about system architecture in great detail, and their resolution must partly be left to future research.

11.6 Acknowledgements

We thank Richard Power, John Bateman, and the anonymous reviewers for insightful comments and advice. This work is part of an ongoing PhD project of the first author and has been supported by the CNPq, the Brazilian Research Council. Parts of the work are based on an analysis of a corpus of Patient Information Leaflets that was developed in the ICONOCLAST and GNOME projects, funded by the UK's EPSRC under grant references GR/L77102 and L51126.)

References

Mira Ariel: 1990, *Accessing Noun-Phrase Antecedents*, Routledge.

The Association of the British Pharmaceutical Industry: 1997, *1996-1997 ABPI Compendium of Patient Information Leaflets.*

Elisabeth André and Thomas Rist: 1994, *Referring to World Objects with text and Pictures.* in: proceedings of Coling'94.

Nicholas Asher: 1993, *Reference to Abstract Objects.* Kluwer Academic Publishers, Dordrecht, The Netherlands.

Jon Barwise and John Etchemendy: 1987, *The Liar; An Essay on Truth and Circularity.* Cambridge University Press.

John Bateman, Judy Delin and Patrick Allen: 2000, *Constraints on Lay-*

out in Multimodal Document Generation. in: proceedings of the INLG-2000 workshop 'Coherence in Generated Multimedia', Mitzpe Ramon, Israel.

Bouayad-Agha, N. Scott, D. R. and Power, R. J. D.: 2000, *Integrating Content and Style in Documents: a case study of Patient Information Leaflets.* Information Design Journal, 9 (2-3), pp.161-176.

Robert Dale and Ehud Reiter: 1995, *Computational interpretations of the Gricean maxims in the generation of referring expressions.* Cognitive Science (19).

Miriam Eckert and Michael Strube: 1999, *Resolving Discourse Deictic Anaphora in Dialogues.* in: proceedings of EACL'99.

Steven K. Feiner and Kathleen R. McKeown: 1990, *Coordinating Text and Graphics in Explanation Generation.* in: proceedings of AAAI-90.

H.P. Grice: 1975, *Logic and Conversation.* Cole and Morgan (Eds.) Syntax and Semantics, Vol.iii: Speech Acts. New York, Academic Press.

Douglas R. Hofstadter: 1985, *Metamagical themes: questing for the essence of mind and pattern.* Penguin Books Ltd, Harmondsworth, England.

K. Inui, T. Tokunaga, and H. Tanaka: 1992, *Text Revision: A Model and its Implementation.* 6th International Workshop on NLG, Trento.

Ruth Kempson, Wilfried Meyer Viol, and Dov Gabbay: 2000, *Dynamic Syntax.* Blackwell.

Emiel Krahmer and Mariët Theune: (This volume), *Efficient Context-Sensitive Generation of Referring Expressions.*

Stephen C. Levinson: 1983, *Pragmatics.* Cambridge University Press.

John Lyons: 1977, *Semantics.* Cambridge University Press.

William C. Mann and Sandra A. Thompson: 1987, *Rhetorical Structure Theory: A Theory of Text Organization.* L. Polanyi (ed.) The Structure of Discourse. Ablex, Norwood, NJ, USA.

Kathleen F. McCoy and Michael Strube: 1999, *Generating Anaphoric Expressions: Pronoun or Definite Description?* in: proceedings of workshop 'The Relation of Discourse/Dialogue Structure and Reference', associated with ACL99. University of Maryland, USA.

Kathleen McKeown et al: 1992, *Generating Cross-References for Multimedia Explanation.* in: proceedings of AAAI-92.

Ivandré Paraboni and Kees van Deemter: 1999, *Issues for the Generation of Document Deixis.* in: proceedings of the workshop 'Deixis, Demonstration and Deictic Belief', ESSLLI 1999, Utrecht, The Netherlands.

Ivandré Paraboni: 2000, *An Algorithm for Generating Document-deictic References.* in: proceedings of the INLG-2000 workshop 'Coherence in Generated Multimedia', Mitzpe Ramon, Israel.

Rebecca Passonneau: 1998, *Interaction of Discourse Structure with Explicitness of Discourse Anaphoric Noun Phrases.* M.Walker, A.Joshi, and E.Prince (Eds.) Centering Theory in Discourse. Clarendon Press, Oxford, UK.

Richard Power and Donia Scott: 1998, *Multilingual Authoring using Feedback Texts.* in: proceedings of COLING/ACL conference, Montreal.

Ehud Reiter: 1994, *Has a consensus NL generation architecture appeared and is it psycholinguistically plausible?* in: proceedings of the 7th International Natural Language Generation Workshop, pp.163-170, Maine U.S.A.

James Shaw and Vasileios Hatzivassiloglou: 1999, *Ordering Among Premodifiers.* in: proceedings of ACL'99, University of Maryland.

Kees van Deemter: 1990, *Forward References in Natural Language.* Journal of Semantics 7: pp.281-300.

Kees van Deemter and Rodger Kibble: 2000, *On Coreferring: Coreference in MUC and Related Annotation Schemes. Computational Linguistics* 26 (4), pp. 629-637.

Kees van Deemter: 2002, *Generating Referring Expressions: Boolean Extensions of the Incremental Algorithm. Computational Linguistics* 28 (1), pp.37-52.

Bonnie Lynn Webber: 1991, *Structure and Ostension in the Interpretation of Discourse deixis.* Language and Cognitive Processes 6(2) May 1991, pp. 107-135.

12

Some Observations on Deixis to Properties

ELIZABETH KLIPPLE AND JOHN GURNEY

12.1 Introduction

In this chapter we discuss deictic reference to properties. [1] For the most part research on reference, demonstratives, and deixis has occupied itself with referring to speakers, hearers, places, times, events, and physical objects. We discuss some rather different forms of deixis, exemplified by:

(1) a. Don't go *that fast.*
    b. Keep going in *this direction.*
    c. The toaster is *this big.* [holding up two hands]
    d. Walk *this far.* [indicating on a map]
    e. I'd like to fly *that high.* [said with an airplane visible in the sky]
    f. Don't sew the hem *that carefully*; you'll never finish.
    g. *This* is too fast. [said while seated in a speeding car]
    h. She's not as tall as *that.* [pointing at a measure on a height chart]

In these examples and nearly all to follow we are interested in the nonanaphoric, nondescriptive readings of the demonstrative phrases.[2]

[1]We have benefited from critical comments by anonymous referees and by participants in the Workshop on Deixis, Demonstration, and Deictic Belief at ESSLLI XI, Utrecht as well as discussions with Paul Pietroski. We are also happy to acknowledge Timothy Gregory, Steve Choy, Dekang Lin, and Robert Winkler for various software.

[2]Many linguists (e.g. Fillmore 1971, Heim and Kratzer 1998, and Lyons 1999), have pointed out that the forms of words used in deixis can also be used nondeictically

Information Sharing: Reference and Presupposition in Language Generation and Interpretation.
Edited by Kees van Deemter and Rodger Kibble.

With that understood, these examples differ from those normally discussed in research on demonstratives in that:

1. They involve reference not to objects, places or times, but to properties of events and objects;
2. Pointing gestures are generally inappropriate with these, although another sort of gesture is sometimes helpful;
3. The overt demonstrative lexemes *that*, *this*, and *so* are often associated with adverbs and adjectives.

Regarding point 1, some clarification of what we mean by the word *properties* may be helpful. People often say that length is a property, and also color, redness, and beauty. People say that physical objects have properties. A tree has height, weight, color, and so on. People also say that a tree has *a* height, *a* weight, and *a* color. We think people are talking about different kinds of things when they use the word *property* in these two ways. In this chapter we are chiefly interested in what one might call particular properties. These include the particular height of a tree, its particular color or color scheme, and its particular weight. Perhaps the tree is four meters tall. Then one of its properties is that height, a height of four meters. We can use these and other forms of language to denote that height.

Particular heights are (perhaps complex) abstract entities. They have numerical aspects but, of course, they are not just numbers; a height is not a number, even though a height of three meters is one meter greater than a height of two meters. A further point of clarification is this: We hold that events also have properties. The speed of a running at some instant is a property of the running event as well as the direction, acceleration, and so on.[3]

We propose that the sentences in (1) are cases of deixis to particular properties. Therefore, achieving successful reference and understanding which property is referred to will depend in a certain way on the imme-

---

when bound by quantifiers or when used as anaphors like *that high* in: *I can jump five feet off the ground. Can you jump that high?* This anaphoric versus deictic difference is generally found with both the more usual deictic reference to objects and places, and our deixis to properties. We are focusing on cases of deixis, but in most cases the same expressions used as deictic demonstratives can be used anaphorically in a sentence or discourse. Also, it should be noted that pronouns such as *he*, *she*, *it*, and *they* can be used as demonstratives, although their more common use may be anaphoric.

[3]Some people (including Klein 1980, Zwarts 1993, and Rullmann 1995) seem to use the term *degree* to name the same thing that we call 'particular property'; although in other works *degree* seems to indicate only something like numerical value. We return to this issue in Section 12.6 where we discuss truth conditions and logical forms.

diate context (Cf. Kaplan 1989).[4]

Deixis to properties raises questions on several fronts: reference, perception, gesture, the lexicon, syntax, and semantics. Our discussion makes observations and proposals about all of these. The scope of this chapter is broad because we think it is worthwhile to think about these components and the relations among them all at one time.

Our discussion will proceed as follows. First, we review the general theory of deixis and reference that we accept, based on the investigations of Kripke 1972, Kaplan 1989, and Dretske 1981, in Section 12.2. Next, we offer arguments for bringing property deixis under this general theory, in Section 12.3. In Section 12.4, we discuss certain semantic properties that are peculiar to adjectives and adverbs, and which influence and interact with our treatment of deixis to properties, which is further elaborated in Section 12.6.

In Section 12.5, we discuss some syntactic issues concerning some typically deictic words, usually called 'demonstratives' in the syntax literature, and consider the syntactic form of AdjPs and AdvPs containing them.

Following that, in Section 12.6, we consider logical forms that could correspond to the sentences and phrases containing deixis to properties. Although demonstrative noun phrases such as *that height* and *this length* can also be used to refer to properties, most of our discussion is about the adverbial and adjectival demonstratives like the ones given in (1), which have been least discussed in the literature. We concentrate on points that matter most to deixis. We do not, therefore, go very far toward integrating this into a complete theory (dealing with comparatives, superlatives, positives, etc.) of the meanings of the types of adjectives and adverbs we have selected to study. We do, however, provide a preliminary discussion in Section 12.6.[5]

We discuss the role of gesture in property deixis in Section 12.7. We will see that the need for gesture is not as great with some sorts of deixis to properties as it is for NPs, and also that the gestures used with property deixis are often not pointing gestures.

Consideration of deixis to properties gives insight into the nature of deixis and demonstratives. We hope to show, however, that it does not raise any special problems for a theory of deixis. We argue that grounded reference is needed in order for a demonstrative expression to succeed. Successful reference through deixis, however, needs to be

[4]See Fillmore 1971, Levinson 1983, and Lyons 1977, for similar but less explicit views.

[5]For work on these issues, though with little emphasis on deixis, see Klein 1980, Ludlow 1989, Larson and Segal 1995, and Zwarts 1993.

distinguished from successful communication of reference; the former can occur without the latter.

Finally, in Section 12.8, we consider all of this with respect to a computational application which we have developed, a natural language interface to a virtual reality (VR) model of the world, the Natural Language and Virtual Reality (NLVR) system. Deictic reference to properties of events arises in this application. We also mention a semi-autonomous robot (developed by colleagues) that detects and interprets some of the gestures used in deixis to properties. In these systems, the contribution of nondescriptive cognition in language understanding is prominent. So the distinction between direct reference and description may be seen more clearly in them than in other computational natural language processing systems, most of which are language bound.

12.2 Referential Theory of Names and Demonstratives

In this section we offer a review of some of the claims of a prominent referential theory of names and demonstratives.[6] This is based on the original work of Kripke 1972 and Kaplan 1989. Our purpose is simply to make some of this theory available for the discussion of property deixis in the following section.

Names include the ones all of us use like *Aristotle*, *John*, and *Baltimore*. Demonstratives include 'the pronouns *I*, *my*, *you*, *he*, *his*, *she*, *it*, the demonstrative pronouns *that*, *this*, the adverbs *here*, *now*, *tomorrow*, *yesterday*, the adjectives *actual*, *present*, and others' (Kaplan 1989). These are simple demonstratives; the complex demonstratives covered by the theory include all the demonstrative noun phrases like *that man*, *this hotel*, *that city*, *this party*. Virtually all work in this tradition deals only with demonstrata (things referred to) that are individuals such as physical objects, times, places, and events. The tradition generally neglects the complex adjectival and adverbial phrases like *that fast* and those in example (1). (We discuss these in Section 12.3.1 and following.)

Kripke and others argue for what we will call the 'Kripke/Kaplan' theory of reference at some length, defending it against an alternative called the 'description theory' of reference, which had been held by most interested parties for most of the 20th century and still remains tempting if not defensible.[7] A rough and ready bit of reasoning in favor of a description theory runs like this: You've never met Aristotle, yet you can talk about him, ask questions, and so on. How is this possible?

[6]Section 12.2 can be skipped by readers who are familiar with Kripke 1972, Kaplan 1989, and Dretske 1981. However, this section is based on our interpretation of these works.

[7]For a sustained defense of the description theory see Neale 1990.

All you know about him are some facts relating Aristotle to Greece, philosophy, Plato, Alexander, etc. So for you, *Aristotle* must amount to nothing more than all these facts. I.e. *Aristotle* simply means *the student of Plato who ....* This kind of thinking may account for some of the pull of the description theory.[8]

The Kripke/Kaplan theory holds that names and deictic expressions are not disguised descriptions, and so it needs to say what they are instead. Here are some of the claims of this theory:

RT1. Names and demonstratives are rigid designators.

One way to articulate this point is the following formula:

(2) $\forall a \forall b [\ulcorner a = b \rightarrow \Box(a = b)\urcorner \text{ is true}]$[9]

where the variables **a** and **b** range over names and deictic demonstratives.

One instance of this rule would state (informally): Suppose you say *Octavius is identical to Augustus* and what you say is true. In that case you are correctly using the names *Octavius* and *Augustus* to refer to the same person. You could also have said *Octavius is necessarily identical to Augustus* or *Octavius must be Augustus* both truly. On the other hand if you said *Octavius might not be Augustus* or *It's possible that Octavius is not Augustus* these would be false.[10]

RT2. Many uses of definite descriptions are not rigid designators.

Suppose you say *The winner of the race is the winner of the long jump* and that is true. In this case you could not truly say *The winner of the race is necessarily identical to the winner of the long jump.* The first winner could have lost the long jump.

RT3. Names when used to refer are not disguised definite descriptions.

You generally cannot substitute a description for a name in an utterance without changing the meaning of the utterance. More on this later in this section.

RT4. Demonstratives when used deictically are not disguised definite descriptions.

You generally cannot substitute a description for a deictic expression

[8] These theories have variants which we do not take the space to articulate here.

[9] A paraphrase reads: All utterances that have the form *If a is identical to b then a is necessarily identical to b* will be true, on condition that names or demonstratives substitute for *a* and *b*.

[10] In all cases the modalities are what Kripke might call metaphysical, not epistemic.

in an utterance without changing the meaning of the utterance. Again, there will be more on this later in this section.

RT5. Names and deictic expressions are directly referential.

If you say *That tree is too big* and there is no object that is in fact the referent of *that tree* then what you said has no truth value. The referent must exist and, of course, be, by some criterion (see CT1 below), the actual referent in order for *that tree* to make a contribution to the meaning of the utterance. On the other hand, if you said *A tree in Kensington fell down yesterday* and Kensington has no trees then what you said is just false, not incomplete or without truth value.

RT1 is an empirical claim about how we, at least sometimes, use names and deixis. We take RT2 also as an empirical claim, though obvious. RT1 is intended to gain in support and likewise lend support to RT3 and RT4 from a number of philosophical arguments. The strongest arguments for all of this are the argument from ignorance and the argument from error (see Kripke 1972). For our purposes we mention two other so-called modal arguments, MA1 and MA2, below. The strategy here is to systematically point out that various proposed likely definite descriptions are not substitutable for a given name or a given deictic expression.

MA1. *Aristotle* does not mean *the philosopher who taught Alexander and was a student of Plato* because it is possible (even if not true) that Aristotle might have never made his initial journey to Athens.

MA2. *That tree* does not mean The tree I am pointing at because (a) if you say *The tree I am now pointing at is that tree*, this is not necessarily true (you might have been pointing at another tree) and (b) if you say *I am now pointing at that tree* this is *not* necessarily true.

MA1 and MA2 are evidence for RT3 and RT4. The rigid designation thesis RT1 would explain why we keep failing to come up with the right definite description that works for a name or a deictic expression. So RT1 explains RT3 and RT4.

Direct support for RT5 comes from the observations it makes about the difference between not completing a proposition and saying something false. Indirect support comes from including it with R1 through R4 in the overall theory. If names and deictic expressions do not succeed in referring via satisfaction of some supposedly equivalent description then they must do the referring more directly.

This leaves an important question: Names and deictic expressions actually can be used to refer to particular people, trees, etc. What makes it the case that when you say *That tree is too tall* you are referring to one tree rather than another, say, the one right next to it? Since *that tree* cannot be captured by any description it would seem that there is no unique description that could serve. The 'causal theory' of reference offers an answer to this question. Here we will use one aspect of a 'flow of information' version of the causal theory loosely based on Dretske 1981.

> CT1. An utterance of a referring expression must be properly informationally related with an individual (entity, time, place, etc.) in order for the expression to count as referring.

In other words, if you say *That tree fell down*, the tree to which you are referring is the one which is itself the source of information that is responsible for the eventual utterance of *that tree.* In the case of deictic expressions like *that tree* we can be more explicit: You need to perceive the tree; it is the perceptual information that counts. This means that it is not enough for the tree to be close by or in the current context (whatever that means).

Here is another gloss on CT1. If you say *That tree is too tall* when faced with two or more trees you are in fact referring to one of them if you in fact had one in mind or intended to refer to one of them. And the one you had in mind was the one you were looking at or thinking about or concentrating on. CT1 tries to explain all this mental talk in terms of information reaching you and ultimately determining your utterance.[11]

12.3 Property Deixis

Our method will be to discuss various examples of property deixis, assimilating them to the above principles that were developed for their deictic cousins. The point will be that parallel considerations of the data support parallel conclusions.

12.3.1 Rigid Property Designators

The argument that property demonstratives are rigid designators proceeds by showing that they are not equivalent to proposed likely definite descriptions. Deictic property demonstratives can take the form of noun phrases *that speed*, adjective phrases *that tall*, and adverb phrases *that*

[11]One consequence of this approach is that a deictic expression succeeds in referring as long as the person uttering it (or otherwise using it) perceives it, regardless of whether a hearer can identify the correct referent as well. Of course, for communication to succeed, the hearer must be able to pick out the speaker's referent, and for this a gesture or some other means of identifying salience may be required; but gestures and salience are not essential to deictic reference itself.

fast. The noun phrases like *this speed* and *that length* are the most parallel to the demonstratives mentioned above in the last section. However, our investigation concentrates not on these noun phrases but rather on adjectival and adverbial phrases like *that fast* and *this big*, which have received less attention in the semantics literature.

This choice of cases to investigate might raise at least initial doubts about our thesis for some people. Sentences like *My tree is that tall* refer to a tree and predicate something of the tree. Predication is often the role of descriptions, so a good proposal might be that the phrase *that tall* is really just a description.

To investigate whether a description theory of deixis to properties will succeed consider first the following two imperatives, the first of which uses a deictic adverb phrase:

(3) a. Always go that fast.
    b. Always go as fast as that car.

Assume you point at a car zooming past. Since you point at the car, it might seem plausible to propose that (3a) means no more and no less than (3b). After all, if a pointing were required, as entertained by Kaplan, it seems you must be pointing at the car. Hence, there may be a hidden deictic reference to the car in (3a) which is not hidden in (3b). Indeed, how could you point at a speed (as would seem to be required for (3a))? We will return to this question about the role of pointing in property deixis in Section 12.7. For now, we would like to observe that (3a) does not mean (3b). If the car is presently going fifty miles per hour, then you need to always go fifty miles per hour in order to do (3a). While to do (3b) you need to go whatever speed the car is going at the time. Compare (3b) to *always work as hard as the fellow next to you.* Our explanation for the failure of the translation is predictable; *that fast* is a rigid designator of that speed of the car, while *as fast as that car* contains a nonrigid description of the speed, although of course the reference to the car itself is rigid.

Example (3b) is not decisive because the description theorist could either propose that (3b) is elliptical for (4) or simply that (4) itself has the meaning of (3a).

(4) Always go as fast as that (car) is going now.

This translation of (3a) attempts to achieve the rigidity of (3a) through a definite description that itself contains two rigid designators (of the car and of the present time) while disallowing any rigid designator of a property.[12]

[12]We could call this a nominalist translation.

Recalling that we regard our proposals as empirically supported explanations of various linguistic facts (this one and several to follow), we do not need to regard our analysis of (3a) as metaphysically necessary. Nevertheless, we can carry the argument about this last sort of attempted translation one step further. Consider an appropriate analog to *I am now pointing at that tree* (the example used in MA2 in Section 12.2):

(5) a. We are now going this fast.
    b. We are now going as fast as we are going now.

In (5b) a plausible definite description translation has been substituted for *this fast.* Assume we are in the car going fifty miles per hour and *this fast* refers to our current speed. Then (5a) is true but not necessarily true. We could have been going thirty miles per hour. However, (5b) is, of course, necessarily true. So (5a) and (5b) have different meanings.

This case is similar to another familiar case that has been used to elucidate rigid designation by indexicals that denote the speaker, his location, and the current time:

(6) I am here now.

(6) is true whenever spoken but not necessarily true. You could have been somewhere else now. Analogously if

(7) That tree is that tall.

succeeds in expressing a proposition, then it is true but not necessarily true. It is not necessary that the tree is thirty-five feet tall.

Based on these cases alone, it seems likely that *this fast* and *that fast* are rigid designators and also that they are not descriptions, hence directly referring.

12.3.2 Direct Property Deixis

In this section we provide reasons for thinking that property demonstratives used deictically are directly referring in Kaplan's sense. These reasons should also help clarify the notion of deictic reference to properties.

1. If deictic property expressions are directly referring, then that explains why they are rigid designators. This point is exactly parallel to the earlier point about other demonstratives and names.

2. There may be no effective rule for constructing the appropriate definite description that works for all cases. Consider the following three cases:

(8) a. Go that way. [pointing North]
    b. He ran that far. [pointing at a marker]

c. I caught a fish this big. [holding up two hands separated]

For a nondeictic translation each of these would need a very different definite description:

(9) a. Go the direction of the vector running through my arm.
b. He ran as far as the distance to that (marker).
c. I caught a fish as big as the distance between my hands.

So why not assume the deictic expressions refer directly rather than standing in for these various definite descriptions?

3. The following sentences each contain one property demonstrative. And each of them must be uttered in the right sort of context in order to succeed in expressing a determinate question.

(10) a. Can you do sums that fast?
b. Are you that honest?
c. Is your tree exactly that tall?

For (10a) you may be watching a whiz kid do arithmetic. For (10b) perhaps you observe someone return a lost umbrella. The point is this: These questions are not felicitous if you are pointing at a kid winning a spelling bee, in (10a); if you observe the fellow simply waiting for a train, in (10b).

Unlike these deictic questions, the following as-A-as questions do not require the above sorts of context (where the property itself is salient).

(11) a. Can you do sums as fast as that (guy)?
b. Are you as honest as that fellow?
c. Is your tree exactly as tall as that (tree)?

This suggests not only that the descriptions and the demonstratives are not equivalent; it also suggests that for (10) the properties (alacrity at sums, honesty) must be in some way contextually perceived (or otherwise cognizable). You need to see the kid adding in order to state or understand the question. Perception of the kid doing arithmetic is what makes it the case that you are referring to the kid's alacrity and not that of someone else. Likewise, if the top half of the tree were obscured by a cloud then (10c) would fail to express a question while (11c) still would.

12.3.3 Perception of Properties

In this section we look at the possible application of CT1 to direct reference to properties.

When you point at a tree and ask *Is your tree that tall?* you are, of course, pointing to the tree. You are pointing to the tree because this is the object that has the property you want to refer to. A good hypothesis is that you need to see (or have other cognitive/perceptual access to) the property; seeing is one route to the nondescriptive access required for all direct reference. Here you do that by looking at the tree. Looking at the tree helps but is not sufficient. If the top of the tree were obscured in a cloud, your attempted deictic reference to its height would fail. You would not see how tall the tree is. There are other expressions ready at hand that presuppose that this kind of perception is possible:

(12) a. Can you see how tall that tree is?
b. Let me hear how quietly you kids can play.
c. I did not feel how warm the stove was.

Most of the properties we have considered have a scalar structure. Some, like height, permit a real number metric. Others, like loveliness, as used in:

(13) My garden is not nearly this lovely.

may not have the full metric of height. Nevertheless, in all of these cases one is referring to a particular property. You are not referring to the abstract properties of height or beauty. You are referring to the particular height or beauty of this tree or this garden. If the tree is fifty feet three inches tall you are referring to a height of fifty feet and three inches whether you know this or not. This is no different than referring to a man who happens to be a train spotter whether you know this about him or not. We will return to this point in Section 12.8, where we discuss our implementation of deictic reference in the VR system.

We are suggesting that people who successfully use deictic reference to properties must often be able to see how tall or lovely or fast something is. This is not the same as seeing *that* something is tall or lovely or fast. In the first place, the thing may not be tall or fast. You can see how fast a slow car is. (We say a little more about the logic of these adjectives and adverbs in the next section.) Nor is it seeing that the thing is, say, fifty feet three inches tall (in the case of the tree). If you see that the tree is fifty feet three inches tall, you know it is that tall; but you may not know this even though you see how tall it is. Also, you may see that the tree is fifty feet three inches tall without seeing the tree or (we would venture) seeing how tall it is. Perhaps you looked it up in a book. We propose that reading the book may not properly ground the deixis in (12a). However, it is clear that devices and instruments can mediate this kind of perception. You can see how hot the boiler is by looking at its temperature gauge.[13]

[13]Without the gauge you need to touch it in order to feel how hot it is. In both cases you are perceiving something. See Dretske 1969 and Dretske 1981 for more complete

The role of human perception in deixis to properties needs further investigation. Short of this, we describe our NLVR system in Section 12.8. NLVR is a simulation of both the deixis and the perception.

12.4 Semantics of Adverbs and Adjectives

In this section we note some observations about scalar properties, adjectives, and adverbs. We restrict the discussion to observations relevant to the deictic uses.

12.4.1 Properties and Scales

As mentioned above, many properties are naturally thought of as having values on a scale. The scale can be assigned actual numerical values, as with temperature, speed, size, weight, distance, and age, because these are properties for which scientists and others have developed scales. Some numerically treated properties are multidimensional, such as color, location on a map or a globe, and perhaps volume; these are more complex, though we will not have space to look into this complication.[14]

Some properties are clearly scalar although science has not (or has not yet or may never) assigned units and numerical values to them; these include goodness, happiness, anger, popularity, readiness, silliness, intelligence, beauty, wetness, hairiness, rareness (of meat)[15] – in fact, this is a very large class, maybe most of the properties one can speak of.

Even though there may exist a well worked out system of numerical measure for a certain property, a speaker of the language does not have to be able to discern the numerical value in order to be able to perceive the property such as a speed, a size, or someone's happiness. (See the comments on reference in Sections 12.2 and 12.3.3.) Indeed, although humans generally cannot discern numerical value, they are very good at judging relative values of physical properties of things they perceive, i.e., they can tell to a high degree of accuracy whether one person is taller than another, whether one car is going faster than another, whether one angle is greater than another, etc.

---

discussion of the differences between seeing something and seeing that something is such and such.

[14]We should note that color, when treated by physics as wavelengths of light, might seem to be a one-dimensional scale; but as it is perceived by humans, and spoken about in language, it is better represented by the color solid, which varies in three dimensions.

[15]Actually, some numerical scales have been attempted for intelligence, as well as states of readiness of emergency teams and for doneness of meat.

12.4.2 Lexical Expression of Properties

When we look more closely at the way lexical items are used to denote properties, it becomes clear that further semantic distinctions come into play. Lexical nouns can be employed to refer to a property kind, e.g. *length*, *speed*, *redness*, and *happiness*. Lexical adjectives and adverbs, for the most part, denote not just a kind of property, but a specific property falling under a kind: *Fast* means not just a speed but high speed; *slow* means not just speed but low speed.

It has often been observed that for modifiers of this type, there is a comparison class or standard that is often implicit (Ludlow 1989, Klein 1980, and Higginbotham 1985).

In the following:

(14) a. That elephant is big.
b. That butterfly is big.

(14a) is most naturally interpreted as *that elephant is big for an elephant*, and (14b) as *that butterfly is big for a butterfly*, and not the other way around. It is possible, still, to interpret these sentences where *big* is interpreted on some absolute or at least independent scale, so polysemy or functional dependence on context exists in adjectives and adverbs according to whether or not the implicit comparison class is employed. We will have more remarks on this in Section 12.6.1.

12.4.3 Scalar Properties and Deixis

There are a few remarks that we would like to make about a certain type of scalar adjective and adverb, because they have an interesting interaction with deictic words and the rest of the 'Degree' category of words[16], that is not shared with other adjectives and adverbs. This particular type of adjective and/or adverb (many can function as either) express numerically measurable scalar properties with lexical items that form antonym pairs: *fast–slow*, *big–little*, *tall–short*, *wide–narrow*, *high–low*, *deep-shallow*, *old–young*[17]. When used alone, these adjectives or adverbs

[16]The 'Degree' category will be motivated syntactically and discussed in Section (12.5).

[17]This class, approximately, is identified in Zwarts 1993, who calls them 'measure degree adjectives'. He distinguishes them from nonmeasure degree adjectives, which include *healthy*, *ill*, *pretty*, *angry*, and the like; this distinction in fact seems to be the same as that between property scales with assigned numerical scales, and those without, discussed above.

Although we agree that the distinction should be made, and find his analysis insightful, we cannot adopt it wholesale because we are not sure the characterization is correct. In particular, we are concerned that his system does not seem to be able to account for the contrast between 'high-range' and 'low-range' adjectives or adverbs (discussed below), which would presumably both be of the 'measure degree' type, and

refer to a value of a specific property which is either in the high range (the 'high-range' member of the pair) or the low range (the 'low-range' member of the pair).

When the 'high-range' member of an antonym pair is used in deixis, it loses its positive connotation, and just indicates the scale (the value being fixed by the demonstrative in a context):

(15) a. He can only go that fast. [said of a turtle]

b. How tall is Jimmy now? [asked about a little boy]

That is, in (15a), there is no implication that the turtle is actually going fast. It is possible to use the 'low-range' member of an antonym pair with a demonstrative, but the adjective or adverb retains the implication that the value must be a low one:

(16) a. I can't walk that slow. [referring to the speed of a turtle]

b. # Can you drive that slow? [referring to a race car at high velocity][18]

c. # How slow does that cheetah run?

On the other hand, for scalar measure properties expressed by more than a pair of adjectives or adverbs the semantic facts are different. For example, temperature, although clearly measurable and scalar, has a large number of associated adjectives. *This cold*, *this hot*, *this cool*, *this warm*, and *this tepid*, all seem to need to be in specific ranges of temperature scale, and none seem to have the same import as *this temperature*.[19] In addition, a great many other adjectives and adverbs, which also seem to involve a scale, always retain the implication of the bare adjective or adverb. These include *full*, *empty*, *red*, *grey*, *wet*, *soft*, *beautiful*, *angry*, and many others.

Another difference between 'high-range' and 'low-range' members of an antonym pair with deixis is that the deictic word or other Degree word itself can be modified (or at least modifiers can precede the demonstrative):

(17) a. It is twice this tall.

b. Go twice that fast.

c. It was five times that tall.

d. We can pick berries three times that fast.

---

also the contrast between temperature adjectives and the other measurable property adjectives (also discussed below).

[18]We use # to mark a semantically anomalous sentence and ⋆ to mark syntactic deviance.

[19]*This warm* can mean *this temperature* for some speakers.

Generally, this is only the case with the 'high-range' member of the scale; it is not so felicitous with the 'low-range' member:

(18) a. ? Go twice this slow.
b. ?? Go half this slow.
c. # It is twice that small.
d. # It is half that small.

Even though (18a), (18b), (18c) and (18d) may not sound terribly bad, it is quite difficult to interpret them.

Interestingly, within the scope of a negative, the 'high-range' polar adjectives seem to regain their implication that the value of the property must be in the high range. Compare

(19) a. Don't go that fast.
b. Don't go that speed.

In (19a) *fast* has an implication (which may be a scalar implicature (Grice 1989)) that is missing from (19b). The implication is that you should go slower than whatever speed *that fast* refers to, even though going faster would not be going the same speed. This implication appears to be missing from (19b). If this is so, then there may be a potential problem for the view proposed above, and for Zwarts 1993, that *that fast* and other positive polarity property deictics lose any reference to the upper end of the scale.[20]

12.5 Syntactic Properties of Deictic Words

In this section we will examine some issues involving the syntactic properties of deictic lexical items, or 'demonstratives'. Use of deictic words with adverbs and adjectives may seem problematic at first glance. Yet, unlike the semantic and deictic properties of phrases like *that fast*, the syntactic behavior of these *has* been discussed adequately in the literature. The occurrence of demonstratives with adverbs and adjectives follows quite naturally under $\overline{\text{X}}$ theory, which proposes that every lexical category has a specifier position.

First, recall that the demonstratives *that* and *this* can serve as either determiners or pronouns, as in:

(20) a. That dog is big.
b. What is that?

[20]The same shift seems to occur with deixis to amounts – with *much*, *many*, *little*, and *few*. Focus also changes readings, and should be controlled for: *Don't eat that MUCH*, *Don't eat THAT much*, *Don't eat THAT little*.

As we have seen above, *that*, *this*, or *so*[21] can also be associated with an adverb or an adjective, as in:

(21) a. I want to go that fast.
b. He is that tall.
c. I would like a piece of wood this long.
d. Don't fly so high.

Jackendoff 1977 proposed that *that*, *this*, and *so*, in this position preceding an Adj or Adv, are members of the category Deg or Degree, which serves as the specifier of the AdvP or AdjP, much as determiners (Det) serve as the specifier of NP. [22] Other nondemonstrative members of the category Deg include *how*, *too*, *as*, *more*, *most*, and *less*.

We will assume refinements of this approach proposed by Abney 1987 and Corver 1991, taking Deg to be a functional head that projects the maximal projection DegP and takes the AdjP or AdvP as complement:

(22) $[_{\text{DegP}}$ spec $[_{\overline{\text{Deg}}}$ Deg^0 $[_{\text{AP}}$ spec $[_{\overline{\text{A}}}$ A^0 PP$]]]]$

Adverbs like *very*, *somewhat*, and *extremely* cannot cooccur with *this* and *that*, which might suggest that they are also of category Deg:

(23) a. ⋆ Go this very fast.
b. ⋆ He is extremely that tall.

However, they are arguably not in this set, but are adverbial modifiers adjoined to the $\overline{\text{Adj}}$ or $\overline{\text{Adv}}$ (Corver 1991), parallel to the difference between determiners and adjectives in the projections of nominals.[23]

That, *this*, and *so* also serve as anaphoric pronominal elements in adjectival or adverbial contexts. Of course, *that* and *this* can be pronouns for nouns, either deictic or anaphoric to NPs.

(24) a. That is a dog.
b. I would like to look at this.

That and *this* can also serve as deictic pronominals which refer to properties. In other words, they can be 'proadjectives ' or 'proadverbs', in some cases.

(25) a. That's too fast.

[21] The semantic properties of *so* are somewhat different from *that* and *this*, but it has similar syntactic properties, so we include it in this section.

[22] Under $\overline{\text{X}}$ theory (Jackendoff 1977, Chomsky 1970) all syntactic categories, N, V, P, and Adj/Adv, have the same basic structure, including a specifier and zero, one, or more complements. Differences in surface structures result from the interaction of other grammatical principles.

[23] Actually, *very* should probably not be lumped into this set without further comment, for its syntactic properties are unique.

b. This is how fast you can go.
c. That is ice cold.
d. Is this fast enough?

(26) a. Go a little faster than that.
b. He is much taller than that.

We can show that *that* in (26a) need not refer to the moving object, but to its speed: If we are driving down the road and I say *this is too fast*, I do not mean that we are too fast, or that this car is too fast, I mean that the speed we are traveling is too fast. This is even clearer if you consider a case where you utter (26a) in a situation where you are coaching a runner, or teaching an ice skater how to perform a spin:

(27) a. That was too slow to make the semifinals.
b. This is how you start a spin.

In these cases, *that* or *this* must refer to a property. The only object available for it to refer to is the runner or ice skater, and it is rude and possibly even ungrammatical to refer to a person as *that*! In this situation, in fact, it is mandatory to use a second-person pronoun to refer to the person.

That and *this* can also be proadverbs or proadjectives in response to a question, and can even be modified:

(28) a. Do you want this much? No, I only want a third of that.
b. Is your tree that tall? No, mine's only half that.
c. Did he go that fast? Actually, I think he went twice that.

However, in other cases, it is not so felicitous to use *that* and *this* as proadverbs or proadjectives. It seems that the generalization is that bare *that* and *this* cannot be pronominal elements which fill the position of an adverb postverbally, although they are more acceptable when they fill the position of a bare-NP adverbial that refers to a property. Compare:

(29) a. Go that fast.
b. ⋆ Go that.
c. Follow that.

In (29c), *follow* is subcategorized for an NP, and a pronominal *that* can occur in this position. In (29b), *go* subcategorizes optionally for various PPs, and allows various modifiers, both adverbs and NP adverbs; still, an overt demonstrative adverbial can occur after *go*, while *that* by itself apparently cannot. This implies that *that* and *this* can not really be proadverbs in this position, but only pronouns, although as pronouns they can refer to properties, as NPs such as *that speed* or *five miles an hour* do:

(30) a. Go that speed.
b. Go five miles an hour.

There are two possible hypotheses as to why ⋆*go that* is so bad. One possibility is the one just suggested, that *that* cannot appear in the position of an adverb, and so it is ungrammatical. Under this hypothesis, bare-NP modifiers can also modify *go*, ⋆*go that* should actually be acceptable if *that* can be interpreted as an NP. This may in fact be the case. Consider the following brief discourses:

(31) a. I want you to go seventy miles per hour.
b. ? I can't go that.

(32) a. I want you to run five miles.
b. I can't run that.

As we have observed, *that* in the implied position of an adverb is less acceptable (and impossible for some speakers); something like (33c) or (33d) is needed instead of (33b):

(33) a. I want you to run extremely fast.
b. ?⋆ I can't run that.
c. I can't run like that.
d. I can't run that way.

However, the data in (25-28) contradict the suggestion that *that* and *this* can never serve as proadjectives or proadverbs; it seems to depend on the position in which they occur. A second hypothesis is that *go that* is actually grammatically well-formed, but it simply does not carry enough information to be interpreted in most contexts. That is, there is a problem for the recoverability of the semantics in these positions.

Often, if the function of proadjective or proadverb is called for, then *like that* or *that way* are the preferred pronominal elements:

(34) a. Can you run like that?
b. I can't run that way.
c. He used to be very shy, but he's not like that anymore.

Thus, *thusly*, and *so* are also used as proadverbs – and were used more thusly in the past (cf. Webster's 1966). *Like this* and *this way* seem to be replacing them; these should probably be considered to be frozen forms which have become proadverbs.

Consider also that other modificational elements, particularly those referring to space and time, have specialized lexemes for deixis and pronominalization, and these sometimes must be used, instead of *that* and *this*.

(35) I want to go to Florida.

(36) a. ⋆ You can't go that.
b. ?? You can't go to that.
c. You can't go there.

(37) We leave at five o'clock.

(38) a. ⋆ I can't go that.
b. ⋆ I can't go at that.
c. I can't go at that time.
d. I can't go then.

Still, when used in other positions, a locative can be pronominalized with either *that* or *there*:

(39) a. Under the table is my cat's favorite place.
b. That is my cat's favorite place.
c. There is my cat's favorite place.

It seems that the reason underlying these facts, as well as those involving deictic adverbials, has to do with preferred use of lexical items with the correct features in various contexts.

We will conclude that the difficulty of use of *this* and *that* as pro-adverbs in postverbal position is not an outright exclusion, but is affected by (1) the existence of more appropriate forms (*that way*, *like this*, and *thus*) and (2) semantic recoverability.

The only example of a property demonstrative that seems to actually require gesture is the word *yea* (also discussed in Fillmore 1971). For example:

(40) a. My toaster is yea big. [said holding up hands to show size]
b. Mary is yea tall. [said holding up one hand to Mary's height]

This does seem to be an instance of a lexeme which (1) can only be used as a demonstrative, not as an anaphor, and (2) must be accompanied by a demonstration. Additionally, it seems to be semantically restricted to physical measure; the following sentences are all extremely odd:[24]

(41) a. # I was going yea fast.
b. # Let's see if you can drive yea smoothly.
c. # Look how happy John is; Mary is yea happy, too.

[24] *Yea* does not seem to exist at all for some English speakers; we have heard the suggestion that it is not present in British English, although we do not have confirmation of this. It seems to be present in the idiolects of the American English speakers we have asked. It does have the feel of being somewhat antiquated or countrified, but it is still quite acceptable.

In this section we have seen that demonstrative words such as *this*, *that*, *there*, etc. can be used either as deictics, or as anaphors coreferring with previous expressions (with the exception of *yea*, which has only a restricted deictic function). Cutting across this distinction, the demonstratives *this*, *that*, and *so* serve either as pronouns (or proadjectives or proadverbs), or as specifiers — determiners (category Det) when used as specifier of the NP, and category Deg when used as specifier of AdjP or AdvP. The use of *this* and *that* as proadjectives or proadverbs is somewhat restricted, but the restrictions are similar to the restrictions on using these anaphorically to places and times. *That way*, *like this*, and *thus* supplement them in postverbal position, similar to the use of *there*, *then*, and the like.

12.6 Representation of Truth Conditions by Logical Form

In this section we discuss representations of truth conditions for all of the examples of demonstrative sentences we have been investigating. We will consider the proposal that these truth conditions be given in a usual first order logical language that we will extend so as to quantify over variables for properties, much as Davidson 1967 and Parsons 1990 argued for extending logical forms to quantify over event variables. In Davidson's case the event variables range over particular events. In our case the property variables will range over the abstract particular properties described in the introduction. This discussion will be somewhat exploratory.

Davidson based his proposal that a quantified event variable should occur in logical form on three main facts: (1) Events, even when denoted by verbs, can be referred back to anaphorically: *John left town. That was unexpected*; (2) Nominals can denote events: *the destruction of the city*; and (3) The detachment inferences: Verbs can be modified by adverbials which can be dropped by what appears to be logical inference. Analysis of perceptual reports about events such as *We saw the boy drown* provides a fourth argument (Higginbotham 1983). All four of these arguments have analogs that support quantifying over properties. We will briefly discuss the first two arguments, and then look at the third in greater detail. The fourth we will leave for future work.

As we have already noted in Section 12.5, almost all demonstrative terms can be either deictic or anaphoric. That this is true for demonstrative property expressions is shown in (42b), (43b), (44), and (45b):

(42) a. I want to go eighty miles per hour.
b. That would be too fast.

(43) a. She sewed the hem artfully.

b. She sewed the cuffs that way too.

(44) Cheetahs can run seventy miles per hour, but horses can't run that fast.

(45) a. Is your table two meters long?
b. No, it's not that big.

These are exactly analogous to the type of example that Davidson used in his first argument, showing that we make anaphoric reference to events, and providing evidence that we need an event variable in the logical form to properly account for this sort of anaphora. Following the same sort of reasoning, we suggest that there is a similar need for a property variable in logical form, to account for anaphoric reference to properties. Thus the logical form for (43a) would be something like:

(46) $\exists e \exists x[\text{sew}(e, \text{she}) \wedge \text{artful}(x, e) \wedge \text{past}(e)]$

The variables **e** and **x** in (43a) are the event variable and the property variable, respectively. In this case, the position of these variables as existentially bound in this way makes them available for later anaphors like *that way* in (43b).

The technical means for representing and computing this variety of anaphoric binding could be achieved either through dynamic binding (as in Chierchia 1995) or discourse representation structures (as in Kamp and Reyle 1993). Using dynamic binding, the scope of the property variable **x** can be made to include the logical form of (43b) when that sentence is added to the discourse. This allows **x** in the logical form **[that(x)]way(x)** to bind with the previous **x**.

Likewise the scope of the event variable **e** could be extended to the logical form of *that took over six minutes* where *that* is anaphoric to the sewing event. This is an example of Davidson's case for postulating event variables. The general rule is: For discourse anaphors there should be an existentially bound variable already in the representations that make up the discourse to that point.[25]

To apply Davidson's second argument to reference to properties, we need only note that we have seen numerous examples of nominals that denote properties, both property kinds and particular properties: *its speed*, *the speed of light*, *the color of grass*, *his height*, *fifty miles per hour*, etc. In the present framework these would require logical forms like **[the(x)]speed(x)** and **[his(x)]height(x)**.

Now we turn to Davidson's third argument. Take the following natural language inference:

[25]This rule needs amendments to deal with embedded structures and presuppositions that we will ignore here.

(47) a. Sam killed the victim cleverly yesterday.

b. Therefore, Sam killed the victim cleverly.

c. Therefore, Sam killed the victim.

From (47a) one can straight away infer both (47b) and (47c). A minimally adequate logical form for (47a) that quantifies over events will explain these inferences as logically valid inferences where one or more of the the conjuncts are simply detached.

(48) $\exists$e[killing(e, sam, victim) $\wedge$ cleverly(e) $\wedge$ yesterday(e)]

We can use the same style of argument to promote quantifying over not only events but their properties (such as speed or quickness):

(49) a. Kitty crawled away extremely slowly.[26]

b. Therefore, Kitty crawled away slowly.

From (49a) one can straight away infer (49b). We propose the following logical form for this inference:

(50) a. $\exists$e$\exists$y[crawling(e, Kitty) $\wedge$ slow(y, e) $\wedge$ extreme(y)]

b. $\exists$e$\exists$y[crawling(e, Kitty) $\wedge$ slow(y, e)]

Again, the fact that the inference from (49a) to (49b) is so compelling can be explained by the validity of logical detachment.

Both of the above reconstructed inferences are parallel to the familiar explanations of the behavior of intersecting adjectives. *I bought a tree* follows from *I bought a tall tree* because *tall* is an intersecting adjective. If the adjective is not intersecting as in *I bought an artificial tree* there is no inference. Logical form would represent *artificial* as an operator rather than a predicate, so logical detachment would not be possible. We have the same distinction among the adverbs. In (49a) *extremely* is an intersecting adverbial modifier of *slowly* and should be represented as a predicate in logical form. But adverbs like *seemingly* and *apparently* are not intersecting so they should not be represented as predicates.

Now we can apply similar logical analysis to the cases of property *deixis*. We saw support in Section 12.5 for a distinction between our Deg words *this* and *that* on the one hand versus *extremely* and the other intersecting adverbial modifiers on the other hand. We will therefore: (a) exploit the analogy between NP determiners and Degs pointed out in that section and (b) make use of the property variable we have just argued for. Given all this, we propose the following logical forms for two of our key examples of deictic reference to properties (namely, (5a) *we are now going this fast* and (17a) *it is twice that tall*).

[26]Kitty is a cat, not a person.

(51) a. ∃e[going(e, we) ∧ now(e) ∧ [this(z)][fast(z, e)]]

b. [twice(z)][[that(z)][tall(z, it)]]

In (51a), [**this(z)**] binds the variable **z**. One way to analyze this is as a deictic binder of the form ∃**z**[**z** = **this**] where **this** acts like a deictic pronoun. This method is mentioned by Larson and Segal 1995 and explicitly proposed in Lepore and Ludwig 2000.

Based on all of the argument up till now the deictic **z** must range over particular properties.[27]

So according to this proposal the logical forms of some adverbs and adjectives specify two arguments, one for an argument of predication and one for the particular property. In (51a) **e** binds with the so-called event variable.[28] Thus a valuation function would assign a particular event to **e** and it would assign an <event, property> pair to **fast(z, e)**.[29]

12.6.1 Other Uses of Scalar Adverbs and Adjectives

Scalar adjectives and adverbs can occur in at least the following three paradigms:

(52) a. She crawled away slowly

b. She crawled this slowly

c. He crawled more slowly than her.

We will call these the positive, deictic, and comparative uses of *slowly*. Can one representation of meaning for *slowly* apply to all three uses? We will briefly compare some proposals about (52a) and (52c) to our above current proposal about the representation of deictic expressions like (52b).

Relativity of Positive Scalar Predicates

In section 12.4.2 we observed that in:

(53) a. Some elephant is small

b. Some butterfly is big

there is relativity to a comparison class or type in the meanings of *big* and *small*. If one desires to account for this relativity in logical form we

[27] In English there are, of course, various ways of denoting particular properties: ten kilometers per hour, my speed, a speed of ten kilometers per hour, a speed of six miles per hour.

[28] Note that the adverb *fast* is a predicate on the event, following a standard Davidsonian treatment of events.

[29] For our purposes and in the NLVR implementation, we employ a system of semantic valuation along the lines developed in Larson and Segal 1995. Thus **val(x, man(x))** = some individual man, rather than, for example, the set of all men. This valuation function is many-valued.

can begin by adding an extra argument to the logical forms for *big* and *small* getting the following logical forms for (53b):

(54) a. ∃x[elephant(x) ∧ small(xx, x)]
b. ∃y[butterfly(y) ∧ big(yy, y)]

Variants of this approach include those proposed by Klein 1980, Higginbotham 1985, and Ludlow 1998. Depending on whose theory you follow, the extra variables are taken to range over kinds corresponding to the type of the thing filling the 'real' argument position of the adjective or adverbs (i.e. elephants or butterflies, in this case), or to range over comparison classes of elephants or butterflies, or to range over standards. The selection of the kind, or comparison class, or standard filling this argument is either a function of something in the sentence, say, the noun *elephant* or in other cases dependent on context.

Now we have logical forms for *small* and *big* that look something like our logical form for *fast*, namely, (51a) **fast(z, e)**. All of these have an extra argument. The question is whether all of these extra arguments are equivalent. Generally, the answer is No (Higginbotham 1985, Ludlow 1989). In these theories, **small(xx, x)** and **big(yy, y)** in (54b) would mean x is small for an xx and y is big for a yy respectively. The variables **xx** and **yy** would have to be instantiated for interpretation, perhaps to **elephants** and **butterflies**.[30]

Along these lines the adverb *fast* in the VP *ran fast* would get a logical form like **fast(running, e)** meaning e is fast for a running event. However, in (51a) the first argument of **fast(z, e)** does not range over types of going or, more generally, types of events (or comparison classes of events of going, etc.). It must range over particular speeds. So the analysis for positives is at variance with our above a low analysis of the deictics.

This apparent incompatibility between the two theories might seem to be related to the difference we noted in Section 12.4.3 between the deictic AP *that fast* and the nondeictic positive AP *fast* and other 'high-range' scalar measure adjectives. The latter implies something is fast. The former seems to merely pick out a point on the speed scale. The question now is how might we integrate the two theories? One option would be to simply bifurcate the semantic representations for scalar adverbs (and adjectives) like *fast*.

(55) a. $\text{fast}_1(\text{s, e})$
b. $\text{fast}_2(\text{c, e})$

[30]Higginbotham 1985 would use this argument place for an abstraction over the appropriate nouns or NPs.

Each form has a second argument that ranges over events. However, the first arguments differ; the two forms select different types of first argument with **s** ranging over particular speeds and **c** ranging over types of event (or comparison class). Also the relations between the first and second arguments differ, as mentioned above. Nevertheless this type of semantic ambiguity captures the difference in truth conditions between the deictic and nondeictic uses.

One interesting problem with this kind of semantic bifurcation is that there now needs to be a way to rule out the following reading of *She walked that fast.*

(56) $\exists$e[walk(e, she) $\wedge$ [that(c)]fast_2(c, e) $\wedge$ past(e)]

This nearly unreadable logical form states that she walked and also the walking was fast for that type, where *that type* rigidly designates a particular type of event or thing. It would be something like saying *She walked cat fast* or *She walked walking fast.*

A second, more obvious, problem for the bifurcation proposal is this. As we observed in Section 12.4.3, many adjectives and adverbs do not behave like *fast*, and do not lose the implications of the bare adjectives when in phrases like *that A* or *how A*.

For instance, with the adverb *slowly*, the following inference holds:

(57) a. She crawled that slowly

b. So she crawled slowly

The inference could not be valid if *slowly* were just taken to be ambiguous, i.e, if (57a) uses $\mathbf{slowly_1(x, e)}$ and (57b) uses $\mathbf{slowly_2(x, e)}$. Recall also that many other adjectives and adverbs, including *hot*, *cold*, *red*, *wet*, *soft*, *beautiful*, *angry*, and so on, retain the implication that leads to the above form of inference.

Next consider a more unified proposal wherein we use one logical form to represent both the positive and deictic uses. Here are candidate logical forms to consider.

(58) a. $\exists$e[run(e, he) $\wedge$ past(e) $\wedge$ [that(s)][slow(s, c, e)]]

b. $\exists$e$\exists$s[run(e, he) $\wedge$ past(e) $\wedge$ slow(s, c, e)]]

The intended interpretation of **slow(s, c, e)** is: (a) **s** is the particular speed of **e**; and (b) **s** is a low speed for something of type **c**, a variable which is understood to range over events of running. So (58a) states that he ran that speed and that speed was slow for a running. And (58b) states that he ran some speed (or other) and the speed was slow for a running. Now if we analyze **that(s)** as $\exists$**s**[**s** = **that**] the inference from (58a) to (58b) will be valid.

This proposal takes care of the ambiguity problem; you always pick the same logical form for *slowly*. It also appears to nicely account for the difference between deictic and nondeictic uses via the two different binders of **s**. In (58a) the variable **s** is bound by the rigid binder introduced by the word *that*. In (58b) the variable can be bound by a rule of existential closure, namely, 'Existentially bind any free variables' (Heim 1982).[31]

Rather than accept (58) as our final proposal we will note two remaining problems with logical forms like (58b) as giving the truth conditions for *he ran slow* and the other adjectives and adverbs.

First, this type of logical form will not now work for the 'high range' scalar measure deictic APs *that fast*, *this tall*, etc. This is because, as we saw above, with these adjectives and adverbs the implication of the bare form is lost and *he ran this fast* does not entail *he ran fast*. Therefore, we may need two meanings for these high range salient scalars. Actually, it may be that *He ran that fast* has two readings: the *he ran that speed* reading that we have been discussing, losing the implication, and also a perhaps less available reading that entails *he ran fast*.[32]

The second remaining problem is that these logical forms may not be able to rule out the anomalous sentences like *He ran half that slow* discussed in Section 12.4.2. This sentence may be syntactically acceptable but semantically uninterpretable.

Scalar Comparatives

Now we come to the comparative uses of scalar adjectives and adverbs such as:

(59) Luise is taller than Otto

One variety of semantic theory of scalar adjectives represents this sentence with the following logical form.[33]

---

[31] This unified proposal may also be the right one for representing the anaphoric use of *that slow*.

[32] We could follow the approach of Klipple (in prep.) that the 'high range' scalar measure adjectives and adverbs have two lexical alternates, which are predictable based on their grammatical class, one with the relevant implication and one where that portion of the meaning, and only that portion, is lost. This follows the general approach to lexical items of Levin 1993, and applies it to adjective classes instead of verb classes. One important feature of this approach is that it identifies this class of adjectives as the unusual class, whereas a large number of other classes of adjectives do not lose the implication of the bare adjectives in any syntactic paradigm.

[33] This example and the logical form are taken from Beck 1997. The logical form is similar to a proposal found in von Stechow 1985 which Beck also attributes to Heim 1985.

(60) $\exists$d[d> 0 $\wedge$ the max d_1[tall-as(d_1, Luise)] = d + the max d_2[tall-as(d_2, Otto)]]

It is common to interpret the variable **d** as ranging over something called degrees. In that case we can read (60) as follows. The expression **the max $\mathbf{d_1}$[tall-as($\mathbf{d_1}$, Luise)]** is a definite description denoting the maximum degree for which the height of Luise is greater than or equal to it. We will call this the maximum height number. So the complete logical form (60) states that the maximum height number for Luise plus some finite degree = the maximum height number for Otto. This probably gets some of the truth conditions right for (59).

Although the predicate **tall-as(x, y)** looks a little like our predicate for the deictic adjective phrase **tall(s, y)** in (51b), the interpretations differ. The second argument in each case will denote an entity. However the first argument in **tall-as(x, y)** denotes degrees, which seem to be numbers, while the first argument in **tall(s, y)** denotes a particular property, say a particular height.

It may be possible to define **tall-as(d, x)** in terms of our **$\mathbf{tall_1}$(s, e)**; the latter is analogous to our **$\mathbf{fast_1}$(s, e)** in (55b). There are two problems that must be faced however. First, as we concluded above the representation **$\mathbf{small_1}$(s, x)** should probably be set aside in favor of a three-argument form **small(s, elephant, x)** in order to unify deictic and positive adjective meanings. Applications of the degree based theory deal almost exclusively with what we have called the 'high-range' scalar measure adjectives. Consideration of 'low-range' and other types of scalar adjectives was another reason we found for disfavoring two-argument forms like **$\mathbf{small_1}$(s, x)**.

Secondly, there may be a problem about using logical forms like (60) as discourse representations. At the beginning of this section we used various considerations to support using property variables. Our first argument was a borrowed version of the Davidsonian argument from anaphora which we applied to examples (42b), (43b), and (44). The existentially bound property variable in the logical forms for these examples licenses anaphora to the manner of sewing, the speed, etc. Now we are asked to consider (60) $\exists$**d[d > 0 $\wedge$ the max $\mathbf{d_1}$[tall-as($\mathbf{d_1}$, Luise)] = d + the max $\mathbf{d_2}$[tall-as($\mathbf{d_2}$, Otto)]]** as the representation for (59) *Luise is taller than Otto.* Here the variable **d** is existentially bound. This variable represents the exact degree by which Luise is taller than Otto. This variable is not embedded within a structure that would block later anaphoric binding. Yet we take it that you cannot say anything following (59) that would be anaphoric to the actual degree by which Luise is taller than Otto. In other words, since you didn't mention the amount by which Luise is taller you cannot go on to anaphorically refer to that amount. This problem suggests that the status and theoretical function of (60) in these theories of comparatives may be at odds with the status and theoretical function of the logical forms we have been suggesting for deixis to properties.

12.7 Gesture

In this section we offer a few observations about gesture. Gesture may be used in deictic reference to properties, but often quite differently from deictic reference to objects. Much deixis to properties does not require gesture, and pointing is often inappropriate. We will conclude from this that gesture with demonstratives is often only an aid to making the intended referent salient, but should not itself be treated as part of the semantics, and gesture should be related to more general considerations of perceptual salience in situations of cooperative communication. Moreover, a gesture with deixis to a property often produces the referent of the deixis itself, as we shall observe below.[34]

A pointing gesture is often inappropriate with properties. In a case where the passenger of a car says to the driver *don't go this fast*, it is hard to imagine any appropriate deictic gesture; yet it is clear from context that the referent is the speed of the car. In saying *I want to fly that high*, a person might point at an airplane in the sky; here, it might be the object that is pointed to, not the property itself. If this is the case, then pointing at the airplane serves to get the hearer to focus on the object that has the property being referred to. Still, if the airplane is large in the visual field, or otherwise quite perceptually salient, the deixis in this sentence can succeed with no pointing or other gesture at all.

In referring to a direction, a person might well point in the direction and say *go that way*; however, this cannot be a case of pointing *to* the direction referred to, but rather it is mimicking the direction vector itself. The same sort of thing occurs in indicating the size of an object which is roughly the size of the body, for example, *it is this long*, with the hands held up parallel to each other at the intended distance from each other. More precisely, what is happening here is that the speaker is introducing

[34]We make no claim about whether these gestures are iconic or conventional signs or entirely natural. Some of these uses and our interpretations of them may not be generalizable beyond American speakers of English. Nevertheless these and future perhaps better informed remarks are important to our goals. We want to have a try at characterizing how linguistic understanding interacts with other cognitive processes, in this case, perception of gestures. We also want to model some aspects of this interaction with our simulation.

an object (his pair of hands) into the perceptual space that itself has the property to which he intends to refer.

The gesture accompanying deixis to manner of motion may be a pantomime; for example, *sharks swim like this* with an accompanying swimming movement of the hand and arm, or, to indicate a dance step, *do it like this* accompanied by the dance step itself (this could also be used to show the manner of performing a dance step which is already known; in fact to indicate movements which are indescribable with words). This sort of deixis carries over to just about any type of physical manner imaginable (building a tool shed, fixing a car, setting a table, and so on).

In most of these latter cases, the gesture is not merely an aid to making the intended referent salient; rather, it is the creation of the referent of the demonstrative expression itself. If you say *do it this way* and do a dance step, you are not using the dance step to refer to something else in the context; you are creating an action which has the desired manner. Similarly if you hold up your hands and say *it is this long.* Even pointing to indicate direction is a case of reference to the gesture itself, not of a gesture indicating something else; if you orient your finger or arm along a certain axis and say *go that way*, you are not pointing at something else which has the desired orientation, you are creating it yourself.

It is also possible to point to other things that indicate the intended property: One can point to an arrow on a map, or a road; one can point to another person doing a dance step, or a picture or drawing of it; one can point to a certain place on a ruler and say *it is this long*; and one can point to a position on the dial of a measuring device or machine as part of deixis (cf. McNeill 1992). This sort of deixis seems to to be deferred; it is deixis to a property via a symbol for that property.

Though this has been only a brief discussion, we tentatively conclude that at least in English, gestures which accompany property deixis can be quite different than the pointing gestures usually discussed. Exploration of deixis to properties should shed light on the types of gesture possible and the role of gesture in deixis itself.

12.8 Simulating Property Deixis

In this section, we explain how the Natural Language and Virtual Reality (NLVR) system implements a simulation of language understanding involving property deixis. Relations between the NLVR system and research on natural language syntax and semantics go two ways: (1) Development of the NLVR system raises problems for further theoretical investigation such as how to interpret users who refer to properties deictically; (2) Computational implementation of deictic theory is, of course, not straightforward. This means that semantic theory leaves something unexplained, namely, how do people do it, how is it possible? We use the NLVR system as a processing model, showing how it might be done in this instance – albeit by a machine rather than a person.

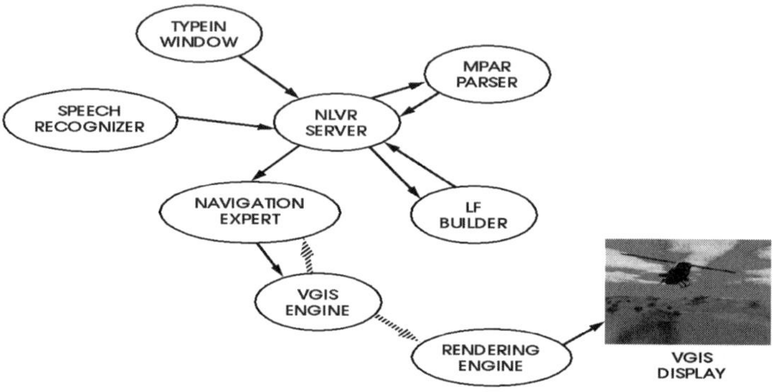

FIGURE 1 The NLVR System using Perceptual Information

Figure 1 is a diagram of the NLVR system connected to a virtual reality (VR) system called the Virtual Graphic Information System (VGIS). The whole system simulates deixis to properties (along with other forms of deixis and reference) in the course of performing a spoken language navigation task. A user navigates his point of view through the virtual world in real-time by uttering sequences of imperatives such as the following:

(61) a. Start heading for the Tiefort Mountains.
b. Look to your right.
c. Drop down to 700 kilometers.
d. Start moving twice this fast.
e. Keep going in this direction for thirty kilometers.

The NLVR system uses a Minimalist parser and interprets the syntactic parse trees during the navigation task.[35] This causes virtual motion through the VR world.[36]

[35]See Gurney, Klipple, and Gregory 1998 and Klipple and Gurney 1998 for more information on NLVR.

[36]For the spoken language navigation task, response to imperatives must be rapid. Parsing time in this dynamic VR environment is normally less than 0.5 seconds. An earlier version of the parser is described in Lin ms. which is available from http://www.cs.umanitoba.ca/~lindek. Total NLVR end to end processing time is normally less than 1.0 second.

The two sentences (61d) and (61e) are typical of deixis to properties. The computational interpretation problem for deixis breaks down into two parts: developing semantic representations for the sentences and finding referencc3 for dcictic expressions.

12.8.1 Representation

To simplify our explanations we will consider less complex sentences like the following:[37]

(62) a. Fly south very fast.
  b. Fly south this fast.

(62b) is a case of deixis without gesture and is directly referring to the speaker's current speed. The LF Builder in Figure 1 delivers Davidsonian quasi-logical forms[38] (with the event variables and property variables of Section 12.6) to the Navigation Expert:

(63) a. imp:[impro-subj:[n:pro:X1],predv:[[v:fly(X2,X1)],
  mods:[t:tense(bare,X2),jvan:[n:south(X3,X2)],
  jvaa:[[a:fast(X4,X2)],jaa:[a:very(X4)]]]]]
 b. imp:[impro-subj:[n:pro:X1],predv:[[v:fly(X2,X1)],
  mods:[t:tense(bare,X2),jvan:[n:south(X3,X2)],
  jvaa:[jdg:[d:this(X4)],[a:fast(X4,X2)]]]]]

Interpretation of both (63a) and (63b) proceeds by binding all of the free variables: **X1**, **X2**, **X3**, and **X4**. In both examples, the event variable **X2** binds to an index of a known VGIS API action (such as ROTATE or TRANSLATE) and the third variable **X3** binds to a numerical representation for a known direction – in this case, 180.0 degrees. Both the index and the number are rigid designators in the system. The variables of the descriptive predicates in the remainder of (63a), the nondeictic example, are interpreted along lines of theories of positive adjectives discussed in Section 12.6.1. Up to this point, there is no property deixis, no direct reference, and no perception of properties.

Now consider the variable **X4** in (63b), the deictic property example. This logical form represents **this(X4)** as a quantifier so that the variable **X4** must bind with a designator for a particular speed which is, of course, one member of the set of all speeds. This makes the interpretation of the phrase *this fast* definite and the deictic situation makes it a case of direct reference. The referent here is not to be found in a data base. It should

[37]The examples in the monologue in (61e) use aspectual verbs making response by the system to these commands too involved to discuss here. Briefly, the Navigation Expert in Figure 1 creates parallel processes (threads) in response to these (and most) commands, thus simulating a reactive behavior type of robot (Brooks 1991).

[38]These are Prolog representations of the logical forms.

be something one perceives. So, whereas (63a) can be interpreted (and the binding of all its variables found) through data base queries (some involving knowledge of default values) and without perception, we need simulated perception for the Navigation Expert in order to bind **X4** in (63b).

12.8.2 Simulated Perception

In order to produce the VR scene, the VGIS engine in Figure 1 must send information about the location and attitude of your virtual viewpoint to the Rendering Engine, along the lower dashed arrow. The Rendering Engine computes with this information and paints the VGIS display with pixels at about sixteen frames per second. When your viewpoint is moving, the scene seems to rush by. You, the speaker who said *fly south this fast*, can, therefore, deictically 'refer' to your speed because you 'perceive' it (you get information about it).[39]

For the Navigation Expert to get the reference of *this fast*, it must simulate perception of your speed. To model this we send the same viewpoint information that VGIS sent to the Rendering Engine back along the upper dashed arrow in Figure 1. This is a data stream which, of course, varies with time and tracks the effects you see on the display. The Navigation Expert represents this viewpoint position information it gets with numbers and calculates speed as, say, ten meters per second. Even though you do not know the speed as ten meters per second, the Expert does. Nevertheless, we have simulated some of the essence of deictic understanding because the information you get about speed originates from the same source as the information the Navigation Expert gets. More importantly, both streams of information co-vary with changes in the source. This is our model of a 'flow of information' needed for our causal theory of reference, CT1 in Section 12.2. It is as if the Expert perceives the speed by looking at a meter while you perceive it by attending to visual flow. Nevertheless, you and the Expert are locked onto and can, therefore, refer directly to the same property. This conforms to points CT1 and RT5; the reference is direct and based on information from its source.

We have not addressed the communication problem and problems of misunderstanding. At its present state of development, the Navigation Expert does very limited pragmatic reasoning to avoid certain misunderstandings of deictic phrases that may arise. It can simulate perception of objects and locations in the scene, however. The method is similar to the above perception of the viewpoint properties. To simulate perceiv-

[39] We say 'refer' and 'perceive' because the situation is virtual.

ing the helicopter in Figure 1, it begins receiving a message stream of information about the position, etc. of the helicopter. This information varies continuously according to the movement of helicopterish pixels across the VGIS display. For example, as the helicopterish pixels move to the left across the display screen, the VGIS engine sends new values for the relative bearing of the helicopter to the Navigation Expert.

12.8.3 Simulated Gesture

A pointing gesture is simulated in NLVR by the user touching the display. So the system can deal with commands like:

(64) a. Go forward that far. [pointing at the helicopter]
     b. Float up that high. [pointing at the top of a mountain]

The navigator that we have implemented uses a very simple (thus fallible) discourse strategy: For proximal deictic expressions assume deixis is made directly to properties of the viewpoint unless a pointing gesture causes perception of some other object. In other words, your moving viewpoint is salient by default. Pointing causes an indicated object to be more salient. For distal deictic expressions, assume the referent is neither you nor a property of you.

12.8.4 A Semi-autonomous Robot

As a point of information we mention another implementation that simulates some aspects of understanding deixis to properties and their characteristic gestures. This is the semi-autonomous robot developed at the Navy Center for Applied Artificial Intelligence (Perzanowski, Schultz, and Adams 1998). This robot uses a range finder to detect gestures. Its repertoire includes:

(65) a. Move over there. [moving one's hand along a vector]
     b. Back up this far. [spreading one's hands to show a distance]
     c. Go to the way point over there. [moving one's hand along a vector towards the way point object]

Only (65b) involves complex demonstrative deixis to a property. However both (65a) and (65b) use nonpointing gestures like the ones we discussed in Section 12.7.

12.9 Conclusions

We conclude that the analysis of phrases like *that fast* or *this big* poses no special problems for the theories of deixis, semantics, or syntax. Existing theories of direct reference, rigid designation, and deictic reference can be extended to cover deixis to properties. However, this result does invite the claim that properties must be perceived. Even though we defended this claim, the role of this kind of perception needs further investigation.

In syntactic theory, the proposal of the category Deg to capture these functional uses of *that* and *this* was made at least as early as the first full examinations of X-bar theory; while the syntactic properties of this category also need further exploration, the fact that some members of Deg are demonstratives is not a difficulty for syntactic theory.

Consideration of these phrases does give insight into the proper semantic treatment of properties. We argued that semantics needs to provide for the possibility of direct reference to properties, very much parallel to the reference to events argued for by Davidson 1967. We made a distinction between property kinds, such as color, and particular properties, such as a height of five feet. Though we were not able to give a full treatment of the semantics of adjectives and adverbs, we integrated our proposed variable which refers directly to the particular property with semantic formulations necessitated by consideration of other semantic properties of adverbs and adjectives, and of comparatives.

Property deixis also sheds light on the relation of gesture to communication with deixis. We observed that while gesture is an aid to deixis, a gesture itself is not required for the semantics of a demonstrative. Gestures that instantiate their referents, not as often discussed in the literature, seem quite common with property deixis.

In place of an explanation as to how deixis to properties succeeds we have implemented the NLVR system. The transparent workings of this simulation suggests one way that some of the requirements for successful deictic reference to properties can be satisfied.

References

Abney, S. 1987. *The English Noun Phrase in its Sentential Aspect.* Doctoral dissertation, MIT, Cambridge, Massachusetts.

Beck, S. 1997. On the Semantics of Comparative Conditionals. *Linguistics and Philosophy* 20(3):229–271.

Brooks, R. A. 1991. Intelligence Without Representation. *Artificial Intelligence* 47(1–3):139–159.

Chierchia, G. 1995. *Dynamics of Meaning: Anaphora, Presupposition, and the Theory of Grammar.* Chicago, Illinois: Chicago University Press.

Chomsky, N. 1970. Remarks on Nominalizations. In *Readings in English Transformational Grammar*, ed. Roderick Jacobs and Peter Rosenbaum. London: Ginn.

Corver, N. 1991. Evidence for DegP. In *Proceedings of the 21st North East Linguistics Society*, 33–47. Amherst, Massachusetts. GLSA.

Davidson, D. 1967. The Logical Form of Action Sentences. In *The Logic of Decision and Action*, ed. Nicholas Rescher. 81–95. Pittsburgh: University of Pittsburgh Press. Republished in Donald Davidson, *Essays on Actions and Events*, Oxford University Press, Oxford, 1980.

Dretske, F. I. 1969. *Seeing and Knowing.* Chicago, Illinois: University of Chicago Press.

Dretske, F. I. 1981. *Knowledge and the Flow of Information.* Cambridge, Massachusetts: The MIT Press.

Fillmore, C. 1971. Santa Cruz Lectures on Deixis. Technical report. Bloomington, Indiana: Indiana University Linguistics Club.

Grice, H. P. 1989. *Studies in the Way of Words.* Cambridge, Massachusetts: Harvard University Press.

Gurney, J., E. Klipple, and T. Gregory. 1998. The Spoken Language Navigation Task. In *Proceedings of the AAAI Workshop on Representations for Multi-Modal Human-Computer Interaction.* Madison, Wisconsin. AAAI.

Heim, I. 1982. *The Semantics of Definite and Indefinite Noun Phrases.* Doctoral dissertation, Linguistics Department, University of Massachusetts, Amherst, Massachusetts.

Heim, I. 1985. Notes on Comparative and Related Constructions. ms., University of Texas, Austin, Texas.

Heim, I., and A. Kratzer. 1998. *Semantics in Generative Grammar.* Oxford: Blackwell.

Higginbotham, J. 1983. The Logic of Perceptual Reports: an Extensional Alternative to Situation Semantics. *Journal of Philosophy* 80:100–127.

Higginbotham, J. 1985. On Semantics. *Linguistic Inquiry* 16(4):547–593.

Jackendoff, R. 1977. *$\bar{X}$ Syntax: A Study of Phrase Structure.* Cambridge, Massachusetts: The MIT Press.

Kamp, H., and U. Reyle. 1993. *From Discourse to Logic: Introduction to Model-theoretic Semantics in Natural Language, Formal Logic and Discourse Representation Theory, Vol. 1.* Dordrecht: Kluwer Academic Publishers.

Kaplan, D. 1989. Demonstratives. In *Themes from Kaplan*, ed. J. Almog, J. Perry, and H. Wettstein. 481–563. New York, New York: Oxford University Press.

Klein, E. 1980. A Semantics for Positive and Comparative Adjectives. *Linguistics and Philosophy* 4(1):1–45.

Klipple, E., and J. Gurney. 1998. Verb Modification and the Lexicon in the Natural Language and Virtual Reality System. In *Proceedings of the Workshop on Lexical Semantic Systems.* Pisa.

Kripke, S. 1972. Naming and Necessity. In *Semantics of Natural Language*, ed. Donald Davidson and Gilbert Harman. Dordrecht, Netherlands: Reidel.

Larson, R., and G. Segal. 1995. *Knowledge of Meaning*. Cambridge, Massachusetts: The MIT Press.

Lepore, E., and K. Ludwig. 2000. The Semantics and Pragmatics of Complex Demonstratives. *Mind* 109(434):199–240.

Levin, B. 1993. *English Verb Classes and Alternations: a Preliminary Investigation*. Chicago, Illinois: University of Chicago Press.

Levinson, S. C. 1983. *Pragmatics*. Cambridge: Cambridge University Press.

Lin, D. Principar—An Efficient, Broad-coverage, Principle-based Parser. ms. University of Manitoba.

Ludlow, P. 1989. Implicit Comparison Classes. *Linguistics and Philosophy* 12(4):519–533.

Lyons, C. 1999. *Definiteness*. Cambridge: Cambridge University Press.

Lyons, J. 1977. *Semantics*. Cambridge: Cambridge University Press.

McNeill, D. 1992. *Hand in Mind*. Chicago, Illinois: University of Chicago Press.

Neal, S. 1990. *Descriptions*. Cambridge, Massachusetts: MIT Press.

Parsons, T. 1990. *Events in the Semantics of English*. Cambridge, Massachusetts: MIT Press.

Perzanowski, D., A. Schultz, and W. Adams. 1998. Integrating Natural Language and Gesture in a Robotics Domain. In *Proceedings of the IEEE International Symposium on Intelligent Control*, 247–252. Gaithersburg, Maryland. IEEE.

Rullmann, H. 1995. *Maximality in the Semantics of Wh-Constructions*. Doctoral dissertation, University of Massachusetts, Amherst.

von Stechow, A. 1985. Comparing Semantic Theories of Comparison. *Journal of Semantics* 3:1–77.

Webster's Third New International Dictionary of the English Unabridged with Seven Language Dictionary. Encyclopædia Britannica, Inc.

Zwarts, J. 1993. A Degree-Based Semantics for Bare Positive Adjectives. In *The Proceedings of the Eleventh West Coast Conference on Formal Linguistics*, ed. Jonathan Mead, 539–552. Stanford, California. Center for the Study of Language and Information.

13

Relevance and Perceptual Constraints in Multimodal Referring Actions

Frédéric Landragin, Antonella De Angeli, Frédéric Wolff, Patrice Lopez and Laurent Romary

13.1 Introduction

13.1.1 Referring actions in multimodal systems

Referring to objects spread on a graphical interface is a typical action in Human-Computer Interaction (HCI). In the direct manipulation paradigm, this action is performed by a simple mouse-mediated pointing as a selection process. Interaction is ambiguity-free, but highly restricted. As a new generation of multimodal systems begins to evolve, the number of communicative actions available for indicating visual targets drastically increases and allows the user to express his intention rather than to perform elementary actions. References can be based on auditory signals (verbal input), motor-visual signals (gestural input), or on a combination thereof (multimodal input). Moreover, each type of input can be exploited through a great flexibility of forms. As an example, consider the following multimodal inputs extracted from a corpus collected by a simulation experiment (Wolff 1999). Very different gestures and verbal utterances perform the same communication goal, i.e., referring to a group of targets (see Figure 1).

Despite their clear usability advantages, the design of multimodal

Information Sharing: Reference and Presupposition in Language Generation and Interpretation.
Edited by Kees van Deemter and Rodger Kibble.

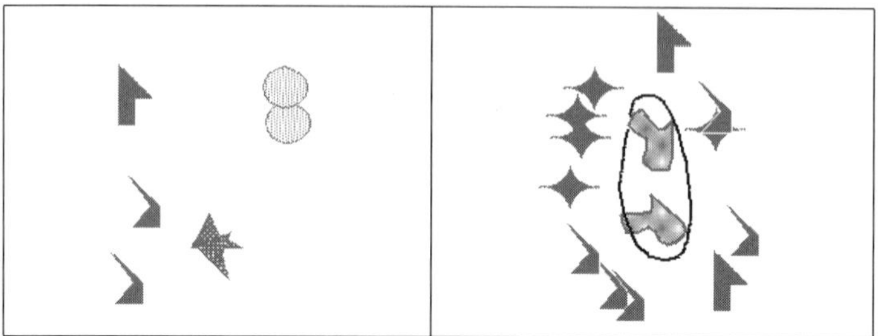

A. "The two pieces with a circle shape..."	B. "These two objects..."

FIGURE 1 Examples of complex multimodal reference to a group of targets.

systems still poses original and challenging problems to HCI researchers. In particular, it requires the development of innovative interaction paradigms to constrain the high variability of natural communication inside computational capabilities. The efficiency of these paradigms strongly depends on their compatibility with cognitive constraints affecting spontaneous behaviour (Oviatt and Cohen 2000). Indeed, although adaptation is a fundamental human ability, several aspects of communication escape conscious control and involve hard-wired or automatic processes. This is the case for instance for intonation, disfluencies, kinaesthetic motor control, cross-modal integration and timing. Automaticity occurs over extensive practice with an activity, when specific routines are built up in memory. Performed beyond conscious awareness, automatic processing is effortless and fast, but also requires great effort to be modified. Even when people learn new solutions (i.e., set up alternative routines in memory), as soon as they are involved in a demanding situation, they spontaneously return to their old ways. As a consequence, errors are very likely to occur. Taking into account actual human capabilities and constraints, it is unrealistic to expect that users will be able to adapt all or some parts of their behaviour to suit system limitations. On the contrary, multimodal systems should favour automatic behaviour by allowing users to directly express their intentions. In this way, the effort required to monitor their own expressions, as well as to plan and perform corresponding actions remains minimal. Usable systems thus require a deep understanding of the factors affecting human spontaneous behaviour.

13.1.2 The ecological approach and its extension

To cope with communication variability, designers need to know the conditions under which specific actions are likely to be produced. Such knowledge can drive the design of effective architectures which are capable of using all the appropriate cues needed to understand users' communicative intentions. Since HCI is highly different from human-human communication (Jönsson and Dählback 1988), empirical research, especially in the form of early simulation, is instrumental to the formalisation of a theory of multimodal interaction (Oviatt 1997, Oviatt et al. 1997, De Angeli et al. 1998). Elsewhere (Wolff et al. 1998, De Angeli et al. 1999a, 1999b) we have presented the ecological approach to multimodal system design, an innovative theoretical framework explaining communication variability as a function of cognitive constraint and contextual knowledge.

The ecological approach claims that gesture variability is linked to visual perception. To reach this conclusion, the approach has revised gestural communication by introducing it into the perception-action cycle (Neisser 1976). This is a well established psychological framework describing how action planning and execution is controlled by perception, and how perception is constantly modified by active exploration of the visual field. Through the analysis of spontaneous communication, we have demonstrated that the cyclic nature of cognition is a powerful conceptual structure for understanding referring gestures (Wolff et al. 1998, De Angeli et al. 1999b).

The ecological approach to multimodal system design assumes that gestures are virtual actions (Kita 2000), re-enactments of real activities in a virtual space. In particular, referring gestures are considered as virtual actions aimed at directing the listener's attention towards a target. These virtual actions do not modify the physical environment in which they are produced, as would do grasping the target and moving it in front of the listener. They modify the dialogue context, inducing the listeners to shift the focus of their attention towards the target. This effect corresponds to the semiotic function of gesture.

In this chapter, we attempt to extend the ecological approach to cope also with verbal language variability. In particular, following Relevance Theory (Sperber and Wilson 1995) we try to understand the link between speech in a discourse context and gesture in a perceptive context. The potential of this extension is confirmed by the results of a simulation study. Exploiting the perceptual constraints, people tend to modify the effect of their utterances.

13.2 Theoretical framework

13.2.1 Affordances and multimodal system design

The ecological approach is an established psychological theory of perception, cognition and action (Gibson 1979) now adapted to multimodal system design (De Angeli et al. 1999b). According to ecological psychology, the perception-action cycle is mediated by *affordances*, that is, optic information about objects that convey functional properties. Affordances represent powerful cues of action. They are not properties of the object, but relations derived by the encounter between information coming from the object and the repertoire of physical actions available to the observer. The mutuality of organism-environment relationship is a major theoretical assumption of the ecological approach. Affordances are characteristic of the environment relative to specific individuals. The same physical layout will have different affordances for different individuals, insofar each individual has a different repertory of acts (Gibson 1979). For example, a stone may afford being thrown by an adult, but not by a child. An extension of the concept of affordances to the world of design was initially proposed by Norman (1988), but its potential in the domain of natural communication is still not well understood.

The ecological approach to multimodal system design extends the concept of affordances to explain the variability of multimodal actions. Its basic assumption is that gestures are determined by the mutuality of information provided by the object to be referred to, and by the set of movements available to the speaker. The innovative aspect of the approach is the importance attributed to visual perception as a fundamental cue for explaining the variability of communicative actions.

13.2.2 Perceptual constraints in multimodal referring actions

Elsewhere, (De Angeli et al. 1998, De Angeli et al. 1999b, Wolff et al. 1998) we have demonstrated that the way a reference action is produced depends on the complexity of extracting the target from the visual context. Gestures are efficient means for coping with the complexity of the visual word. They are deeply connected to visual perception.

In 2D environments where targets are on the same surface, a gesture can pass through the targets to be referred to, or it can define a borderline between the targets to be referred to and the other targets. The first case corresponds to an *elective* gesture (some examples are shown in Figure 2). The second case corresponds to a *separating* gesture (an example was shown in Figure 1-B). When targets are grouped, several gestures can indicate the targets one by one, or one global gesture can be used to indicate the entire group. The first case corresponds to an *individual*

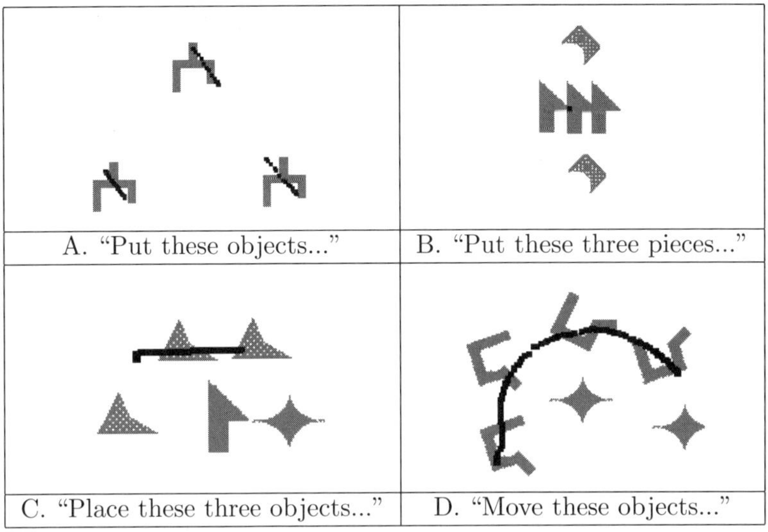

FIGURE 2 Examples of elective gesture for group designation.

access, an example of which is shown in Figure 2-A. The second case corresponds to a *group access*, cf. Figure 2-B. Gestures can take several *forms* like pointing, scribbling, targeting, or circling. Gesture form is not linked to access type. No gestural category was associated with a particular type access. Single circlings, targetings and even pointings were used to refer to groups of objects. Especially in the cases of targeting and pointing, this feature leads to ambiguities (i.e., competition of possible candidates to referents identification). Resolving such ambiguities assumes to take into account implicit information on which depends the referring action, i.e., perceptual groups.

Type, granularity, form and size tend to be adapted to the visual context (size and layout of the objects). Visual cues are features which help solve ambiguities often arising from spontaneous gesturing. Considering only the gesture and the visual context, Figure 2 shows:

- An example of type access ambiguity (does the small pointing in Figure 2-B indicate a single target or the group of three?).
- An example of scope ambiguity (how many targets are referred to in Figure 2-C: two, or three by including the nearest remaining target of the same shape?).
- And an example of pattern ambiguity (does the gesture in Figure 2-D draw an incomplete circle around the star-shaped targets, or pass through the four others to refer to them by a targeting form?).

An important factor for disambiguation is the visual *salience*. When an object or a group is salient, it is more susceptible to be referred to by a simple gesture. This is the case when it is isolated or when it has visual characteristics which distinguish it from the other objects and attract the user's intention more easily. In Figure 2-B for example, the group salience is very high and induces a group access. In a multimodal context, the verbal referring expression is another factor of disambiguation. The adjective "three" used in Figure 2-B and Figure 2-C is sufficient for comprehension.

13.2.3 Relevance in multimodal referring actions

Another basic assumption of our model is that human beings are efficient communicators. According to the *cognitive* principle of relevance (Sperber and Wilson 1995), "human cognition tends to be geared to the maximisation of relevance." *Relevance* is a property of inputs to cognitive processes, embodying the notion of *contextual effect* and *processing effort*. Processing an input yields some contextual effects when it affects the context of previous assumptions on the topic. There are three types of effects: *(i)* contextual implication; *(ii)* strengthening or weakening of existing assumptions; *(iii)* contradiction and elimination of existing assumptions. The relation between effects and relevance is the following: the greater the effects, the greater the relevance. However, processing the input involves some mental effort. For the same effects: the smaller the effort needed to achieve them, the greater the relevance. Since the maximal effects can sometimes be achieved only at the price of an enormous effort, Sperber and Wilson introduce a distinction between maximal and optimal relevance. In a communicative situation and for an individual, optimal relevance corresponds to adequate effects for no unjustifiable effort. Assuming that human beings are efficient communicators supposes that they optimise the relevance of their communication acts. This brings us to the *communicative* principle of relevance: "Every act of ostensive communication communicates a presumption of its own optimal relevance." (Sperber and Wilson 1995)

This principle can be transposed to HCI because of the spontaneous character of the interaction. It applies to multimodal communication because communication relies upon information which is distributed among gesture and language, the whole responding to the communication theory that is relevance. Applying Relevance Theory to multimodal referring actions, we expect that users select the most efficient referring strategy. In this reduced context, we need to specify the notions of relevance, contextual effects and processing effort. Effects correspond to everything that helps to resolve the referring action, i.e., to connect objects to words and gestures. Effects are obtained by two notions: the amount of new data deduced from the referring action and the importance of these data, with respect to the intention of reference. It seems possible to compute an evaluation of effects. Each word or gesture brings a piece of information which helps the resolution. As a consequence, we count them and we take into account the reference task context and the perceptual context by weighting. Processing effort could be modelled by three notions: the number of inference steps to deduce the new data from the referring action, the complexity of this deduction and the date of used information to deduce the new data (memory access). Scoring the processing effort is a more complex problem which presumes to model cognitive processes. This point is discussed at the end of the chapter. Relevance can somehow be viewed as a measure of the ratio effects/effort. The most relevant referring hypothesis appears to be the one corresponding to the largest ratio value. Optimising the relevance implies maximising the ratio. The main problem in a multimodal context is the manner of weighting effects and effort, considering the particularities of each modality and their integration.

13.2.4 Objective

Applying the concept of affordances to multimodal communication, we expect that referring actions will be affected by the visual characteristics of the target. We assume that semantic features are distributed across language, vision and gesture to optimise communication relevance. All together, these modalities supply different and complementary information for composing meaning. The main complexity of multimodal reference is the heterogeneity of the referring expressions, exploiting advantages of both language and gesture. We mentioned earlier that in the context of a multimodal spoken interface, we need to consider the integration of gesture and language. Here, we wish to study the variability of referring expressions in light of Relevance Theory. Since this theory was developed in general terms, we argue that it can be applied towards understanding heterogeneous multimodal referring expressions. Our objectives are therefore:

- To study whether our estimation of relevance agrees with the actual data. Can we evaluate the relevance of referring expressions in a multimodal context? Is it a discriminant factor?
- And to identify the factors and constraints which could help find the referring expression with the optimal relevance dynamically. Such factors would allow us to determine and to optimize the reference resolution process in the context of intelligent multimodal

interfaces.

Our approach is empirical and this study is more a description of prospective ongoing work than the development of a general model. This chapter addresses the evaluation of the effect of perception on multimodal referring actions, according to a descriptive scoring methodology.

13.3 Simulation study and hypothesis

13.3.1 Simulation study

A Wizard of Oz simulation was run to collect a corpus of spontaneous multimodal actions (Wolff 1999, Wolff et al. 1998, De Angeli et al. 1999b). In this technique, a human (the wizard) plays the role of the computer behind the interface in order to test the efficiency of the planned capacities of a dialog system before its implementation. Seven students from the University of Nancy participated in the simulation experiment as volunteers. They were French native speakers. Engaging a dialogue with the simulated system, they were required to move groups of objects into appropriate boxes. The interaction was based on speech and gesture, mediated by a microphone and an electronic pen. The experimental instructions provided to participants were only related to the task and not to the mode of interaction. In order to assure the spontaneous character of the interaction, users were free to use speech and gesture as they wished. This is important because our goal was to collect the largest possible variety of multimodal referring expressions for our corpus. To inhibit unimodal verbal references, the objects to be moved into the boxes were abstract-shaped figures, i.e., having no linguistic term associated with them (De Angeli et al. 1998). The shapes could be targets or distractors. The targets were collections of two or three identically shaped stimuli to be moved into the box displaying their shape. The distractors were exclusively used in relation to perceptual field organization and were not to be moved. The perceptual organization of the visual field was manipulated according to the principles of Gestalt Theory (Wertheimer 1922–1923, Kanizsa 1979) which describe the laws underlying spontaneous grouping. The manipulation was based on *similarity* (the objects are grouped on the basis of their salient physical attributes, such as shape and color); *proximity* (the objects are grouped on the basis of their relative proximity); *good continuation* (the groups presenting continuous outlines are more salient than those with discontinuous ones).

The experiment contrasted high salience groups with low salience groups. In the first case, targets were easily perceived as an homogeneous group, clearly separated from surroundings called distractors (see

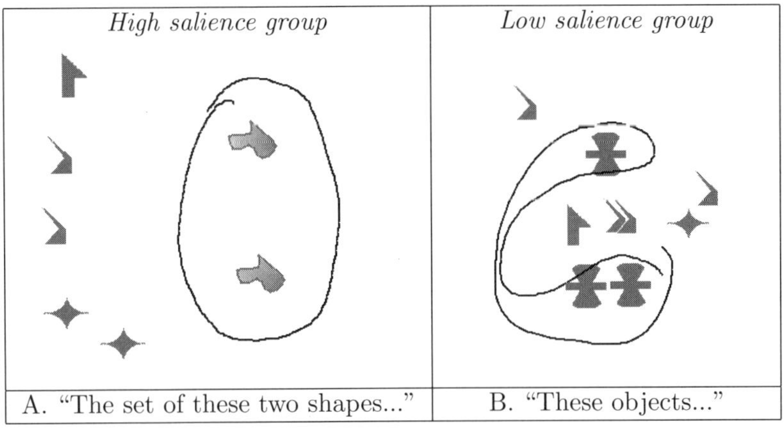

FIGURE 3 Examples of separating gesture for the designation of a high salience group or a low salience group.

Figure 3-A). In the latter case, targets were spontaneously perceived as elements of a broader heterogeneous group including distractors (see Figure 3-B). The distinction between high salience and low salience is extracted by evaluating the three gestalt grouping criteria and by comparing them. The proximity criterion is evaluated as true when *(i)* there is no distractor between the figures of the group and *(ii)* all distances between each of the figures of the group and each of the other figures are greater than the compactness value of the group, i.e., the maximum distance between two figures of the group. The circling gesture in Figure 3-A points out a high salience group. The two shapes are similar and, even if they are not so close, they are nearer to one another than to any other shapes or distractors. So the similarity and the proximity criteria are both evaluated as true. As we have only two targets, there is no need to evaluate good continuation and therefore the group salience is set to high. The gesture in Figure 3-B points out a low salience group of the three targets with the same shape. Proximity and good continuation, both evaluated as false, are in opposition to similarity.

13.3.2 Hypothesis

Our main hypothesis is that group salience is an important predictive cue to access type. When group salience is very high, the gesture can be highly simplified. For example, a simple pointing gesture can refer to the entire group unambiguously, as seen in Figure 2-B. (In Figure 3-A, a simple pointing gesture is not conceivable but the circling gesture is also simplified due to the broad spacing. Rapidity and imprecision had no repercussion on the identification). On the contrary, low salient groups afford almost only individual access (if the user chooses group access anyway, the gesture will be very complex as shown in Figure 3-B, which is a singular example).

13.4 Data coding

13.4.1 Linguistic scoring

Our approach of Relevance Theory modelling applied to multimodal referencing supposes to compute both cognitive contextual effects and processing effort. A measurement of contextual effects seems particularly interesting because, when applied to automatic comprehension in multimodal dialogue systems, it could help to resolve the referring action. In order to study verbalisations occurring with gestural references, we have parsed our transcribed corpus with a Lexicalized Tree Adjoining Grammar (LTAG) using the tools described in (Lopez 2000) and computed a score for each referring expression. We used the definition of derivation of Schabes and Shieber (1994) and linguistic principles of Abeillé et al. (1999) for LTAG. These choices allow the result of the parsing (the derivation tree) to be equivalent to a classical semantic dependency graph. Since each node in the derivation tree represents one and only one predicate, semantically empty words are not present in the derivation tree. Consequently the number of new pieces of data is obtained by the number of nodes in the dependency tree resulting from the parsing of the referring expression.

The importance of the predicates for the reference task is taken into account by weighting. This weighting w is subjective and depends on the application. For example, in our simulation we never have only one kind of object. Distractors are always heterogeneous shapes occurring at each visual scene step. So words such as *object* (contrary to words such as *circle*) provide no information for the identification of a piece in the visual scene and correspond to a score of $w = 0$. We consider that for the semantic head of the linguistic referring expression, we have $w = 0$ for abstract nouns in this application context. Considering the simulation application, the list of transcribed abstract nouns is as follows: *object, form, piece* and *figure* (in French: "objet", "forme", "pièce" and "figure"). For the weighting of the other nouns and of the modifiers, we have introduced these general rules depending on the level of specification of the object:

- $w = 1$, for non-abstract nouns *(triangle, circle)*.
- $w = 1$, for adjectives *(grey)* as they provide a piece of information about an object to be referred to.

- $w = 1$, for conjunctions *(and)* as they provide a piece of information about how their elements are linked.
- $w = 1$, for prepositions *(with, without)* as they define the role of the objects in the global predicate.
- $w = 0$, for an indefinite determiner *(a)* which provides no information for the reference task.

The main problem concerns the other determiners (definite ones), the demonstrative articles and pronouns, and the deictic marks which in French can be concatenated at the end of a word ("cet objet-**ci** et cet objet-**là**", *this object and that object*). No rule can be defined for the weighting of these words if we do not consider the multimodal context (i.e., is there a gesture or not?). Consequently a score taking only the linguistic part into account cannot be defined, and the complete rules for scoring the linguistic part of multimodal referring expressions will be introduced in section 13.4.3.

13.4.2 Gestural scoring

The experimental conditions concern visual salience, and our hypothesis is based on this salience and on the access type of the gesture. Perceptual constraints are therefore taken into account in the gesture and we base our scoring on its access type.

In our corpus, the gestural part of each multimodal command is tabulated according to the strategy adopted to identify the corresponding group. Gestures are scored as *group accesses* when more than one object is accessed by only one gesture. In this case the user's intention is to point out the group in which the referents are to be found. This intention and the corresponding amount of data constitute the effects. Gestures are scored as *individual accesses* when each gesture of the multimodal expression indicates only one object.

13.4.3 Multimodal scoring

Considering that a demonstrative article in the verbal part of a multimodal referring expression produces more effects than a definite one (because a demonstrative holds a piece of information useful to link gesture and language), we can now introduce the following rules for the weighting of the determiners and articles in a multimodal context:

- $w = 0.5$, for definite determiners ("le", *the*) which indicate a more precise denomination of the referred object.
- $w = 1$, for demonstrative articles ("ce", *this*) which allow to determine a direct relation between the verbal reference and a referring gesture and indicate that the reference is expressed by the two

modalities.

- $w = 0.5$, for deictic marks which determine a link with a referring gesture.
- $w = 1$, for demonstrative pronouns ("celui-ci", *this one*; "celui-là", *that one*; "ceux-là", *those* or *those ones*) for similar reasons to the previous item.

Applying these rules, we get for example the following results: "les objets-là" = "ces objets" = "ceux-là" < "ces objets-là". For an expression which gives no information about the object to refer to like "un objet" *(an object)*, we have $w = 0$ and thus a null contextual effect. On the other hand, for a rich expression like "ce petit triangle" *(this small triangle)*, we have large contextual effects ($w = 3$). Now we have a complete set of rules to score the linguistic part of multimodal referring expressions. Two illustrative examples are shown in Figure 4.

13.5 Results

13.5.1 Corpus analysis

A corpus of 522 multimodal commands has been analysed. All the Figures in this chapter illustrate expressions from this corpus. To test the role of perception on the verbal utterance, we have extracted a sample of 98 significant multimodal referring expressions equally distributed between the two group conditions (De Angeli et al. 1997). In particular, we do not keep the unimodal referring expressions and duplicates. Consequently our sample is not statistically representative of the corpus, but this has no repercussion on our analysis for several reasons. First, our approach focuses on the spontaneous character of the communicative act and thus on its variability. Our goal is to show that relevance is a criterion to make sense of this variability. Consequently the sample only needs to be representative of the variability and we do not address the fact that someone used the odd expression more or less frequently. This approach justifies why we think we can make do with seven subjects. Considering the possible types of referring expressions, we were of the opinion that after seven simulation sessions a satisfactory variability was reached, i.e., increasing the size of the corpus would not lead to an increase in the number of different multimodal referring expressions. Moreover, we do not want statistical results on the frequency of use of each type of referring expression. A person-oriented dialogue system must understand the most complex and significant expressions, and not only the most likely.

Our hypothesis concerns the group salience which was supposed to be a predictive cue for gesture access type. As a preliminary result which

verbal referring expression	"cet objet et celui-ci" *(this object and this one)*	"les deux objets, formes grises à petits pois" *(the two objects, grey shapes with small points)*
derivation tree	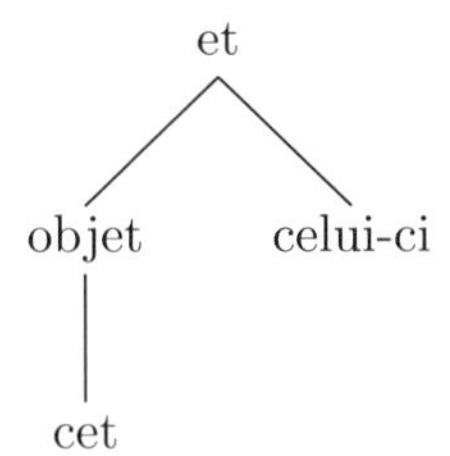	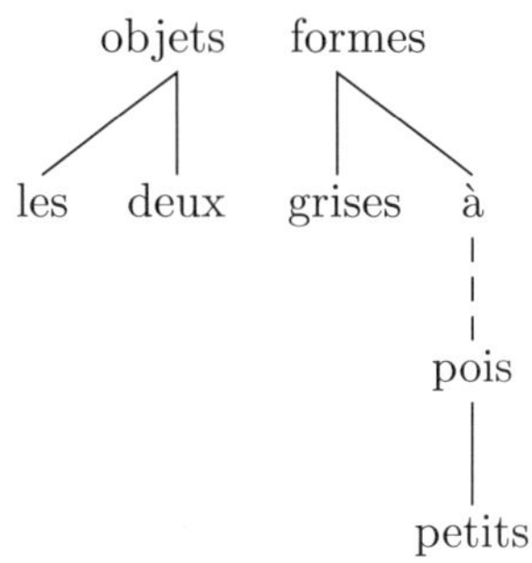
new data scoring	4	8
linguistic scoring	$1+0+1+1=\mathbf{3}$	$0.5+1+0$ $+0+1+1+1+1=\mathbf{5.5}$
gesture(s)	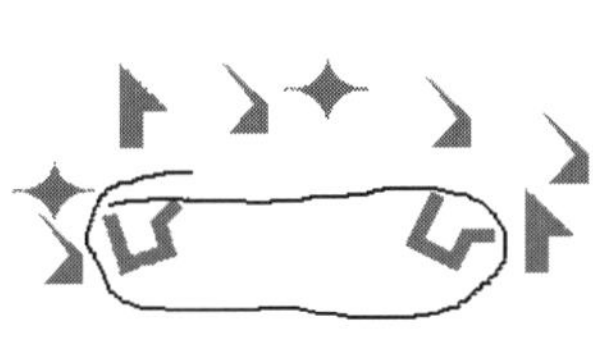	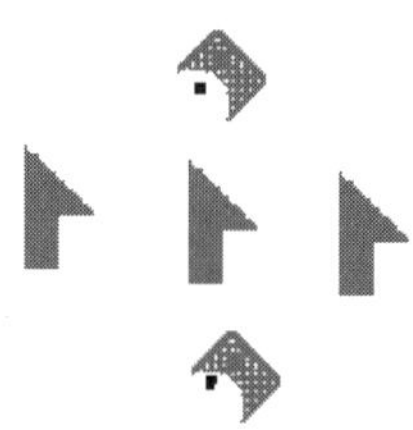
gestural scoring	group access	individual access
	A. *Example of a coordination in the referring expression, with one long gesture (low group-salience).*	B. *Example of a precision in the referring expression, with two pointing gestures (low group-salience).*

FIGURE 4 Examples of multimodal scoring.

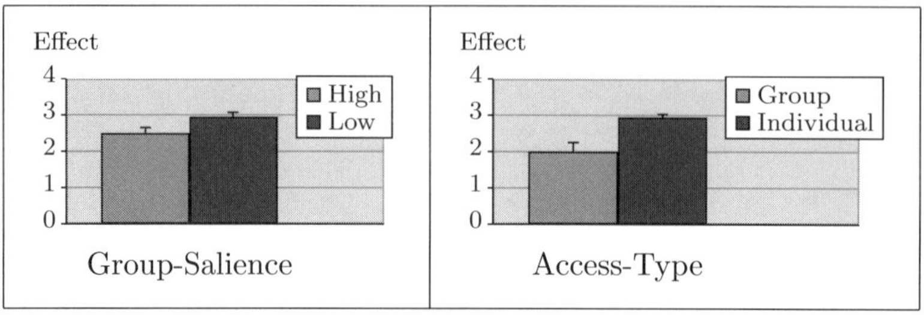

FIGURE 5 Contextual effects as a function of Group-Salience and Access-Type (Error bars represent mean standard errors).

must still be verified, we found that perception has an effect not only on the gesture, but also on the verbalization. This effect is twofold: *implicit* cues and *explicit* cues may affect the verbal part of the referring expression. It is implicit when the verbal expression is affected by the visual layout of the object to be referred to (in high salience conditions, verbalization is simplified). It is explicit when the verbal expression is affected by the gesture. We can observe that a simple group gesture is accompanied by a simple verbalization, and a complex gesture requires a complex verbalization. Here we have tested the twofold effect by:

- Comparing the effects of verbal expressions produced under the two group salience conditions (implicit cues).
- Comparing the effects of verbal expressions produced together with both gestural access types (explicit cues).

The average value of the contextual effects in our sample is 2.66, with a standard deviation of 1.17. The distribution ranges from 1 to 6 and is affected by a substantial positive skewedness, which is difficult to normalise by transformation. Because of this statistical characteristic, the two effects were tested separately using non-parametric statistics (see Figure 5). This procedure allows us to process low-quality data, with respect to variables for which the parameters of the population are unknown (hence, the name non-parametric). To evaluate our hypothesis, the Mann-Whitney U test (Blalock 1979) was applied. It allows testing differences between groups, verifying whether two sampled populations are from the same population. The observations from both groups are combined and ranked (in the case of ties an average rank is assigned). Then, the number of times a score from group 1 precedes a score from group 2 and vice versa is calculated. The logic behind the test is trivial. If two groups do not differ, then the first observation should come from group 1, the second from 2, the third from 1, the fourth from 2 and so on.

Instead, if the two samples come from different populations, their rank orders should differ. The Mann-Whitney statistical value U is obtained by counting the number of times a value from the group with the smaller sample precedes a value from the group with the larger sample. The probability value (p) associated with the U statistic depends on the total number of observations (N). The p value is the basis for deciding if a statistical result like the one observed would occur by chance. Saying that a correlation is significant at the 0.05 level means that you can be 95% confident that the results are due to a real difference in the population and not to chance factors.

For the implicit cues hypothesis, the Mann-Whitney U test shows a strong influence of group salience on contextual effects, $U = 687$ ($N = 87$); $p < .05$. Under the low salience conditions, users produced complex verbalizations; whereas under high salience conditions, verbalizations were significantly simplified. This result supports our hypothesis that humans spontaneously plan their verbal references having a representation of the visual context in mind. When the group is more easily perceptible, they need less complex referring expressions to convey their intentions, since they can exploit implicit information. As a corollary, we can deduce that humans naturally attribute their own perceptual capabilities to an artificial interlocutor.

The influence of explicit visual cues on contextual effects was straightforward, $U = 324,5$ ($N = 84$); $p < .001$. The analysis shows that, for multimodal reference, complexity of gestural and verbal expressions are linked. A simple referring gesture (direct group access) comes jointly with a simple verbalization, generally a deictic. A complex gesture (individual access that indirectly builds the group) needs a complex verbalization. In the latter case, the linguistic part provides temporal links for simplifying the complex spatial designations. The results are consistent with previous findings (Wolff et al. 1998, De Angeli et al. 1999b) showing a high correlation between the reference strategies adopted by verbal and gestural languages to identify targets. In particular, gestural group access was always accompanied by a plural deictic anchor or target descriptions (i.e., *these objects, the two isolated objects, the two forms*). Moreover, only one out of three multimodal expressions were formed by an individual access accompanied by a plural verbal reference.

For the implementation of dialogue systems, these results are important because they point out the significance of taking perceptual constraints into account. Even if the task of our study leads to referring actions on sets of similar objects (and this could have favoured the perception of salient groups), it appears that visual perception gives some hints to interpret gestures and verbal expressions. This could lead to more comprehensive systems.

13.5.2 Effects and effort and their use in multimodal systems

We argue first that evaluating contextual effects and processing effort can aid comprehension. Sperber and Wilson (1995) consider that an evaluation of effects and effort with counting operations is not representative of human abilities. Humans are not able to pass judgment on the quantity of obtained effects or effort. Nevertheless, if it is possible to provide such capacities to a dialogue system, the automatic comprehension process will be improved because:

1. It could identify heuristics to prune the referring search space. Given several candidates for a multimodal referring expression, a post-evaluation of their relevance can show preferential procedures and their significant parameters for the reference resolution.
2. It could question the result of a reference resolution when its relevance is low.
3. It could detect the ill-chosen utterances that reveal a particular behaviour of the user.
4. It could be helpful to go back in the dialogue history to find the source of a misunderstanding.

To sum up, managing scores is a way of representing complex processes in communication.

Secondly, in automatic generation, an evaluation of relevance appears to be the ideal criterion for choosing among the large range of available referring expressions. More precisely, it is a criterion to minimize the number of backtracks in the generation search space. The main problem in generation is the impossibility of generating all of the possible expressions before chosing one of them. Moreover, the possible referring expressions in a multimodal context explode, considering the great number of gestural forms and the great number of verbal expressions. Exploratory choices must be made with the possibility of looking back and questioning these choices. By taking perceptual constraints into account and using relevance evaluation, we argue that the most efficient choices will be made from the very beginning of the process.

13.6 Future work

To evaluate contextual effects, we have proposed scoring rules for the linguistic part of multimodal referring expressions. This is enough to point out the link between perception and verbalization, but not to present a real metric for multimodal input. With this intention we also need to extend the score to the contextual effects of gestures. As seen in section 13.2.3, effects are obtained by two notions: the amount of new data deduced from the referring action and the importance of these data, with respect to the intention of reference. We can evaluate the number of new pieces of data deduced from a gesture by enumerating each particularity that brings a piece of information helpful for the referent identification. Considering the possible types of gestures we collected in our corpus, it is the case of a stop in the gesture or an abrupt change of direction. The notion of *singularity* (Bellalem and Romary 1995) includes these particularities and provides a framework to analyse them (a semantic feature is associated with each singularity). Then we need to evaluate the importance of these data. A weighting could be introduced for this purpose taking into account the perceptual context (position of the targets, salience, group). Then the scores may be confronted and the correlation between perception, gesture and language may be tested.

The processing effort of a referring action is of course more complicated to compute than the contextual effects which only require a descriptive methodology. Evaluation of the processing effort requires a general theory of reference that takes into account multimodal communication. In order to correctly interpret this kind of natural referring actions, the system has to represent and use jointly for each objects of the application different kinds of information: linguistic, pragmatic and perceptive. To conclude considering the proposed contextual effects scoring, we argue that Mental Representation Theory (Reboul 1998) could provide a framework able to compute the processing effort, to represent such information and to use it for reference resolution in accordance with Relevance Theory. The goal of this general theory of reference, inspired by Sag and Hankamer (1984), is to explain the processing of object and event reference resolutions using a specific world representation called *mental representations*. This data structure gathers all information needed to resolve references, including perceptive information. Using a small set of rules, these mental representations are updated after each new utterance and allow to resolve heterogeneous references as spatial designation. As seen in section 13.2.3, processing effort includes the number of inference steps to deduce the new data from the referring action, the complexity of this deduction and the date of used information. Mental Representation Theory could lead to an evaluation of these notions. Inference has an important role in the operations over mental representations, and the accessibility of information is modelled by the notion of *domain of reference*. A domain of reference is a subset of the set of mental representations for a given individual at a given time (it is very much like the notion of context in Relevance Theory). Considering this notion, we plan to develop a general methodology for our scoring.

The implementation of dialogue systems integrating Mental Representations, scores of contextual effects and processing effort, is one of our main ongoing projects.

13.7 Conclusion

In this chapter, we have tried, in the context of a sound theoretical background, to evaluate the precise role of perception in multimodal systems. From the field of psychology, we have extended the ecological approach to show how demonstrative gestures could be seen as the realization of specific affordances induced by the gestalt properties of objects. From a more linguistic point of view, we have extended Relevance Theory to consider multimodal referring expressions, which has led us to define a tentative scoring measure of such expressions to evaluate their relevance. Although the results we presented seem promising, the calculus is still rather coarse and has to be considered within the context of a real modelling of the notion of relevance in multimodal dialogue.

References

Abeillé, A., Candito, M.-H. and Kinyon, A. 1999. FTAG: Current Status and Parsing Scheme. In *Proc. of Venezia per il Trattamento Automatico delle Lingue* (VEXTAL), Venice.

Bellalem, N. and Romary, L. 1995. Reference Interpretation in a Multimodal Environment Combining Speech and Gesture. In *Proc. of First International Workshop on Intelligence and Multimodality in Multimedia Interfaces*, Edinburgh.

Blalock, H. M. 1979. *Social Statistics.* New York: McGraw-Hill.

De Angeli, A., Gerbino, W., Petrelli, D. and Cassano, G. 1998. Visual Display, Pointing and Natural Communication: The Power of Multimodal Interaction. In *Proc. of International Working Conference on Advanced Visual Interfaces* (AVI98), l'Aquila.

De Angeli, A., Gerbino, W., Romary, L. and Wolff, F. 1999a. The Ecological Approach to Multimodal System Design. In A. Braffort et al. (Eds.): *Gesture-Based Communication in Human-Computer Interaction, Lecture Notes in Artificial Intelligence 1739*, Berlin: Springer-Verlag.

De Angeli, A., Romary, L. and Wolff, F. 1999b. Ecological Interfaces: Extending the Pointing Paradigm by Visual Context. In P. Bouquet et al. (Eds.): *Modeling and Using Context, Lecture Notes in Artificial Intelligence 1688*, Berlin: Springer-Verlag.

Gibson, J. J. 1979. *The Ecological Approach to Visual Perception.* Boston: Houghton Mifflin.

Jönsson, A. and Dählback, N. 1988. Talking to a Computer is not like Talking to your Best Friend. In *Proc. of the Scandinavian Conference on Artificial Intelligence*, Tromsø.

Kanizsa, G. 1979. *Organization in Vision*. New York: Praeger.

Kita, S. 2000. How Representational Gestures Help Speaking. In D. McNeill (Ed.): *Language and Gesture*, New York: Cambridge University Press.

Lopez, P. 2000. LTAG Workbench: A General Framework for LTAG. In *Proc. of 5th International Workshop on Tree Adjoining Grammars and Related Formalisms* (TAG+5), Paris.

Neisser, U. 1976. *Cognition and Reality*. San Francisco: Freeman & Co.

Norman, D. 1988. *The Psychology of Everyday Things*. New York: Basic Books.

Oviatt, S. 1997. Multimodal Interactive Maps: Designing for Human Performance. *Human-Computer Interaction 12*, pp.93-129.

Oviatt, S., De Angeli, A. and Kuhn, K. 1997. Integration and Synchronization of Input Modes during Multimodal Human-Computer Interaction. In *Proc. of Conference on Human Factors in Computing Systems* (CHI'97), New York: ACM Press. Also in E. André (Ed.): *Proc. of the ACL Workshop on Referring Phenomena in a Multimedia Context and their Computational Treatment* (ACL/EACL-97), Madrid.

Oviatt, S. and Cohen, P. 2000. Multimodal Interfaces that Process what Comes Naturally. *Communication of the ACM*, vol.43, no.3, pp.45-53.

Reboul, A. 1998. A Relevance Theoretic Approach to Reference. In *Proc. of Relevance Theory Workshop*, Luton.

Sag, I. and Hankamer, J. 1984. Toward a Theory of Anaphoric Processing. *Linguistics and Philosophy 7*, pp.325-345.

Schabes, Y. and Shieber, S. 1994. An Alternative Conception of Tree-Adjoining Derivation. *Computational Linguistics 20*, pp.91-124.

Sperber, D. and Wilson, D. 1995. *Relevance. Communication and Cognition* (2nd edition). Oxford: Blackwell.

Wertheimer, M. 1922. Untersuchungen zur Lehre von der Gestalt I. *Psychologische Forschung 1*, pp.47-58.

Wertheimer, M. 1923. Untersuchungen zur Lehre von der Gestalt II. *Psychologische Forschung 4*, pp.301-350.

Wolff, F., De Angeli, A. and Romary, L. 1998. Acting on a Visual World: The Role of Perception in Multimodal HCI. In *Proc. of AAAI Workshop on Multimodal Representation*, Madison.

Wolff, F. 1999. *Analyse contextuelle des gestes de désignation en dialogue homme-machine*. Doctoral dissertation, Henri Poincaré University, Nancy.

Index